SAS® Companion for the MVS Environment

Version 6
Second Edition

Kui Zhang
6/1998

SAS®

SAS Institute Inc.
SAS Campus Drive
Cary, NC 27513

The correct bibliographic citation for this manual is as follows: SAS Institute Inc., *SAS® Companion for the MVS Environment, Version 6, Second Edition*, Cary, NC: SAS Institute Inc., 1996. 503 pp.

SAS® Companion for the MVS Environment, Version 6, Second Edition

The SAS® System is an integrated system of software providing complete control over data access, management, analysis, and presentation. Base SAS software is the foundation of the SAS System. Products within the SAS System include SAS/ACCESS®, SAS/AF®, SAS/ASSIST®, SAS/BUDGET™, SAS/CALC®, SAS/CONNECT®, SAS/CPE®, SAS/DMI®, SAS/EIS®, SAS/ENGLISH®, SAS/ETS®, SAS/FINANCE™, SAS/FSP®, SAS/GRAPH®, SAS/IMAGE®, SAS/IML®, SAS/IMS-DL/I®, SAS/INSIGHT®, SAS/LAB®, SAS/NVISION®, SAS/OR®, SAS/PH-Clinical®, SAS/QC®, SAS/REPLAY-CICS®, SAS/SESSION®, SAS/SHARE®, SAS/SPECTRAVIEW®, SAS/STAT®, SAS/TOOLKIT®, SAS/TRADER®, SAS/TUTOR®, SAS/DB2™, SAS/GEO™, SAS/GIS™, SAS/PH-Kinetics™, SAS/SHARE*NET™, and SAS/SQL-DS™ software. Other SAS Institute products are SYSTEM 2000® Data Management Software, with basic SYSTEM 2000, CREATE™, Multi-User™, QueX™, Screen Writer™, and CICS interface software; InfoTap® software; NeoVisuals® software; JMP®, JMP IN®, and JMP Serve® software; SAS/RTERM® software; and the SAS/C® Compiler and the SAS/CX® Compiler; Video Reality™ software; VisualSpace™ software; and Emulus® software. MultiVendor Architecture™ and MVA™ are trademarks of SAS Institute Inc. SAS Institute also offers SAS Consulting®, SAS Video Productions®, Ambassador Select®, and On-Site Ambassador® services. *Authorline®*, Books by Users™, The Encore Series™, *JMPer Cable®*, *Observations®*, *SAS Communications®*, *SAS Training®*, *SAS Views®*, the SASware Ballot®, and SelecText™ documentation are published by SAS Institute Inc. The SAS Video Productions logo, the Books by Users SAS Institute's Author Service logo, and The Encore Series logo are registered service marks or registered trademarks of SAS Institute Inc. The Helplus logo, the SelecText logo, the SAS Online Samples logo, the Video Reality logo, and the Quality Partner logo are service marks or trademarks of SAS Institute Inc. All trademarks above are registered trademarks or trademarks of SAS Institute Inc. in the USA and other countries. ® indicates USA registration.

The Institute is a private company devoted to the support and further development of its software and related services.

IBM®, CMS®, DB2®, MVS®, OS/2®, PS/2®, and SAA® are registered trademarks or trademarks of International Business Machines Corporation. ORACLE® is a registered trademark of Oracle Corporation. ® indicates USA registration.

Other brand and product names are registered trademarks or trademarks of their respective companies.

Doc P19, 042296

Contents

Credits   ix

Part 1 · Running the SAS System under MVS   1

Chapter 1 · Initializing and Configuring the SAS System   3

Invoking SAS under MVS   4

Connecting to SAS under MVS   5

Customizing Your SAS Session   6

Specifying Operating System Data Sets   13

SAS System Files   14

Reserved MVS DDnames   23

Chapter 2 · Allocating SAS Data Libraries   25

Introduction   25

Allocating SAS Data Libraries Internally   28

Allocating SAS Data Libraries Externally   30

How SAS Assigns an Engine When No Engine Is Specified   32

Allocating Generation Data Sets   33

Allocating Multivolume SAS Data Libraries   33

Assigning Multiple Librefs to a Single SAS Data Library   38

Deallocating SAS Data Libraries   38

Listing Your Current Librefs   39

Estimating the Size of a SAS Data Set   39

Estimating the Size of a SAS Index   41

Chapter 3 · Accessing V6 and V6SEQ SAS Data Libraries   43

Overview of the V6 and V6SEQ Engines   43

Using the V6 Engine   45

Using the V6SEQ Engine   49

Chapter 4 · Accessing BMDP, SPSS, and OSIRIS Files   53

The BMDP, SPSS, and OSIRIS Engines   53

Restrictions on the Use of These Engines   53

Accessing BMDP Files   54

Accessing SPSS Files   55

Accessing OSIRIS Files   56

Chapter 5 · Allocating External Files   59

Introduction   59

Ways of Allocating External Files   59

Using the FILENAME Statement to Allocate External Files   60

Using the JCL DD Statement to Allocate External Files   62

Using the TSO Allocate Command to Allocate External Files   63

Allocating External Files on Tape   63

Allocating Generation Data Sets   64

Allocating Nonstandard External Files   65

Concatenating External Files   66

Displaying Information about External Files   66

Deallocating External Files   66

Chapter 6 · Accessing External Files   69

Referring to External Files   70

Writing to External Files   70

Reading from External Files   78

Accessing Nonstandard Files   83

Accessing OpenEdition MVS Hierarchical File System Files   84

Writing Your Own I/O Access Methods   90

Accessing SAS Statements from a Program   91

Using the INFILE/FILE User Exit Facility   91

Chapter 7 · Routing the SAS Log and SAS Procedure Output   93

Default Routings   93

Routing to External Files with the PRINTTO Procedure   95

Routing to External Files with SAS System Options   96

Routing to External Files with Commands   97

Routing to External Files with DD Statements   98

Routing to a Printer   98

Routing Output to a Remote Destination   101

Part 2 · Application Considerations   103

Chapter 8 · SAS Interfaces to ISPF and REXX   105

SAS Interface to ISPF   106

SAS Interface to REXX   122

Chapter 9 · Transporting SAS Files to and from MVS   131

Introduction   131

General Steps   132

Transporting SAS Data Sets   132

Transporting SAS Catalogs   134

Guidelines for Transporting SAS Files   136

Identifying and Resolving Problems   138

Additional Sources of Information   140

Chapter 10 · Data Representation   141

Representation of Numeric Variables   141

Using the LENGTH Statement to Save Storage Space   143

How Character Values are Stored   144

Chapter 11 · Identifying and Resolving Problems   145

Support for the SAS System   145

Solving Problems under MVS   147

Chapter 12 · Optimizing Performance   151

Introduction   151

Collecting Performance Statistics   152

Optimizing I/O   152

Efficient Sorting   157

Some SAS System Options That Can Affect Performance   157

Managing Memory   158

Loading SAS Modules Efficiently   159

Other Considerations for Improving Performance   160

Part 3 · Host-Specific Features of the SAS Language   163

Chapter 13 · CALL Routines   165

Chapter 14 · Data Set Options   167

Summary of SAS Data Set Options   168

Chapter 15 · Functions   171

Chapter 16 · Informats and Formats   173

Considerations for Using Informats and Formats under MVS   173

Numeric Informats   175

Numeric Formats   182

Chapter 17 · Macro Facility   191

Macro Variables   191

Macro Statements   193

Macro Functions   194

Autocall Libraries   194

Stored Compiled Macro Facility   196

Other Host-Specific Aspects of the Macro Facility   197

Additional Sources of Information   198

Chapter 18 · Procedures   199

Chapter 19 · Statements   261

Chapter 20 · System Options   299

A Note about System Option Values   299

Summary Table of SAS System Options   396

Chapter 21 · Windows and Window Features   411

Host-Specific Windows   411

Host-Specific Frames of the FORM Subsystem   416

Command-Line Commands   419

Windowing Options under MVS   423

Display Manager Under MVS – Terminal Support   424

Part 4 · Appendices   429

Appendix 1 · Accessing V5 and V5SEQ SAS Data Libraries   431

Overview of the V5 and V5SEQ Engines   431

Using the V5 Engine   432

Using the V5SEQ Engine   436

Appendix 2 · Using the INFILE/FILE User Exit Facility   441

Introduction   441

Writing a User Exit Module   441

Function Descriptions   445

SAS Service Routines   451

Building Your User Exit Module   453

Activating an INFILE/FILE User Exit   453

Sample Program   453

Appendix 3 · Host-System Subgroup Error Messages   465

Introduction   465

Messages from the SASCP Command Processor   465

Messages from the TSO Command Executor   467

Messages from the Internal CALL Command Processor   469

Glossary   471

Index   483

Credits

Documentation

Design and Production	Design, Production, and Printing Services
Documentation Coordination	Lisa M. Ripperton
MVS Documentation Review	Thomas J. Hahl, Kevin Hobbs, Dale D. Ingold, John R. Kohl, N. Elizabeth Malcom, Lisa M. Ripperton, W. David Shinn, Sandi Smith, Annette R. Tharpe, Helen Weeks, Christina M. Williams
Style Programming	Publications Technology Department
Technical Review	Anne Albright, Dawn M. Amos, Stephen M. Beatrous, Daniel C. Berry, Patricia L. Berryman, Sherri H. Claes, David A. Driggs, Ceci Edmiston, Mark K. Gass, Nancy L. Goodling, Daniel B. Hamrick, Annette T. Harris, Keefe Hayes, William F. Heffner, Phil Herold, Kevin Hobbs, Christina A. Hobbs, Cynthia A. Hunley, Tim Hunter, Dale D. Ingold, Brenda C. Kalt, Richard D. Langston, Pauline M. Leveille, Renee Lorden, Cathy A. Maahs-Fladung, James McNealy, LaVon Missell, Jason Moore, Pei-Lan Morgenroth, Susan M. O'Connor, Joseph M. Piechota, Terry D. Poole, Meg Pounds, Linda S. Proctor, Kent Reeve, Lisa M. Ripperton, W. David Shinn, Dan Squillace, Daniel S. Taylor, Annette R. Tharpe, Thomas P. Weber, Helen Weeks, Randal K. Whitehead, Christina M. Williams
Writing and Editing	John R. Kohl, Hanna Schoenrock, Joan M. Stout, Helen Weeks

Software Development and Support

The host-specific features and subsystems of SAS software under MVS are designed, coded, built, tested, and supported by the MVS Host Department within the Host Systems Research and Development Division. The primary software developers and support personnel for the 6.09 Enhanced Release are identified here.

Development	Daniel C. Berry, Mark K. Gass, Keefe Hayes, Phil Herold, Arthur L. Hunt, Tim Hunter, Dale D. Ingold, Steve Jenisch, Richard D. Langston, Lisa M. Ripperton, George H. Stafford, Thomas P. Weber
Installation Procedure	David A. Juras, Anne-Marie Olinger, Guy L. Olinger, Cynthia D. Schnupper, Cheryl L. Turney
Porting and Source Management	Stephen E. Blankinship, David A. Juras, Cheryl L. Turney, Kevin S. Walton, Robert J. Wooten, Kenneth N. Wright
Quality Assurance	Anne Albright, Dawn M. Amos, Ceci Edmiston, Cynthia A. Hunley, Pauline M. Leveille, Allen S. Malone, James McNealy, Joy Polzin, Annette R. Tharpe

Technical Support	Richard H. Anderson, Cindy D. Brock-Bailey, David B. Caudle, Ginny Dunn, Amber Elam, Daniel B. Hamrick, Kevin Hobbs, Marc Howell, Charles A. Jacobs, Susan Marshall, Rick Matthews, Jason Moore, Denise J. Moorman, Susan Nine, Lynn H. Patrick, Joseph M. Piechota, Terry D. Poole, Joy Reel, Katrina Rempson, Jon C. Schiltz, Eileen Shea, Jeffrey R. Stead, Marilyn Tomasic
Testing	Pei-Lan Morgenroth, Lisa M. Ripperton, Daniel S. Taylor, Christina M. Williams
Tools	Stephen E. Blankinship, Arthur L. Hunt, David A. Juras, Pei-Lan Morgenroth, Guy L. Olinger, Lisa M. Ripperton, Daniel S. Taylor, Cheryl L. Turney, Kevin S. Walton, Robert J. Wooten, Kenneth N. Wright

Part 1

Running the SAS® System under MVS

Chapter 1   Initializing and Configuring the SAS® System

Chapter 2   Allocating SAS® Data Libraries

Chapter 3   Accessing V6 and V6SEQ SAS® Data Libraries

Chapter 4   Accessing BMDP, SPSS, and OSIRIS Files

Chapter 5   Allocating External Files

Chapter 6   Accessing External Files

Chapter 7   Routing the SAS® Log and SAS® Procedure Output

Chapter 1 Initializing and Configuring the SAS® System

Invoking SAS under MVS   4
Invoking SAS under TSO: the SAS CLIST   4
Invoking SAS in Batch Mode: the SAS Cataloged Procedure   4
Logging On to the SAS System Directly   5

Connecting to SAS under MVS   5

Customizing Your SAS Session   6
Configuration Files   7
    Creating a User Configuration File   7
    Specifying a User Configuration File   8
Autoexec Files   8
    Displaying Autoexec Statements in the SAS Log   8
    Using an Autoexec File under TSO   9
    Using an Autoexec File in Batch Mode   9
SASUSER Library   9
    Creating Your Own SASUSER Libraries   9
    Specifying Your Own SASUSER Library   10
SAS System Options   11
    Specifying or Changing System Option Settings   11
    Displaying System Option Settings   12
    Precedence for Option Specifications   13

Specifying Operating System Data Sets   13
Handling of Nonstandard Member Names   14

SAS System Files   14
WORK Library   14
    Increasing the Size of the WORK Library   15
    Deleting Temporary SAS Data Sets   16
    Directing Temporary SAS Data Sets to the USER Library   16
SAS Log File   17
    Changing the Contents of the SAS Log   18
    Changing the Appearance of the SAS Log   18
SAS Procedure Output File   19
    Changing the Appearance of Procedure Output   19
Parmcards File   20
Summary Table of SAS System Files   20

Reserved MVS DDnames   23

Invoking SAS under MVS

Invoking SAS under TSO: the SAS CLIST

To invoke SAS under TSO, you execute the SAS CLIST by typing a command (usually **SAS**) at the READY prompt. The SAS CLIST is an external file that contains TSO commands and control instructions.

At each site, the command that you use and the SAS CLIST itself may have been modified by your SAS Software Consultant, so you should ask your consultant for site-specific information about the CLIST.

The SAS CLIST starts a display manager session, an interactive line mode session, or a noninteractive session, depending on the defaults that have been specified in the CLIST. To override the mode of running SAS that is specified in the CLIST, you use commands similar to those shown in Table 1.1. (Again, the exact commands that you use may be site-specific.)

Table 1.1   *Commands for Invoking SAS*

Mode	How to Invoke	How to Terminate	Description
Display Manager	`sas options('dms')`	`bye` or `endsas`	enables you to write and execute SAS programs and to view the SAS log and SAS procedure output in an interactive windowing environment. This is the default mode at most sites. If it is the default at your site, then you can invoke it by entering **sas** with no options.
interactive line mode	`sas options('nodms')`	`/*` or `endsas;` statement	prompts you to enter SAS statements at your terminal, one line at a time.
noninteractive line mode	`sas input("'my.sas.program'")`	n/a	executes under interactive MVS, but it is called noninteractive because the program runs with no intervention from the terminal.

Invoking SAS in Batch Mode: the SAS Cataloged Procedure

To invoke SAS during a batch job, you use a JCL EXEC statement that executes the SAS cataloged procedure. The SAS cataloged procedure invokes SAS. By specifying parameters in the JCL EXEC statement, you can modify the way in which the SAS System is invoked.

At each site, the JCL EXEC statement that you use and the cataloged procedure itself may have been modified by your SAS Software Consultant, so you should ask your SAS Software Consultant for site-specific information.

Logging On to the SAS System Directly

MVS sites can choose to substitute the SAS System for the standard TSO terminal monitor program, enabling users to log on to SAS directly. If SAS comes up automatically when you log in, then your system may have already been set up to log on to SAS directly.

By automatically invoking the SAS System or a SAS application when users log on, site administrators can insulate users from the TSO environment. Because SAS is running as its own terminal monitor program, TSO commands are not accessible to users. This reduces memory usage slightly.

This method of invoking SAS also provides the following advantages:

□ sites can restrict user access to the TSO environment

□ novice users do not have to learn how to work in the TSO environment

For complete information about this method of invoking SAS, see *Installation Instructions and System Manager's Guide.*

Connecting to SAS under MVS

Under MVS, you can access or connect to a SAS session in any of the following ways:

3270 terminals
You can use devices that support extended data streams as well as those that do not. See "Display Manager Under MVS – Terminal Support" on page 424 for more information about terminal support.

terminal emulators
Terminal emulators that you can use to access SAS on MVS include Emulus (available from SAS Institute) and EXTRA, Rumba, Communications Manager, and so forth (available from other vendors).*

SAS/CONNECT software
SAS/CONNECT supports cooperative and distributed processing between MVS and Windows, OS/2, MAC, UNIX, OpenVMS, CMS, and VSE. It supports several advanced communications protocols (including TCP/IP, APPC, TELNET, EHLLAPI, ASYNC, and 3270), enabling local clients that are running SAS to communicate with one or more SAS applications or programs that are running in remote environments. For more information, see *SAS/CONNECT Software: Usage and Reference, Version 6, Second Edition.*

SAS/SHARE software
SAS/SHARE enables local and remote clients in a heterogeneous network to update SAS data concurrently. It also provides a low-overhead method for multiple remote clients to read local SAS data. For more information, see *SAS/SHARE Software: Usage*

---

* Although Emulus software is available from SAS Institute, it operates independently of the SAS System and its applications. It offers enhancements to 3270 terminal operations as well as extended, interactive features for users of SAS graphics applications, such as SAS/INSIGHT software.

and Reference, Version 6, First Edition and SAS Technical Report P-260, *SAS/SHARE Software for the MVS Environment, Release 6.08.*

SAS/SESSION

SAS/SESSION enables terminal users who are connected to the Customer Information Control System (CICS) to communicate with the SAS System in an MVS/ESA environment. It uses the LU6.2 (APPC/MVS) protocol. SAS Software Consultants will find more information about SAS/SESSION in Appendix P, "Implementing SAS/SESSION for CICS Software" in *Installation Instructions and System Manager's Guide.*

Customizing Your SAS Session

Whether you are using interactive processing under TSO or batch processing, you may want to customize certain aspects of the SAS System. For example, you may want to change the line size or page size for your output, or you may want to see performance statistics for your SAS programs.

You can customize the SAS System for your session in five ways:

□ Under TSO, pass operands into the SAS CLIST that your site uses to invoke SAS. (See "Invoking SAS under TSO: the SAS CLIST" on page 4.) This method is usually used for one-time overrides of CLIST operands. Here is an example:

```
sas options('nocenter linesize=80') config('''my.config.file''')
```

□ In batch mode, pass parameters into the SAS cataloged procedure that your site uses to invoke SAS. (See "Invoking SAS in Batch Mode: the SAS Cataloged Procedure" on page 4.) This method is usually used for one-time overrides of parameters in the cataloged procedure. Here is an example:

```
//MYJOB   EXEC SAS,OPTIONS='NOCENTER LINESIZE=80',
//            CONFIG='MY.CONFIG.FILE'
```

□ Specify SAS system options in a user configuration file. (See "Configuration Files" on page 7.) This method is useful if you, as an individual user, always want to override the values of system options that are specified in your site's system configuration file.

□ Execute SAS statements (such as OPTIONS, LIBNAME, and FILENAME statements) in an autoexec file. (See "Autoexec Files" on page 8.) This method is most useful for specifying options and allocating files that pertain to a particular SAS application.

□ In interactive mode, specify a SASUSER library that contains a user profile catalog. (See "SASUSER Library" on page 9.)

See "Precedence for Option Specifications" on page 13 for information about the order of precedence for these methods.

Configuration Files

A *configuration file* contains SAS system options that are set automatically when you invoke SAS. SAS uses two types of configuration files:

□ the system configuration file, which is used by all users at your site by default. Your SAS Software Consultant sets up the system configuration file for your site.

□ a user configuration file, which is generally used by an individual user or department.

When you allocate a system or user configuration file, you must specify LRECL=80 and RECFM=FB.

Creating a User Configuration File

To create a user configuration file, use any text editor to write SAS system options into an operating system data set. The configuration file can be either a sequential data set or a member of a partitioned data set that contains 80-byte fixed-length records.

Whichever type of data set you choose, specify one or more system options in each line. If you specify more than one system option on a line, use either a blank or a comma to separate the options.

Some options can be thought of as on (enabled) or off (disabled). Specifying just the keyword enables the option; specifying the keyword prefixed with NO disables the option. For example, the configuration file might contain these option specifications:

```
NOCENTER
NOSTIMER
NOSTATS
```

All of these options are disabled.

Options that take a value must be specified in the following way:

```
option-name=value
```

For example, a configuration file might contain the following lines:

```
LINESIZE=80
PAGESIZE=60
```

Note: When you specify SAS system options in a configuration file, blank spaces are not permitted before or after an equal sign. Comment lines must start with an asterisk in column 1.

A configuration file can contain any system option except the CONFIG= option. If CONFIG= appears in a configuration file, it is ignored; no error or warning message appears.

Specifying a User Configuration File

To tell SAS where to find your user configuration file, do the following:

□ If you use the SAS CLIST to invoke SAS under TSO, use the CONFIG operand. For example:

```
sas config('''my.config.file''')
```

□ If you use the SAS cataloged procedure to invoke SAS in batch mode, use the CONFIG= parameter. For example:

```
//S1  EXEC SAS,CONFIG='MY.CONFIG.FILE'
```

The user configuration file that you specify is executed along with the system configuration file that your installation uses. This happens because the SAS CLIST or the SAS cataloged procedure concatenates the file that you specified to the system configuration file.

Note: The SAS system options that you specify in the user configuration file override system options that are specified in the system configuration file.

Autoexec Files

Under MVS, an *autoexec file* can be either a sequential data set or a member of a partitioned data set. Unlike configuration files, which contain SAS system options, an autoexec file contains SAS statements. These statements are executed immediately after the SAS System has been fully initialized and before any SAS input source statements have been processed. For example, an autoexec file could contain the following lines:

```
options fullstats pagesize=60 linesize=80;
libname mylib 'userid.my.lib';
dm 'clock';
```

The OPTIONS statement sets some SAS system options, the LIBNAME statement assigns a libref, and the DM statement executes a display manager command.

Note: Some SAS system options can be specified only when you invoke SAS. These system options cannot be specified in an OPTIONS statement; therefore, they cannot be specified in an autoexec file. See Chapter 20 for information about SAS system options and about where they can be specified.

Displaying Autoexec Statements in the SAS Log

SAS statements that are submitted from an autoexec file usually are not displayed in the SAS log. However, if you specify the ECHOAUTO system option when you invoke SAS, then SAS writes (or "echoes") the autoexec statements to the SAS log as they are executed.

Using an Autoexec File under TSO

Under TSO, use the AUTOEXEC operand when you invoke SAS to tell SAS where to find your autoexec file. For example, the following command invokes SAS and tells SAS to use an autoexec file named MY.EXEC.FILE:

```
sas autoexec('''my.exec.file''')
```

Using an Autoexec File in Batch Mode

To specify an autoexec file in a batch job, use a JCL DD statement to assign the DDname SASEXEC to your autoexec file. This DD statement must follow the JCL EXEC statement that invokes the SAS cataloged procedure. For example, the following two lines of JCL can be used to accomplish the same results in a batch job as the previous example did under TSO:

```
//MYJOB     EXEC SAS
//SASEXEC   DD DSN=MY.EXEC.FILE,DISP=SHR
```

SASUSER Library

The SASUSER library contains SAS catalogs that enable you to customize certain features of the SAS System while your SAS session is running and to save these changes. For example, in base SAS software, any changes that you make to function key settings or to window attributes are stored in a catalog named SASUSER.PROFILE. The SASUSER library can also contain personal catalogs for other SAS software products. You can also store SAS data files, SAS data views, SAS programs, SAS/ACCESS descriptor files, and additional SAS catalogs in your SASUSER library.

When you use the SAS CLIST that is supplied by SAS Institute to invoke SAS under TSO, the CLIST allocates an operating system data set to be used as the SASUSER library during your SAS session. The SASUSER library is normally used only in interactive processing; the SAS cataloged procedure, which invokes SAS in batch processing, does not allocate a SASUSER library.

In addition to storing function key settings and window attributes, the SASUSER.PROFILE catalog is used to store your DEFAULT.FORM. The DEFAULT.FORM is created by the FORM subsystem. It is used to control the default destination of all output that is generated by the PRINT command during a display manager session. (See "Using the PRINT Command and the FORM Subsystem" on page 99 and *SAS Language: Reference, Version 6, First Edition*, for information about the FORM subsystem.)

Note: If your SAS CLIST has been modified so that it does not create a SASUSER library, SAS creates a PROFILE catalog that is used to store profile information for use during a single SAS session. This catalog is placed in the WORK library and is deleted at the end of your session; it is not available to a subsequent SAS session.

Creating Your Own SASUSER Libraries

By creating your own SASUSER libraries, you can customize the SAS System to meet the requirements of a number of different types of jobs. For example, suppose you want to create a user profile for a particular type of task that requires a unique set of key definitions.

In order to do this, you must first create a SAS data library that can be used as the SASUSER library.*

The easiest way to accomplish this is to start a SAS session and then use a LIBNAME statement to create the library, as explained in "Allocating SAS Data Libraries Internally" on page 28. For example, to create a SAS data library with an operating system data set name of ABC.MY.SASUSER, submit the following LIBNAME statement:

```
libname newlib 'abc.my.sasuser' disp=new;
```

Notice that a libref of NEWLIB was used in this example. SASUSER is a reserved libref and cannot be reassigned during a SAS session.

You can also use the TSO ALLOCATE command to create an operating system data set for use as your SASUSER library. By using the ALLOCATE command, you can avoid having to start a SAS session to use the LIBNAME statement; however, you must be familiar with TSO commands and with DCB (data control block) attributes in order to use the ALLOCATE command effectively. Here is a typical ALLOCATE command for the SASUSER library that provides satisfactory performance at many sites:

```
alloc fi(newlib) da('abc.my.sasuser') new catalog space(80 20) dsorg(ps)
      recfm(f s) blksize(6144) reu
```

When you enter this ALLOCATE command from the READY prompt, an operating system data set named ABC.MY.SASUSER is created with the correct attributes for a SAS data library.

In order to use the new SAS data library as the SASUSER library, you must end your SAS session and start a second session. When you start a second session, you can use the SASUSER CLIST operand to specify ABC.MY.SASUSER as the SASUSER library. (See the next section.)

Specifying Your Own SASUSER Library

After creating your own permanent SAS data library, designate that library as your SASUSER library. You can do this in either of the following ways:

□ Use the SASUSER CLIST operand to specify the operating system data set name of your SAS data library. For example, if you had created a library with an operating system name of ABC.MY.SASUSER, then you would use the following CLIST command to invoke SAS:

```
sas sasuser('''abc.my.sasuser''')
```

When you enter this command, the libref SASUSER is associated with the SAS data library whose operating system data set name is ABC.MY.SASUSER. Any profile changes that you make during your session are saved in the SAS catalog SASUSER.PROFILE, which is a member of the SASUSER library. These changes will be retained when you end your SAS session.

□ Use the SASUSER= system option to specify the DDname that identifies your SAS data library. (See "SASUSER=" on page 370.)

---

* This must be a Version 6 SAS data library that is created with the V6 engine.

Both of these methods require that you identify the SAS data library when you invoke SAS; you cannot change the SASUSER library during a SAS session.

SAS System Options

SAS system options control many aspects of your SAS session, including output destinations, the efficiency of program execution, and the attributes of SAS files and data libraries.

After a system option is set, it affects all subsequent DATA and PROC steps in a program until it is respecified with a different value. For example, the CENTER|NOCENTER option affects all output from a program, regardless of the number of steps in the program.

Specifying or Changing System Option Settings

The default values for SAS system options are appropriate for many of your SAS programs. If you need to specify or change the value of a system option, you can do so in the following ways:

□ Create a user configuration file to specify values for the SAS system options whose default values you want to override. See "Creating a User Configuration File" on page 7 for details.

□ Under TSO, you can specify any SAS system option following the OPTIONS parameter in the SAS CLIST command:

```
sas options('option-list')
```

For options that can be on or off, just list the keyword that corresponds to the appropriate setting. For options that take a value, list the keyword identifying the option followed by an equal sign and the option value, as in the following example:

```
sas options('nodate config=myconfig')
```

□ In batch mode, you can specify any SAS system option in the EXEC SAS statement:

```
// EXEC SAS,OPTIONS='option-list'
```

For example:

```
// EXEC SAS,OPTIONS='OPLIST LINESIZE=80 NOCENTER NOSTATS'
```

□ Specify SAS system options in an OPTIONS statement in an autoexec file, which is executed when you invoke SAS, or in an OPTIONS statement at any point during a SAS session. The options are reset for the duration of the SAS session or until you change them with another OPTIONS statement. The OPTIONS statement has the following form:

OPTIONS *option-list*;

For example:

```
options nodate linesize=72;
```

See Table 20.1 on page 398 to find out whether a particular option can be specified in the OPTIONS statement. For more information about autoexec files, see "Autoexec Files" on page 8. For more information about the OPTIONS statement, see *SAS Language and Procedures: Usage, Version 6, First Edition.*

□ Change SAS system options from within the OPTIONS window. On the command line of a display manager or interactive procedure window, enter the keyword OPTIONS. The OPTIONS window appears. Place the cursor on any option setting and type over the existing value. The value will be saved for the duration of the SAS session only. Not all options are listed in the OPTIONS window. See "OPTIONS Window" on page 13 for more information.

Default Options Table and Restricted Options Table

Your SAS Software Consultant may have created a default options table and/or a restricted options table. These tables are documented in *Installation Instructions and System Manager's Guide*, and they can affect the settings of SAS system options for your SAS sessions.

□ The default options table can contain any option; its only purpose is to eliminate the need for a system configuration file.

□ The restricted options table can contain any option. You cannot override the settings of the invocation options that are specified in this table.

Contact your SAS Software Consultant for more information.

Displaying System Option Settings

To display the current settings of SAS system options, use the OPTIONS procedure or the OPTIONS window.

Some options may seem to have default values even though the default value listed in Chapter 20 is none. This happens when the option is set in a system configuration file, in the system default options table, or in the system restricted options table.

OPTIONS Procedure

The OPTIONS procedure writes to the SAS log all system options that are available under MVS. By default, the procedure lists one option per line with a brief explanation of what the option does. To list the options with no explanation, use the SHORT option:

```
proc options short;
run;
```

Under MVS, PROC OPTIONS also supports some additional options for listing system options that are specific to SAS/ACCESS interfaces or to the SAS interface to ISPF. See "OPTIONS" on page 218 for details.

OPTIONS Window

To display the OPTIONS window, enter `OPTIONS` from the command line of any display manager window. The OPTIONS window displays the settings of many SAS system options. However, it does not list the following system options:

□ those that are valid only at SAS invocation

□ those that are specific to your host operating system

□ those that are available on all host operating systems, but whose values are host-specific.

See Table 20.1 on page 398 to find out whether a particular option is listed in the OPTIONS window.

Precedence for Option Specifications

When the same option is set in more than one place, the order of precedence is as follows:

1. OPTIONS window or OPTIONS statement (submitted from a SAS session or job).

2. restricted options table, if there is one. (Note: This table cannot contain any options that you could also specify in the OPTIONS window or OPTIONS statement.)

3. SAS invocation, including invocation by way of an EXEC SAS JCL statement (in batch) or by way of the SAS CLIST command (under TSO)

4. user configuration file, if there is one

5. system configuration file (as the SAS System is initialized)

6. default options table, if there is one

For example, options that you specify during your SAS session (in the OPTIONS window or via an OPTIONS statement) take precedence over options that you specified when you invoked SAS. Options that you specify with the SAS CLIST command take precedence over settings in the configuration file. The settings in the user configuration file take precedence over settings in the system configuration file and in the default options table.

Specifying Operating System Data Sets

Wherever you specify the name of an operating system data set *internally* (in a SAS LIBNAME or FILENAME statement, for example), the name can be in any of these forms:

□ a fully qualified data set name such as 'SAS.SAS6.AUTOEXEC' or 'MY.PDS(MEMBER)'

□ a partially qualified data set name such as '.CNTL'. SAS inserts the value of the SYSPREF= system option (which is usually *userid* by default) in front of the period. (See "SYSPREF=" on page 388.) In the following example, an OPTIONS statement is used to assign a value of USER12.SAS6 to the SYSPREF= system option. When SAS executes the FILENAME statement, it interprets '.RAW.DATAX' as 'USER12.SAS6.RAW.DATAX'.

```
options syspref=user12.sas6;
filename raw2 '.raw.datax' disp=old;
```

□   a temporary data set name such as '&MYTEMP'.

Note that names of operating system data sets must always be enclosed in quotes.

Handling of Nonstandard Member Names

You can use the SAS system option FILEEXT= to specify how extensions in member names of partitioned data sets are to be handled. See "FILEEXT=" on page 320 for more information.

SAS System Files

Configuration files (described in "Configuration Files" on page 7) and SASUSER files (described in "SASUSER Library" on page 9) are only two of several SAS system files that are automatically identified to your session by either the SAS CLIST (under TSO) or the SAS cataloged procedure (in batch). This section describes several other SAS system files that are significant to SAS users under MVS.

For brief descriptions of all the SAS system files that are frequently used by the SAS CLIST or by the SAS cataloged procedure, see Table 1.3 on page 20.

WORK Library

By default, the WORK library is a temporary SAS data library that contains temporary SAS data sets, utility files (created by some SAS procedures, such as PROC SORT and PROC TABULATE), your user profile, and other items that SAS uses in processing your current job. Anytime you assign a one-level name to a SAS data set, the data set is stored in the WORK library by default.

The WORK library is automatically defined by the SAS System at the beginning of your SAS job or session, unless you invoke SAS under TSO and specify the GO operand. By default, the entire WORK library is deleted at the end of each SAS job or session.

The WORK library must exist on a disk device in Version 6 format so that it can be accessed by the V6 engine. (See "Using the V6 Engine" on page 45 for information about the V6 engine.) Under MVS, the operating system data set that is associated with the DDname WORK is allocated by the SAS CLIST or by the SAS cataloged procedure.

Space is the aspect of the WORK library that is most likely to require your consideration. Both the SAS cataloged procedure and the SAS CLIST include parameters that enable you to specify how much space to allocate to the work library. In the cataloged procedure and CLIST that are supplied by SAS Institute, the space allocation for the WORK library is as follows:

```
SPACE=(6144,(500,200))
```

That is, the space is allocated in 6144-byte blocks, with a primary allocation of 500 blocks and a secondary allocation of 200 blocks. (Your installation may use different values; see the JCL from one of your SAS jobs to get a listing of the cataloged procedure that your SAS jobs use.) This space is enough for many SAS jobs. However, if you have many large temporary SAS data sets, or if you use a procedure that has many large utility files (for example, a PROC FREQ step with a complex TABLES statement that you run against a large SAS data set), you may run out of space in the WORK library. If you run out of space in batch mode, your PROC or DATA step terminates prematurely and issues a message similar to the one shown in Output 1.1. In an interactive session, a dialog window asks you to specify what action to take.

Output 1.1
Insufficient WORK
Space Message

```
ERROR: Insufficient space in file WORK.DATASET.DATA.
NOTE: The SAS System stopped processing this step because of errors.
NOTE: SAS set option OBS=0 and will continue to check statements.
      This may cause NOTE: No observations in data set.
WARNING: The data set WORK.DATASET may be incomplete.  When this step
         was stopped there were 22360 observations and 4 variables.
ERROR: Errors printed on page 1.
NOTE: SAS Institute Inc., SAS Campus Drive, Cary, NC 27513
```

Here are three possible solutions to this problem:

□ Use a larger WORK library. (See the next section, "Increasing the Size of the WORK Library".)

□ Delete each temporary SAS data set as soon as you no longer need it. (See "Deleting Temporary SAS Data Sets" on page 16.)

□ Direct the temporary SAS data sets to a different SAS data library so that data space in the WORK library is conserved for items that must be stored there. (See "Directing Temporary SAS Data Sets to the USER Library" on page 16.)

You can also combine these methods.

Increasing the Size of the WORK Library

Batch Mode Method
To increase the size of the WORK library in a batch job, include the WORK parameter in the EXEC statement in your JCL. The following SAS job allocates 1000 blocks of primary and 400 blocks of secondary space—twice as much as the default WORK allocations:

```
//HUGE JOB accounting-information
// EXEC SAS,WORK='1000,400'
//SYSIN DD *

SAS statements

/*
//
```

Interactive Mode Method
If you invoke SAS interactively, then include the WORK operand in the SAS CLIST command, as in the following example:

```
sas work('1000,400')
```

Deleting Temporary SAS Data Sets

Under MVS, *temporary SAS data set* means a data set that is stored in a temporary SAS data library. That is, you cannot designate the data set itself as temporary, but the data set takes on the attribute of the library in which it is stored.

One simple way to conserve space in the WORK library is to delete each temporary SAS data set with a PROC DATASETS step after you no longer need it. However, there are two problems with this method.

□ You can cause errors in a job by deleting a SAS data set before the job is finished with it.

□ If you need several very large temporary SAS data sets in your job at the same time, you may run out of space before you reach a point at which you can delete any SAS data sets.

An alternative to deleting the temporary SAS data sets is to direct them to a different SAS data library, as described in the next section.

Directing Temporary SAS Data Sets to the USER Library

You can use the USER= system option to store temporary data sets in the USER library rather than in the WORK library. You can make the USER library as large as you need it to be.

Note: Utility data sets that are created by the SAS procedures continue to be stored in the WORK library. However, any data sets that have one-level names and that are created by your SAS programs will be stored in the USER library.

You can use a temporary or permanent operating system data set for the library, and you can put the library either on disk or on tape. The operating system data set can be either a Version 5 or Version 6 SAS data library. If it is a Version 5 SAS data library, then it provides support for data sets but not for catalogs. Table 1.2 summarizes differences between the WORK and USER libraries.

Table 1.2
Differences between the WORK and USER Libraries

Library	Type of O.S. Data Set	Storage Medium	Format
WORK	temporary	disk	V6
USER	temporary or permanent	disk or tape	V6 or V5

The following example illustrates the use of the USER= system option. The numbered lines of code are explained below.

```
         filename giant 'company.survey.tvdata';
         libname result 'my.tv.sasdata';
❶       libname temp '&tvtemp' space=(cyl,(6,2));
❷       options user=temp;

❸       data totalusa;
            infile giant;
            input home_id region income viewers cable;
            if home_id=. then delete;
         run;

❹       proc freq;
            tables region*income*viewers*cable
❺              / noprint out=result.freqdata;
         run;
```

❶ The LIBNAME statement associates the libref TEMP with the temporary operating system data set &TVTEMP.

❷ In the OPTIONS statement, the USER= system option designates the TEMP libref as the temporary SAS data library. Any data sets that have one-level names and that are created by your SAS program will be stored in this library.

❸ A one-level name is used in the DATA statement. When the DATA step is processed, the SAS data set TEMP.TOTALUSA is created.

❹ Because the large TOTALUSA data set was directed to the TEMP library, there is more space available in the WORK library for the utility files that the FREQ procedure requires.

❺ The SAS data set FREQDATA contains the results of the FREQ procedure. A two-level name is used to store FREQDATA in the permanent SAS data library MY.TV.SASDATA.

SAS Log File

The SAS log file is a temporary operating system data set that has a DDname of SASLOG in both the SAS cataloged procedure and the SAS CLIST. In batch mode, the SAS cataloged procedure assigns default data control block (DCB) characteristics to this file as follows:

BLKSIZE=141
LRECL=137
RECFM=VBA

Under TSO, either interactively or noninteractively, the SASLOG file is routed to the terminal by default. In a display manager session, the SAS log is directed to the LOG window.

See Chapter 7, "Routing the SAS Log and SAS Procedure Output," for more information about the SAS log and about how to route output in a batch job.

Changing the Contents of the SAS Log

The particular information that appears in the SAS log depends on the settings of several SAS system options. See "Collecting Performance Statistics" on page 152 for more information.

In addition, the following portable system options affect the contents of the SAS log:

ECHOAUTO
> controls whether the SAS source statements in the autoexec file are written (echoed) to the SAS log.

MPRINT
> controls whether SAS statements that are generated by macros are displayed.

MLOGIC
> controls whether macro trace information is written to the SAS log when macros are executed.

NEWS=
> specifies an external file that contains messages to be written to the SAS log when the SAS System is initialized. Typically, the file contains information such as news items about the system.

NOTES
> controls whether NOTES are printed in the log. NOTES is the default setting for all methods of running SAS. Do not specify NONOTES unless your SAS program is completely debugged.

OPLIST
> specifies whether options given at SAS invocation are written to the SAS log.

SOURCE
> controls whether SAS source statements are written to the log. NOSOURCE is the default setting for SAS interactive line mode; otherwise, SOURCE is the default.

SOURCE2
> controls whether secondary source statements from files that are included by %INCLUDE statements are written to the SAS log.

SYMBOLGEN
> controls whether the macro processor displays the results of resolving macro references.

Changing the Appearance of the SAS Log

The following portable system options are used to change the appearance of the SAS log:

DATE
> controls whether the date and time, based on when the SAS job or session began, are written at the top of each page of the SAS log and of any print file that the SAS System creates. Use NODATE to suppress printing of the date and time.

LINESIZE=
> specifies the line size (printer line width) for the SAS log and the SAS procedure output file. LS= is an alias for this option. LINESIZE= values can range from 64 through 256.

NUMBER
> controls whether the log pages are numbered. NUMBER is the default. Use the
> NONUMBER option to suppress page numbers.

OVP
> controls whether lines in SAS output are overprinted.

SAS Procedure Output File

Whenever a SAS program executes a PROC step that produces printed output, SAS sends
the output to the procedure output file. Under TSO, either interactively or noninteractively,
the procedure output file is routed to the terminal by default. In a display manager session,
output is directed to the OUTPUT window.

In batch mode, the SAS procedure output file is identified in the cataloged procedure by
the DDname SASLIST. Unless you specify otherwise, SAS writes most procedure output to
this file. (A few procedures, such as the OPTIONS procedure, route output directly to the
SAS log by default.) PUT statement output may also be directed to this file by a FILE
statement that uses the fileref PRINT. (PRINT is a special fileref that can be specified in the
FILE statement.)

The following DCB characteristics of the procedure output file are controlled by the
cataloged procedure, typically with the following values:

> BLKSIZE=264
> LRECL=260
> RECFM=VBA

The SAS procedure output file is often called the *print file*; however, note that any data
set that contains carriage-control information (identified by a trailing A as part of the
RECFM= specification) can be called a print file.

Changing the Appearance of Procedure Output

The following portable system options are used to change the appearance of procedure
output:

CENTER
> controls whether the printed results are centered or left-aligned on the procedure output
> page. CENTER is the default; NOCENTER specifies left alignment.

DATE
> controls whether the date and time, based on when the SAS job or session began, are
> written at the top of each page of the SAS log and of any print file that the SAS System
> creates. Use NODATE to suppress printing of the date and time.

LINESIZE=
> specifies the line size (printer line width) for the SAS log and the SAS procedure output
> file. LS= is an alias for this option. LINESIZE= values can range from 64 through 256.

NUMBER
> controls whether the page number is printed on the first title line of each SAS printed output page. NUMBER is the default. Use the NONUMBER option to suppress page numbers.

PAGENO=
> specifies a beginning page number for the next page of output that the SAS System produces.

PAGESIZE=
> specifies how many lines to print on each page of SAS output. PS= is an alias for this option. In a display manager mode or interactive line mode session, the PAGESIZE= option defaults to the terminal screen size, if this information is available from the operating system. PAGESIZE= values can range from 15 through 500.

Parmcards File

The parmcards file is a temporary operating system data set that is identified by the DDname SASPARM. It is created automatically by the SAS cataloged procedure and by the SAS CLIST. SAS uses the parmcards file for internal processing. Lines that follow a PARMCARDS statement in a PROC step are first written to the parmcards file; then they are read into the procedure. The PARMCARDS statement is used in the BMDP and EXPLODE procedures.

Summary Table of SAS System Files

Table 1.3 lists all of the SAS system files that are frequently used in the SAS CLIST or in the SAS cataloged procedure. In the CLIST and cataloged procedure, logical names are associated with operating system data sets. The logical names listed in Table 1.3 are those that are used by the standard SAS CLIST or cataloged procedure. Your installation may have changed these names.

The system option column of Table 1.3 lists the SAS system options that you can pass into the SAS CLIST (using the OPTIONS operand) or into the SAS cataloged procedure (using the OPTIONS parameter) when you invoke SAS. You can use these system options to change the defaults that were established by the CLIST or by the cataloged procedure. (See "Specifying or Changing System Option Settings" on page 11.)

Table 1.3 *SAS System Files*

Default Logical Name	Purpose	System Option	CLIST Operands	Type of OS Data Set
CONFIG	system configuration file	CONFIG=*DDname*	DDCONFIG(*DDname*)	sequential data set or PDS member; must be FB, LRECL=80

Description: contains system options that are processed automatically when you invoke SAS. The system configuration file is usually maintained by your data center.

CONFIG	user configuration file	CONFIG=*DDname*	CONFIG(*dsn*) DDCONFIG(*DDname*)	sequential data set or PDS member; must be FB, LRECL=80

Description: also contains system options that are processed automatically when you invoke SAS. Your user configuration file is concatenated to the system configuration file.

LIBRARY	format library (V6)	n/a	n/a	SAS data library

Description: contains V6 formats and informats.

SAMPSIO	sample SAS data library	n/a	n/a	SAS data library

Description: is the SAS data library that is accessed by SAS programs in the sample library provided by SAS Institute.

SAS*nnnnn*	command processor file	n/a	n/a	sequential data set or PDS member

Description: is used by the SASCP command in the SAS CLIST.

SASAUTOS	system autocall library	n/a	MAUTS(*dsn*)	PDS

Description: contains source for SAS macros that were written by your data center or provided by SAS Institute.

SASAUTOS	user autocall library	SASAUTOS=*specification**	SASAUTOS(*dsn*) DDSASAUT(*DDname*)	PDS

Description: contains a user-defined autocall library to which the system autocall library is concatenated.

SASEXEC	autoexec file	AUTOEXEC=*DDname*	AUTOEXEC(*dsn*) DDAUTOEX(*DDname*)	sequential data set or PDS member

Description: contains statements that are executed automatically when you invoke SAS.

* SASAUTOS: *specification* can be a fileref, a partitioned data set name enclosed in quotes, or a series of file specifications enclosed in parentheses. See "SASAUTOS=" on page 367.

Table 1.3 (*continued*)

Default Logical Name	Purpose	System Option	CLIST Operands	Type of OS Data Set
SASHELP	HELP library	SASHELP= *DDname*	SASHELP(*dsn*) DDSASHLP(*DDname*)	SAS data library

Description: contains system default catalogs and Help system information.

SASLIB	format library (V5)	SASLIB= *DDname*	n/a	load library

Description: a load library that contains Version 5, Version 6, or both Version 5 and Version 6 user-written procedures, formats, informats, and functions. It is searched before the SAS System load library.

SASLIST	procedure output file	PRINT= *DDname*	PRINT(*dsn*) DDPRINT(*DDname*)	sequential data set or PDS member

Description: contains SAS procedure output.

SASLOG	log file	LOG= *DDname*	LOG(*dsn*) DDLOG(*DDname*)	sequential data set or PDS member

Description: SAS log file.

SASMSG	system message file	SASMSG= *DDname*	SASMSG(*dsn*) DDSASMSG(*DDname*)	PDS

Description: contains SAS system messages.

SASPARM	parmcards file	PARMCARD= *DDname*	PARMCARD(*size*) DDPARMCD(*DDname*)	sequential data set or PDS member

Description: a temporary data set that is used by some procedures. The PARMCARD= system option assigns a DDname to the parmcards file; the PARMCARD CLIST operand specifies the file size. You can use the DDPARMCD operand to specify an alternate name for the parmcards file via the CLIST.

SASSNAP	SNAP dump file	n/a	n/a	sequential data set or PDS member

Description: SNAP output from dump taken during abend recovery.

SASSWK*nn*	sort work files	DYNALLOC SORTWKDD= SORTWKNO=	n/a	sequential

Description: temporary files that are used by the host sort utility when sorting large amounts of data.

(*continued*)

Table 1.3 *(continued)*

Default Logical Name	Purpose	System Option	CLIST Operands	Type of OS Data Set
SASUSER	SASUSER library	SASUSER= *DDname*	SASUSER(*dsn*) DDSASUSR(*DDname*)	SAS data library
Description: contains the user profile catalog and other personal catalogs.				
STEPLIB	STEPLIB library	n/a	LOAD(*dsn*) SASLOAD(*dsn*)	load library
Description: a load library that contains SAS procedure and user-written load modules. (Allocate with a STEPLIB DD statement in a batch job.)				
SYSIN	primary input file	SYSIN= *DDname*	INPUT(*dsn*) DDSYSIN(*DDname*)	sequential data set or PDS member
Description: contains SAS statements. The primary input file can be specified with the INPUT operand under TSO, or allocated with a DD statement in a batch job.				
USER	USER library	USER= *DDname* | *dsn*	n/a	SAS data library
Description: specifies a SAS data library in which to store SAS data sets that have one-level names (instead of storing them in the WORK library).				
WORK	WORK library	WORK= *DDname*	DDWORK(*DDname*)	SAS data library
Description: contains temporary SAS files that are created by the SAS System during your session.				

Reserved MVS DDnames

In addition to the logical names shown in Table 1.3, which have a special meaning to the SAS System, you should be aware of the following reserved DDnames, which have a special meaning to the operating system:

JOBCAT
: specifies a private catalog that the operating system is to use instead of the system catalog for the duration of the job (including jobs with more than one job step).

JOBLIB
: performs the same function as STEPLIB (described in Table 1.3) except that it can be used in a job that has more than one job step.

PROCLIB
: specifies a private library of cataloged procedures to be searched before the system library of cataloged procedures is searched. See your SAS Software Consultant for information about whether the PROCLIB DDname convention is used at your facility.

SORTLIB
: is used by some host sort utilities.

SORTMSG

   is used by some host sort utilities to print messages.

SORTWK*nn*

   specifies sort work data sets for the host sort utility. If allocated, this will be used instead of the SASSWK*nn* data sets.

STEPCAT

   specifies a private catalog that the operating system is to use instead of the system catalog for the current job step.

SYSABEND

   specifies a data set to contain the output from a system dump.

SYSHELP

   is used by TSO HELP libraries (not the SAS HELP facility).

SYSLIB

   is used by some IBM system utility programs.

SYSMDUMP

   specifies a data set to contain output from a system dump.

SYSOUT

   is used by some utility programs to identify an output data set.

SYSPRINT

   is used by some utility programs to identify a data set for listings and messages that may be sent to the printer.

SYSUADS

   is used by some TSO commands that may be invoked under the SAS System.

SYSUDUMP

   specifies a data set to contain output from a system dump.

SYS*nnnnn*

   is reserved for internal use (for dynamic allocation) by the operating system.

Chapter 2 Allocating SAS® Data Libraries

Introduction   25
Ways of Allocating SAS Data Libraries   26
SAS Library Engines   26
SAS View Engines   27

Allocating SAS Data Libraries Internally   28
Advantages of Allocating SAS Data Libraries Internally   28
LIBNAME Statement Syntax   29
LIBNAME Statement Examples   30

Allocating SAS Data Libraries Externally   30
JCL DD Statement Examples   31
TSO ALLOCATE Command Examples   31
Using a DDname as a Libref   32
Using the LIBNAME Statement with Externally Allocated SAS Data Libraries   32

How SAS Assigns an Engine When No Engine Is Specified   32

Allocating Generation Data Sets   33

Allocating Multivolume SAS Data Libraries   33
General Guidelines   33
Allocating a SAS Data Library on Multiple DASD Volumes   34
Extending a SAS Data Library to Multiple DASD Volumes   35
Allocating an Existing Multivolume SAS Data Library   36
Allocating Multivolume SAS Data Libraries in an SMS Environment   36
    Allocating an Existing Multivolume SAS Data Library in an SMS Environment   37
Allocating a Multivolume Generation Data Group   37

Assigning Multiple Librefs to a Single SAS Data Library   38

Deallocating SAS Data Libraries   38

Listing Your Current Librefs   39

Estimating the Size of a SAS Data Set   39
Using the CONTENTS Procedure to Determine Observation Length   39

Estimating the Size of a SAS Index   41

Introduction

Under MVS, a SAS data library is a specially formatted operating system data set that contains only SAS files. When you allocate an *existing* SAS data library, you are simply making it available to your SAS program and assigning a logical name to it for the duration of your SAS session. When you allocate a *new* SAS data library, you are actually creating the data library. Therefore, in addition to assigning a logical name to the operating system data set, you specify parameters such as block size, disposition, and space allocation. If you do not specify these additional parameters, SAS uses default values that are derived from SAS system options.

The logical name that you assign to your SAS data library is called a *libref* if you use the SAS LIBNAME statement to allocate the library, or a *DDname* if you use the JCL DD statement or the TSO ALLOCATE command to allocate the library. Thereafter, you can use the libref or DDname as a convenient way of referring to the library.

Ways of Allocating SAS Data Libraries

Under MVS, you can allocate a new or existing SAS data library in the following ways:

- □ *internally* (within a SAS session), using a LIBNAME statement
- □ *externally*, using a JCL DD statement or a TSO ALLOCATE command.

See "Allocating SAS Data Libraries Internally" on page 28 and "Allocating SAS Data Libraries Externally" on page 30 for more information about these methods.

SAS Library Engines

The SAS System provides different engines that enable you to access and, in most cases, to update files of different types and different formats. See *SAS Language: Reference* for a complete discussion of the SAS System's multiple engine architecture and the different types of engines that are provided on all host operating systems.

When you allocate a SAS data library internally, you use the *engine* parameter of the LIBNAME statement to specify the appropriate engine for each SAS data library that you want to access. (See "LIBNAME Statement Syntax" on page 29.) Or SAS can determine which engine to use, based on the procedures described in "How SAS Assigns an Engine When No Engine Is Specified" on page 32.

When you allocate a SAS data library externally, SAS assigns an engine to the library. You can override the default by subsequently using the LIBNAME statement to associate a different engine with the library. See "Using the LIBNAME Statement with Externally Allocated SAS Data Libraries" on page 32.

Table 2.1 lists the library engines that have MVS-specific aspects and tells you where to look for more information about them.

Table 2.1 *SAS Library Engines for MVS*

Engine	Description	Where Documented
V6	accesses SAS files in Version 6 disk format. You can also use the aliases BASE, V609, V608, V607, and V606 to specify this engine.	"Using the V6 Engine" on page 45
V6SEQ	accesses SAS files in Version 6 sequential format, including sequential format on tape and sequential format on disk. You can also use the alias TAPE to specify this engine.	"Using the V6SEQ Engine" on page 49

(continued)

Table 2.1 (*continued*)

Engine	Description	Where Documented
V5	accesses SAS files in Version 5 disk format	"Accessing V5 and V5SEQ SAS Data Libraries" on page 431
V5SEQ	accesses SAS files in Version 5 sequential format, including sequential format on tape and sequential format on disk	"Accessing V5 and V5SEQ SAS Data Libraries" on page 431
BMDP OSIRIS SPSS	provide read-only access to BMDP, OSIRIS, and SPSS (including SPSS-X) files, respectively	"Accessing BMDP, SPSS, and OSIRIS Files" on page 53
REMOTE	is used by SAS/CONNECT and SAS/SHARE software to access remote files	*SAS/CONNECT Software: Usage and Reference, Version 6, Second Edition* and *SAS/SHARE Software: Usage and Reference, Version 6, First Edition*
XPORT	transports SAS files from one operating system to another	"Transporting SAS Data Sets" on page 132

SAS View Engines

SAS view engines enable the SAS System to read SAS data views that are described by the SQL procedure or by SAS/ACCESS software. These engines support the SAS data set model only and are not specified in the LIBNAME statement.

Under MVS, the following view engines are supported:

ADB   accesses ADABAS database files.

DB2   accesses DB2 database files.

DDB   accesses CA-DATACOM/DB database files.

IDMS   accesses CA-IDMS database files.

IMS   accesses IMS-DL/I database files.

ORACLE   accesses ORACLE database files.

SQL   accesses data sets that are described by the SQL procedure.

For more information about the SQL view engine, see *SAS Guide to the SQL Procedure: Usage and Reference, Version 6, First Edition.* For information about the other view engines, see the appropriate SAS/ACCESS software documentation.

Allocating SAS Data Libraries Internally

The LIBNAME statement allocates the operating system data set, associates it with an engine, and assigns a libref to it. The assignment lasts for the duration of the SAS job or session unless you clear it. (See "Deallocating SAS Data Libraries" on page 38 for information about clearing a libref.)

Advantages of Allocating SAS Data Libraries Internally

Although you can use a JCL DD statement or a TSO ALLOCATE command to allocate SAS files *externally*, the LIBNAME statement can do much more. Here are several reasons why it is better to allocate SAS data libraries internally with the LIBNAME statement:

□ The LIBNAME statement provides an easy way to do dynamic allocation in the batch environment. SAS programs that have LIBNAME statements instead of external allocations can be executed either in the TSO environment or in the batch environment.

□ The JCL DD statement and the TSO ALLOCATE command are not portable to other operating systems. The LIBNAME statement is portable with minor changes to the *OS-data-set-name* and options parameters.

□ If you use the LIBNAME statement, you can allocate your data library for only as long as you need it, and then "free" (deallocate) it. By contrast, DDnames that are allocated externally remain allocated for the duration of the SAS session or job. (The LIBNAME CLEAR statement clears an externally allocated libref, but it does not deallocate the file. See "Deallocating SAS Data Libraries" on page 38.)

□ DDnames that are allocated externally cannot be reassigned later by a LIBNAME statement. You would receive an error message in the SAS log stating that the DDname is currently assigned.

□ By using macro statements and the LIBNAME statement, you can conditionally allocate files.

□ You cannot assign an engine when you allocate a file externally. SAS uses the procedure described in "How SAS Assigns an Engine When No Engine Is Specified" on page 32 to determine which engine to use; however, it is more efficient to specify an engine explicitly in a LIBNAME statement. Also, the following SAS engines must be specified in a LIBNAME statement because they are not assigned by default: XPORT, BMDP, SPSS, OSIRIS, V5SEQ, and REMOTE.

□ DDnames that are allocated externally are not included in the list that is produced by the LIBNAME LIST statement nor in the LIBNAME window until after they have been used as librefs in your SAS session. (See "Listing Your Current Librefs" on page 39.)

LIBNAME Statement Syntax

This section provides a brief overview of LIBNAME statement syntax. For complete information about the LIBNAME statement, see "LIBNAME" on page 289.

The general form of the LIBNAME statement is:

LIBNAME *libref* <*engine*> <*'OS-data-set-name'*> <*engine/host-options*>;

libref

> is a logical name by which the library is referenced during your SAS session. The libref must begin with a letter and must contain 1-8 characters consisting of letters or numbers. SAS reserves some names as librefs for special system libraries. See "SAS System Files" on page 14 for more information.
>
> When choosing a libref, follow the rules for SAS names, but do not use underscores. To read, update, or create files that belong to a permanent SAS data library, you must include the libref as the first part of a two-level SAS member name in your program statements, as follows:*
>
> `libref.member`
>
> *libref* could also be a DDname that was specified in a JCL DD statement or in a TSO ALLOCATE command. The first time the DDname of a SAS data library is used in a SAS statement or procedure, SAS assigns it as a libref for the SAS data library.

engine

> tells SAS which engine to use for accessing the library. Valid engine names for MVS include V6 (or its alias, BASE), V6SEQ (or its alias, TAPE), V5, V5SEQ, XPORT, REMOTE, BMDP, OSIRIS, and SPSS. See "SAS Library Engines" on page 26 for more information. If you do not specify an engine, SAS uses the procedures described in "How SAS Assigns an Engine When No Engine Is Specified" on page 32 to assign an engine for you. If the engine name that you supply does not match the actual format or attributes of the data library, then any attempt to access the library will fail.

'OS-data-set-name'

> is the operating system data set name of the SAS data library, enclosed in quotes. See "Specifying Operating System Data Sets" on page 13. You can omit this argument if you are merely specifying the engine for a previously allocated DDname.

engine/host options

> are options that apply to the SAS data library. The host-specific options that are available depend on which engine you are using to access the data library. See "SAS Library Engines" on page 26 for more information about SAS engines. Specify as many options as you need. Separate them with a blank space. For a complete list of available options, see "LIBNAME" on page 289.

---

*   An exception is a SAS file in the USER library. In this case, you can use a one-level name. See "Directing Temporary SAS Data Sets to the USER Library" on page 16 for more information about the USER library.

LIBNAME Statement Examples

Allocating an existing SAS data library:
  The following LIBNAME statement allocates the existing SAS data library
  LIBRARY.CATALOG.DATA and assigns the libref BOOKS to it:

```
libname books 'library.catalog.data';
```

Allocating a new SAS data library:
  The following LIBNAME statement allocates the new SAS data library
  prefix.NEW.SASDATA. The *prefix* will be taken from the value of the SYSPREF=
  system option, as explained in "Specifying Operating System Data Sets" on page 13.
  The LIBNAME statement assigns the libref NEWLIB to the data library.

```
libname newlib '.new.sasdata' disp=(new,catlg) unit=3380 vol=xyz828
space=(cyl,(10,3)) blksize=23040;
```

Because the operating system data set did not previously exist, appropriate values are
specified for DISP=, UNIT=, and other engine/host options. The engine name is not
specified explicitly, so SAS assigns the default engine to the libref. (The default engine
is the engine that is specified by the SAS system option ENGINE=. See "ENGINE="
on page 316.) SAS uses these values to dynamically allocate the data set; then it assigns
the libref to the data set.
  Note: If you do not specify default values for DCB attributes when you allocate a
new operating system data set with the LIBNAME statement, the SAS System supplies
default values. See "Internal Allocation: V6 Engine" on page 47 and "Internal
Allocation: V6SEQ Engine" on page 50 for details.

Specifying additional options for a previously allocated SAS data set:
  See "Using the LIBNAME Statement with Externally Allocated SAS Data Libraries"
  on page 32.

Allocating SAS Data Libraries Externally

There are several advantages to allocating SAS data libraries internally (see "Advantages of
Allocating SAS Data Libraries Internally" on page 28). However, you can also use either a
JCL DD statement or a TSO command to allocate a SAS data library externally and to
assign a DDname to it.
  Note: If you do not use the LIBNAME statement to specify an engine for a data set
that was allocated externally (as described in "Using the LIBNAME Statement with
Externally Allocated SAS Data Libraries" on page 32), then SAS uses the procedures
described in "How SAS Assigns an Engine When No Engine Is Specified" on page 32 to
determine which engine to use.

JCL DD Statement Examples

Allocating an existing SAS data library:
> The following JCL DD statement allocates the cataloged data set
> LIBRARY.CATALOG.DATA and assigns the DDname BOOKS to it:

```
//BOOKS DD DSN=LIBRARY.CATALOG.DATA,DISP=OLD
```

Allocating a new SAS data library:
> This example allocates a new SAS data library on tape:

```
//INTAPE DD DSN=USERID.V6.SEQDATA,UNIT=TAPE,
// LABEL=(1,SL),DCB=(RECFM=U,LRECL=32756,BLKSIZE=32760),
// DISP=(NEW,KEEP),VOL=SER=XXXXXX
```

> Notice that DCB attributes are specified. When you allocate a new SAS data library
> externally, you must either specify DCB attributes or accept the default DCB attributes
> that SAS supplies. See "DCB Attributes for the V6 Engine" on page 46 and "DCB
> Attributes for the V6SEQ Engine" on page 50 for details.

Specifying additional options for a previously allocated SAS data library:
> See "Using the LIBNAME Statement with Externally Allocated SAS Data Libraries"
> on page 32.

TSO ALLOCATE Command Examples

Allocating an existing SAS data library:
> The following TSO ALLOCATE command allocates the cataloged data set
> LIBRARY.CATALOG.DATA and assigns the DDname BOOKS to it:

```
alloc file(books) da('library.catalog.data') old
```

> The following command performs the same allocation, this time using the SAS X
> statement to submit the TSO ALLOC command (see "X" on page 297 for details about
> the X statement):

```
x alloc file(books) da('library.catalog.data') old;
```

Allocating a new SAS data library:
> The following example allocates a new sequential SAS data library on disk:

```
alloc fi(intape) da(v6.seqdata) dsorg(ps) recfm(u) blksize(6144) new
```

> Notice that DCB attributes are specified. When you allocate a new SAS data library
> externally, you must either specify DCB attributes or accept the default DCB attributes
> that SAS supplies. See "DCB Attributes for the V6 Engine" on page 46 and "DCB
> Attributes for the V6SEQ Engine" on page 50 for details.

Specifying additional options for a previously allocated SAS data library:
> See "Using the LIBNAME Statement with Externally Allocated SAS Data Libraries"
> on page 32.

Using a DDname as a Libref

After a DDname has been assigned, you can use it in a SAS job in the same way you would use a libref. For example:

```
proc contents data=books._all_;
run;
```

The first time the DDname BOOKS is used in this manner, SAS assigns it as a libref for the SAS data library.

When a DDname is allocated externally, it is not listed by the LIBNAME LIST statement nor in the LIBNAME window until after you have used it as a libref in your SAS session. (See "Listing Your Current Librefs" on page 39.)

Using the LIBNAME Statement with Externally Allocated SAS Data Libraries

You can use the LIBNAME statement to specify an engine for a data library that was previously allocated externally. For example, suppose you used an X statement to submit the following TSO ALLOCATE command, which allocates the SAS data library QUARTER1.MAILING.LIST:

```
x alloc f(mail) da('quarter1.mailing.list') old;
```

You could later use the LIBNAME statement to associate an engine with the library as follows:

```
libname mail v6seq;
```

This LIBNAME statement associates the Version 6 sequential engine with the data library that is referred to by the DDname MAIL. You can then read to and write from the sequential format data library QUARTER1.MAILING.LIST. You do not need to specify the data set name in this example, as long as MAIL is the DDname for QUARTER1.MAILING.LIST. If you do specify the data set name, the name must match the data set name that was already allocated to that DDname.

How SAS Assigns an Engine When No Engine Is Specified

In some cases, you may choose not to specify an engine name in the LIBNAME statement, or you may choose not to issue a LIBNAME statement for a data library that was allocated externally. For these situations, you need to know how SAS assigns an engine to the library.

□ For a new SAS data library on disk, SAS uses the value of the ENGINE= system option as the engine. (Exception: For a new *sequential-format* data library on disk, you must include the engine name in the LIBNAME statement.)

□   For an existing SAS data library on disk, SAS examines the library's DCB attributes to determine which engine to use.

  □   If DSORG=PS and RECFM=FS, SAS uses the V6 engine.

  □   If DSORG=DA, SAS uses the V5 engine.

  □   If DSORG=PS and RECFM=U, SAS uses the current value of the SEQENGINE= system option.

  □   If either DSORG= or RECFM= is undefined, SAS uses the current value of the ENGINE= system option.

□   For new tape data sets, SAS uses the current value of the SEQENGINE= system option.

□   For existing tape data sets, instead of looking at the characteristics of the tape, SAS opens the file and reads the first record to determine whether it should use V6SEQ or V5SEQ.

Allocating Generation Data Sets

A generation data set (or *generation*) is a version of a data set that is stored as a member of a generation data group. (For detailed information about generation data groups, see your IBM documentation.) Both SAS data libraries and standard external files can be stored and managed as generation data groups. The methods of allocating and accessing generations are the same for SAS data libraries as they are for external files. For more information, see "Allocating Generation Data Sets" on page 64 and "Allocating a Multivolume Generation Data Group" on page 37.

Allocating Multivolume SAS Data Libraries

A Version 6 SAS data library on disk may span volumes. The operating system data set that contains the SAS data library may exist on multiple DASD volumes, but it is processed by SAS software as one logical entity. This capability greatly increases the storage capacity of a data library. This section provides the information you need to run a batch job that creates a multivolume SAS data library.

   Note: If you need to allocate multivolume SAS data libraries in an SMS environment, see "Allocating Multivolume SAS Data Libraries in an SMS Environment" on page 36 instead.

General Guidelines

When creating a multivolume SAS data library, observe the following guidelines:

□   A data library can span no more than five volumes.

□   Unless you are allocating the multivolume data library in an SMS environment, you are not required to specify all of the volumes for the library when you first allocate the library. You can add more volumes as a data library grows.

□   A multivolume data library must be allocated on devices of the same type (for example, all 3380s or all 3390s). However, the control units that are attached to the devices may support a mix of standard CKD and extended CKD (ECKD) capabilities. SAS software optimizes I/O operations at the device level by exploiting the capabilities of the primary control unit that is attached to the volume that is being accessed.

□   It is recommended that entire DASD volumes be allocated to multivolume data libraries. SAS software opens a separate data control block (DCB) on each DASD volume. This means that you must specify a primary space allocation for each volume. Secondary allocation space is not obtained for a multivolume SAS data library, so it is not practical to use DASD volumes that have heavily fragmented free space.

□   If your installation runs periodic full-volume backups, you must ensure that the other volumes in a multivolume data library are not updated while a backup of one of the volumes is running; otherwise, data integrity cannot be guaranteed if you attempt to restore the library from the full-volume backups. The best way to ensure data integrity is to back up the data library as a complete unit in volume sequence order and to restrict data library access to "read only" during the backup operation. This ensures integrity if a restore operation is required, because the data library can be restored logically in volume sequence order.

□   When restoring a multivolume data library, you do not need to restore the library to the same volumes that it previously existed on. A data library can even be restored to multiple volumes of a different device type than it previously existed on, as long as the restore utility places the maximum number of blocks of the given block size on each track of the new device.

Allocating a SAS Data Library on Multiple DASD Volumes

When a multivolume SAS data library is initially allocated, an individual JCL DD statement is required for each volume. Follow these DD statements with another DD statement that catalogs the data library on all volumes. After you have allocated the library, the cataloged volume sequence must remain the same in order for proper access to occur.

   The following example allocates a data library on five single-density 3380 volumes. In this example, the DDnames LIBVOL1 through LIBVOL5 and CATVOLS are used to illustrate the sequence in which the data library volumes are initially allocated and cataloged. However, any valid DDnames can be used.

```
//LIBVOL1   DD DSN=SAS.MVDATLIB,UNIT=3380,
//             DISP=(NEW,KEEP,KEEP),
//             DCB=(DSORG=PS,RECFM=FS,BLKSIZE=23040,LRECL=23040),
//             SPACE=(CYL,(884)),
//             VOL=SER=(VOL001)
//LIBVOL2   DD DSN=SAS.MVDATLIB,UNIT=3380,
//             DISP=(NEW,KEEP,KEEP),
//             DCB=(DSORG=PS,RECFM=FS,BLKSIZE=23040,LRECL=23040),
//             SPACE=(CYL,(884)),
//             VOL=SER=(VOL002)
```

```
//LIBVOL3   DD DSN=SAS.MVDATLIB,UNIT=3380,
//             DISP=(NEW,KEEP,KEEP),
//             DCB=(DSORG=PS,RECFM=FS,BLKSIZE=23040,LRECL=23040),
//             SPACE=(CYL,(884)),
//             VOL=SER=(VOL003)
//LIBVOL4   DD DSN=SAS.MVDATLIB,UNIT=3380,
//             DISP=(NEW,KEEP,KEEP),
//             DCB=(DSORG=PS,RECFM=FS,BLKSIZE=23040,LRECL=23040),
//             SPACE=(CYL,(884)),
//             VOL=SER=(VOL004)
//LIBVOL5   DD DSN=SAS.MVDATLIB,UNIT=3380,
//             DISP=(NEW,KEEP,KEEP),
//             DCB=(DSORG=PS,RECFM=FS,BLKSIZE=23040,LRECL=23040),
//             SPACE=(CYL,(884)),
//             VOL=SER=(VOL005)
//CATVOLS   DD DSN=SAS.MVDATLIB,UNIT=3380,
//             DISP=(OLD,CATLG,KEEP),
//             VOL=SER=(VOL001,VOL002,VOL003,VOL004,VOL005)
```

Extending a SAS Data Library to Multiple DASD Volumes

In the following example, a SAS data library is created on one volume but is extended onto a second and finally a third DASD volume. Using this method, a SAS data library may be extended to a total of five DASD volumes.

When a new DASD volume is added, the existing volume sequence order of the data library must be properly maintained. Always add the new volume serial number at the end of the VOL=SER= list in the DD statement that recatalogs the data library. (In this example, the CATVOLS DDname is again used for the DD statements that recatalog the data library.)

```
//* Create a new single-volume library
//LIBVOL1    DD DSN=SAS.MVDATLIB,UNIT=3380,
//              DISP=(NEW,CATLG,KEEP),
//              DCB=(DSORG=PS,RECFM=FS,BLKSIZE=23040,LRECL=23040),
//              SPACE=(CYL,(884)),
//              VOL=SER=(VOL001)
.
.
.
//* Later, extend the existing SAS data library to a second volume
//UNCATLIB   DD DSN=SAS.MVDATLIB,
//              DISP=(OLD,UNCATLG,KEEP)
//LIBVOL2    DD DSN=SAS.MVDATLIB,UNIT=3380,
//              DISP=(NEW,KEEP,KEEP),
//              DCB=(DSORG=PS,RECFM=FS,BLKSIZE=23040,LRECL=23040),
//              SPACE=(CYL,(884)),
//              VOL=SER=(VOL002)
```

```
//CATVOLS   DD DSN=SAS.MVDATLIB,UNIT=3380,
//             DISP=(OLD,CATLG,KEEP),
//             VOL=SER=(VOL001,VOL002)
.
.
.

//* Still later, further extend the existing data library to a third volume
//UNCATLIB  DD DSN=SAS.MVDATLIB,
//             DISP=(OLD,UNCATLG,KEEP)
//LIBVOL3   DD DSN=SAS.MVDATLIB,UNIT=3380,
//             DISP=(NEW,KEEP,KEEP),
//             DCB=(DSORG=PS,RECFM=FS,BLKSIZE=23040,LRECL=23040),
//             SPACE=(CYL,(884)),
//             VOL=SER=(VOL003)
//CATVOLS   DD DSN=SAS.MVDATLIB,UNIT=3380,
//             DISP=(OLD,CATLG,KEEP),
//             VOL=SER=(VOL001,VOL002,VOL003)
```

Allocating an Existing Multivolume SAS Data Library

After a multivolume SAS data library has been initially allocated or extended to additional DASD volumes, any of the following statements can be used for allocation as long as the data library is cataloged in volume sequence order.

```
//USEVOLS   DD DSN=SAS.MVDATLIB,DISP=OLD

x alloc fi(usevols) da('sas.mvdatlib') shr;

libname usevols 'sas.mvdatlib';
```

Cataloging a multivolume SAS data library ensures that SAS can process it properly without requiring the VOL=SER= list each time the library is allocated for use.

Allocating Multivolume SAS Data Libraries in an SMS Environment

If you are allocating new multivolume SAS libraries in an SMS environment, then you will be unable to use the allocation method described in "Allocating Multivolume SAS Data Libraries" on page 33. This is because SMS generally restricts the user both from specifying particular volsers and from creating and keeping uncataloged data sets. Therefore, your SMS system administrator will need to set up a storage class that allows multi-unit allocations and that has the GUARANTEED SPACE attribute. The GUARANTEED SPACE attribute ensures that the primary space amount for your request is allocated on each candidate volume when the multivolume data set is allocated.

The following examples allocate a permanent and a temporary multivolume library in an SMS environment in which the SASMV storage class has been defined by the system administrator and has been assigned the GUARANTEED SPACE attribute. Each volume will have the 400 cylinder primary space allocation.

permanent multivolume library:

```
//IEFBR14  EXEC PGM=IEFBR14
//DD1      DD DSN=SAS.PERMLIB,DISP=(,CATLG),
//         UNIT=(DISK,2),SPACE=(CYL,400),STORCLAS=SASMV,
//         DCB=(RECFM=FS,LRECL=6144,BLKSIZE=6144)
```

temporary multivolume library:

```
//SAS      EXEC SAS
//WORK     DD DSN=&&WORK,DISP=(,DELETE),
//         UNIT=(SYSDA,2),SPACE=(CYL,400),STORCLAS=SASMV,
//         DCB=(RECFM=FS,LRECL=6144,BLKSIZE=6144)
```

Note: You cannot dynamically add volumes in an SMS environment, so you should allocate the maximum number of volumes in the original allocation. Alternatively, you can back up the original library and redefine it with more volumes, then restore the library using the COPY procedure.

Unless otherwise indicated, all of the guidelines listed in "General Guidelines" on page 33 apply to allocating multivolume SAS data libraries in an SMS environment as well.

For detailed information about SMS, see your IBM documentation.

Allocating an Existing Multivolume SAS Data Library in an SMS Environment

The information in "Allocating an Existing Multivolume SAS Data Library" on page 36 applies to the SMS environment as well. See that section for details.

Allocating a Multivolume Generation Data Group

As explained in "Allocating Generation Data Sets" on page 64, a SAS data library can be stored and managed as a generation data group (GDG). To allocate a GDG that spans multiple volumes, use either of the following methods:

SMS   Define the GDG with a standard IDCAMS job. Ensure that the job does *not* contain a DD card for the data set; otherwise, the DEFINE GENERATION DATA GROUP statement generates duplicate data set messages and fails. (When you use the GUARANTEED SPACE attribute in an SMS environment, data set information is allocated on all designated packs; the DEFINE recognizes that information has been duplicated and fails.) When creating a new generation, use the relative form of the data set name in your DD card (for example, DSN=XXX.SAS.GDG(+1)). Abide by all SAS SMS multivolume restrictions.

IEFBR14   Define the GDG with a standard IDCAMS job. When creating a new generation, observe the guidelines provided in "Allocating Multivolume SAS Data Libraries" on page 33 and use the absolute form of the data set name (for example, DSN=XXX.MULTI.GDG.G0001V00).

Assigning Multiple Librefs to a Single SAS Data Library

You can assign more than one libref to the same operating system data set. Any assigned libref may be used to access the data library. In fact, you can use the librefs interchangeably.

For example, suppose that in two different programs you used different librefs for the same data sets. Later you develop a new program from parts of the two old programs, or you include two different programs with the %INCLUDE statement. In the new program, you could simply assign the two original librefs to each data set and proceed.

Note: Even when multiple librefs are assigned to the same operating system data set, the operating system allocates the data set only once. The first logical name (libref or DDname) that you assign is used as the DDname in the operating system allocation.

Deallocating SAS Data Libraries

The method you use to deallocate a SAS data library depends on how it was allocated.

□   To deallocate a SAS data library that was allocated with a LIBNAME statement, issue a LIBNAME statement in the following form, using the libref for the data library that you want to deallocate:

LIBNAME *libref* <CLEAR>;

This statement deassigns the libref and deallocates the library only if there are no other librefs assigned to that library.

Note: Libraries that were allocated by a LIBNAME statement are deallocated automatically at the end of your SAS session.

□   To deallocate a library that was allocated with a TSO command, first issue a LIBNAME statement to "clear" (deassign) the libref, as shown above. Then issue an operating system command that "frees" (deallocates) the data set.

For example, suppose that a SAS data library with the libref MYLIB is stored in the operating system data set MYID.RECENT.DATA. The following two statements would clear the libref and free the operating system data set:

```
libname mylib clear;
x tso free da('myid.recent.data');
```

If the data library is currently being used by a DATA step or PROC, the LIBNAME statement fails.

Note: If multiple librefs have been assigned to the same operating system data set, the data set is not freed until all librefs assigned to the data set have been cleared.

Listing Your Current Librefs

You can use either the LIBNAME command or a form of the LIBNAME statement to list your current librefs. In both cases, DDnames for externally allocated data libraries are also listed, but only after you have used them as librefs in your SAS session. (See "Using a DDname as a Libref" on page 32.)

□ When you issue the LIBNAME command from a SAS display manager window, the LIBNAME window is displayed. The LIBNAME window lists all the librefs that are currently assigned for your session.

The LIBNAME window displays the full operating system data set name of the SAS data library, as well as the engine that is used to access the data library. See "LIBNAME" on page 414 for an example of a LIBNAME window under MVS.

□ The following form of the LIBNAME statement writes to the SAS log the attributes of all the librefs that are currently assigned for your session:

```
LIBNAME _ALL_ LIST;
```

Estimating the Size of a SAS Data Set

To obtain a rough estimate of how much space you need for a disk-format SAS data set that was created by the V6 engine, follow these steps:

Note: This procedure is valid only for *uncompressed* native SAS data files that were created with the V6 engine.

1. Use PROC CONTENTS to determine the size of each observation. (See the next section.)

2. Multiply the size of each observation by the number of observations.

3. Add 10% for overhead.

4. The result of this calculation will be in bytes. You can convert this value to tracks based on the capacity of your data storage device.

For additional information about estimating the size of a SAS data set, see Chapter 4 of *Tuning SAS Applications in the MVS Environment*, by Michael Raithel. This book is available from SAS Institute as part of the Books by Users program.

Using the CONTENTS Procedure to Determine Observation Length

To determine the length of each observation in a Version 6 SAS data set, you can create a Version 6 SAS data set that contains one observation. Then run the CONTENTS procedure to determine the observation length. The CONTENTS procedure displays engine/host-dependent information, including page size, and the number of observations per page for uncompressed SAS data sets. For example, the following input produces a SAS data set plus PROC CONTENTS output:

```
data oranges;
    input variety $ flavor texture looks;
    cards;
navel 9 8 6
;

proc contents data=oranges;
run;
```

The output is shown in Output 2.1.

Output 2.1
CONTENTS
Procedure Output

```
                            The SAS System                          1

                            CONTENTS PROCEDURE

Data Set Name: WORK.ORANGES              Observations:        1
Member Type:   DATA                      Variables:           4
Engine:        V609                      Indexes:             0
Created:       14:27 Tuesday, March 5, 1996  Observation Length:  32
Last Modified: 14:27 Tuesday, March 5, 1996  Deleted Observations: 0
Protection:                              Compressed:          NO
Data Set Type:                           Sorted:              NO
Label:

                -----Engine/Host Dependent Information-----

Data Set Page Size:        6144
Number of Data Set Pages:  1
File Format:               607
First Data Page:           1
Max Obs per Page:          139
Obs in First Data Page:    4
Physical Name:             SYS96065.T142625.RA000.USERID.R0000180
Release Created:           6.090450
Release Last Modified:     6.090450
Created by:                USERID
Last Modified by:          USERID
Subextents:                1
Total Blocks Used:         1

          -----Alphabetic List of Variables and Attributes-----

            #    Variable   Type   Len   Pos
            -----------------------------------
            2    FLAVOR     Num    8     8
            4    LOOKS      Num    8     24
            3    TEXTURE    Num    8     16
            1    VARIETY    Char   8     0
```

The only values that you need to pay attention to are **Observation Length** and **Compressed**:

Observation Length
   is the record size in bytes.

Compressed
   has the value NO if records are not compressed; it has the value YES if records are compressed. (If the records are compressed, do not use the procedure given in "Estimating the Size of a SAS Data Set" on page 39.)

Estimating the Size of a SAS Index

Under MVS, you can use the following formula to obtain a rough estimate of the size of a simple index:

```
size=(unique) * (8) * (length) * (1.15)
```

unique
    is the number of unique values of the key variable

8
    is the number of bytes of overhead for each unique value in the index

length
    is the length of the key variable, in bytes

1.15
    is a multiplication factor for general index overhead

Note: The result of this calculation will be in bytes. You can convert this value to tracks based on the capacity of your data storage device.

42

Chapter 3 Accessing V6 and V6SEQ SAS® Data Libraries

Overview of the V6 and V6SEQ Engines   *43*
Utilities That You Can Use with Version 6 SAS Data Libraries   *44*

Using the V6 Engine   *45*
When to Use This Engine   *45*
How to Select the V6 Engine   *45*
DCB Attributes for the V6 Engine   *46*
   External Allocation: V6 Engine   *46*
   Internal Allocation: V6 Engine   *47*
Engine/Host Options for the V6 Engine   *47*
CONTENTS Procedure Output   *48*

Using the V6SEQ Engine   *49*
When to Use This Engine   *49*
How to Select the V6SEQ Engine   *49*
DCB Attributes for the V6SEQ Engine   *50*
   External Allocation: V6SEQ Engine   *50*
   Internal Allocation: V6SEQ Engine   *50*
Engine/Host Options for the V6SEQ Engine   *51*
CONTENTS Procedure Output   *52*

Overview of the V6 and V6SEQ Engines

You use the V6 and V6SEQ engines to access V6 and V6SEQ SAS data libraries, respectively. Table 3.1 on page 44 summarizes some useful information about these engines.

For information about portable features of the SAS System that are used by these engines, see *SAS Language: Reference.* For information about host-specific features, see the appropriate chapter in this book.

For general information about SAS library engines, see "SAS Library Engines" on page 26 and *SAS Language: Reference.*

	V6 Engine	V6SEQ Engine
Table 3.1 *Overview of the V6 and V6SEQ Engines*		
DCB Attributes	DSORG=PS RECFM=FS BLKSIZE=*value** LRECL=same value as BLKSIZE	DSORG=PS RECFM=U BLKSIZE=*value*** LRECL=any value
Member Types Supported	ACCESS CATALOG DATA*** PROGRAM VIEW	ACCESS† CATALOG† DATA PROGRAM† VIEW†
Engine/Host Options	BLKSIZE= DISP= SPACE= UNIT= VOLSER=	BLKSIZE= DISP= SPACE= UNIT= VOLSER=
Portable Data Set Options	all	all
MVS-Specific Data Set Options	n/a	FILEDISP=
Portable System Options	BUFNO= BUFSIZE= COMPRESS= REUSE=	BUFSIZE= TAPECLOSE=
MVS-Specific System Options	BLKSIZE= BLKSIZE()= FILEDEV= FILESPPRI= FILESPSEC= FILEUNIT= FILEVOL= SYSPREF=	FILEDEV= FILESPPRI= FILESPSEC= FILEUNIT= FILEVOL= SYSPREF=

* where *value* can be from 4096 to 32256 in increments of 512. The default is 6144.
** where *value* is up to the maximum for your device type
*** including indexing capabilities
† limited support: you can use the V6SEQ engine to move or transport these member types, but you cannot use the V6SEQ engine to access the information within these members

Utilities That You Can Use with Version 6 SAS Data Libraries

You can use standard MVS utilities such as IEBGENER, ISPF/PDF 3.3, or DF/HSM to copy or move SAS data libraries that were created with the V6 engine or with the V6SEQ engine. As long as the block size of the data library that you are copying is not greater than the track capacity of the target device, a V6 or V6SEQ data library may be transferred between unlike device types (for example, 3350 to 3380). This makes it easier to use DASD management software such as IBM's DF/HSM, FDR by Innovation Data Processing, or DMS/OS by Sterling Software.

Using the V6 Engine

A V6 SAS data library is an operating system data set that has a special internal format. This internal format enables you to access any of the SAS data sets in the library directly, without searching through other SAS data sets. You can also read or write more than one SAS data set in a disk-format data library in a single DATA step.

When to Use This Engine

You use the V6 engine to create SAS data libraries on disk and to read from, write to, or update those libraries. The V6 engine also enables you to index and compress observations. (For more information about indexes, see *SAS Language: Reference*. For more information about compressing observations, see *SAS Language: Reference* and "Determine whether you should compress your data" on page 153.)

The V6 engine is the default engine for SAS data libraries, unless the default engine has been changed with the SAS system option ENGINE=. This engine is also the only engine under MVS that provides full support for catalogs in Version 6 and for members of type ACCESS, PROGRAM, and VIEW. It also supports multivolume SAS data libraries on disk. See "Allocating Multivolume SAS Data Libraries" on page 33.

Here are some other important characteristics of the V6 engine:

□ It makes efficient use of DASD space because it uses fixed-length physical blocks and enables you to have more than one SAS file per track.

□ You can use standard utilities to move or copy a V6 data library between unlike device types. This can be done only if the block size of the library is less than or equal to the track size of the target device.

□ It provides a convenient way for you to reduce the elapsed time for SAS jobs. Setting the BUFNO= system option or data set option to a value greater than 1 causes multiple pages to be transferred during a single DASD I/O operation. This can substantially reduce the elapsed time for SAS jobs. However, multiple pages are not transferred when an index is used in a "read" operation.

□ It exploits memory above the 16-megabyte line. I/O buffers for permanent V6 data libraries are allocated above the 16-megabyte line.

□ After a V6 data library is opened, it remains open until the libref is cleared, or until you end the SAS session. At step boundaries within a SAS session, SAS ensures data integrity by writing any necessary control information to the data set.

How to Select the V6 Engine

There are three ways to select the V6 engine:

□ Specify V6 as the value of the *engine* argument in the LIBNAME statement.
   Note: Use BASE as the engine name if you write programs that create new SAS data libraries and you want to create the data libraries in the latest available format. In the 6.09 Enhanced release, BASE is an alias for V6, and it will be an alias for newer engines in subsequent releases.

□ For existing V6 SAS data libraries on disk, specify no value for *engine* in the LIBNAME statement. SAS then examines the data set attributes and selects the V6

engine automatically. SAS also selects the V6 engine automatically if you omit the
LIBNAME statement and use a JCL DD statement or a TSO ALLOCATE command to
allocate the library.

□   Set the value of the SAS system option ENGINE= to V6. This option tells SAS which
engine to use as the default when you allocate a new operating system data set without
specifying an engine.

DCB Attributes for the V6 Engine

The operating system data set label contains DCB information that describes the data set's
characteristics. The operating system writes the DCB information when it creates the library,
using either values that are supplied by the user, or the values of several SAS system
options. Both the SAS System and MVS utility programs use this DCB information during
processing.

The following sections provide additional information about DCB parameters for the
V6 engine. Also see "DCB Attribute Options" on page 275 for more information.

External Allocation: V6 Engine

If you use a JCL DD statement or a TSO ALLOCATE command to allocate a new V6 SAS
data library, and if you choose to specify DCB attributes, then you must specify the
following DCB attributes:

□   DSORG=PS

□   RECFM=FS

□   BLKSIZE=4096 to 32256 in increments of 512 (The default is 6144.)

□   LRECL=*value*, where *value* is the same as the value for BLKSIZE=.

If you do not specify DCB attributes for a new V6 SAS data library, then SAS supplies
the above DCB attributes whenever the V6 engine has been either explicitly or implicitly
assigned. (See "How to Select the V6 Engine" on page 45 and "How SAS Assigns an
Engine When No Engine Is Specified" on page 32 for details about how engines are
assigned.)

When allocating a V6 data library, choose an appropriate block size. Here are some
guidelines. (See also "Optimizing I/O" on page 152.)

□   If most members of the library will have large numbers of observations, choose the
optimal block size for the device. (For a 3380, this value is 23040. For a 3390, it is
27648. See your IBM documentation for the optimal block sizes of other devices.) The
result is the minimum amount of overhead that is required to map and transfer library
DASD blocks, because there will be fewer total blocks to handle.

□   If most members of the library will contain few observations, or if their size and number
of observations vary widely, choose a smaller block size such as 6144. This increases
the opportunity for apportioning DASD space among library members, and it generally
makes better use of DASD space.

If no block size is specified when a SAS data library is physically opened for the first
time, SAS uses the value of the BLKSIZE= system option. If that value is 0, then SAS uses
the BLKSIZE(*device-type*)= system option. If the value of BLKSIZE(*device-type*)= is 0,

SAS uses a block size of 6144 by default.

If you specify a block size that is not an integral multiple of 512, then the number is rounded down to an integral multiple of 512.

Internal Allocation: V6 Engine

If you use the LIBNAME statement to allocate a new V6 SAS data library, SAS supplies the following DCB attributes for you:

□ DSORG=PS

□ RECFM=FS

□ BLKSIZE=6144

□ LRECL=6144

You can override the default value of the BLKSIZE= system option by using the BLKSIZE= option in the LIBNAME statement.

Note: If the SAS system option BLKALLOC is in effect, then SAS assigns BLKSIZE= and LRECL= values when the SAS data library is allocated. If NOBLKALLOC is in effect, then SAS assigns BLKSIZE= and LRECL= values when the library is first accessed.

Engine/Host Options for the V6 Engine

The engine/host options that you can supply in the LIBNAME statement correspond to the JCL or TSO parameters that you would specify if you allocated the SAS data library externally. For the V6 engine, you can specify any of the engine/host options shown in Table 3.1 on page 44. (For more information about these options and their values, see the description of *engine/host options* under "LIBNAME" on page 289.) Or you can accept the default values that are derived from the corresponding SAS system options, as follows:

□ If you do not specify a value for DISP=, the default for existing data sets is DISP=(OLD,KEEP,KEEP). For new data sets, the default depends on how you are allocating the library:

   □ If you are allocating the library with a LIBNAME statement or with a TSO ALLOCATE command, disposition defaults to DISP=(NEW,CATLG,DELETE).

   □ If you are allocating the library with a JCL DD statement, disposition defaults to DISP=(NEW,DELETE,DELETE).

In an interactive environment, if you use a LIBNAME statement to allocate a data library that does not exist and you do not specify a value for DISP=, one of the following actions occurs:

   □ If the SAS system option FILEPROMPT is in effect (the default), then a requestor window asks whether you want to create the operating system data set. If you reply **Yes**, you are asked whether you want to catalog the data set when it is deallocated, or to delete it.

   □ If the SAS system option NOFILEPROMPT is in effect, an error message is written to the SAS log.

□   If you do not specify values for the SPACE= parameters, SAS uses the current values of the SAS system options FILEUNIT=, FILESPPRI=, and FILESPSEC=. The defaults are SPACE=(CYL,(1,1)).

□   If you do not specify a value for VOLSER=, SAS uses the current value of the SAS system option FILEVOL=, if a value for FILEVOL= has been specified at your site.

□   If you do not specify a value for UNIT=, SAS uses the current value of the SAS system option FILEDEV=. The default is SYSDA.

Note: The default values shown are those that are supplied by SAS. Your SAS system administrator may have changed the default values for your site.

For temporary data libraries, you do not need to specify any options, but you can override any of the default values.

CONTENTS Procedure Output

The PROC CONTENTS output in Output 3.1 shows information that is generated by the V6 engine.

Output 3.1
PROC CONTENTS
Output Generated
by the V6 Engine

```
                            The SAS System                            1

                          CONTENTS PROCEDURE

        Data Set Name: WORK.ORANGES              Observations:         4
        Member Type:   DATA                      Variables:            5
        Engine:        V609                       Indexes:              0
        Created:       14:27 Tuesday, March 5, 1996   Observation Length:   40
        Last Modified: 14:27 Tuesday, March 5, 1996   Deleted Observations: 0
        Protection:                              Compressed:          NO
        Data Set Type:                           Sorted:              NO
        Label:

                   -----Engine/Host Dependent Information-----

        Data Set Page Size:      6144
        Number of Data Set Pages: 1
        File Format:             607
        First Data Page:         1
        Max Obs per Page:        152
        Obs in First Data Page:  4
        Physical Name:           SYS96065.T142625.RA000.USERID.R0000180
        Release Created:         6.090450
        Release Last Modified:   6.090450
        Created by:              USERID
        Last Modified by:        USERID
        Subextents:              1
        Total Blocks Used:       1

                -----Alphabetic List of Variables and Attributes-----

                    #    Variable    Type    Len    Pos
                    ----------------------------------
                    2    FLAVOR      Num      8      8
                    4    LOOKS       Num      8      24
                    3    TEXTURE     Num      8      16
                    5    TOTAL       Num      8      32
                    1    VARIETY     Char     8      0
```

Using the V6SEQ Engine

When to Use This Engine

Use the V6SEQ engine to create sequential-format SAS data libraries either on disk or on tape, and to access files in sequential data libraries. The primary purpose of this engine is to enable you to back up Version 6 SAS data sets, catalogs, or whole data libraries. The V6SEQ engine makes it possible to back up applications that contain both SAS data sets and SAS catalogs. The V6SEQ engine also enables you to transport a tape-format library to another MVS or CMS system via tape or shared DASD. Finally, you can use this engine to create a multivolume sequential-format SAS data library on tape or disk.

In contrast to the V6 engine, V6SEQ has the following limitations:

□ It does not support indexing nor compression of observations.

□ Because a V6SEQ SAS data library does not contain a directory, SAS cannot access an individual data set directly. It must read through all preceding SAS data sets in order to reach a requested data set. Direct access to individual observations (using the POINT= or KEY= options in the SET or MODIFY statements) also is not supported.

□ In a single DATA step or PROC step, you can use only one SAS data set from a particular sequential SAS data library.

Unlike disk-format libraries, sequential libraries are always closed at step boundaries.

How to Select the V6SEQ Engine

There are three ways to select this engine:

□ Specify V6SEQ as the value of the *engine* argument in the LIBNAME statement.
    Note: Use TAPE as the engine name if you write programs that create new SAS data libraries and you want to create the data libraries in the latest available format. In the 6.09 Enhanced release, TAPE is an alias for V6SEQ, and it will be an alias for newer sequential engines in subsequent releases.

□ For existing V6SEQ SAS data libraries on tape, specify no value for *engine* in the LIBNAME statement. This engine is selected automatically if you do not provide a value for the engine argument and you are allocating the library internally. This engine is also selected automatically if you omit the LIBNAME statement and allocate the library externally.

□ Set the value of the SEQENGINE= system option to SASV6SEQ. The DCB attributes of the allocated data set must indicate a sequential format SAS data library.

DCB Attributes for the V6SEQ Engine

The operating system data set label contains DCB information which describes the data library's characteristics. The operating system writes the DCB information when it creates the library, using either values that are supplied by the user, or the values of several SAS system options. Both the SAS System and MVS utility programs use this DCB information during processing.

See "DCB Attribute Options" on page 275 for more information about DCB attributes.

External Allocation: V6SEQ Engine

If you use a JCL DD statement or a TSO ALLOCATE command to allocate a new V6SEQ data library on disk or on tape, and if you choose to specify DCB attributes, then you must specify the following DCB attributes:

□ DSORG=PS

□ RECFM=U

□ BLKSIZE=*value*, where *value* is up to the maximum for your device type.

If you do not specify DCB attributes for a new V6SEQ SAS data library, then SAS supplies the above DCB attributes whenever the V6SEQ engine has been either explicitly or implicitly assigned. (See "How to Select the V6SEQ Engine" on page 49 and "How SAS Assigns an Engine When No Engine Is Specified" on page 32 for details about how engines are assigned.)

Note: In order to use the TSO ALLOCATE command to allocate a data set on tape, your user ID must have MOUNT authority.

Internal Allocation: V6SEQ Engine

If you use the LIBNAME statement to allocate a new V6SEQ data library on disk or on tape, SAS supplies the following DCB attributes for you:

□ DSORG=PS

□ RECFM=U

In addition, if no block size is specified when a SAS data library is physically opened for the first time, SAS uses the value of the BLKSIZE= system option. If that value is 0, then SAS uses the BLKSIZE(*device-type*)= system option. If the value of BLKSIZE(*device-type*)= is 0, SAS uses the largest block size that the device supports.

Note: If the SAS system option BLKALLOC is in effect, then SAS assigns BLKSIZE= and LRECL= values when the SAS data library is allocated. If NOBLKALLOC is in effect, then SAS assigns BLKSIZE= and LRECL= values when the library is first accessed.

Engine/Host Options for the V6SEQ Engine

The engine/host options that you can supply in the LIBNAME statement correspond to the JCL or TSO parameters that you would specify if you allocated the SAS data library externally. For the V6SEQ engine, you can specify any of the engine/host options shown in Table 3.1 on page 44. (For more information about these options and their values, see the description of *engine/host options* under "LIBNAME" on page 289.) Or you can accept the default values that are derived from the corresponding SAS system options, as follows:

□ If you do not specify a value for DISP=, the default for existing data sets is DISP=(OLD,KEEP,KEEP). For new data sets, the default is DISP=(NEW,CATLG,DELETE). If you specify only DISP=NEW and omit the normal disposition parameter, the following defaults occur:

  □ If you are allocating the library with a LIBNAME statement or with a TSO ALLOCATE command, normal disposition defaults to CATLG.

  □ If you are allocating the library with a JCL DD statement, normal disposition defaults to DELETE for new data sets.

  In an interactive environment, when you use a LIBNAME statement to allocate a data library that does not exist and you do not specify a value for DISP=, one of the following actions occurs:

  □ If the SAS system option FILEPROMPT is in effect (the default), then a requestor window asks whether you want to create the operating system data set. If you reply **Yes**, you are asked whether you want to catalog the data set when it is deallocated, or to delete it.

  □ If the SAS system option NOFILEPROMPT is in effect, an error message is written to the SAS log.

□ If you do not specify values for the SPACE= parameters, SAS uses the current values of the SAS system options FILEUNIT=, FILESPPRI=, and FILESPSEC=. The defaults are SPACE=(CYL,(1,1)).

□ If you do not specify a value for VOLSER=, SAS uses the current value of the SAS system option FILEVOL=, if a value for FILEVOL= has been specified at your site.

□ If you do not specify a value for UNIT=, SAS uses the current value of the SAS system option FILEDEV=. The default is SYSDA.

Note: The default values shown are those that are supplied by SAS. Your SAS system administrator may have changed the default values for your site.

For temporary data libraries, you do not need to specify any options, but you can override any of the default values.

CONTENTS Procedure Output

The PROC CONTENTS output in Output 3.2 shows information that is generated by the V6SEQ engine.

Output 3.2
PROC CONTENTS
Output Generated
by the V6SEQ
Engine

```
                              The SAS System

                            CONTENTS PROCEDURE

     Data Set Name: SEQ.ORANGES              Observations:          .
     Member Type:   DATA                     Variables:             5
     Engine:        V6SEQ                     Indexes:               0
     Created:       14:48 Tuesday, March 5, 1996   Observation Length:  40
     Last Modified: .                         Deleted Observations: 0
     Protection:                              Compressed:            NO
     Data Set Type:                           Sorted:                NO
     Label:

               -----Engine/Host Dependent Information-----

               Data Set Page Size: 32000
               Physical Name:      USERID.MVS.SEQ
               Release Created:    6.090450
               Created by:         USERID

          -----Alphabetic List of Variables and Attributes-----

          #     Variable   Type    Len    Pos
          -----------------------------------
          2     FLAVOR     Num       8      8
          4     LOOKS      Num       8     24
          3     TEXTURE    Num       8     16
          5     TOTAL      Num       8     32
          1     VARIETY    Char      8      0
```

Chapter 4 Accessing BMDP, SPSS, and OSIRIS Files

The BMDP, SPSS, and OSIRIS Engines 53

Restrictions on the Use of These Engines 53

Accessing BMDP Files 54
Assigning a Libref to a BMDP File 54
Referencing BMDP Files 54
Examples of Accessing BMDP Files 54

Accessing SPSS Files 55
Assigning a Libref to an SPSS File 55
Referencing SPSS Files 55
Examples of Accessing SPSS Files 56

Accessing OSIRIS Files 56
Assigning a Libref to an OSIRIS File 56
Referencing OSIRIS Files 57
Examples of Accessing OSIRIS Files 57

The BMDP, SPSS, and OSIRIS Engines

The following read-only engines enable you to access files that were created with other vendors' software as if those files were written by the SAS System:

BMDP   accesses system files that were created with BMDP Statistical Software.

SPSS   accesses SPSS files that were created under Release 9 of SPSS as well as SPSS-X system files and portable files.

OSIRIS   accesses OSIRIS files.

You can use these engines in any SAS applications or procedures that do not require random access. For example, by using one of the engines with PROC CONTENTS and its _ALL_ option, you can determine the contents of an entire SPSS file at once.

Restrictions on the Use of These Engines

Because these are sequential engines, they cannot be used with the POINT= option of the SET statement, nor with the FSBROWSE, FSEDIT, or FSVIEW procedures in SAS/FSP software. However, you can use PROC COPY or a DATA step to copy a BMDP, SPSS, or OSIRIS file to a SAS data set, and then either use POINT= or use SAS/FSP to browse or edit the file.

Accessing BMDP Files

The BMDP engine can read only BMDP "save" files that were created on the same operating system. For example, the BMDP engine under MVS cannot read BMDP files that were created under the OpenVMS operating system.

Assigning a Libref to a BMDP File

In order to access a BMDP file, you must use the LIBNAME statement to assign a libref to the file. Specify the BMDP engine in the LIBNAME statement as follows:

LIBNAME *libref* BMDP '*OS-data-set-name*';

libref	is a SAS libref.
BMDP	is the BMDP engine.
OS-data-set-name	is the operating system data set name of the BMDP file.

You do not need to use a LIBNAME statement before running PROC CONVERT if you are using PROC CONVERT to convert a BMDP file to a SAS data file. (See "CONVERT" on page 211.)

Note that the LIBNAME statement has no options for the BMDP engine.

If you previously used a TSO ALLOC command or a JCL DD statement to assign a DDname to the BMDP file, you can omit the *OS-data-set-name* in the LIBNAME statement and use the DDname as the libref. (See "Examples of Accessing BMDP Files," later in this section.)

Referencing BMDP Files

Because there can be multiple "save" files in a single physical BMDP file, you use the value of the BMDP CODE= argument as the name of the SAS data file. For example, if the BMDP "save" file contains CODE=ABC and CODE=DEF, and if the libref is XXX, you reference the files as XXX.ABC and XXX.DEF. All BMDP CONTENT types are treated the same, so even if file DEF has CONTENT=CORR under BMDP, SAS treats it as CONTENT=DATA.

In your SAS program, if you want to access the first BMDP "save" file in the operating system data set, or if there is only one "save" file, you can refer to the file as _FIRST_. This approach is convenient if you do not know the BMDP CODE= name.

Examples of Accessing BMDP Files

Suppose the operating system data set MY.BMDP.FILE contains the "save" file ABC. The following statements assign a libref to the data set and then run PROC CONTENTS and PROC PRINT on the BMDP file:

```
libname xxx bmdp 'my.bmdp.file';
proc contents data=xxx.abc;
proc print data=xxx.abc;
run;
```

In the next example, the TSO ALLOC command associates a DDname with the name of the operating system data set that comprises the BMDP *OS-data-set-name*. The operating system data set name is omitted in the LIBNAME statement, because the libref that is used is the same as the DDname in the TSO statement. The PROC PRINT statement prints the data for the first "save" file in the physical file.

```
tso alloc f(xxx) da('my.bmdp.file') shr reu;
libname xxx bmdp;
proc print data=xxx._first_;
run;
```

Accessing SPSS Files

The SPSS engine supports native and portable file formats for both SPSS and SPSS-X files. The engine automatically determines which type of SPSS file it is reading and reads the file accordingly.

This engine can read only SPSS data files that were created under the same operating system. For example, the SPSS engine under MVS cannot read SPSS files that were created under the OpenVMS operating system. The only exception is an SPSS portable file, which can originate from any operating system.

Assigning a Libref to an SPSS File

In order to access an SPSS file, you must use the LIBNAME statement to assign a libref to the file. Specify the SPSS engine in the LIBNAME statement as follows:

LIBNAME *libref* SPSS '*OS-data-set-name*';

libref	is a SAS libref.
SPSS	is the SPSS engine.
OS-data-set-name	is the operating system data set name of the SPSS file.

You do not need to use a LIBNAME statement before running PROC CONVERT if you are using PROC CONVERT to convert an SPSS file to a SAS data file. (See "CONVERT" on page 211.)

Note that the LIBNAME statement has no options for the SPSS engine.

If you previously used a TSO ALLOC command or a JCL DD statement to assign a DDname to the SPSS file, you can omit the *OS-data-set-name* in the LIBNAME statement and use the DDname as the libref. (See "Examples of Accessing SPSS Files," later in this section.)

Referencing SPSS Files

SPSS data files do not have names. For these files, use a member name of your choice in SAS programs.

SPSS data files have only one logical member per file. Therefore, you can use _FIRST_ in your SAS programs to refer to the first data file.

Examples of Accessing SPSS Files

Suppose you want to read the operating system data set MY.SPSSX.FILE. The following statements assign a libref to the data set and then run PROC CONTENTS and PROC PRINT on the SPSS file:

```
libname xxx spss 'my.spssx.file';
proc contents data=xxx._first_;
proc print data=xxx._first_;
run;
```

In the next example, the TSO ALLOC command associates a DDname with the name of the operating system data set that comprises the SPSS *OS-data-set-name*. The operating system data set name is omitted in the LIBNAME statement, because the libref that is used is the same as the DDname in the TSO command. The PROC PRINT statement prints the data in the first member of the SPSS data file.

```
tso alloc f(xxx) da('my.spssx.file') shr reu;
libname xxx spss;
proc print data=xxx._first_;
run;
```

Accessing OSIRIS Files

Although OSIRIS runs only under MVS and CMS, the SAS OSIRIS engine accepts an MVS data dictionary from any other operating system that is running the SAS System. The layout of an OSIRIS data dictionary is the same on all operating systems. The data dictionary and data files should not be converted between EBCDIC and ASCII, however, because the OSIRIS engine expects EBCDIC data.

Assigning a Libref to an OSIRIS File

In order to access an OSIRIS file, you must use the LIBNAME statement to assign a libref to the file. Specify the OSIRIS engine in the LIBNAME statement as follows:

LIBNAME *libref* OSIRIS *'OS-data-set-name'* DICT=*'dictionary-file-name'*;

libref	is a SAS libref.
OSIRIS	is the OSIRIS engine.
OS-data-set-name	is the operating system data set name of the data file.
dictionary-file-name	is the operating system data set name of the dictionary file. The *dictionary-file-name* can also be a DDname. However, if you use a DDname for the *dictionary-file-name*, do not use quotes.

You do not need to use a LIBNAME statement before running PROC CONVERT if you are using PROC CONVERT to convert an OSIRIS file to a SAS data file. (See "CONVERT" on page 211.)

If you previously used a TSO ALLOC command or a JCL DD statement to assign a DDname to the OSIRIS file, you can omit the *OS-data-set-name* in the LIBNAME statement. However, you must still use the DICT= option, because the engine requires both files. (See "Examples of Accessing OSIRIS Files," later in this section.)

Referencing OSIRIS Files

OSIRIS data files do not have individual names. Therefore, for these files you can use a member name of your choice in SAS programs. You can also use the member name _FIRST_ for an OSIRIS file.

Under OSIRIS, the contents of the dictionary file determine the file layout of the data file. A data file has no other specific layout.

You can use a dictionary file with an OSIRIS data file only if the data file conforms to the format that the dictionary file describes. Generally, each data file should have its own DICT file.

Examples of Accessing OSIRIS Files

Suppose you want to read the data file MY.OSIRIS.DATA, and the data dictionary is MY.OSIRIS.DICT. The following statements assign a libref to the data file and then run PROC CONTENTS and PROC PRINT on the file:

```
libname xxx osiris 'my.osiris.data' dict='my.osiris.dict';
proc contents data=xxx._first_;
proc print data=xxx._first_;
run;
```

The next example uses JCL. In this example, the DD statements can be omitted if the physical names are referenced in the LIBNAME statement.

```
//       JOB
//       EXEC  SAS
//OSIR   DD  DSN=MY.OSIRIS.DATA,DISP=SHR
//DICT   DD  DSN=MY.OSIRIS.DICT,DISP=SHR
//SYSIN  DD  *

   /* Any one of the following libname statements can be used. */
libname osir osiris dict=dict;
libname xxx osiris 'my.osiris.data' dict=dict;
libname osir osiris dict='my.osiris.dict';

proc print data=osir._first_;    /* if osir libref is used */
proc print data=xxx._first_;     /* if xxx libref is used  */
//
```

58

Chapter **5** Allocating External Files

Introduction   59

Ways of Allocating External Files   59

Using the FILENAME Statement to Allocate External Files   60
FILENAME Statement Syntax   61
FILENAME Statement Examples   61

Using the JCL DD Statement to Allocate External Files   62

Using the TSO Allocate Command to Allocate External Files   63

Allocating External Files on Tape   63

Allocating Generation Data Sets   64
Allocating a New Generation of a Generation Data Group   64
Allocating an Existing Generation of a Generation Data Group   64

Allocating Nonstandard External Files   65
Allocating ISAM Files   65
Allocating OpenEdition MVS Hierarchical File System Files   66
Allocating SMS PDSEs   66

Concatenating External Files   66

Displaying Information about External Files   66

Deallocating External Files   66

Introduction

External files are files whose format is determined by the operating system rather than by the SAS System. External files include raw data files, JCL libraries, files that contain SAS programming statements, and load libraries. In batch and noninteractive line modes, the SAS log and procedure output files are also external files.

Ways of Allocating External Files

In order to work with an external file in the SAS System, you must first allocate the file. You can allocate either a new data set or an existing data set. The only difference is that, if you are creating a new data set, you must specify that it is new and you must describe its structure and format.

You can allocate external files in the following ways:

☐   If you plan to use an external file only once in your SAS program, then you can allocate it by simply specifying the operating system data set name in a SAS statement or command. For example, this display manager INCLUDE command allocates an existing sequential data set and includes it into the PROGRAM EDITOR window:

```
include 'myid.report.data'
```

Similarly, this PROC PRINTTO statement allocates a new PDS member:

```
proc printto print='userid.output.data(rockport)' new;
```

□ If you plan to use the same external file several times in your SAS program, then use one of the following methods to allocate the file.

SAS FILENAME statement
You can use this method in all modes for most types of files. See the next section, "Using the FILENAME Statement to Allocate External Files," for more information.

JCL DD statement
You can use this method if you use MVS in batch mode. See "Using the JCL DD Statement to Allocate External Files" on page 62 for more information.
Note: Unlike the other two methods, if you use the JCL DD statement to allocate a file, there is no way to deallocate the file until the job ends.

TSO ALLOCATE command
You can use this method if you use MVS under TSO. See "Using the TSO Allocate Command to Allocate External Files" on page 63 for more information.

Each of these three methods establishes a *fileref* or a DDname that you can subsequently use to refer to the file instead of specifying the data set name again. See "Referring to External Files" on page 70 for more information.

Using the FILENAME Statement to Allocate External Files

The FILENAME statement associates a SAS fileref (file reference name) with the operating system's name for an external file. This is equivalent to allocating an operating system data set externally (using a JCL DD statement or a TSO ALLOCATE command) and assigning a fileref to it.

In an interactive environment, if you issue a FILENAME statement for a standard external file that does not exist and do not specify DISP=NEW, one of the following actions occurs:

□ If the SAS system option FILEPROMPT is in effect (the default), then a requestor window asks whether you want to create the external file. If you reply **Yes**, SAS creates the external file, using any attributes that you specified in the FILENAME statement. If you do not specify any attributes, SAS uses the values of the SAS system options FILEDEV=, FILEVOL=, FILEUNIT=, FILESPPRI=, and FILESPSEC=. See Chapter 20, "System Options," for information about these options.

□ If the SAS system option NOFILEPROMPT is in effect, an error message is written to the SAS log.

FILENAME Statement Syntax

This section provides only a brief overview of FILENAME statement syntax. For complete information about the FILENAME statement, see "FILENAME" on page 270.

The syntax of the FILENAME statement is

FILENAME *fileref* *<device-type>* '*OS-data-set-name*' *<options . . . >*;

fileref
> identifies the external file. The *fileref* must conform to the rules for DDnames. That is, it can consist of one to eight letters, numbers, or the national characters $, @, and #; the first character must be either a letter or a national character. You can subsequently use the fileref to refer to this file in your SAS session or batch job. (See "Referring to External Files" on page 70.)

device-type
> enables you to route output to an output device, disk or tape file by specifying device type. If *device-type* is not defined for a new file, its value is taken from the SAS system option FILEDEV=.

'*OS-data-set-name*' | ('*OS-data-set-name-1*'. . .'*OS-data-set-name-n*')
> is the operating system data set name of the SAS data library, enclosed in quotes (see "Specifying Operating System Data Sets" on page 13), or it can be a concatenation of operating system data set names. For a concatenation, enclose each data set name in quotes, and enclose the entire group of file-specifications in parentheses.

options
> include standard options such as file disposition as well as options for SYSOUT data sets such as the destination for output and the number of copies desired. These options are described in detail in "FILENAME" on page 270. Generally, values for options may be specified either with or without quotes. However, values that contain special characters must be enclosed in quotes.

FILENAME Statement Examples

Type of File	New or Existing File?	Example
sequential	existing	`filename raw 'myid.raw.datax' disp=old;`

	new	`filename x 'userid.newdata' disp=new`
		`    space=(trk,(5,1)) unit=3380 volume=xyzabc`
		`    recfm=fb lrecl=80 blksize=6160;`

partitioned	existing	`filename raw 'sas.raw.data(mem1)' disp=old;`

	new	`filename dogcat 'userid.sas6.physn(optwrk)'`
		`    disp=new space=(trk,(1,3,1))`
		`    volume=xxx111 recfm=fb lrecl=255`
		`    blksize=6120 dsorg=po;`

(continued)

Type of File	New or Existing File?	Example
temporary	new	`filename nextone '&mytemp' disp=new` `    space=(trk,(3)) lrecl=80 blksize=6160;`
tape	existing	`filename mytape 'prod.data' vol=myvol` `    unit=tape label=(1,SL);`

	new	`filename tranfile 'sas.cport.file' label=(1,SL)`
		`    vol='042627' unit=cart blksize=8000`
		`    disp=(new,keep);`

concatenated	existing	`filename concat12` `    ('prod.payroll.data' 'prod.trans(may)');`

terminal	n/a	`filename term1 '*';`
		`            or`
		`filename term2 terminal;`

printer	n/a	`filename prnt unit=printer sysout=a;`

Using the JCL DD Statement to Allocate External Files

The syntax of the JCL DD statement is

> //*DDname* DD DSN=*data-set-name,options*

options include options such as file disposition as well as options that describe the format of the file.

Here are some examples:

□ Allocating an existing sequential data set:

```
//BOOKS DD DSN=LIBRARY.CATALOG.DATA,DISP=SHR
```

□ Allocating a new sequential data set:

```
//REPORT  DD DSN=LIBRARY.REPORT.FEB08,DISP=(NEW,CATLG),
//          SPACE=(CYL,(1,1)),UNIT=SYSDA,
//          DCB=(LRECL=80,RECFM=FB,BLKSIZE=6160)
```

□ Concatenating sequential data sets:

```
//INPUT   DD DSN=LIBRARY.DATA.QTR1,DISP=SHR
//        DD DSN=LIBRARY.DATA.QTR2,DISP=SHR
//        DD DSN=LIBRARY.DATA.QTR3,DISP=SHR
//        DD DSN=LIBRARY.DATA.QTR4,DISP=SHR
```

For complete information about the JCL DD statement, see IBM's *MVS/ESA JCL User's Guide* (GC28-1653-04) and the *MVS/ESA JCL Reference* (GC28-1654-04).

Using the TSO Allocate Command to Allocate External Files

The syntax of the TSO ALLOCATE command is

ALLOC FILE(*DDname*) DA('*data-set-name*') *options*

options include options such as file disposition as well as options that describe the format of the file.

Here are some examples:

□ Allocating an existing member of a PDS:

```
alloc fi(in1) da('my.pds(mem1)') shr
```

□ Allocating a new sequential data set:

```
alloc fi(report) da('library.report.feb08') new sp(1,1) cyl lrecl(80)
     recfm(f b) blksize(6160)
```

□ Concatenating sequential data sets:

```
alloc fi(input) da('library.data.qtr1' 'library.data.qtr2'
     'library.data.qtr3' 'library.data.qtr4') shr
```

For complete information about the TSO ALLOCATE command, see IBM's *TSO Extensions Version 2 Command Reference* (SC28-1881-05).

Allocating External Files on Tape

Because tapes are used primarily in batch mode, the FILENAME statement gives only limited support for parameters that are normally associated with data sets on tape. However, you can use the FILENAME statement to allocate a *cataloged* tape file, provided that you specify the data set name and disposition (as you would normally do in a JCL DD statement). To allocate an *uncataloged* tape file, do the following:

□ For a data set on an IBM standard-label tape (label type SL, the most common type), you must specify the data set name, UNIT= parameter, and volume serial number. You may also specify the label number and type, and the disposition, or you can allow default values to be used for these parameters. For example:

```
filename mytape 'prod.data' vol=myvol unit=tape label=(2,SL);
```

□ For a data set on a nonlabeled tape (label type NL) you must supply the above information plus DCB information. (See "DCB Attribute Options" on page 275 for details.) For example:

```
filename tranfile 'sas.cport.data' disp=(new,keep) unit=tape vol=xvol
     label=(1,NL) recfm=fb lrecl=80 blksize=8000;
```

Allocating Generation Data Sets

A generation data set (or *generation*) is a version of a data set that is stored as a member of a generation data group. (For detailed information about generation data groups, see your IBM documentation.) Both standard external files and SAS data libraries can be stored and managed as generation data groups. The following sections describe the various methods of allocating new and existing generations.

See also "Allocating a Multivolume Generation Data Group" on page 37.

Allocating a New Generation of a Generation Data Group

To allocate a *new* generation of a generation data group, use one of the following methods:

□ In a JCL DD statement, you can specify either the relative form of the data set name or the absolute form.

Relative form:

```
//DD1    DD DSN=PROD.GDG(+1),DISP=(NEW,CATLG)
```

Absolute form:

```
//DD1    DD DSN=PROD.GDG.G0008V00,DISP=(NEW,CATLG)
```

□ In a SAS FILENAME statement (for external files), a SAS LIBNAME statement (for SAS data libraries), or a TSO ALLOCATE command, you must specify the absolute form of the data set name.

FILENAME statement:

```
filename dd1 'prod.gdg.g0008v00' disp=(new,catlg);
```

LIBNAME statement:

```
libname dd1 'prod.gdg.g0008v00' disp=(new,catlg);
```

TSO ALLOCATE command:

```
alloc fi(dd1) da('prod.gdg.g0008v00') new
```

Allocating an Existing Generation of a Generation Data Group

To access an *existing* generation of a generation data group, you can use either the relative form of the data set name or the absolute form in a FILENAME statement, LIBNAME statement, JCL DD statement, or TSO ALLOCATE command.

□ Relative form:

FILENAME statement:

```
filename gdgds 'my.gdg.data(-1)';
```

LIBNAME statement:

```
libname gdgds 'my.gdg.data(-1)';
```

JCL DD statement:

```
//DD1    DD DSN=PROD.GDG(-1),DISP=SHR
```

TSO ALLOCATE command:

```
alloc fi(dd1) da('prod.gdg(-1)') shr
```

□ Absolute form:

FILENAME statement:

```
filename gdgds 'my.gdg.data.g0008v01';
```

LIBNAME statement:

```
libname gdgds 'my.gdg.data.g0008v01';
```

JCL DD statement:

```
//DD1    DD DSN=PROD.GDG.G0008V01,DISP=SHR
```

TSO ALLOCATE command:

```
alloc fi(dd1) da('prod.gdg.g0008v01') shr
```

Allocating Nonstandard External Files

Allocating ISAM Files

To allocate a *new* ISAM file, you must use either a JCL DD statement or the TSO ALLOCATE command; you cannot use the FILENAME statement. However, you can use the FILENAME statement to allocate an existing ISAM file.

Allocating OpenEdition MVS Hierarchical File System Files

See "Accessing OpenEdition MVS Hierarchical File System Files" on page 84 for details.

Allocating SMS PDSEs

To allocate an SMS PDSE, specify the appropriate SMS options in the FILENAME statement. (See "Options That Specify SMS Keywords" on page 279.)

You can use a PDSE (Partitioned Data Set Extended) wherever you can use a PDS.

Concatenating External Files

Multiple sequential data sets can be concatenated via JCL DD statements, a TSO ALLOCATE command, or a FILENAME statement. (When accessing concatenated files, performance is better when either of the first two methods is used.) See the examples in "Using the FILENAME Statement to Allocate External Files" on page 60, "Using the JCL DD Statement to Allocate External Files" on page 62, and "Using the TSO Allocate Command to Allocate External Files" on page 63. Also see "Reading Concatenated Data Sets" on page 81.

Displaying Information about External Files

In all host environments, when you are in display manager mode, you can issue the FILENAME command from the command line to display the FILENAME window. This window lists all current SAS filerefs plus the name of the operating system data set to which each fileref has been assigned. Files that were allocated externally (with a JCL DD statement or with the TSO ALLOCATE command) are listed only after you have used them as filerefs in your SAS session. For more information about the FILENAME window, see *SAS Language: Reference.*

Under MVS, three additional windows—FNAME, DSINFO, and MEMLIST—also provide information about external files. For information about these windows, see "Host-Specific Windows" on page 411.

Deallocating External Files

The method that you use to deallocate a file depends on which method you used to allocate it:

□   If you used the FILENAME statement to allocate the file, then use the FILENAME statement with the CLEAR argument to deallocate it:

```
filename books clear;
```

Note: The CLEAR argument is optional. Specifying **FILENAME** *fileref;* has the same effect.

□ If you used the JCL DD statement to allocate the file, then the file is automatically deallocated when the job step ends. (There is no way to deallocate the file before the job step ends.)

□ If you used the TSO ALLOCATE command to allocate the file, then use the TSO FREE command:

```
free fi(books)
```

Chapter **6** Accessing External Files

Referring to External Files *70*

Writing to External Files *70*
FILE Statement 71
 FILE Statement Examples 72
Writing to Sequential Data Sets 72
Writing to Members of Partitioned Data Sets 73
Writing to a Printer 73
Writing to the Internal Reader 74
Writing to a Temporary Data Set 74
Using the FILE Statement to Specify Data Set Attributes 74
Using the Data Set Attributes of an Input File 75
Using the FILE Statement to Specify Data Set Disposition 75
 Appending Data with the MOD Option 75
 Appending Data with the MOD Disposition 76
Writing to Print Data Sets 76
Designating a Print Data Set as a Nonprint Data Set 77

Reading from External Files *78*
INFILE Statement 78
 INFILE Statement Examples 79
Reading from a Sequential File 79
Reading from a Member of a Partitioned Data Set 80
Reading from the Terminal 80
Reading Concatenated Data Sets 81
Reading from Multiple External Files 81
Reading from Print Data Sets 82
Getting Information about an Input Data Set 82

Accessing Nonstandard Files *83*
Accessing IMS-DL/I and CA-IDMS Databases 83
Accessing ISAM Files 83
Accessing VSAM Data Sets 83
Accessing the Volume Table of Contents (VTOC) 84

Accessing OpenEdition MVS Hierarchical File System Files *84*
Allocating HFS Files 85
Allocating an HFS Directory 85
Specifying File-Access Permissions and Attributes 85
Using HFS File Names in SAS Statements and Commands 86
 Concatenating HFS Files 87
Accessing a Particular File in an HFS Directory 87
Piping Data between SAS and OpenEdition MVS Commands 87
Host-Specific Options for HFS Files 88
Using the X Statement to Issue OpenEdition MVS Commands 89
Restrictions in SAS System Support for OpenEdition MVS 90

Writing Your Own I/O Access Methods *90*

Accessing SAS Statements from a Program *91*

Using the INFILE/FILE User Exit Facility *91*

Referring to External Files

After allocating an external file, you can use the fileref or DDname of the file as a convenient way of referring to that file in any subsequent SAS language statement or command. (Note: The first time the DDname of an external file is used in a SAS statement or procedure, SAS assigns it as a fileref for the external file. Therefore, any information provided here about filerefs also applies to the DDnames of external files.) In the following example, the FILENAME statement associates the fileref REPORT with the sequential data set MYID.NEWDATA. The FILE statement later uses the fileref rather than the data set name to refer to the data set.

```
filename report 'myid.newdata' disp=old;
data _null_;
   file report;
   put ...;
run;
```

Here is a similar example in which a JCL DD statement associates the DDname IN with a member of a partitioned data set. The INFILE statement later uses the DDname rather than the data set name and member name to refer to the PDS member.

```
//IN DD DSN=MYID.NEWDATA(TRIAL1),DISP=SHR
//SYSIN DD *
data out;
   infile in;
   input ...;
run;
```

When referring to a member of a PDS, you also have the option of specifying only the data set name in the FILENAME or DD statement. Then, in subsequent references, you specify the member name with the fileref. For example:

```
//IN DD DSN=MYID.NEWDATA,DISP=SHR
//SYSIN DD *
data out;
   infile in(trial1);
   input ...;
run;
```

If an external data set is not cataloged, you must also provide the volume serial number. See "FILENAME" on page 270 for more information about other options that you can specify.

Writing to External Files

After allocating an external file, you can use the FILE statement or the FILE command to write to the file. This section describes the FILE statement. For information about the FILE command, see *SAS Language: Reference.*

FILE Statement

The FILE statement specifies the current output file for PUT statements in the DATA step. (See *SAS Language: Reference* for a complete description of the PUT statement.)

When multiple FILE statements are present, the PUT statement builds and writes output lines to the file that was specified in the most recent FILE statement. If no FILE statement was specified, the PUT statement writes to the SAS log.

The specified output file must be an external file, not a SAS data library. This external file can be a sequential data set on disk or tape, a member of a partitioned data set (PDS), or the terminal. It can also be a VSAM file, a file in the Hierarchical File System of OpenEdition MVS, or an IMS-DL/I database file.

The FILE statement is executable; therefore, you can use it in conditional processing (in an IF/THEN statement, for example).

As with INFILE, it is possible to alternately access multiple external files. See the example in "Reading from Multiple External Files" on page 81. However, because of PDS structure, you cannot write to multiple members of a single PDS at the same time.

Under MVS, SAS uses the IBM ENQUEUE/DEQUEUE facility to prevent multiple users from writing to the same operating system data set simultaneously. This facility also prevents the SAS System and ISPF from overwriting each other.

FILE Statement Syntax

This section provides a brief overview of FILE statement syntax. For complete information about the FILE statement, see "FILE" on page 264.

The syntax of the FILE statement is

FILE *file-specification* *<type>* *<options . . . >*;

file-specification
   identifies the file. It can be in the following forms:

Form	Example
fileref	`report`
fileref(*member*)	`report(feb)`
'*OS-data-set-name*'	`'library.daily.report'`
'*OS-data-set-name(member)*'	`'library.daily.output(report1)'`
reserved filerefs	`LOG` or `PRINT`

   See "Specifying Operating System Data Sets" on page 13 for details about different ways of specifying *OS-data-set-name*.

type
   specifies the type of file. Nonstandard (host-specific) file types that you can specify for MVS are:

   DLI   for IMS-DL/I databases (see "Accessing IMS-DL/I and CA-IDMS Databases" on page 83)

HFS and PIPE	for files in the Hierarchical File System (see "Accessing OpenEdition MVS Hierarchical File System Files" on page 84)
VSAM	for VSAM files (see "Accessing VSAM Data Sets" on page 83).

options

describe the output file's characteristics and specify how it is to be written with a PUT statement. Many of these options are not host-dependent and are documented in *SAS Language: Reference*. For information about MVS-specific options, see "FILE" on page 264. You can use these options to do the following:

□ define variables that will contain information about the external file

□ specify special open and close processing

□ specify file characteristics.

FILE Statement Examples

Type of Data Set	Example
sequential	`file 'my.new.dataset';`

member of a PDS	`file out(newdata);`
	or
	`file 'my.new.dataset(newdata)';`

sequential or member of a PDS*	`file report;`
VSAM	`file payroll vsam;`
IMS	`file psb dli;`
SAS log	`file log;`

* depending on what the fileref is associated with

Writing to Sequential Data Sets

The disposition of a sequential data set can be OLD, MOD, or SHR. Using OLD eliminates the possibility of another job writing to the data set at the same time your job is writing to it.

If you specify OLD or SHR, SAS begins writing at the beginning of the data set, replacing existing information. To append new information to the existing information, specify the MOD option in the FILE statement.

The following example assigns the fileref RAW to the data set MYID.RAW.DATAX and uses the fileref in a simple DATA step:

```
filename raw 'myid.raw.datax' disp=old;
data _null_;
   file raw;
   msgline='write this line';
   put msgline;
run;
```

Writing to Members of Partitioned Data Sets

To write to a member of a PDS, include the member name along with the data set name in the FILE statement, the FILENAME statement, the TSO ALLOCATE command, or the JCL DD statement. Omitting the member name causes an error message because SAS tries to treat the PDS as a sequential data set.

The disposition of the PDS member can be OLD or SHR; you cannot use a disposition of MOD for a member of a PDS. In both cases, SAS begins writing at the beginning of the member, replacing existing information. Using OLD eliminates the possibility of another job writing into the member at the same time your job is writing into it.

In a single DATA step you can write to only one member of a particular PDS; however, you can write to members of separate PDSs. To write to more than one member of a given PDS, you must use a separate DATA step for each member.

The following example assigns the fileref RAW to the PDS member MEM1 and then uses the fileref in a simple DATA step:

```
filename raw 'myid.raw.data(mem1)' disp=old;
data _null_;
   file raw;
   put 'write this line';
run;
```

Writing to a Printer

This example uses the FILENAME and FILE statements to route output to a printer.

```
filename prnt unit=printer sysout=a;
data _null_;
   file prnt;
   put 'text to write';
run;
```

Writing to the Internal Reader

This example uses the FILENAME and FILE statements to write to an internal reader.

```
filename injcl '.misc.jcl' disp=shr;

filename outrdr sysout=a pgm=intrdr recfm=fb lrecl=80;

data _null_;
  infile injcl(myjcl);
  file outrdr noprint notitles;
  input;
  put _infile_;
run;
```

Writing to a Temporary Data Set

The following examples use the FILENAME and FILE statements to write to a temporary data set.

□   This example shows how to use default attributes to define a temporary file:

```
filename tempfile '&mytemp' ;
data out;
    file tempfile;
    put ...;
run;
```

□   The next example defines a temporary file and specifies some of its attributes:

```
filename nextone '&mytemp' disp=new
    lrecl=80 blksize=320 space=(trk,(3));
data out;
    file nextone;
    put ...;
run;
```

Using the FILE Statement to Specify Data Set Attributes

You can specify data set attributes in the FILE statement as well as in the FILENAME statement. SAS supplies default values for any attributes that you do not specify. (For information about default values, see "Overview of DCB Attributes" on page 277 and "DCB Option Descriptions" on page 275.)

   This example specifies values for LRECL= and RECFM= in the FILE statement and allows SAS to use the default value for BLKSIZE=:

```
filename x 'userid.newdata' disp=new space=(trk,(5,1))
          volume=xyz111;
data out;
   file x lrecl=80 recfm=fb;
   put ... ;
run;
```

Using the Data Set Attributes of an Input File

In this example, data are read from the input file; then the data are written to an output file, using the same file characteristics. The DCB option in the FILE statement tells SAS to use the same data set attributes for the output file as were used for the input file.

```
filename in  'userid.input';
filename out 'userid.output';

data;
   infile in;
   input;
   file out dcb=in;
   put _infile_;
run;
```

Using the FILE Statement to Specify Data Set Disposition

Appending Data with the MOD Option

In this example, the MOD option is used to append data to the end of an external file.

```
filename out 'user.output';

data _null_;
   file out;
   put ... ;     /* New data are written to 'user.output'      */
run;

data _null_;
   file out mod;
   put ... ;     /* Data are appended to the end of 'user.output' */
run;
```

Appending Data with the MOD Disposition

This example is similar to the previous one except that instead of using the MOD option, the DISP= option is used. The OLD option is then used to overwrite the data.

```
filename out 'user.output' disp=mod;

data _null_;
   file out;
   put ... ;     /* Data are appended to end of 'user.output'         */
run;

data _null_;
   file out old;
   put ... ;     /* Data are written at the beginning of 'user.output' */
run;

data _null_;
   file out;
   put ... ;     /* Data are written at the beginning of 'user.output' */
run;

data _null_;
   file out mod;
   put ... ;     /* Data are appended to the end of 'user.output'       */
run;
```

Writing to Print Data Sets

A print data set contains carriage-control information (also called ASA control characters) in column 1 of each line. These characters (blank, 0, − , + , and 1) control the operation of a printer, causing it to skip lines, to begin a new page, and so on. They do not normally appear on a printout. A nonprint data set does not contain any carriage-control characters.

When you write to a print data set, SAS shifts all column specifications in the PUT statement one column to the right in order to accommodate the carriage-control characters in column 1. Therefore, if you expect to print an external file, you should designate the file as a print data set either when you allocate it or when you write to it.

□   To designate a data set as a print data set when you *allocate* it, use the RECFM= option in the FILENAME statement, the JCL DD statement, or the TSO ALLOCATE command. Adding the letter A to the end of the value for the RECFM= option (RECFM=FBA or RECFM=VBA, for example) causes SAS to include carriage control characters in the data set that is being created. See "FILENAME" on page 270 for complete information about the RECFM= option.

□   When you *write to* a data set that was not designated as a print data set when it was allocated, you can designate it as a print data set in several ways, depending on what you plan to do with the data set. Here are some examples:

  □   Use the PRINT option in the FILE statement, as in

```
file saveit print;
```

SAVEIT is the fileref of the data set. The PRINT option in the FILE statement adds carriage-control characters in column 1 of any external file; this is the simplest way to create a print data set.

□ Use PRINT as the fileref in the FILE statement (different from the PRINT option above), as in

```
file print;
```

The PRINT fileref in the FILE statement causes SAS to write the information either to the standard SAS procedure output file (SASLIST), or to another output file if you have used a PROC PRINTTO statement to redirect your output. (See "PRINTTO" on page 230 and Chapter 7, "Routing the SAS Log and SAS Procedure Output," for information about PROC PRINTTO.) In either case, this file contains carriage-control characters by default. You can suppress the carriage-control characters by specifying the NOPRINT option in the FILE statement (see the next section, "Designating a Print Data Set as a Nonprint Data Set").

□ Use the letter A as part of the value in the RECFM= option in the FILE statement:

```
file saveit recfm=vba;
```

As in the FILENAME statement, the letter A in the RECFM= option of the SAS FILE statement causes SAS to include carriage-control characters in the data set that is being created. SAS also changes the record format of the target data set.

For information about how to process print files as input, see "Reading from Print Data Sets" on page 82.

Designating a Print Data Set as a Nonprint Data Set

If a data set has been allocated as a print data set, you can use the NOPRINT option in the FILE statement to designate it as a nonprint data set (without carriage-control information). For example, suppose you specified RECFM=VBA, indicating a print data set, when you allocated a file and that you assigned the fileref OUTDD to the file. The following SAS statement designates OUTDD as a nonprint data set:

```
file outdd noprint;
```

To write lines without carriage-control information to the SAS procedure output file, specify

```
file print noprint;
```

The NOPRINT option is also useful when you use a DATA step to copy a data set that already contains carriage-control information. In this case, use NOPRINT to prevent SAS from adding an additional column of carriage-control information.

Reading from External Files

After you allocate an external file, you can read from the file in a SAS DATA step by specifying it in the INFILE statement, the INCLUDE command, or the %INCLUDE statement.

This section describes the INFILE statement. For information about the INCLUDE command, the %INCLUDE statement, and the DATA step, see *SAS Language: Reference.*

INFILE Statement

In a SAS DATA step, the INFILE statement specifies which external file is to be read by a subsequent INPUT statement. Every external file that you want to read must have a corresponding INFILE statement. The external file can be a sequential data set on disk or tape, a member of a partitioned data set (PDS), or any of several nonstandard file types (see the description of the *type* argument in the next section, "INFILE Statement Syntax"). The file can also be entered from a terminal.

The INFILE statement is executable. Therefore, it can be used in conditional processing—in an IF/THEN statement, for example.

When multiple INFILE statements are present, the INPUT statement reads from the external file that was specified by the most recent INFILE statement. (See *SAS Language: Reference* for a complete description of the INPUT statement.)

INFILE Statement Syntax

This section provides a brief overview of INFILE statement syntax. For complete information about the INFILE statement, see "INFILE" on page 284.

The syntax of the INFILE statement is

INFILE *file-specification* <*type*> <*options* . . . >;

file-specification
  identifies the file. It may be in the following forms:

Form	Example
fileref	report
fileref(*member*)	report(feb)
'*OS-data-set-name*'	'library.daily.report'
'*OS-data-set-name(member)*'	'library.daily.source(report1)'
reserved fileref	CARDS

See "Specifying Operating System Data Sets" on page 13 for details about different ways of specifying *OS-data-set-name.*

type
  specifies the type of file. Nonstandard (host-specific) file types that you can specify for MVS are DLI, HFS, IDMS, ISAM, PIPE, VSAM, and VTOC. For information about

these file types, see "Accessing Nonstandard Files" on page 83 and "Accessing OpenEdition MVS Hierarchical File System Files" on page 84.

options

describe the input file's characteristics and specify how it is to be read with an INPUT statement. Many of these options are not host-dependent and are documented in *SAS Language: Reference*. Those that are host-specific are documented in "INFILE" on page 284. You can use these options to do the following:

□ define variables that will contain information about the external file

□ specify special open and close processing

□ specify file characteristics.

INFILE Statement Examples

Type of Data Set	Example
sequential	`infile 'library.daily.data';`

member of a PDS	`infile report(feb);`
	or
	`infile 'library.daily.source(report1)';`

sequential or member of a PDS*	`infile data;`
IMS	`infile psb dli;`
in-stream	`infile cards;`

* depending on what the fileref is associated with

Reading from a Sequential File

This example assigns the fileref RAW to the data set MYID.RAW.DATAX and uses the fileref in a simple DATA step:

```
filename raw 'myid.raw.datax' disp=shr;
data out;
   infile raw;
   input ... ;
run;
```

This example is similar to the previous one, except that it specifies a value for the SYSPREF= system option and then uses a partially qualified data set name in the FILENAME statement:

```
options syspref=sys2.sas6;
filename raw2 '.raw.datax' disp=shr;
```

```
data out;
   infile raw2;
   input ... ;
run;
```

See "Specifying Operating System Data Sets" on page 13 for information about using SYSPREF= and partially qualified data set names.

Reading from a Member of a Partitioned Data Set

This example specifies the PDS name in the FILENAME statement and then specifies the member name in parentheses following the fileref in the INFILE statement:

```
filename mypds 'user.my.pds';
data out;
   infile mypds(mydata);
   input ... ;
run;
```

This example specifies both the PDS name and the member name in the FILENAME statement. Therefore, only the fileref is specified in the INFILE statement:

```
filename mymember 'user.my.pds(mydata)';
data out;
   infile mymember;
   input ... ;
run;
```

Reading from the Terminal

If you run SAS in interactive line mode or in noninteractive mode, you can read input from the terminal. These examples illustrate ways to define a terminal file. In the first example, TERMINAL is specified as the device type in the FILENAME statement.

```
filename term1 terminal;
data one;
   infile term1;
   input ... ;
run;        /* Enter "/*" to signify end-of-file    */
```

In the next example, an asterisk is used in place of an operating system data set name to indicate that the file will be entered from the terminal.

```
filename term2  '*';
data out;
   infile term2;
   input ... ;
run;        /* Enter "/*" to signify end-of-file    */
```

Reading Concatenated Data Sets

Multiple sequential data sets can be concatenated (via a JCL DD statement, a TSO ALLOCATE command, or a FILENAME statement) and read consecutively using one pair of INFILE/INPUT statements.

Sequential data sets and individual PDS members can also be concatenated, as in the following example:

```
x alloc fi(in1) da('my.data1' 'my.pds(mem)' 'my.data2');
data mydata;
   infile in1;
   input ... ;
   /* SAS statements */
run;
```

Here is an example of using the FILENAME statement to concatenate data sets:

```
filename in1 ('my.data1' 'my.pds(mem)' 'my.data2');
```

You can also concatenate external files that are stored on different types of devices and that have different characteristics.

If PDSs are concatenated and a member is specified in the INFILE statement, then SAS searches each PDS for that member. SAS searches in the order in which the PDSs appear in the DD statement, the ALLOCATE command, or the FILENAME statement. If the member is present in more than one of the PDSs, SAS retrieves the first one that it finds.

Reading from Multiple External Files

You can read from multiple external files either sequentially or alternately from multiple filerefs.

□ To read from multiple external files *sequentially,* use the END= option or the EOF= option in each INFILE statement to direct program control to a new file after each file has been read. For example:

```
filename outrdr sysout=a pgm=intrdr recfm=fb lrecl=80;
data _null_;
   length dsn $ 44;
   input dsn $;
   infile dummy filevar=dsn end=end;
   file outrdr noprint notitles;
   do until(end);
      input;
      put _infile_;
      end;
cards;
PROD.PAYROLL.JCL(BACKUP)
PROD.PAYROLL.JCL(TRANS)
PROD.PAYROLL.JCL(PRINT)
;
run;
```

See *SAS Language: Reference* for more information about the END= and EOF= options of the INFILE statement.

□ In order to *alternately* access multiple external files, the files must have different filerefs. You can partially process one file, go to a different file, and return to the original file. An INFILE statement must be executed each time you want to access a file, even if you are returning to a file that was previously accessed. The DATA step terminates when SAS encounters the EOF of any of the files. Consider the following example:

```
filename exfile1 'my.file.ex1';
filename exfile2 'my.file.ex2';
data mydata;
    infile exfile1;
    input ... ;

    /* SAS statements */

    infile exfile2;
    input ... ;

    /* SAS statements */

    infile exfile1;
    input ... ;

    /* SAS statements */

run;
```

When there is more than one INFILE statement for the same fileref, with options specified in each INFILE statement, the options apply cumulatively to successive files.
Note: Multiple files inside concatenations cannot be accessed in this manner.

Reading from Print Data Sets

When reading from a print data set, you can tell SAS to ignore the carriage-control character that is in column 1 of print data sets by specifying the SAS system option FILECC. For more information, see "FILECC" on page 318.

Getting Information about an Input Data Set

In the following example, data set information is printed in the SAS log. Control blocks are printed in hexadecimal format. Note that only the first 100 bytes of the JFCB are printed. The example can be used with either a sequential data set or a PDS.

```
filename in 'user.data';
data out;
    infile in jfcb=jf dscb=ds volumes=vol ucbname=ucb
           devtype=dev;
```

```
        if (_n_ = 1) then
            put @1 'Data Set Name:' @17 jf $52.    /
                @4 'Volume ='       @20 vol $30.    /
                @4 'JFCB ='         @20 jf $hex200. /
                @4 'DSCB ='         @20 ds $hex188. /
                @4 'Devtype ='      @20 dev $hex48. /
                @4 'Device Addr ='  @20 ucb $3.     ;
    run;
```

Accessing Nonstandard Files

Accessing IMS-DL/I and CA-IDMS Databases

Both the SAS/ACCESS interface to IMS-DL/I and the SAS/ACCESS interface to CA-IDMS include a DATA step interface. Extensions for certain SAS statements (such as INFILE, FILE, PUT, and INPUT) enable you to format database-specific calls in a SAS DATA step. Therefore, you can access the IMS or CA-IDMS data directly, without using SAS/ACCESS view descriptors. If your site licenses these interfaces, see *SAS/ACCESS Interface to IMS-DL/I: Usage and Reference, Version 6, Second Edition* and SAS Technical Report P-269, *SAS/ACCESS Interface to CA-IDMS: DATA Step Interface, 6.09 Enhanced Release* for more information.

Note: The DATA step interface for IMS-DL/I is a "read/write" interface. The DATA step interface for CA-IDMS is "read" only.

Accessing ISAM Files

To read an ISAM file sequentially, include the ISAM keyword on the INFILE statement as in the following example:

```
data newdata;
    infile isamfile isam;
    input;
    /*  SAS statements */
run;
```

Accessing VSAM Data Sets

Use the VSAM option to indicate that a fileref points to a VSAM external file.

□   To *read* a VSAM file with an INPUT statement, specify the VSAM option in an INFILE statement:

```
filename in1 'prod.payroll';
data mydata;
    infile in1 vsam;
    input ...;
    /* SAS statements */
run;
```

□ To *write* to an empty VSAM file with a PUT statement, specify the VSAM option in a FILE statement:

```
filename out 'myid.newdata' disp=old;
data current;
    file out vsam;
    put ...;
    /* SAS statements */
run;
```

□ To *update* a VSAM data set, include an INFILE statement and a FILE statement that point to the same fileref, and specify the VSAM type option in the DATA step:

```
filename mydata 'myid.newdata' disp=old;
data newdata;
    file mydata vsam;
    infile mydata vsam;
    /* SAS statements */
run;
```

Many VSAM-specific options are available with the INFILE and FILE statements. See "VSAM Options for the FILE and INFILE Statements under MVS" on page 268 for details. For complete information about accessing VSAM data sets, see *SAS Guide to VSAM Processing, Version 6, First Edition.*

Accessing the Volume Table of Contents (VTOC)

To access a disk's Volume Table of Contents (VTOC), specify the VTOC option in an INFILE statement. See "VTOC Options for the INFILE Statement under MVS" on page 288 for more information.

Accessing OpenEdition MVS Hierarchical File System Files

The Hierarchical File System (HFS) is a directory-based file system that is very similar to the file systems used in UNIX. It is part of OpenEdition MVS, an addition to the MVS/ESA operating system that provides conformance to the ANSI POSIX.1 standard.

The SAS System under MVS enables you to read and write HFS files and to pipe data between SAS and OpenEdition MVS commands.

Allocating HFS Files

You can allocate an HFS file either externally (using a JCL DD statement or the TSO
ALLOCATE command) or internally (using the SAS FILENAME statement). For
information about allocating HFS files externally, see *MVS/ESA OpenEdition MVS User's
Guide.*

When you use the FILENAME statement to allocate an HFS file, you specify that the
file is in the HFS in either of the following ways:

□ Include a slash in the path name:

```
filename input '/u/sasusr/data/testset.dat';
```

□ Specify HFS as the file type:

```
filename input hfs 'testset.dat';
```

You can also do both—that is, specify the HFS file type *and* use a slash in the path name.

If you do not specify the entire path name of the HFS file, then the directory component
of the path name is the working directory that was current when the file was allocated, not
when the fileref is used. For example, if your working directory was
`/usr/local/sasusr` when you allocated the file, then the following statement
associates the INPUT fileref with the path `/usr/local/sasusr/testset.dat` .

```
filename input hfs 'testset.dat';
```

If you change your current working directory to `/usr/local/sasusr/testdata`
then the following statement still refers to `/usr/local/sasusr/testset.dat`, not to
`/usr/local/sasusr/testdata/testset.dat`.

```
infile input;
```

Allocating an HFS Directory

To allocate a *new* HFS directory, you must use either a JCL DD statement or a TSO
ALLOCATE command. (See *MVS/ESA OpenEdition MVS User's Guide.*) To allocate an
existing HFS directory, simply specify a directory in place of the file names in the above
FILENAME statement examples.

To open a particular file in a directory for input or output, you must specify the file
name in the SAS INFILE or FILE statement, as described in "Accessing a Particular File in
an HFS Directory" on page 87.

Specifying File-Access Permissions and Attributes

How you specify file-access permissions and attributes depends on which method you use to
allocate an HFS file:

□ When you use a JCL DD statement or a TSO ALLOCATE command to allocate an
HFS file, you can use the PATHMODE and PATHOPTS options to specify file-access

permissions and attributes for the file. If you later use the file's DDname in a SAS session, SAS uses the values of those options when it opens the file.

For example, if you use the following TSO ALLOCATE command to allocate the DDname INDATA, then SAS issues an "insufficient authorization" error message and does not permit the file to be opened for output. (The ORDONLY value of PATHOPTS specifies "open for reading only.")

```
alloc file(indata) path('/u/sasusr/data/testset.dat')
              pathopts(ordonly)
```

In other words, you could use the DDname INDATA in a SAS INFILE statement, but not in a FILE statement. Similarly, if you specify OWRONLY, then you can use the DDname in a FILE statement but not in an INFILE statement.

► *Caution* . . . . **PATHOPTS values OAPPEND and OTRUNC take precedence over FILE statement options OLD and MOD.**
If you specify OAPPEND ("add new data to the end of the file"), the FILE statement option OLD does not override this behavior. Similarly, if you specify OTRUNC ("if the file exists, erase it and re-create it"), the FILE statement options OLD and MOD do not override this behavior. (See page 266 for details about these FILE statement options.) ▲

□ If you use the FILENAME statement to allocate an HFS file, or if you use a JCL DD statement or a TSO ALLOCATE command but do not specify values for PATHMODE and PATHOPTS, then SAS uses the following values for those options:

   □ For PATHMODE, SAS uses the file-access mode `-rw-rw-rw-`; however, this mode may be modified by the current file-mode creation mask. (For detailed information about the file-mode creation mask, see *MVS/ESA OpenEdition MVS User's Guide.*)

   □ For PATHOPTS, the file-access mode that SAS supplies depends on how the fileref or DDname is being used:

      □ If the fileref or DDname appears only in a FILE statement, SAS opens the file for writing only, and if the file does not exist, SAS creates it.

      □ If the fileref appears only in an INFILE statement, SAS opens the file for reading only.

      □ If the fileref appears in both FILE and INFILE statements within the same DATA step, SAS opens the file for reading and writing. For the FILE statement, SAS also creates the file if it does not already exist.

Using HFS File Names in SAS Statements and Commands

To use an actual HFS file name (rather than a fileref or DDname) in a SAS statement or command, include a slash in the path name. You can use an HFS file name anywhere that an external file name can be used, such as in a FILE or INFILE statement, or in an INCLUDE or FILE display manager command. If the file is in the current directory, specify the directory component as `./`. For example:

```
include './testprg.sas'
```

Concatenating HFS Files

To associate a fileref with a concatenation of HFS files or directories, enclose the path names in parentheses. The fileref can be opened only for input. For example:

```
filename testdata ('data/testset1.dat' 'data/testset2.dat');
```

All of the path names in the concatenation must be for HFS files or directories. If your program reads data from different types of files in the same DATA step, you can use the EOF= option in each INFILE statement to direct program control to a new INFILE statement after each file has been read. (See *SAS Language: Reference* for more information about the EOF= option of the INFILE statement.)

Accessing a Particular File in an HFS Directory

If you have associated a fileref with an HFS directory or with a concatenation of HFS directories, you can open a particular file in the directory for reading or writing by using an INFILE or FILE statement in the form shown below:

```
infile fileref(file);
file   fileref(file);
```

If you do not enclose *file* in quotes, then SAS appends a file extension to the file name. In the INCLUDE and FILE display manager commands, the file extension is ".sas". In the INFILE and FILE statements, the file extension is ".dat".

If the file is opened for input, SAS searches all of the directories that are associated with the fileref in the order in which they appear in the FILENAME statement. If the file is opened for output, SAS creates the file in the first directory that was specified. If the file is opened for updating but does not exist, SAS creates the file in the first directory.

Piping Data between SAS and OpenEdition MVS Commands

To pipe data between SAS and OpenEdition MVS commands, you first specify the PIPE file type and the command in a FILENAME statement. Enclose the command in single quotes. For example, this FILENAME statement assigns the command `ls -lr` to the fileref OEMVSCMD:

```
filename oemvscmd pipe 'ls -lr';
```

To send the output from the command as input to the SAS System, you then specify the fileref in an INFILE statement. To use output from SAS as input to the command, you specify the fileref in a FILE statement.

You can associate more than one command with a single fileref. Commands are executed in the order in which they appear in the FILENAME statement. For example:

```
filename oemvscmd pipe ('ls *.sas' 'ls *.data');
```

Piping Data from an OpenEdition MVS Command to SAS

When a pipe is opened for input by the INFILE statement, any output that the command writes to standard output or to standard error is available for input. For example, here is a DATA step that reads the output of the `ls -l` command and saves it in a SAS data set:

```
filename oemvscmd pipe 'ls -l';
data dirlist;
   infile oemvscmd truncover;
   input mode $ 1-10 nlinks 12-14 user $ 16-23 group $25-32
         size 34-40 lastmod $ 42-53 name $ 54-253;
run;
```

Piping Data from SAS to an OpenEdition MVS Command

When a pipe is opened for output by the FILE statement, any lines that are written to the pipe by the PUT statement are sent to the command's standard input. For example, here is a DATA step that uses the OpenEdition MVS `od` command to write the contents of the file in hexadecimal format to the HFS file `dat/dump.dat` :

```
filename oemvscmd pipe 'od -x -tc - >dat/dump.dat';
data _null_;
   file oemvscmd;
   input line $ 1-60;
   put line;
cards;
The SAS System is an integrated system of software products,
enabling you to perform data management, data analysis, and
data presentation tasks.
;
run;
```

Host-Specific Options for HFS Files

Table 6.1 shows which host-specific options are recognized by the FILENAME, FILE, and INFILE statements for HFS files and pipes. No other options are recognized, including such MVS-specific options as DISP, CLOSE, and DCB. Descriptions of the options follow the table.

Table 6.1
Host-Specific
Options for HFS
Files and Pipes

Option	FILENAME	FILE	INFILE
OLD	X	X	
MOD	X	X	
LRECL=	X	X	X
RECFM=	X	X	X

OLD
> replaces the previous contents of the file. This is the default. This option has no effect on a pipe.

MOD
> appends the output lines to the file. This option has no effect on a pipe.

LRECL=*value*
> specifies the maximum number of characters in a line (unless the file has been opened with RECFM=N). The default is 255. Lines longer than *value* are truncated. *value* must be between 1 and 32767, inclusive.

RECFM=*record-format*
> specifies the record format of the file. Valid values are:

F	specifies that all lines in the file have the length specified in the LRECL option. In output files, lines that are shorter than the LRECL value are padded on the right with blanks.
V | D	specifies that the lines in the file are of variable length, ranging from 1 character to the number of characters specified by LRECL=. This is the default.
P	specifies that the file has variable-length records and is in print format.
N	specifies that the file is in binary format. The file is treated as a byte stream; that is, line boundaries are not recognized.

Using the X Statement to Issue OpenEdition MVS Commands

To start the OpenEdition MVS shell, issue the following X statement:

```
x omvs;
```

Note: OpenEdition MVS commands are case-sensitive.

You can also use the X statement to issue the following OpenEdition MVS commands:

`x cd` *directory*`;`
> changes the current working directory to *directory*. If *directory* is omitted, the current working directory is changed to the working directory that was initially assigned to your login name.

`x umask` *mask*`;`
> changes the current file-mode creation mask value to *mask*. According to UNIX conventions, *mask* is a one- to three-digit octal number. The file-mode creation mask modifies the file mode of new files. Each 1 bit in the file-mode creation mask causes the corresponding permission bit in the file mode to be disabled. If a bit is 0 in the mask, the corresponding file-mode bit can be enabled. For HFS files that are created by SAS, the file mode for new files is "-rw-rw-rw-"; however, this mode is modified by the current file-mode creation mask. For example, `x umask 022` ensures that each newly created file can be written to only by its owner. (For detailed information about the file-mode creation mask, see *MVS/ESA OpenEdition MVS User's Guide.*)

The new value is displayed in the SAS log. If *mask* is not specified, the current value is simply displayed in the SAS log; the current file-mode creation mask value remains unchanged.

```
x pwd;
```
displays your current working directory in the SAS log.

To issue a TSO command or CLIST that has the same name as one of the OpenEdition MVS commands (a CLIST named CD, for example), either enter the command using uppercase characters, or use the `TSO:` prefix and enclose the command in quotes, as in the following examples:

```
x CD option1 option2 ...;

x 'tso:cd option1 option2 ...';
```

For more information about the X statement, see "X" on page 297.

Restrictions in SAS System Support for OpenEdition MVS

□ It is not possible to run SAS under the OpenEdition MVS shell. However, you can run the shell after you initialize SAS by using the `x omvs;` statement.

□ You can place a SAS data library, SAS catalog, or SAS data set in the HFS only if it is in transport format. (See "Transporting SAS Files to and from MVS" on page 131.)

Writing Your Own I/O Access Methods

You can write your own I/O access method to replace the default SAS access method. This feature enables you to redirect external file I/O to a user-written program.

In the following example, the user-written access method, SASREADC, reads an entry from a SAS catalog. The PGMPARM= option is used to pass a parameter to the access method.

```
filename myentry 'pgm=sasreadc' pgmparm='libref.catalog.entry.type';
```

You can then access the catalog entry just as you would access an external file (using the %INCLUDE statement, for example).

Note: The user-written I/O access method applies only to external files, not to SAS data sets.

See your SAS software consultant for additional information about writing I/O access methods.

Accessing SAS Statements from a Program

You can redirect your SAS statements to come from an external program rather than from a file by using the SYSINP= and PGMPARM= system options. SYSINP= specifies the name of the program, and PGMPARM= specifies a parameter that is passed to the program. For more information, see "SYSINP=" on page 387 and "PGMPARM=" on page 362.

Using the INFILE/FILE User Exit Facility

User exit modules enable you to inspect, modify, delete, or insert records in a DATA step. Here are some examples of how they may be used:

□ encrypting and decrypting data

□ compressing and decompressing data

□ translating data from one character-encoding system to another.

This is an advanced topic. See Appendix 2 for details.

Chapter 7 Routing the SAS® Log and SAS® Procedure Output

Default Routings 93

Routing to External Files with the PRINTTO Procedure 95
Rerouting to the Default Destination 95

Routing to External Files with SAS System Options 96
Routing Your SAS Log or Procedure Output to an External File 96
Copying Your SAS Log or Procedure Output to an External File 97

Routing to External Files with Commands 97
Using the FILE Command 97

Routing to External Files with DD Statements 98

Routing to a Printer 98
Using the PRINTTO Procedure 98
Using the PRINT Command and the FORM Subsystem 99
   Specifying a Form 99
   Modifying Your Default Form 99
   Adding a Form 100
Using the PRTFILE and PRINT Commands 100

Routing Output to a Remote Destination 101

Default Routings

For each SAS job or session, the SAS System automatically creates two types of output:

SAS log file
: contains information about the processing of SAS statements. As each program step executes, notes are written to the SAS log along with any applicable error or warning messages. (For more information, see "SAS Log File" on page 17.)

SAS procedure output file
: is also called the *print file*. Whenever a SAS program executes a PROC step that produces printed output, SAS sends the output to the procedure output file. (For more information, see "SAS Procedure Output File" on page 19.)

Table 7.1 shows the default routings of the SAS log and procedure output files.

Table 7.1
Default Routings of the SAS Log and Procedure Output Files

Processing Mode	SAS Log File	Procedure Output File
batch	printer	printer
display manager (TSO)	LOG window	OUTPUT window
interactive line (TSO)	terminal	terminal
noninteractive (TSO)	terminal	terminal

These default routings are specified in the SAS cataloged procedure and in the SAS CLIST, which you use to invoke SAS in batch mode and under TSO, respectively. Your system administrator may have changed these default routings.

This chapter explains how to change the routing of these files. Use Table 7.2 to help you decide which method you should choose to change the routing.

Table 7.2 *Decision Table: Changing the Default Destination*

To route your SAS log or procedure output to...	Using this mode of processing...	Use this method...	See...
a printer	any mode	FILENAME statement and PRINTTO procedure	"Using the PRINTTO Procedure" on page 98
	display manager under TSO	PRINT command and FORM subsystem	"Using the PRINT Command and the FORM Subsystem" on page 99
		PRTFILE and PRINT commands	"Using the PRTFILE and PRINT Commands" on page 100
an external file	any mode	PRINTTO procedure	"Routing to External Files with the PRINTTO Procedure" on page 95
	batch	LOG= and PRINT= system options	"Routing Your SAS Log or Procedure Output to an External File" on page 96
		SASLOG DD and SASLIST DD statements	"Routing to External Files with DD Statements" on page 98
its usual location *and* to an external file	any mode	ALTLOG= and ALTPRINT= system options	"Routing to External Files with SAS System Options" on page 96
	display manager under TSO	FILE command	"Using the FILE Command" on page 97
a remote destination	any mode	FILENAME statement and PRINTTO procedure	"Routing Output to a Remote Destination" on page 101

Routing to External Files with the PRINTTO Procedure

Using the PRINTTO procedure with its LOG= and PRINT= options, you can route the SAS log or SAS procedure output to an external file from any mode. You can specify the name of the external file in the PROC PRINTTO statement. For example, the following statement routes procedure output to MYID.OUTPUT.DATA(MEMBER):

```
proc printto print='myid.output.data(member)' new;
```

However, if you plan to specify the same external file several times in your SAS program, you can allocate the file using a FILENAME statement, a JCL DD statement, or the TSO ALLOCATE command. (See Chapter 5 for details and examples.) Once the external file is allocated, use the PROC PRINTTO statement options LOG= or PRINT= at any point in your SAS session to direct the log or procedure output to the external file. Specify the fileref or the DDname that is associated with the external file. Here is an example that uses FILENAME statements to allocate external files for both the log and the procedure output:

```
filename printout 'myid.output.prtdata' disp=old;
filename logout 'myid.output.logdata' disp=old;

proc printto print=printout log=logout new;
```

The log and procedure output continue to be routed to the designated external file until another PROC PRINTTO statement reroutes them.

The NEW option causes any existing information in the file to be cleared. If you omit the NEW option from the PROC PRINTTO statement, the SAS log or procedure output is *appended* to existing sequential data sets. You must specify NEW when routing to a partitioned data set because you cannot append data to a partitioned data set member.

If you want to route both the log and procedure output to partitioned data set members, the members must be in different data sets. SAS does not allow you to write to two members of one partitioned data set at the same time.

Rerouting to the Default Destination

To reroute the log and procedure output to their default destinations, submit the following statements:

```
proc printto;
run;
```

See Table 7.1 on page 93 for a list of the default destinations.

Routing to External Files with SAS System Options

You can use SAS system options to change the destination of the SAS log and procedure output. The options that you use depend on which of the following tasks you want to accomplish:

□ routing your SAS log or procedure output to an external file instead of to their default destinations (see the next section, "Routing Your SAS Log or Procedure Output to an External File")

□ routing the log or output both to their default destinations and to an external file (see "Copying Your SAS Log or Procedure Output to an External File" on page 97)

Specify the options in any of the following ways:

□ when you invoke the SAS CLIST

□ in the JCL EXEC statement

□ in a configuration file.

See "Specifying or Changing System Option Settings" on page 11 for more information about specifying SAS system options.

Before using the options described in this section, you must allocate the appropriate data sets to your TSO session or batch job. See "Ways of Allocating External Files" on page 59 for details about allocating external files.

Routing Your SAS Log or Procedure Output to an External File

Use the LOG= and PRINT= system options to change the destination of your SAS log or procedure output. The log and procedure output then are *not* routed to their default destinations.

When you invoke the SAS System, use the LOG= and PRINT= options to specify the DDnames of the allocated data sets.

□ TSO (SAS CLIST):

```
alloc fi(logout) da('myid.output.logdata') old
alloc fi(printout) da('myid.output.prtdata') old

sas options('log=logout print=printout') input('''myid.sas.program''')
```

These TSO ALLOCATE commands must be submitted *prior* to invoking SAS.

□ Batch (JCL EXEC statement):

```
//SASSTEP  EXEC SAS,OPTIONS='LOG=LOGOUT PRINT=PRINTOUT'
//LOGOUT   DD  DSN=MYID.OUTPUT.LOGDATA,DISP=OLD
//PRINTOUT DD  DSN=MYID.OUTPUT.PRTDATA,DISP=OLD
//SYSIN    DD  DSN=MYID.SAS.PROGRAM,DISP=SHR
```

LOG= and PRINT= are normally used in batch, noninteractive, and interactive line modes. These system options have no effect in display manager mode. If you are running in display manager mode, use the ALTLOG= and ALTPRINT= system options (see the next section).

Copying Your SAS Log or Procedure Output to an External File

Use the ALTLOG= and ALTPRINT= system options to send a copy of your SAS log or procedure output to an external file. The log and procedure output are also displayed in the LOG and OUTPUT windows as usual (if you are in display manager), or otherwise routed to their default destinations.

When you invoke SAS, use the ALTLOG= and ALTPRINT= options to specify the DDnames of the allocated data sets.

```
sas options('altprint=printout altlog=logout')
```

This method works in all modes of running SAS. See the previous section for complete examples.

Routing to External Files with Commands

Using the FILE Command

You can use the FILE command to copy the contents of many different display manager windows to external files. Issue the FILE command on the command line of the window whose contents you want to copy. For example, to copy the contents of the LOG window to a sequential data set, issue the following command on the command line of the LOG window:

```
file 'myid.log.out'
```

If the sequential file does not exist, a requestor window asks you whether you want to create the file and whether you want to catalog it. If the file does exist, a requestor window asks you whether you want to replace it or to append data to the existing data.

You can also use the FILE command to copy the contents of a window to a partitioned data set (PDS) member:

```
file 'myid.log.out1(test)'
```

If you have already associated a fileref or DDname with your PDS, you can use the fileref or DDname in the command, followed by the member name in parentheses:

```
file mylib(test)
```

If the member that you specify already exists, it is overwritten because you cannot append data to existing PDS members.

Routing to External Files with DD Statements

In an MVS batch job, you can use the SASLOG DD and SASLIST DD statements to change the destination of the SAS log and procedure output file. These statements override the DD statements in the SAS cataloged procedure; therefore, the position of these statements in your JCL is important. You must place the SASLOG DD statement and the SASLIST DD statement in the same order as they appear in the SAS cataloged procedure. Also, these statements must follow the JCL EXEC statement, and they must precede the DD statements for any DDnames that are not included in the cataloged procedure (such as SYSIN).

For example, the following job routes the SAS log to member DEPT of an existing partitioned data set and routes the procedure output to an existing sequential data set:

```
//REPORT  JOB accounting-information,MSGLEVEL=(1,1)
//SASSTEP EXEC SAS,OPTIONS='LINESIZE=80 NOSTATS'
//SASLOG  DD DSN=MYID.MONTHLY.REPORT(DEPT),DISP=OLD
//SASLIST DD DSN=MYID.MONTHLY.OUTPUT,DISP=MOD
//SYSIN  DD *

SAS statements

//
```

Note: SASLOG and SASLIST are the default DDnames of the SAS log and procedure output files. If these DDnames have been changed in your site's SAS cataloged procedure, then use your site's DDnames in place of SASLOG and SASLIST.

▶ *Caution* . . . .   *The SAS cataloged procedure selects default DCB characteristics unless you specify them in the SASLOG or SASLIST DD statement.*
If you are routing the SAS log to a member of a partitioned data set whose DCB characteristics are different from those given in "SAS Log File" on page 17, you must include the existing DCB characteristics in the SASLOG DD statement. Similarly, if you are routing the SAS procedure output to a member of a partitioned data set whose DCB characteristics are different from those given in "SAS Procedure Output File" on page 19, you must include the existing DCB characteristics in the SASLIST DD statement. Otherwise, the existing DCB characteristics of the partitioned data set will be changed to the characteristics that are specified for SASLOG or SASLIST in the SAS cataloged procedure, making the other members of the partitioned data set unreadable. ▲

Routing to a Printer

Using the PRINTTO Procedure

You can use the FILENAME statement in conjunction with the PRINTTO procedure to route your output directly to a printer. Use the SYSOUT= option in the FILENAME statement to direct your output to the system printer. Then specify the fileref with the PRINT= or LOG= option in the PROC PRINTTO statement. The following example establishes a fileref and uses it in the PROC PRINTTO statement to reroute the procedure output:

```
filename output sysout=a;
proc printto print=output;
```

Usually, SYSOUT=A specifies that the destination is a printer; however, this is determined by the data center personnel at your site.

Using the PRINT Command and the FORM Subsystem

Use the PRINT command to route the contents of a display manager window to your default printer. This is the easiest method of printing output. For example, issue the PRINT command from the command line of your OUTPUT window to send the contents of that window to your default printer.

The default printer—as well as other aspects of your output such as printer margins, printer control language, and font control information—are controlled by the FORM subsystem. The FORM subsystem consists of six frames that are described in detail in *SAS Language: Reference.* You use these frames to define a form for each printer that is available to you at your site. You can also define multiple forms for the same printer. (See "Adding a Form" on page 100.) Your SAS Software Consultant can give you information about your default form and about any other forms that have been defined at your site.

Specifying a Form

To route the contents of a display manager window to a printer that is not your default printer, you can use the FORM= option with the PRINT command. Use this option to specify a form that has been defined for a different printer. For example, to copy output to a printer destination that is described in a form named MYOUTPUT, you would enter the following command-line command:

```
print form=myoutput
```

Modifying Your Default Form

To change the default destination printer and to customize other features of the output that the PRINT command generates, you can modify the default form that the FORM subsystem uses. To modify your default form, do the following:

1. Enter `fsforms default` from the command line to display your default form. If your SASUSER.PROFILE catalog contains a form named DEFAULT, then that form is displayed. If you do not have a form named DEFAULT, then the Printer Selection frame is displayed.

2. Select a printer from the Printer Selection frame. When you select a printer, SAS copies the default form for that printer into your SASUSER.PROFILE catalog.
    Note: Printer information is site-specific; see your system administrator if you need help with selecting a printer.

3. Make other changes to the default form, if desired, by changing the information in the other frames of the FORM subsystem. Issue the **NEXTSCR** command to scroll to the next FORM frame, and issue the **PREVSCR** command to scroll to the previous frame. Two of these frames, the Print File Parameters frames, are used to specify host-specific

printer information; they are described in "Host-Specific Frames of the FORM Subsystem" on page 416. The other frames are described in *SAS Language: Reference*.

4. Enter the END command to save your changes.

Adding a Form

You can also add additional forms to the FORM subsystem. These forms can then be used with the PRINT command, as described in "Specifying a Form" on page 99, and they can be modified in the same manner as described in "Modifying Your Default Form" on page 99. For example, to create a form named MYOUTPUT, do the following:

1. Enter `fsforms myoutput` from the command line.

2. Selecting a printer from the Printer Selection frame.

3. Use the NEXTSCR and PREVSCR commands to scroll through the other frames of the FORM subsystem. Use these other frames to provide additional information that will be associated with the MYOUTPUT form.

4. Enter the END command to save your changes.

Using the PRTFILE and PRINT Commands

You can also use the PRTFILE command, followed by the PRINT command, to print the contents of display manager windows. This method enables you to override some of the defaults that are established by the FORM subsystem, such as the destination or the SYSOUT class.

PRTFILE establishes the destination, and PRINT sends the contents of the window to that destination. If you don't specify a destination with the PRTFILE command, PRINT automatically sends the window contents to your default printer. (See "Using the PRINT Command and the FORM Subsystem" on page 99 for details about using the PRINT command alone.)

For example, to print the contents of your OUTPUT window on RMT5 instead of on your default printer, follow this procedure:

1. From the PROGRAM EDITOR window, submit a FILENAME statement to allocate a destination file for the output. You can use the DEST= and SYSOUT= options to specify the destination and SYSOUT class, respectively. You can also direct the output to the HOLD queue by specifying the HOLD option. (See "SYSOUT Data Set Options for the FILENAME Statement" on page 280 for information about other options that you can specify.) For example:

   ```
   filename myrpt dest=rmt5 sysout=a hold;
   ```

   Note: The destination printer that you specify in the FILENAME statement must be the same type of printer as your default printer.

2. From the command line of any display manager window, issue the PRTFILE command, specifying the fileref from your FILENAME statement. For example:

   ```
   prtfile myrpt
   ```

3. From the command line of the window whose contents you want to print, issue the `PRINT` **command.**

4. **If you want to print the contents of any other windows, issue the `PRINT`** command from the command line of those windows. A requestor window warns you that the destination file already exists. Enter **A** in the requestor window to append the window contents to the destination file.

5. From the command line of the first window that you printed, issue the `FREE` command.

6. From the PROGRAM EDITOR window, submit a FILENAME statement to clear (deassign) the fileref. Your output is not actually printed until you perform this step. For example:

```
filename myrpt clear;
```

Routing Output to a Remote Destination

You can use the DEST= option of the FILENAME statement to route output to a remote destination. The destination can be a work station, a local or remote printer, or other device.

In order to route your output to a remote destination, you must know the remote station ID of the device that will receive your output. The station ID is an identifying label that is established by your data center; it is one to eight characters in length. You must also know the appropriate SYSOUT class for output that is directed to the remote device. Your data center personnel can provide you with this information.

After determining the remote station ID and the SYSOUT class, you use either the TSO ALLOCATE command or a SAS FILENAME statement to establish a DDname or fileref for the destination. Then use the DDname or fileref with the PRINTTO procedure to route your output. Here is an example that routes the procedure output file to a remote printer:

```
filename output sysout=a dest=6670xyz1;
proc printto print=output;
proc print data=oranges;
run;
```

The FILENAME statement includes the options SYSOUT=A and DEST=6670XYZ1. The values of these options are site-specific. In this case, the output class, A, specifies that the output will be directed to a printer. The remote station ID, 6670XYZ1, links the fileref to a particular printer.

The PROC PRINTTO statement then specifies the fileref OUTPUT in the PRINT= option. This option routes the procedure output file to the destination that was associated with the fileref OUTPUT in the FILENAME statement. When the PRINT procedure is executed, SAS sends the procedure output to the job entry subsystem (JES); the output is not displayed in the OUTPUT window. JES holds the output until the file identified by the fileref OUTPUT is freed. Then the output is printed at the remote destination.

To route the SAS log to a remote destination, use the same procedure, but use the LOG= option instead of the PRINT= option with the PROC PRINTTO statement.

Part 2
Application Considerations

Chapter 8   SAS® Interfaces to ISPF and REXX

Chapter 9   Transporting SAS® Files to and from MVS

Chapter 10   Data Representation

Chapter 11   Identifying and Resolving Problems

Chapter 12   Optimizing Performance

104

Chapter **8** SAS® Interfaces to ISPF and REXX

SAS Interface to ISPF   106
Software Requirements   106
Enabling the Interface   106
Invoking ISPF Services   106
    Using the ISPEXEC CALL Routine   107
    Using the ISPLINK CALL Routine   107
    Testing ISPEXEC and ISPLINK Return Codes   108
    Using ISPF Dialog Development Models   108
Using Special SAS System Options with the Interface   108
    Changing the Status of ISPF Interface Options during Execution of a DATA Step   109
Using the ISPF Editor from Your SAS Session   110
    Copying ISPF EDIT Models to Your SAS Session   110
Using Special Facilities for Passing Parameters to ISPF   111
    Variable-Naming Conventions   111
    Specifying Fixed Binary Parameters   111
    Passing Parameters That Are Longer Than 200 Bytes   112
    Bypassing Parameter Processing   113
Accessing SAS Variables from ISPF   114
    VDEFINE, VDELETE, and VRESET Services   114
    Handling of SAS Variables   114
    Examples   116
Tips and Common Problems to Avoid   116
    Checking for Invalid Values in SAS Variables   116
    Truncated Values for Numeric Variables   117
    Uninitialized Variables   117
    Character Values Passed for Numeric Variables   117
Testing ISPF Applications   117
Sample Application   118
    Employee Records Application   118
    First Employee Record Application Panel   120
    Second Employee Record Application Panel   121

SAS Interface to REXX   122
Enabling the Interface   122
Invoking a REXX Exec   123
Interacting with the SAS Session from a REXX Exec   124
    Routing Messages from REXX Execs to the SAS Log   124
    The GETEXEC DATA Step Function   124
    The PUTEXEC DATA Step Routine   124
    Checking Return Codes in REXX Execs   125
Changing the Host Command Environment   125
Comparing the REXX Interface to the X Statement   126
Comparing SAS REXX Execs to ISPF Edit Macros   126
Examples of REXX Execs   127
    A Simple REXX Exec   127
    Using the GETEXEC DATA Step Function   127
    Using the PUTEXEC DATA Step Routine   128
    Checking the SAS Return Code in a REXX Exec   129

SAS Interface to ISPF

The SAS interface to ISPF consists of CALL routines, system options, and other facilities that enable you to write interactive ISPF applications in the SAS language or in a combination of the SAS language and other languages that are supported by ISPF. This interface replaces the Version 5 product, SAS/DMI. It provides access to ISPF both from SAS Display Manager and from SAS/AF Screen Control Language (SCL).

Using this interface, you can implement interactive applications that can be used even by novice users. Users need only know how to log on to a 3270 or 3290 terminal. All other information can be supplied as part of the application itself.

For SAS programmers, using this interface is often preferable to using other languages to implement interactive ISPF applications, because existing SAS data files and applications can be exploited. The interface also reduces the need for the SAS programmer to learn another language.

For detailed information about ISPF, see the IBM documents *ISPF Dialog Developer's Guide and Reference* and *ISPF Reference Summary*.

Software Requirements

Table 8.1 summarizes the software requirements for using the interface.

Table 8.1
Software Requirements for Using the SAS Interface to ISPF

Software	Version Required
Base SAS Software	SAS System Release 6.08 or later
Operating System	MVS/SP Version 2 or later TSO/E Version 2 or later
ISPF	ISPF Version 2 or later

Enabling the Interface

The interface is available to you whenever you invoke SAS in the MVS environment under ISPF. There is no separate procedure for enabling the interface.

Invoking ISPF Services

The interface provides CALL routines that enable you to use ISPF services from a SAS DATA step. The ISPF services facilitate many other tasks. For example, they provide an efficient way to convert SAS files to ISPF tables and ISPF tables to SAS files. They also enable display input to be validated by the ISPF panel processing section and/or by the SAS DATA step, giving cross-variable-checking capability.

The IBM documents *ISPF Dialog Developer's Guide and Reference* and *ISPF Reference Summary* describe the ISPF services and their syntax conventions. To invoke these services, you can use either the ISPLINK CALL routine or the ISPEXEC CALL routine. However, ISPEXEC has the following limitations:

□   The following ISPF services *cannot* be invoked from ISPEXEC:

      GRERROR
      GRINIT
      GRTERM
      VCOPY
      VDEFINE
      VDELETE
      VREPLACE
      VRESET

□   The SAS services described in "Changing the Status of ISPF Interface Options during Execution of a DATA Step" on page 109 cannot be invoked from ISPEXEC.

□   You cannot use abbreviated variable lists (described in "Variable-Naming Conventions" on page 111) with ISPEXEC.

Remember that SAS restricts the length of each parameter to 200 characters, and that ISPF restricts a name list to 254 names. However, see "Passing Parameters That Are Longer Than 200 Bytes" on page 112 if you need to pass longer parameters.

Using the ISPEXEC CALL Routine

To invoke ISPEXEC from a SAS DATA step, use a CALL statement with one of these formats:

```
call ispexec(value1,value2 );

call ispexec(,value2 );

call ispexec(value2 );
```

where *value1* and *value2* are variables, literals, or expressions to be passed as parameters to ISPF. Use the same parameters that you would use with an ISPF ISPEXEC.

Value1, if specified, is the length of *value2*. If you use the second or third form of the call, the ISPF interface provides this value.

Value2 is a character string that contains the service name and parameters, specified as they would be in a CLIST. Parameters can be specified as symbolic ISPF variables that will be replaced with the ISPF variable values at run time. Only one scan for symbolic variables is done, and the resulting service request must not exceed 512 bytes in length.

Note: If you use symbolic ISPF variables, remember that both SAS and ISPF use ampersands to define symbolic variables. Enclose the ISPF symbolic variable specifications in single quotes to prevent them from being replaced by SAS.

Using the ISPLINK CALL Routine

To invoke ISPLINK from a SAS DATA step, use a CALL statement with this format:

```
call isplink(value1, . . . ,value15 );
```

where *value1,...,value15* are variables, literals, or expressions to be passed as parameters to ISPF. You use the same parameters that you would use with an ISPF ISPLINK. See "Using Special Facilities for Passing Parameters to ISPF" on page 111 for a description of special parameter considerations.

Trailing blanks are sometimes used by ISPF to determine the end of a parameter; they are optional because the interface supplies them. If more than 15 positional parameters are required (for example, TBSTATS can have up to 17 parameters), parameters 15 through 20 can be specified in *value15*. The values must be separated by commas. The interface will parse *value15* into parameters 15 through 20.

Testing ISPEXEC and ISPLINK Return Codes

Each ISPEXEC or ISPLINK CALL subroutine results in a return code that is described in IBM's *ISPF Dialog Developer's Guide and Reference* manual. You can test the return code with the SAS numeric variable ISP_RC. Because this variable is set by ISPEXEC or ISPLINK, the SAS compiler produces a `Note: Variable` *varname* `is uninitialized` message. To avoid receiving this message, specify the following SAS statement in your program:

```
retain isp_rc 0;
```

Using ISPF Dialog Development Models

A standard ISPF function called Dialog Development Models uses the ISPF EDIT facility to simplify the development of programs. (See the chapter on "Using Edit Models" in the IBM manual *ISPF Edit and Edit Macros*. See also "Using the ISPF Editor from Your SAS Session" on page 110 and "Copying ISPF EDIT Models to Your SAS Session" on page 110.)

If you specify PL/I as the model class, the statements that the model facility produces will be in the proper SAS form. To simplify the use of the Dialog Development Models, the PL/I return code variable, PLIRETV, is recognized and used by the interface in the same way as ISP_RC. The following examples could have been created using the `SELECT` Edit model:

```
data _null_;
   call ispexec('SELECT PANEL(ISR@PRIM)');
   if pliretv¬=0 then put pliretv=;
run;

data _null_;
   call isplink('SELECT',' ','PANEL(ISR@PRIM)');
   if pliretv¬=0 then put pliretv=;
run;
```

Using Special SAS System Options with the Interface

The SAS interface to ISPF includes the following SAS system options. These options are useful in developing and debugging ISPF applications. Most of them are used in conjunction with the ISPF VDEFINE service, which is described in "VDEFINE, VDELETE, and VRESET Services" on page 114.

ISPCAPS	ISPMSG=	ISPVDEFA	ISPVTMSG=
ISPCHARF	ISPNOTES	ISPVDLT	ISPVTNAM=
ISPCSR=	ISPNZTRC	ISPVDTRC	ISPVTPNL=
ISPEXECV=	ISPPT	ISPVIMSG=	ISPVTRAP
ISPMISS=	ISPTRACE	ISPVRMSG=	ISPVTVARS=

To determine which of these options are in effect for your SAS session, submit the following statements from the PROGRAM EDITOR window and view the output in the LOG window.

```
proc options isp;
run;
```

You specify these options as you would specify any other SAS system option. (See "Specifying or Changing System Option Settings" on page 11.) For detailed information about these options, see Chapter 20, "System Options."

Changing the Status of ISPF Interface Options during Execution of a DATA Step

You can use the interface's SAS service in conjunction with the ISPLINK CALL routine to change the status of some of the SAS system options that relate to the ISPF interface. For example, the following ISPLINK CALL specifies the ISPNZTRC system option:

```
call isplink ('SAS','ISPNZTRC');
```

The system options whose status can be changed in this manner are listed in Table 8.2. See Chapter 20, "System Options," for detailed descriptions of these options.

Note: For compatibility with SAS/DMI, you can use the DMI service to change the status of the corresponding system option.

Table 8.2
SAS Services and Their SAS/DMI Equivalents

SAS Service	Equivalent DMI Service
('SAS','ISPCAPS')	('DMI','CAPS')
('SAS','NOISPCAPS')	('DMI','NOCAPS')
('SAS','ISPCHARF')	('DMI','CHARFORMATTED')
('SAS','NOISPCHARF')	('DMI','NOCHARFORMATTED')
('SAS','ISPNOTES')	('DMI','NOTES')
('SAS','NOISPNOTES')	('DMI','NONOTES')
('SAS','ISPNZTRC')	('DMI','NZRCTRACE')
('SAS','NOISPNZTRC')	('DMI','NONZRCTRACE')
('SAS','ISPPT')	('DMI','PT')
('SAS','NOISPPT')	('DMI','NOPT')

(continued)

Table 8.2   *(continued)*

SAS Service	Equivalent DMI Service
('SAS','ISPTRACE')	('DMI','TRACE')
('SAS','NOISPTRACE')	('DMI','NOTRACE')
('SAS','ISPVDTRC')	('DMI','VDEFTRACE')
('SAS','NOISPVDTRC')	('DMI','NOVDEFTRACE')
('SAS','ISPVDLT')	('DMI','VDELVDEF')
('SAS','NOISPVDLT')	('DMI','NOVDELVDEF')
('SAS','ISPVTRAP')	('DMI','VTRAP')
('SAS','NOISPVTRAP')	('DMI','NOVTRAP')

Using the ISPF Editor from Your SAS Session

If you prefer to use the ISPF editor rather than the SAS editor, or if you need to use the ISPF editor in order to use edit models (see the next section, "Copying ISPF EDIT Models to Your SAS Session"), you can use the SAS System's HOSTEDIT command. Under MVS, the HOSTEDIT command temporarily suspends the current SAS session and initiates a session of the ISPF editor or browser. See "HOSTEDIT" on page 419 for details.

Copying ISPF EDIT Models to Your SAS Session

A major advantage of being able to access the ISPF editor with the HOSTEDIT command is that it enables you to access ISPF EDIT models, modify them as necessary, and then copy them to your SAS PROGRAM EDITOR window.

To access an ISPF EDIT model, do the following:

1. Invoke SAS from ISPF and enter HOSTEDIT on the command line of the PROGRAM EDITOR window.

2. Enter `MODEL CLASS PLI` on the ISPF editor command line.

3. Enter `MODEL` plus the model name to include a particular model (for example, `MODEL TBDISPL`), or enter `MODEL` alone and specify a model from the list of EDIT models that appears.

You can then modify the model as necessary and use the END command to save it back to your PROGRAM EDITOR window.

For more information about the ISPF EDIT facility and EDIT models, refer to the IBM manual *ISPF Edit and Edit Macros*.

Using Special Facilities for Passing Parameters to ISPF

The interface provides special facilities and services that simplify the coding and processing of parameters for ISPF services. These facilities include:

- □ variable-naming conventions that simplify the specification of variables to ISPF

- □ methods for specifying fixed binary parameters

- □ a way to pass parameters that are longer than the usual 200-byte limit

- □ a way to bypass parameter processing

Variable-Naming Conventions

To simplify the specification of variables to ISPF, the interface recognizes _ALL_ or an asterisk (*) to reference all variable names. Variable names can also be selected by their prefixes. When a name ends in a colon, all variables that begin with the specified name are referenced.

You can also use other types of SAS variable lists, including numbered range lists (for example, x1-xn) and name range lists (x-numeric-a), as described in the chapter on "Rules of the SAS Language" in *SAS Language: Reference* .

When a variable list is passed to the VDEFINE service (see "VDEFINE, VDELETE, and VRESET Services" on page 114), the special naming conventions refer to all variables in the current DATA step that are legal ISPF variable names. (Note: A name that contains an underscore is not a legal ISPF variable name.) SAS arrays, temporary DATA step variables such as FIRST.*variable* and LAST.*variable*, and the variable PLIRETV are not considered candidates for VDEFINE. The special naming conventions for services other than VDEFINE refer only to the list of currently defined variables and *not* to all of the variables in the DATA step.

Specifically, the special variable-naming conventions can be used in the following places:

- □ in the second parameter for the VCOPY, VDEFINE, VDELETE, VERASE, VGET, VMASK, VPUT, and VREPLACE services

- □ in the third parameter for the TBADD, TBCREATE, TBMOD, TBPUT, TBSARG, and TBSCAN services

- □ in the fourth parameter for the TBCREATE service.

Specifying Fixed Binary Parameters

The interface supports the use of simple numeric constants or variables in ISPF service parameters for services that require numeric parameters. However, for compatibility with SAS/DMI, the following two ways of creating fullword fixed binary parameters in SAS DATA steps are also supported:

```
length fixed10 $4;
retain fixed10;
if _n_=1 then fixed10=put(10,pib4.);
```

or

```
retain fixed10 '0000000a'x;
```

In addition, you can specify a hexadecimal value as a literal parameter by enclosing the value in single or double quotes and entering the letter X after the closing quote.

Some of the services that have numeric parameters are CONTROL, TBDISPL, TBCREATE, TBQUERY, TBSKIP, VDEFINE, and VCOPY.

Note: Never use a blank or null value for a numeric parameter.

The ISPF SELECT service has a special parameter list because it requires a fullword fixed binary parameter that specifies the length of the buffer. The SAS interface to ISPF provides this length parameter, but if you use the ISPLINK CALL routine to invoke the SELECT service, then you must reserve the parameter's place in the parameter list. Use either a comma or two single quotes with a blank between them (' ') to represent the parameter, as in the following example:

```
isplink('SELECT', ,'CMD(%MYDIALOG)');
```

If you use the ISPEXEC CALL routine to invoke the SELECT service, then you do not need to reserve the parameter's place:

```
ispexec('SELECT CMD(%MYDIALOG)');
```

Passing Parameters That Are Longer Than 200 Bytes

SAS limits the length of a CALL routine parameter to 200 bytes, but it is sometimes necessary to pass more than 200 bytes as an ISPF service request parameter. For this reason, the interface has a special parameter form that allows parameters up to 65,535 bytes long for both ISPLINK and ISPEXEC calls.

When a parameter longer than 200 bytes is required, use the following form in place of the parameter:

=varname=length

where *varname* is the name of a SAS character variable in the current DATA step, and *length* is the length of *varname*, expressed as a two-byte binary value. Blanks are not permitted before or after the equal signs.

Using this parameter form does not change ISPF parameter restrictions. For example, ISPEXEC allows a maximum of 512 bytes in its second parameter regardless of how you specify the parameter.

Example

Here is an example that demonstrates the use of parameters greater than 200 bytes: Assume that you want to copy an ISPF table named MASTER into a table named MYTABLE. You do not know the names of the variables contained in the table, but there is an ISPF service named TBQUERY that can be used to obtain this information. TBQUERY returns a list of names enclosed in parentheses and separated by blanks. A return code of 16 indicates that the list of names has been truncated because of insufficient space.

The numbered lines of code are explained following the example.

```
      data _null_;
❶        array anyname $128 longlist longl_1 longl_2 longl_3;
❷        retain longlist longl_1 longl_2 longl_3 ' ';

      more SAS statements

❸        call isplink('VDEFINE','LONGLIST',,,512);
❹        call ispexec('TBQUERY MASTER NAMES(LONGLIST)');
         if isp_rc ne 0 then do;

      more SAS statements

         end;
❺        call isplink('TBCREATE','MYTABLE',,'=LONGLIST='||PUT(512,PIB2.));

      more SAS statements
```

❶ The variables are defined in an ARRAY statement in order to ensure that SAS assigns contiguous memory locations for the variables. The variables must be of the same type and length. A length of 128 bytes is assigned to the variable LONGLIST and to the three variables that follow, so that the total length of the four is 512 bytes for the list of at least 56 names.

❷ The RETAIN statement suppresses the **NOTE: Variable** *varname* **is undefined** message from the SAS compiler (see "Uninitialized Variables" on page 117). Either all or none of the variables must be specified in the RETAIN statement, because if you specify some variables but omit others, the variables may be assigned to non-contiguous memory.

❸ The VDEFINE service is called to define the variable LONGLIST with an explicit length of 512 bytes. See "VDEFINE, VDELETE, and VRESET Services" on page 114 for a discussion of the VDEFINE parameters.

❹ The CALL statement to the TBQUERY service stores the list of names in LONGLIST. Note that this call is to ISPEXEC, which is much simpler than using the ISPLINK call for TBQUERY.

❺ If the service return code is zero (normal completion), then the error-termination routine is bypassed and the TBCREATE service is invoked. The fourth parameter of this call is in the special interface form, which points to the actual parameter and specifies the length of the parameter. The program then copies the table MASTER row by row.

Note: Because ISPF limits the number of names in a table to 254, allowing 2287 bytes (9 bytes per name, including one byte for a separator or closing parenthesis, plus one byte for the opening parenthesis) should be sufficient for any table.

Bypassing Parameter Processing

There may be times when parameters must be passed to ISPF without modification. If the interface encounters a parameter whose first position contains a PL/I "not" symbol (¬), then the parameter that follows the "not" symbol is passed to ISPF unchanged. This facility prevents the parameter from being translated to uppercase and prevents names from being replaced within the parameter.

Accessing SAS Variables from ISPF

This section describes how the SAS interface to ISPF processes three ISPF services—
VDEFINE, VDELETE, and VRESET. These services are used to grant and revoke ISPF
access to variables in the SAS DATA step. This section also provides an explanation of how
SAS numeric and character variables are handled by VDEFINE, and it includes examples of
how VDEFINE and VDELETE are used.

VDEFINE, VDELETE, and VRESET Services

The ISPF VDEFINE service is used to give ISPF access to variables in the SAS DATA step.
When you call the VDEFINE service, the interface adds the SAS variables that you specify
to its list of defined variables.

The ISPF VDEFINE service allows you to specify seven parameters. The form is

```
'VDEFINE', namelist , variable , format , length , optionlist , userdata
```

The interface provides the values for *variable, format, length,* and *userdata* . You need only
specify *namelist* .

The *optionlist* parameter is optional and can be used when you are defining either SAS
character variables or SAS numeric variables. The two VDEFINE options that you can
specify are COPY and NOBSCAN. The LIST option is not supported. COPY allows the
value of the variable that is being defined to be initialized to the value of a dialog variable
that has the same name in the function pool, shared pool, or profile pool. The NOBSCAN
option prevents ISPF from stripping trailing blanks from variables.

To define all SAS variables in the current DATA step, use the following statement:

```
call isplink('VDEFINE','_ALL_');
```

For more information about specifying variables, see "Variable-Naming Conventions" on
page 111.

The VDELETE service ends ISPF access to specified variables in the SAS DATA step,
and the interface drops the variables from the list of defined variables that it maintains. The
interface recognizes the end of a SAS DATA step and deletes any variables that remain on
its list of defined variables.

The VRESET service ends ISPF access to *all* variables that have been passed to the
VDEFINE service. However, in addition to removing *all* variables that the user has passed
to VDEFINE, VRESET also removes variables that the interface has passed to VDEFINE.
To prevent variables that it is using from being removed, the interface changes VRESET to
('VDELETE','_ALL_').

Handling of SAS Variables

SAS provides unique services that you can use when defining numeric and character
variables to ISPF with the VDEFINE service.

Numeric Variables

Numeric SAS variables are in doubleword floating-point format. You may pass them to the VDEFINE service with either the FLOAT format or the USER format. If you use the FLOAT format, you should specify (or let the interface provide) a length of 8, because all SAS numeric variables have a length of 8 during the execution of the SAS DATA step. *

   Note: When the FLOAT format is used, certain features of the SAS interface to ISPF are unavailable: SAS formats and informats that are associated with the variable are not used, null values are not changed to the special missing value "._" (period underscore), and accessing of variables cannot be traced with the ISPVTRAP option.

   Because earlier releases of ISPF did not support the FLOAT format, SAS (and previously, SAS/DMI) supports the use of the USER format. If you specify the USER format, or if you let SAS default to it, then SAS provides a user exit that uses any format and/or informat associated with the variable. If no format or informat is associated with the variable, then the default SAS format and/or informat are used.

Character Variables

In addition to containing strings of printable characters, SAS character variables can actually contain any data value. Hence, you may use any valid ISPF VDEFINE format with a SAS character variable. ISPF treats the variable accordingly. Within the SAS DATA step, the SAS functions INPUT or PUT can be used to perform data conversion as required. The SAS system option ISPCHARF | NOISPCHARF determines whether explicit SAS informats and formats are used to convert SAS character variable values when they are used as ISPF variables. The following list explains how this option determines whether the SAS variable formats are to be used when a variable is passed to the VDEFINE service:

□   If the SAS system option NOISPCHARF is in effect when a SAS character variable is passed to the VDEFINE service, the SAS character variable is defined to ISPF with a *format* of CHAR, and both ISPF and SAS reference and modify the values of these variables directly in main storage.

□   If the SAS system option ISPCHARF is in effect when a SAS character variable is passed to the VDEFINE service, and if the SAS variable has an explicit SAS informat or format, then the SAS character variable is defined to ISPF with a *format* of USER, and the interface uses the SAS informat or format in its conversion routine whenever ISPF references the variable. The interface also applies the following rules:

   □   If the variable contains an invalid value for the SAS informat, the variable is set to the value of the SAS system option MISSING=.

   □   If the variable contains an invalid value for the SAS format, ISPF receives the value of the SAS system option MISSING= for the variable.

   □   If no value is specified for an ISPF character variable, the variable is set to the value of the ISPMISS= option.

   If an application requires an ISPF dialog variable that is longer than the maximum SAS character variable length of 200, then the *length* parameter of VDEFINE can be specified

---

*   For numeric variables, the LENGTH statement applies to the length of the variables when they are stored in a SAS data set, not to the length of the variables in memory while the DATA step is executing.

and associated with the variables that are being defined to ISPF. In order to prevent the data from being overwritten, you must do the following:

□ Create multiple variables whose total length equals or exceeds the length required.

□ Ensure that the SAS compiler assigns storage for the variables contiguously by using SAS ARRAY statements to arrange the variables as needed. Either all or none of the variables must be specified in the RETAIN statement.

It is good practice to code the SAS ARRAY and RETAIN statements for these extra-long variables immediately following the SAS DATA statement.

The following example shows how ISPF dialog variables named LONG1 and LONG2, each 256 bytes long, would be defined.

```
data _null_;
   array anyname1 $128 long1 long1_c;
   array anyname2 $128 long2 long2_c;
   retain long1 long1_c long2 long2_c  ' ';
   call isplink('VDEFINE','(LONG1 LONG2)',,,256);
```

Examples

The following statement defines to ISPF all variables in the current DATA step that begin with the letters PPR:

```
call isplink('VDEFINE','PPR:');
```

The next statement defines the variables SASAPPLN, ZCMD, and ZPREFIX to ISPF. The variables are to be initialized with the values from variables of the same name that already exist in the variable pools.

```
call isplink('VDEFINE','(SASAPPLN  ZCMD  ZPREFIX)',,,,'COPY');
```

This next statement removes all previously defined variables from the variable pool, making them inaccessible to ISPF:

```
call isplink('VDELETE','_ALL_');
```

Tips and Common Problems to Avoid

Checking for Invalid Values in SAS Variables

If a SAS variable in an ISPF table or display has a specified informat, invalid values are replaced with missing values. When you create ISPF panels through which a user can enter or modify SAS values, the values can be checked for validity either with the action section of the panel or with the SAS DATA step. If missing values are not appropriate, you can redisplay the panel (along with an appropriate error message) and prompt the user to re-enter the invalid values correctly.

Checking for Null Values in ISPF Variables

The special missing value of underscore indicates an ISPF variable with a length of 0. (Null values are valid for ISPF values.) The special missing value of underscore distinguishes between an invalid value from an informat (which will have a missing value) and a value that was not provided.

Truncated Values for Numeric Variables

To avoid truncating the values of numeric variables, you must either provide a format whose length does not exceed the size of the display field, or you must increase the length of the display field itself. If no format is associated with a numeric variable, the default format width is 12 characters.

Uninitialized Variables

When a variable is neither specified with an initial value in a RETAIN statement nor appears on the left side of the equal sign in an assignment statement, the SAS log shows the **Note: Variable** *varname* **is uninitialized** message. For example, the following statements would result in the message **NOTE: Variable ZCMD is uninitialized**.

```
data _null_;
length zcmd $200;
call isplink('VDEFINE','ZCMD');
call isplink('DISPLAY','ISRTSO');
put zcmd=;
run;
```

However, in this example the message is misleading, because the call to ISPF actually assigns a value to ZCMD. To prevent the message from being generated, put the variable in a RETAIN statement with an initial value, or use the variable in an assignment statement. For example, the following RETAIN statement assigns an initial value (a blank) to the variable ZCMD:

```
retain zcmd
```

Character Values Passed for Numeric Variables

Under SAS/DMI (the Version 5 predecessor to the SAS interface to ISPF), it was not possible to pass numeric values directly to ISPF services for which numeric values are required. Instead, an alternate method was provided (see "Specifying Fixed Binary Parameters" on page 111). The alternate method is still supported but is not required. Therefore, if you used SAS/DMI to develop ISPF applications, you may prefer to modify those applications so that numeric values are passed directly to these ISPF services instead.

Testing ISPF Applications

When you are testing code that uses ISPF services, there are techniques and facilities that can greatly simplify the testing process. Chapter 2 of the IBM manual *ISPF Dialog Developer's Guide and Reference* describes the ISPF dialog test modes. This facility provides aids for testing functions, panels, variables, messages, tables, and skeletons.

In addition, the SAS System provides the MPRINT system option to help you find coding errors. If you want to see the SAS statements that are generated by SAS macros, specify MPRINT in a SAS OPTIONS statement. (The MPRINT system option is documented in *SAS Language: Reference*).

The ISPF parameters are written to the SAS log when the ISPTRACE option is specified. The tracing can also be turned on and off with the ISPLINK CALL subroutine, as in the following example:

```
call isplink('SAS','NOISPTRACE');   /* stops tracing of ISPF parameters */
```

Sample Application

The IBM manual *ISPF Dialog Management Examples* (ISPF Version 3.3) provides examples of ISPF applications written in APL2, COBOL, FORTRAN, PASCAL, PL/I, and as CLISTs.

This section shows how one of those applications would be written in the SAS language.

Employee Records Application

```
data _null_;
    length empser $6 fname lname $16 addr1 addr2 addr3 addr4 $40 pha $3
        phnum msg typechg chktype $8 i state $1;
    retain empser fname lname i addr1 addr2 addr3 addr4 pha phnum msg
        typechg chktype ' ' state '1' pliretv 0;
    call isplink('VDEFINE',                    /* Define variables      */
        '(EMPSER FNAME LNAME I ADDR: PHA PHNUM TYPECHG CHKTYPE)');
    msg=' ';                                   /* Initialize message    */
call isplink('TBCREATE',                       /* If table doesn't exist*/
        'SASEMPTB','(EMPSER)',                 /* create it             */
        '(LNAME FNAME I ADDR: PHA PHNUM)',
        'NOWRITE');                            /* Don't save the table  */
do while (state¬='4');                         /* Loop until term set   */
    call isplink('DISPLAY','SASEMPLA',msg);    /* Select employee       */
    if pliretv=8 then state='4';               /* End key then terminate*/
    else do;                                   /* Enter key pressed     */
      msg=' ';                                 /* Reset message         */
      state='2';                               /* Process employee panel*/
      call isplink('TBGET','SASEMPTB');        /* Obtain employee data  */
      if pliretv=0 then                        /* If record exists then */
        typechg='U';                           /*   set update flag     */
      else do;                                 /* Record does not exist */
        typechg='N';                           /*   set type=new        */
        lname=' ';fname=' ';i=' ';             /* Initialize panel vars */
        addr1=' ';addr2=' ';addr3=' ';
        addr4=' ';pha=' ';phnum=' ';
      end;
      chktype=typechg;                         /* Save type of change   */
      call isplink('DISPLAY','SASEMPLB');      /* Display employee data */
```

```
    if pliretv¬=8 then do;              /* End key not pressed    */
      if typechg='N' then do;              /* If new employee       */
        call isplink('TBADD','SASEMPTB');  /*   add to table        */
        msg='SASX217';                     /*                       */
        end;                               /*                       */
      else do;                             /*                       */
        if typechg='U' then do;            /* If update requested   */
          call isplink('TBPUT','SASEMPTB'); /*   update table       */
          msg='SASX218';                   /*                       */
          end;                             /*                       */
        else do;                           /*                       */
          call isplink('TBDELETE','SASEMPTB'); /* deleted message   */
          msg='SASX219';                   /*                       */
          end;                             /*                       */
        end;                             /* End table mods          */
      end;                               /* End 2nd panel process   */
    end;                                 /* End 1st panel process   */
  if msg¬=' ' then call isplink('LOG',msg); /* Log message          */
end;                                     /* End do loop             */
call isplink('TBCLOSE','SASEMPTB');      /* Close table             */
call isplink('VDELETE','_ALL_');         /* Delete all variables    */
run;
```

Contents of Member SASEMPLA in ISPPLIB

```
%---------------------------- EMPLOYEE SERIAL --------------------------------
%COMMAND ====>_ZCMD
+
%ENTER EMPLOYEE SERIAL BELOW:
+
+
+
+   EMPLOYEE SERIAL%===>_EMPSER+   (MUST BE 6 NUMERIC DIGITS)
+
+
+
+PRESS%ENTER+TO DISPLAY EMPLOYEE RECORD.
+ENTER%END COMMAND+TO RETURN TO PREVIOUS MENU.
)PROC
  VER (&EMPSER,NONBLANK)
  VER (&EMPSER,PICT,NNNNNN)
)END
```

First Employee Record Application Panel

Display 8.1
First Employee
Record Application
Panel

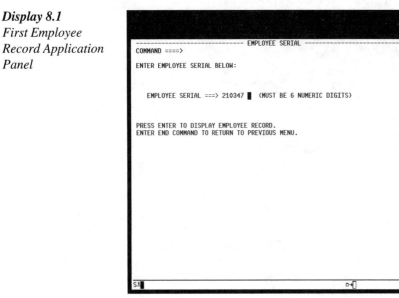

Contents of Member SASEMPLB in ISPPLIB

```
%------------------------------ EMPLOYEE RECORDS ------------------------------
%COMMAND ====>_ZCMD
+
+    EMPLOYEE SERIAL: &EMPSER
+
+    EMPLOYEE NAME:%===>_TYPECHG +   (NEW, UPDATE, OR DELETE)
+      LAST   %===>_LNAME            +
+      FIRST  %===>_FNAME            +
+      INITIAL%===>_I+
+
+    HOME ADDRESS:
+      LINE 1%===>_ADDR1                                    +
+      LINE 2%===>_ADDR2                                    +
+      LINE 3%===>_ADDR3                                    +
+      LINE 4%===>_ADDR4                                    +
+
+    HOME PHONE:
+      AREA CODE   %===>_PHA+
+      LOCAL NUMBER%===>_PHNUM    +
+
)INIT
  .CURSOR = TYPECHG
  IF (&PHA = ' ')
    &PHA = 914
  &TYPECHG = TRANS(&TYPECHG N,NEW U,UPDATE D,DELETE)
)PROC
  &TYPECHG = TRUNC (&TYPECHG,1)
  IF (&TYPECHG = N)
```

```
   IF (&CHKTYPE ¬= N)
      .MSG = SASX211
 IF (&TYPECHG ¬= N)
   IF (&CHKTYPE = N)
      .MSG = SASX212
 VER (&LNAME,ALPHA)
 VER (&FNAME,ALPHA)
 VER (&I,ALPHA)
 VER (&PHA,NUM)
 VER (&PHNUM,PICT,'NNN-NNNN')
 IF (&TYPECHG = N,U)
   VER (&LNAME,NONBLANK,MSG=SASX214)
   VER (&FNAME,NONBLANK,MSG=SASX213)
   VER (&ADDR1,NONBLANK,MSG=SASX215)
   VER (&ADDR2,NONBLANK,MSG=SASX215)
   VER (&ADDR3,NONBLANK,MSG=SASX215)
)END
```

Second Employee Record Application Panel

Display 8.2
Second Employee
Record Application
Panel

Contents of Member SASX21 in ISPMLIB

```
SASX210  'INVALID TYPE OF CHANGE'                           .ALARM=YES
'TYPE OF CHANGE MUST BE NEW, UPDATE, OR DELETE.'

SASX211  'TYPE ''NEW'' INVALID'                             .ALARM=YES
'EMPLOYEE SERIAL &EMPSER ALREADY EXISTS.  CANNOT BE SPECIFIED AS NEW.'

SASX212  'UPDATE OR DELETE INVALID'                         .ALARM=YES
'EMPLOYEE SERIAL &EMPSER IS NEW.  CANNOT SPECIFY UPDATE OR DELETE.'
```

```
SASX213  'ENTER FIRST NAME'                              .ALARM=YES
'EMPLOYEE NAME MUST BE ENTERED FOR TYPE OF CHANGE = NEW OR UPDATE.'

SASX214  'ENTER LAST NAME'                               .ALARM=YES
'EMPLOYEE NAME MUST BE ENTERED FOR TYPE OF CHANGE = NEW OR UPDATE.'

SASX215  'ENTER HOME ADDRESS'                            .ALARM=YES
'HOME ADDRESS MUST BE ENTERED FOR TYPE OF CHANGE = NEW OR UPDATE.'

SASX217  '&EMPSER ADDED'
'EMPLOYEE &LNAME, &FNAME &I ADDED TO FILE.'

SASX218  '&EMPSER UPDATED'
'EMPLOYEE &LNAME, &FNAME &I UPDATED.'

SASX219  '&EMPSER DELETED'
'EMPLOYEE &LNAME, &FNAME &I DELETED.'
```

SAS Interface to REXX

REXX, the procedure language for computing platforms that conform to the IBM Systems
Application Architecture (SAA), is well known for combining powerful programming
features with ease of use. By enabling SAS users to supplement the SAS language with
REXX, the SAS System's interface to REXX provides new SAS programming possibilities
in the MVS environment.

Enabling the Interface

The SAS system options REXXMAC and REXXLOC control the REXX interface.

□ The REXXMAC option enables or disables the REXX interface. If REXXMAC is in
   effect, then the REXX interface is enabled. This means that when SAS encounters an
   unrecognized statement, it searches for a REXX exec whose name matches the first
   word of the unrecognized statement. If the default, NOREXXMAC, is in effect, then the
   REXX interface is disabled. This means that when SAS encounters an unrecognized
   statement, a "statement is not valid" error occurs. You can specify this option in the
   configuration file, when you invoke SAS, or in the OPTIONS statement.

□ When the REXXMAC option is in effect, the REXXLOC= option specifies the
   DDname of the REXX exec library to be searched for any SAS REXX execs. The
   default is REXXLOC=SASREXX. You can specify this option either in the
   configuration file or when you invoke SAS.

Invoking a REXX Exec

SAS REXX execs are REXX programs. They are stored in a library that is allocated to the SASREXX fileref (or to another fileref, as specified by the SAS system option REXXLOC=). A REXX exec is submitted as part of a SAS program in the same way as any other global SAS statement.

To run a REXX exec from within SAS, do the following:

1. Put the REXX exec in a partitioned data set and allocate that PDS to the DDname SASREXX.

2. Either invoke SAS with the REXXMAC option or specify the REXXMAC option later in an OPTIONS statement.

3. Code a statement that begins with the name of the REXX exec.
   Note: You can invoke a REXX exec from an SCL program, but you should enclose the statement in a SUBMIT block. Otherwise, the exec will be executed at compile-time rather than at run-time.

The following example invokes a REXX exec called **YOUREXEC**, which resides in **YOUR.REXX.LIBRARY**. This example works in both batch and TSO environments.

```
options rexxmac;
filename sasrexx 'your.rexx.library' disp=shr;
yourexec;
```

In batch, you can also use a JCL DD statement to allocate the REXX library externally:

```
//jobname JOB   ...
//        EXEC SAS
//SASREXX  DD  DSN=YOUR.REXX.LIBRARY,DISP=SHR
//SYSIN    DD  *
options rexxmac;
yourexec;
/*
//
```

A REXX exec can have zero, one, or multiple arguments. You call the exec by specifying its name, followed by arguments (if any), followed by a semicolon. You can place the exec anywhere that a global SAS statement, such as an OPTIONS or TITLE statement, can be placed.

The exec is invoked when the DATA step is compiled. This means that it is executed only once, rather than for each observation in the DATA step.

"A Simple REXX Exec" on page 127 provides an example of a REXX exec called VERIFY that takes as its argument a single data set name. This REXX exec can be invoked by submitting the following statement from a SAS program:

```
verify data.set.name;
```

A SAS REXX exec submits SAS statements through the SAS subcommand environment by specifying or defaulting to 'SAS' as its "address". When a REXX exec receives control, the default subcommand environment for that program is 'SAS'. As illustrated in this example, any SAS language statement can then be passed to SAS for execution.

Interacting with the SAS Session from a REXX Exec

One of the main advantages of using the REXX interface is that it provides three kinds of communication between the REXX exec and the SAS session:

□ The REXX exec can route messages to the SAS log.

□ You can retrieve and set the value of any variable in the submitting REXX exec by using the GETEXEC DATA step function and the PUTEXEC DATA step routine.

□ You can check the return code from a SAS step in the REXX exec that submits it.

Routing Messages from REXX Execs to the SAS Log

A set of SAS directives enables a REXX exec to print to the SAS log. SAS directives use a leading ++ sequence to differentiate them from normal SAS language statements that are submitted to the SAS subcommand environment.

Three directives are available:

address SAS '++SASLOG'
    causes all subsequent SAS statements to be printed to the SAS log.

address SAS '++NOLOG'
    stops subsequent SAS language statements from being printed to the SAS log.

address SAS '++SASLOG *message-text*'
    places *message-text* into the SAS log and causes subsequent submitted statements to be printed to the SAS log. The message text can include quoted strings or REXX variables. Strings that are enclosed in single quotes are converted to uppercase, whereas strings that are enclosed in double quotes are not. For REXX variables that are not contained in quoted strings, SAS substitutes the values of those variables.

The GETEXEC DATA Step Function

You can use the GETEXEC function in SAS statements that are submitted to the SAS subcommand environment to retrieve the value of any variable in the submitting REXX exec. The syntax of the GETEXEC function is as follows:

$value$ = GETEXEC(*REXX-variable*)

where *REXX-variable* is a SAS expression that represents the name of a REXX variable in uppercase and *value* receives the value of the specified REXX variable.

See "Using the GETEXEC DATA Step Function" on page 127 for an example of the GETEXEC function.

The PUTEXEC DATA Step Routine

You can call the PUTEXEC routine in SAS statements that are submitted to the SAS subcommand environment to assign the value of any variable in the submitting REXX EXEC. The syntax of the PUTEXEC routine is as follows:

CALL PUTEXEC(*REXX-variable, value*)

where *REXX-variable* is a SAS expression that represents the name of a REXX variable in uppercase and *value* is a SAS expression representing the value to be assigned to the specified REXX variable.

See "Using the PUTEXEC DATA Step Routine" on page 128 for an example of the PUTEXEC routine.

Checking Return Codes in REXX Execs

The REXX special variable RC is always set when any command string is submitted to an external environment.

SAS REXX execs are slightly different from ordinary execs, however, in the way RC is set. When an ordinary exec submits MVS commands, the RC variable is set to the command return code when control returns to REXX. The strings that are submitted to SAS, however, are not necessarily complete execution units. The SAS System collects SAS language elements until a RUN statement is encountered, at which point the SAS step is executed. While partial program fragments are being submitted, the RC is set to 0. The SAS return code is not assigned to the REXX variable RC until the string that contains the RUN statement is submitted.

The RC value is set to the value of the &SYSERR SAS System macro variable. See "Checking the SAS Return Code in a REXX Exec" on page 129 for an example of how the REXX variable RC can be tested after a SAS step has been executed.

Changing the Host Command Environment

When a REXX EXEC that is invoked under SAS receives control, the default host command environment for that program is 'SAS'. You can use the ADDRESS instruction followed by the name of an environment to change to a different host command environment:

```
address tso
address sas
address mvs
```

See "Using the GETEXEC DATA Step Function" on page 127 for an example of using the ADDRESS instruction to execute a TSO statement.

You can also use the ADDRESS built-in function to determine which host command environment is currently active:

```
hcmdenv = address()
```

Use the SUBCOM command to determine whether a host command environment is available before trying to issue commands to that environment. The following example checks to see whether SAS is available:

```
/*  REXX */
address mvs "subcom sas"
say "subcom sas rc:" rc
if rc = 1
   then sas="not "
   else sas=""
say "sas environment is "sas"available"
```

Comparing the REXX Interface to the X Statement

The X statement (described on page 297) can be used to invoke a REXX exec. However, compared to the REXX interface, the X statement has the following limitations:

□ With the X statement, the command that you invoke has no way to communicate information back to the SAS session.

□ With the X statement, you have to press Enter to return to SAS.

□ The X statement is available only when SAS is running in the TSO environment. A REXX exec can be invoked from a SAS program running in the batch environment, though it cannot issue TSO commands in the batch environment.

Comparing SAS REXX Execs to ISPF Edit Macros

In their structure and invocation, SAS REXX execs are analogous to ISPF EDIT macros.

□ SAS REXX execs are REXX programs in a library that is allocated to the SASREXX fileref (or to another fileref, as specified by the SAS system option REXXLOC=). They are submitted as part of a SAS program in the same way as any other global SAS statement. A SAS REXX exec submits SAS statements through the SAS subcommand environment by specifying or defaulting to 'SAS' as its "address".

□ ISPF edit macros may be REXX programs in the standard command procedure library (SYSPROC, SYSEXEC, or other). They are started from an ISPF EDIT command line in the same way as any other ISPF EDIT subcommand. An ISPF EDIT macro submits editor subcommands through the ISREDIT subcommand environment by specifying or defaulting to 'ISREDIT' as its "address" (the destination environment for a command string).

Examples of REXX Execs

A Simple REXX Exec

This REXX exec, called VERIFY, takes as its argument a single data set name. The REXX exec checks to see whether the data set exists. If so, the REXX exec routes a message to the SAS log to that effect. If the data set does not exist, the REXX exec creates the data set and then sends an appropriate message to the SAS log.

```
/*------------------ REXX exec VERIFY ------------------*/
Parse Upper Arg fname .

retcode = Listdsi("'"fname"'")
If retcode = 0 Then Do
   Address SAS  "++SASLOG" fname "already exists"
   End
Else Do
   Address TSO "ALLOC FI(#TEMP#) DA('"fname"')
                RECFM(F B) LRECL(80) BLKSIZE(6160)
                DSORG(PS) SPACE(10 5) TRACK NEW"
   Address SAS  "++SASLOG" fname "created"
   Address TSO "FREE  FI(#TEMP#)"
   End

Exit
```

Using the GETEXEC DATA Step Function

This REXX exec executes a TSO command, processes its output, and puts the results in a SAS data set.

```
/*------------------ REXX exec DELDIR ------------------*/
Parse Upper Arg file_prefx .

/*---------- Execute the TSO LISTC Command ------------*/
x = Outtrap('list.')
Address TSO "LISTC L('"file_prefx"') "

/*------- Process Output from the LISTC Command -------*/
idx = 0
file_del.= ''

Do line = 1 To list.0 By 1
   Parse Var list.line word1 word2 word3
   If word1 = 'NONVSAM' Then Do
      fname = word3
      Address TSO  "DELETE '"fname"'"
      idx = idx + 1
      file_del.idx  = fname
      file_stat.idx = 'DELETED'
      End
   End
```

```
/*------- Pass a DATA step into the SAS System --------*/
Address SAS '++SASLOG'

"data results (keep = dsname status);                    "
" total = getexec('IDX');                                "
" put 'Total MVS files deleted: ' total;                 "
" do i = 1 to total;                                      "
"   dsname = getexec('FILE_DEL.' || trim(left(i)));       "
"   status = getexec('FILE_STAT.' || trim(left(i)));      "
"   output;                                               "
"   end;                                                  "
" run;                                                    "


/*------------- Execute a SAS Procedure --------------*/
" proc print;                                             "
" run;                                                    "


/*------------- Return to the SAS System -------------*/
Exit
```

Using the PUTEXEC DATA Step Routine

This REXX exec reads a set of high-level qualifiers from a SAS data set and writes them to
REXX stem variables so that they can be processed by the REXX exec. Then the REXX
exec loops through the high-level qualifiers, calling the DELDIR routine for each one in
turn.

```
/*------------------ REXX exec DELMANY ---------------*/

/* Accepts as arguments up to 5 high-level qualifiers  */

Parse Upper Arg arg1 arg2 arg3 arg4 arg5 .

hlq.=''

/*------- Pass a DATA step into the SAS System --------*/
Address SAS '++SASLOG'

" data prefixes;                                         "
"    input prefix $ 1-20;                                "
"    cards;                                              "
""arg1
""arg2
""arg3
""arg4
""arg5
"run;                                                    "
" data _null_;                                           "
" set prefixes;                                          "
" rexxvar = 'HLQ.' || trim(left(_N_));                   "
" call putexec(trim(rexxvar),prefix);                    "
" call putexec('HLQ.0', trim(left(_N_)));                "
" run;                                                   "
```

```
/*-------------- Call the DELDIR REXX exec ------------*/
Do idx = 1 To hlq.0
   a=2
   pre = hlq.idx
   Call deldir pre
   End

/*-------------- Return to the SAS System -------------*/
Exit rc
```

Checking the SAS Return Code in a REXX Exec

This REXX exec, called SHOWRC, demonstrates how the REXX variable RC can be tested after a SAS step has run:

```
/*----------------- REXX exec SHOWRC -------------------*/

/* Accepts as argument a SAS data set                  */

Parse Upper Arg ds_name .

Address SAS '++SASLOG'
"data newdata;                                          "
"   set "ds_name";                                      "
"   run;                                                "

If rc = 0 Then
   Say 'SAS DATA step completed successfully'
Else
   Say 'SAS DATA step terminated with rc=' rc

Exit
```

Chapter 9 Transporting SAS® Files to and from MVS

Introduction 131

General Steps 132

Transporting SAS Data Sets 132
Converting SAS Data Sets to Transport Format on MVS 132
Importing SAS Data Sets on MVS 133
Using the XPORT Engine with the SAS DATA Step 134

Transporting SAS Catalogs 134
Converting SAS Catalogs to Transport Format on MVS 135
Importing SAS Catalogs on MVS 136

Guidelines for Transporting SAS Files 136
Specifying DCB Characteristics 136
Moving Files via Communications Software 137
Moving Files via Tape 138

Identifying and Resolving Problems 138
Interpreting ASCII Data Correctly on an EBCDIC Host 139
Examining a Transport File in Hexadecimal Format 140

Additional Sources of Information 140

Introduction

Different computer architectures typically have binary incompatibilities such as different representations for floating-point numbers or different character-encoding standards. Therefore, if you need to move SAS files to machines that are running different operating systems, you usually must convert those files to and from a neutral, intermediary format called *transport format.* The only exception is that transport format is not required when moving *tape-format* libraries between MVS and CMS.

A converted file is called a *transport file,* and the process of moving a file from one host operating system to another is called *transporting.*

Note: The following types of SAS files are host-dependent and therefore cannot be transported: indexes, views, access descriptors, and stored programs.

The SAS System provides three ways to transport files: the XPORT engine, the CPORT and CIMPORT procedures, and the separately licensed SAS/CONNECT product. This chapter discusses only the first two methods. For information about SAS/CONNECT, see *SAS/CONNECT Software: Usage and Reference, Version 6, Second Edition.*

General Steps

Here is the general procedure for transporting a SAS file from one host to another:

1. On the sending host, convert the file to transport format.

2. Move the transport file to the receiving host via tape, diskette, or communications software.*

3. On the receiving host, import the transport file—that is, convert it to the file format that is used on the receiving host.

For steps 1 and 3, the specific procedures differ depending on whether you are transporting data sets or catalogs. You generally should use the XPORT engine for transporting SAS data sets, and the CPORT/CIMPORT procedures for transporting catalogs. See "Transporting SAS Data Sets" (below) and "Transporting SAS Catalogs" on page 134 for details.

Transporting SAS Data Sets

The XPORT engine is the recommended tool for transporting SAS data sets. You can use it to transfer entire SAS data libraries that contain only data sets, or you can select individual SAS data sets from a library. You cannot use it to transport SAS *catalogs*. The transport format that the XPORT engine creates is the same for all SAS releases on all hosts. Therefore, a transport file that is in this format can be moved to any release of the SAS System on any host.

Converting SAS Data Sets to Transport Format on MVS

To convert one or more SAS data sets to transport format, specify the XPORT engine in a LIBNAME statement and then use the COPY procedure. The transport file is then ready to be moved to another host.

The following example writes a transport file to tape on MVS. This program copies all SAS data sets in the SAS data library referenced by the libref OLD to the file referenced by the libref TRAN.

```
//EXAMP1 JOB (,X101),'SMITH,B.',TIME=(0,5)
//STEP1 EXEC SAS
//TRAN DD DISP=NEW,UNIT=TAPE,
//     VOL=SER=TRAN01,LABEL=(1,NL),
//     DCB=(RECFM=FB,LRECL=80,BLKSIZE=8000)
//SYSIN DD *
libname old 'actxyz.sales91.sasdata';
libname tran xport;
```

---

* In this context, communications software means software such as FTP that is used for sending or receiving data files.

```
proc copy in=old out=tran memtype=data;
run;
/*
```

A nonlabeled tape is specified because different operating systems process tape labels differently, which can cause complications when you import the transport file on some hosts. To ensure that there is never any question about which DCB characteristics have been specified, SAS Institute recommends that you always use the DCB characteristics shown in this example when you are transporting files via nonlabeled tapes.

Note: To convert only selected SAS data sets in the library to transport format, use the COPY procedure's SELECT statement.

Importing SAS Data Sets on MVS

After moving the transport file to your receiving host (via tape, diskette, or communications software), you must import the file. The following example uses the XPORT engine to import a transport file from tape on MVS.* The transport file must be one that was created by the XPORT engine (not by PROC CPORT); otherwise, the XPORT engine cannot read it.

The following program copies all SAS data sets except DEPT10 and DEPT12 from the transport file to the library that is referenced by the fileref NEW. Note that the recommended DCB characteristics are again used for the TRAN file.

```
//EXAMP2 JOB (,X101),'SMITH,B.',TIME=(0,5)
//STEP1 EXEC SAS
//TRAN DD DISP=OLD,UNIT=TAPE,
//    VOL=SER=TRAN02,LABEL=(1,NL),
//    DCB=(RECFM=FB,LRECL=80,BLKSIZE=8000)
//NEW DD DSN=ACTXYZ.EMPLOYEE.SASDATA,
//    DISP=(NEW,CATLG),UNIT=SYSDA,SPACE=(TRK,(20,5))
//SYSIN DD *
libname tran xport;

proc copy in=tran out=new;
   exclude dept10 dept12;
run;
/*
```

---

* If you are moving the transport file from MVS to a different host, see the SAS Companion for the receiving host for details and examples.

Using the XPORT Engine with the SAS DATA Step

You can also convert a SAS data set to transport format by using the XPORT engine in conjunction with the SAS DATA step. In this method, you specify the XPORT engine on the LIBNAME statement for the transport file. Then use the SAS DATA step to create the file as you would a SAS data set. The following example creates a data set in transport format.

```
libname tran xport;
data tran.test1;
   set sasuser.test1;
   other-SAS-statements
run;
```

One disadvantage to this method is that you can create only one data set at a time. Also, you must specify the name of a particular data set in your program.

Note: In addition to PROC COPY and the SAS DATA step, you can use the XPORT engine in conjunction with any SAS procedure that reads or writes SAS data sets. Simply specify the XPORT option in the LIBNAME statement before using the libref in the PROC statement.

Transporting SAS Catalogs

Use the CPORT and CIMPORT procedures to transport SAS catalogs. You can use these procedures to transport most types of SAS catalog entries except for compiled macros and IML modules. Those files must be created again after their associated data sets have been installed on the receiving host. Also, because different hosts have different windows and keys, WSAVE catalog entries are not portable, and KEYS entries are not always portable.

The CPORT/CIMPORT transport format is different from the transport format that is created by the XPORT engine. The CPORT/CIMPORT transport format is recognized by the release on which it was produced or by *later* releases. Because of enhancements that have been made to catalog structures, you *sometimes* cannot move catalogs to earlier releases of the SAS System under MVS. For example, if you use PROC CPORT to create a transport file in the 6.09 Enhanced release, you cannot import that file in Release 6.07. However, from hosts that are running Release 6.11 or later of the SAS System, you can use the V608 option with PROC CPORT to convert most 6.11 catalog entry types to a transport file that can then be imported by PROC CIMPORT on 6.08 and 6.09 hosts. The exception, of course, is that you cannot transport a 6.11 catalog entry to a 6.08 or 6.09 host if the 6.08 or 6.09 release does not support that catalog entry type. See the PROC CPORT documentation in *SAS Software: Changes and Enhancements, Release 6.11* for more information.

Note: You can also use the CPORT and CIMPORT procedures to transport SAS *data sets*. However, if you plan to use the transport files on earlier releases of the SAS System or in other software, use the XPORT engine instead.* The XPORT engine also enables you to select particular data sets from a library; with PROC CPORT, you can select an entire SAS data library, individual catalogs from a library, or *one* individual data set, but you cannot select multiple individual data sets from a library.

Converting SAS Catalogs to Transport Format on MVS

To convert SAS catalogs, or SAS data libraries that contain catalogs, to transport format, use the CPORT procedure. The following MVS example creates a transport file that contains SAS catalogs. This program copies all SAS catalogs from the SAS data library referenced by the libref OLD to the file referenced by the fileref PORTFILE.

```
//EXAMP3 JOB (,X101),'SMITH,B.',TIME=(0,5)
//STEP1 EXEC SAS
//PORTFILE DD DISP=NEW,UNIT=TAPE,
//    VOL=SER=TRAN11,LABEL=(1,NL),
//    DCB=(RECFM=FB,LRECL=80,BLKSIZE=8000)
//SYSIN DD *
libname old 'actxyz.mylib.sascat';

proc cport library=old file=portfile memtype=catalog
           tape;
run;
/*
```

Please note the following:

□   The CPORT procedure requires correct DCB characteristics (as shown) for the transport file.

□   If the MEMTYPE=CATALOG option is removed, all catalogs and data sets in the SAS data library are copied to the transport file.

□   When creating a transport file on tape, you must include the TAPE option in the PROC CPORT statement. Omit this option if you are creating a transport file on disk.

---

*   The XPORT engine's transport format is more likely to be recognized by other software products, because SAS Institute makes the format specifications available to other software vendors. The PROC CPORT/CIMPORT transport format is more complex and is subject to change with each release of the SAS System.

Importing SAS Catalogs on MVS

After moving a transport file to MVS from another host (via tape, diskette, or communications software), you must import the file.* To import a transport file that was created by PROC CPORT, you use PROC CIMPORT. PROC CIMPORT cannot read a transport file that was created by the XPORT engine.

The following MVS program copies all SAS files from the transport file referenced by the fileref PORTFILE to the library referenced by the fileref NEW. When you import a transport file from tape, you must include the TAPE option in the PROC CIMPORT statement.

```
//EXAMP4 JOB (,X101),'SMITH,B.',TIME=(0,5)
//STEP1 EXEC SAS
//PORTFILE DD DISP=OLD,UNIT=TAPE,
//   VOL=SER=TRAN12,LABEL=(1,NL),
//   DCB=(RECFM=FB,LRECL=80,BLKSIZE=8000)
//NEW DD DSN=ACTXYZ.NEWLIB.SASDATA,DISP=(NEW,CATLG),
//    UNIT=SYSDA,SPACE=(TRK,(30,5))
//SYSIN DD *
proc cimport library=new infile=portfile tape;
run;
/*
```

Guidelines for Transporting SAS Files

In order to transport files successfully, follow the guidelines provided in this section. Many of these guidelines also apply to transporting files on other host operating systems.

Specifying DCB Characteristics

□   When you create or import a transport file, be sure to specify the correct DCB (Data Control Block) characteristics. When you reference a transport file under MVS, you should specify the following DCB characteristics:

DCB=(RECFM=FB,LRECL=80,BLKSIZE=8000)

Use these characteristics whether you are using the XPORT engine, PROC CPORT, or PROC CIMPORT.

□   If you use communications software to move the file from another host to MVS, the transport file occasionally arrives on MVS with improper DCB characteristics. If the communications software does not allow you to specify file characteristics, try the following approach:

1.   On MVS, allocate an empty file that has the correct DCB specifications.

---

*   If you are moving the transport file from MVS to a different host, see the SAS Companion for the receiving host for details and examples.

2. Use a program like the following to initialize a transport file. (It doesn't matter what you write to the file, because the file will be overwritten by the "good" transport file in step 3.)

```
//EXAMP5 JOB (,X101),'SMITH,B.',TIME=(,3)
/*JOBPARM FETCH
//STEP1 EXEC SAS
//TRANFILE DD DSN=USERID.XPT6.FILE,
//          DCB=(LRECL=80,BLKSIZE=8000,RECFM=FB),
//          DISP=(NEW,CATLG),SPACE=(TRK,(3,3)),UNIT=SYSDA
//SYSIN DD *
libname tranfile xport;
data tranfile.temp;
   do i=1 to 10;
   output;
end;
run;
/*
```

3. Using binary transfer, move the transport file from the other host to the new file on MVS.

□ If for some reason you do not know the DCB characteristics of a file *on disk* that you need to import, here are some ways to obtain that information:

□ From ISPF, choose 3.2 (DATA SET UTILITY) from the menu and supply the data set name.

□ From TSO, enter the LISTDS command on the TSO command line:

```
LISTDS 'data-set-name'
```

□ From SAS Display Manager, use the DSINFO window. (See "DSINFO" on page 411.)

Moving Files via Communications Software

□ When transporting a file via communications software, always use BINARY format (sometimes called IMAGE format). This ensures that the file is moved byte-for-byte without modification.

□ Some communications software or COPY utilities insert a carriage-control character at the end of each record. However, if a carriage-control character, or any other character, is inserted in a transport file, the file becomes corrupted and cannot be imported.

□ When moving a SAS transport file to MVS via communications software, the file must be stored with a record length of 80, a record format of FB, and a block size of 8000.

□ When you use communications software to move a file, you may be more successful if you invoke the software from the receiving host rather than from the sending host. Communications software on the receiving host is more likely to have the options that you need in order to create the file with the correct file attributes.

Moving Files via Tape

As noted earlier, transport format is not required when you are moving tape-format libraries between MVS and CMS. But for moving files via tape between other hosts, observe the following guidelines.

□ When transporting a file via tape, always use a nonlabeled tape. Because tape labels are processed differently on different hosts, reading a file from a standard labeled tape may be somewhat complicated on the receiving host.

□ You may encounter problems during importing if your transport file spans more than one tape. (Again, complications may arise because of differences in how different hosts process multivolume tapes.) Therefore, instead of using multivolume tapes, split the original library into two or more libraries and create a separate, unlabeled tape for each one. You can combine the resulting libraries on the receiving host.

Identifying and Resolving Problems

□ You cannot use PROC CIMPORT to import a transport file unless the file was created by PROC CPORT. To determine whether the transport file was created by PROC CPORT, inspect the first portion of the file. On both ASCII and EBCDIC platforms, the header records of both the CPORT/CIMPORT transport format and the XPORT transport format are stored in ASCII format. On an IBM EBCDIC platform such as MVS, you can run a SAS program that interprets the header records correctly as ASCII data (see "Interpreting ASCII Data Correctly on an EBCDIC Host" on page 139), or you can examine the file in hexadecimal format (see "Examining a Transport File in Hexadecimal Format" on page 140).

For a transport file that was created by PROC CPORT, the first 50 characters *in ASCII format* are as follows:

COMPRESSED **COMPRESSED** **COMPRESSED** **COM

If the transport file was created by the XPORT engine, the first 50 characters *in ASCII format* are as follows:

HEADER RECORD*******LIBRARY HEADER RECORD!!!!!!!00

In hexadecimal format, the first 50 bytes of a CPORT transport file are as follows:

2A2A434F4D505245535345442A2A202A2A434F4D5052455353
45442A2A202A2A434F4D505245535345442A2A202A2A434F4D

In hexadecimal format, the first 50 bytes of an XPORT transport file are as follows:

484541444552205245434F52442A2A2A2A2A2A2A4C49425241
525920484541444552205245434F524421212121212121213030

□ If the receiving host cannot import the transport file, try to import the file on the same host that created it. If the original host cannot import a file that it created, then the transport file was created incorrectly. It is a good idea to always test a transport file by importing it on the host that created it; if there is a problem, it is important to recognize the problem immediately.

□ If you suspect that a transport file has been corrupted, it may be helpful to view the file in hexadecimal format after it has been moved to the receiving host. (See "Examining a Transport File in Hexadecimal Format" on page 140.) To inspect your file, follow these steps:

1. Create a sample transport file (one that is known to be correct) on the receiving host.

2. Examine the sample file, noting what it looks like in hexadecimal format.

3. Examine the other transport file (the one in question) to see whether the hexadecimal values correspond to the hexadecimal values in the correct file. If the other transport file has been corrupted, you may find that the corrupted file bears no resemblance to the correct file, that carriage-control characters have been inserted into the corrupted file, or that other differences are immediately apparent.

Interpreting ASCII Data Correctly on an EBCDIC Host

By default, all data stored on MVS and other EBCDIC hosts is assumed to be in EBCDIC format and is interpreted accordingly. To interpret the first portion of a transport file correctly as ASCII data, you can use the following program.

Note: This program does not convert the file to ASCII. It simply interprets the first 5 records in the file as ASCII values and writes them to the SAS log. The actual transport file should never be modified in any way.

```
//PEEK     JOB (,X101),'SMITH,B.',TIME=(,3)
/*JOBPARM FETCH
//STEP1    EXEC SAS
//TRANFILE DD DSN=USERID.XPT6.FILE,DISP=OLD
//SYSIN DD *
data _null_;
infile tranfile obs=5;
input theline $ascii80.;
put theline;
run;
/*
```

Examining a Transport File in Hexadecimal Format

If you use ISPF, the easiest way to examine a transport file in hexadecimal format is to do the following:

1.   Select item 1 (BROWSE) from the ISPF menu.

2.   Specify the data set that you want to browse.

3.   Enter HEX ON from the command line of the editor.

Alternatively, you can use the following SAS program under MVS to display the first 20 80-byte records of a transport file in hexadecimal format.

```
data _null_;
  infile 'transport-file-name';
  input;
  list;
  put '---------------------------------------------';
  if _n_ > 20 then stop;
run;
```

Additional Sources of Information

For more information about transporting files, see the following documents:

□   SAS Technical Report P-195, *Transporting SAS Files between Host Systems*

□   *SAS Procedures Guide, Version 6, Third Edition*

□   *SAS Language: Reference, Version 6, First Edition.*

Chapter **10** Data Representation

Representation of Numeric Variables   141
Representation of Floating-Point Numbers   141
Representation of Integers   143

Using the LENGTH Statement to Save Storage Space   143

How Character Values are Stored   144

Representation of Numeric Variables

The way in which numbers are represented in your SAS programs affects both the magnitude and the precision of your numeric calculations. The factors that affect your calculations are discussed in detail in *SAS Language: Reference.* When processing in an MVS environment, the most important factor you should be aware of is the way in which floating-point numbers and integers are stored.

Representation of Floating-Point Numbers

All numeric values are stored in SAS data sets and are maintained internally in floating-point (real binary) representation. Floating-point representation is an implementation of what is generally known as scientific notation, in which values are represented as numbers between 0 and 1 times a power of 10. For example, 1234 is .1234 times 10 to the 4th power, which is the same as the following expression:

$$\underbrace{.1234}_{\text{mantissa}} * \underbrace{10}_{\text{base}} ** \underbrace{4}_{\text{exponent}}$$

Under MVS, floating-point representation (unlike scientific notation) uses a base of 16 rather than base 10. IBM mainframe systems all use the same floating-point representation, which is made up of 4, 8, or 16 bytes. SAS always uses 8 bytes, as follows:

```
SEEEEEEE MMMMMMMM MMMMMMMM MMMMMMMM MMMMMMMM MMMMMMMM MMMMMMMM MMMMMMMM

 byte 1   byte 2   byte 3   byte 4   byte 5   byte 6   byte 7   byte 8
```

This representation corresponds to bytes of data, with each character occupying 1 bit. The S in byte 1 is the sign bit of the number. If the sign bit is zero, the number is positive. Conversely, if the sign bit is one, the number is negative. The seven E characters in byte 1 represent a binary integer that is known as the *characteristic*. The characteristic represents a signed exponent and is obtained by adding the bias to the actual exponent. The bias is defined as an offset that is used to allow for both negative and positive exponents with the bias representing 0. If a bias was not used, an additional sign bit for the exponent would have to be allocated. For example, IBM mainframes employ a bias of 40 (base 16). A characteristic with the value 42 represents an exponent of +2, whereas a characteristic of 37 represents an exponent of -3.

The remaining M characters in bytes 2 through 8 represent the bits of the mantissa. There is an implied *radix point* before the most significant bit of the mantissa, which also implies that the mantissa is always strictly less than 1. The term radix point is used instead of decimal point, because decimal point implies that we are working with decimal (base 10) numbers, which may not be the case.

The exponent has a base associated with it. Do not confuse this with the base in which the exponent is represented. The exponent is always represented in binary, but the exponent is used to determine what power of the exponent's base should be multiplied by the mantissa. In the case of the IBM mainframes, the exponent's base is 16.

Each bit in the mantissa represents a fraction whose numerator is 1 and whose denominator is a power of 2. For example, the most significant bit in byte 2 represents 1/2 ** 1, the next most significant bit represents 1/2 ** 2, and so on. In other words, the mantissa is the sum of a series of fractions such as 1/2, 1/4, 1/8, and so on. Therefore, in order for any floating-point number to be represented exactly, you must be able to express it as the previously mentioned sum. For example, 100 is represented as the following expression:

```
(1/4 + 1/8 + 1/64) * (16 ** 2)
```

The following two examples illustrate how the above expression is obtained. The first example is in base 10. In decimal notation, the value 100 is represented as follows:

```
100.
```

The period in this number is the radix point. The mantissa must be less than 1; therefore, you normalize this value by shifting the number three places to the right, which produces the following value:

```
.100
```

Because the number was shifted three places to the right, 3 is the exponent, which results in the following expression:

```
.100*10**3=100
```

The second example is in base 16. In hexadecimal notation, 100 (base 10) is written as follows:

```
64.
```

The period in this number is the radix point. Shifting the number two places to the left produces the following value:

```
.64
```

Shifting the number two places also indicates an exponent of 2. Rewriting the number in binary produces the following value:

```
.01100100
```

Finally, the value .01100100 can be represented in the following expression:

$$\frac{1}{2^2} + \frac{1}{2^3} + \frac{1}{2^6} = \frac{1}{4} + \frac{1}{8} + \frac{1}{64}$$

In this example, the exponent is 2. To represent the exponent, you add the bias of 64 to the exponent. The hexadecimal representation of the resulting value, 66, is 42. The binary representation is as follows:

```
01000010 01100100 00000000 00000000 00000000 00000000 00000000 00000000
```

Floating-point numbers that have negative exponents are represented with characteristics that are less than '40'x. When you subtract '40'x from a number that is less than '40'x, the difference is a negative value that represents the exponent. An example of such a number is the floating-point representation of $.03125_{10}$, which is

```
'3F80000000000000'x
```

Subtracting '40'x from the characteristic '3F'x, gives an exponent of -1_{16}. This exponent is applied to the 14-digit fraction, '80000000000000'x, giving a value of $.08_{16}$, which is equal to $.03125_{10}$.

Representation of Integers

Like other numeric values, SAS maintains integer variables in floating-point (real binary) representation. But under MVS, numeric integer values are typically represented as binary (fixed-point) values using two's complement representation. SAS can read and write these values using informats and formats, but it does not process them internally in this form.

You can use the IB$w.d$ informat and format to read and write these binary values. Each integer uses 4 bytes (32 bits) of storage space; thus, the range of values that can be represented is from -2,147,483,648 to 2,147,483,647.

Using the LENGTH Statement to Save Storage Space

By default, when SAS writes a numeric variable to a SAS data set, it writes the number in IBM double-wide floating-point format (as described in "Representation of Floating-Point Numbers" on page 141). In this format, 8 bytes are required for storing a number in a SAS data set with full precision. However, you can use the LENGTH statement in the DATA step to specify that you want to store a particular numeric variable in fewer bytes.

Using the LENGTH statement can greatly reduce the amount of space required for storing your data. For example, if you were storing a series of test scores whose values could range from 0 to 100, you could use numeric variables with a length of 2 bytes. This would save 6 bytes of storage per variable for each observation in your data set.

However, you must use the LENGTH statement cautiously in order to avoid losing significant data. One byte is always used to store the exponent and the sign. The remaining bytes are used for the mantissa. When you store a numeric variable in fewer than 8 bytes, the least significant digits of the mantissa are truncated. If the part of the mantissa that is truncated contains any non-zero digits, then precision is lost.

Use the LENGTH statement only for variables whose values are always integers. Fractional numbers lose precision if they are truncated. In addition, you must ensure that the values of your variable will always be represented exactly in the number of bytes that you specify. You can use Table 10.1 to determine the largest integer that can be stored in numeric variables of various lengths.

Table 10.1
Significant Digits and Largest Integer by Length for SAS Variables under MVS

Length in Bytes	Significant Digits Retained	Largest Integer Represented Exactly
2	2	256
3	4	65,536
4	7	16,777,216
5	9	4,294,967,296
6	12	1,099,511,627,776
7	14	281,474,946,710,656
8	16	72,057,594,037,927,936

Note: No warning is issued when the length that you specify in the LENGTH statement results in truncated data.

How Character Values are Stored

Alphanumeric characters are stored in a computer using a character-encoding system. The two single-byte character-encoding systems that are most widely used in data processing are ASCII and EBCDIC. IBM mainframe computers use the EBCDIC system. The EBCDIC system can be used to represent 256 different characters. Each character is assigned a unique hexadecimal value between 00 and FF.

Table 10.2 shows the EBCDIC code for commonly used characters.

Table 10.2
EBCDIC Code: Commonly Used Characters

Hex	Character	Hex	Character	Hex	Character	Hex	Character
'40'x	space	'95'x	n	'C4'x	D	'E3'x	T
'4B'x	.	'96'x	o	'C5'x	E	'E4'x	U
'4E'x	+	'97'x	p	'C6'x	F	'E5'x	V
'60'x	−	'98'x	q	'C7'x	G	'E6'x	W
'81'x	a	'99'x	r	'C8'x	H	'E7'x	X
'82'x	b	'A2'x	s	'C9'x	I	'E8'x	Y
'83'x	c	'A3'x	t	'D0'x	}	'E9'x	Z
'84'x	d	'A4'x	u	'D1'x	J	'F0'x	0
'85'x	e	'A5'x	v	'D2'x	K	'F1'x	1
'86'x	f	'A6'x	w	'D3'x	L	'F2'x	2
'87'x	g	'A7'x	x	'D4'x	M	'F3'x	3
'88'x	h	'A8'x	y	'D5'x	N	'F4'x	4
'89'x	i	'A9'x	z	'D6'x	O	'F5'x	5
'91'x	j	'C0'x	{	'D7'x	P	'F6'x	6
'92'x	k	'C1'x	A	'D8'x	Q	'F7'x	7
'93'x	l	'C2'x	B	'D9'x	R	'F8'x	8
'94'x	m	'C3'x	C	'E2'x	S	'F9'x	9

Chapter **11** Identifying and Resolving Problems

Support for the SAS System   145
Working with Your SAS Software Consultant   145
   The SITEINFO Window   146
SAS Technical Support   146

Solving Problems under MVS   147
Problems Associated with the MVS Operating System   147
Solving Problems within the SAS System   147
   Examining the SAS Log   147
   Using SAS System Documentation   148
   Using Online Help   148
   DATA Step Debugger   148
   Using SAS Statements and Procedures to Identify Problems   148
   Host-System Subgroup Error Messages   149

Support for the SAS System

Support for the SAS System is shared by SAS Institute and your installation or site. The Institute provides maintenance for the software; the SAS Software Representative and SAS Software Consultant(s) at your installation are responsible for providing you with direct user support.

☐ The SAS Software Representative receives all shipments and correspondence and distributes them to the appropriate personnel at your site. There is typically one Representative per site.

☐ SAS Software Consultants are knowledgeable SAS users who support the other users at your site. Each SAS Software Consultant should have a copy of *SAS Consultant's Guide: Supporting the SAS System, Second Edition,* which contains detailed information about reporting problems and about the extensive resources that are provided by the SAS Technical Support Division. The SAS Technical Support Division is available to assist your SAS Software Consultant with problems that you encounter.

Working with Your SAS Software Consultant

At each site, one or more SAS Software Consultants have been designated as the "first point of contact" for SAS users who need help resolving problems. If you do not know the names of your SAS Software Consultants, you can obtain this information from the display manager SITEINFO window (see "The SITEINFO Window" on page 146).

If the SAS Software Consultant is unable to resolve your problem, then he or she will contact the SAS Technical Support Division for you. In order to provide the most efficient service possible, the Institute asks that you do not contact Technical Support directly.

The SITEINFO Window

The SITEINFO window generally includes the name of your SAS Software Consultant and the names of SAS products that are installed at your site, as well as some of the information that your SAS Software Consultant needs when he or she contacts Technical Support. To access this window, issue the SITEINFO command on the command line of any display manager window.

Output 11.1 shows the template for the SITEINFO window that is shipped with the SAS System. This template is modified for each site; therefore, the information that the SITEINFO contains varies.

Output 11.1
SITEINFO Window

```
* SAS Licensed Installation Information:

    Site Number:
     Site Name:

  Please provide the above information with all communications
  with the Technical Support Division of SAS Institute, Inc.

* Installation Name and Address:

      Name:
    Address:

    Telephone:

* SAS Software Representative (this is the person to whom SAS
  Institute directs all communication about products installed
  at this site):

      Name:
    Telephone:

* Installation Consulting Group:

      Product           Name              Telephone

       Base
       Graph
         .
         .
         .

  Request for help with SAS programming problems should be
  directed to your installation's consulting group.

* Requests for information concerning SAS courses or other
  educational services should be directed to the following
  individual and/or group:

      Name:
    Telephone:

* A list of SAS Institute Software products available at this site
  can be seen by issuing the PROD command from the SETINIT window.
```

SAS Technical Support

The SAS Technical Support Division can assist with suspected internal errors in the SAS System and with possible system incompatibilities. It can also help answer questions about SAS statement syntax, general logic problems, and procedures and their output. However, the Technical Support Division cannot assist with special-interest applications, with writing user programs, or with teaching new users. It is also unable to provide support for general statistical methodology or for the design of experiments.

Solving Problems under MVS

As you use the SAS System under MVS, you might encounter many different kinds of problems. Problems might occur within the context of your SAS program, or they might actually be with some component of the operating system or with computer resources rather than with the SAS System. For example, problems might be related to job control language or to a TSO command.

Problems Associated with the MVS Operating System

If a problem is detected by the operating system, you get messages from the operating system in the job log or on the terminal screen (rather than in the SAS log). In this case, you might need to consult an appropriate IBM manual or your on-site systems staff to determine what the problem is and how to solve it.

Most error messages indicate which part of the operating system is detecting the problem. Here are some of the most common message groups, along with the operating system component or utility that issues them:

CSV*xxxx*	MVS load module management routines
ICE*xxxxx*	IBM sort utility
ICH*xxxx*	RACF system-security component of MVS
IDC*xxxxx*	catalog-management component of MVS
IEC*xxxxx*	MVS data-management routines
IKJ*xxxx*	TSO terminal monitor program (TMP)
WER*xxxxx*	SYNCSORT program

Consult the appropriate system manual to determine the source of the problem.

Solving Problems within the SAS System

Several resources are available to help you if you determine that your problem is within the SAS System. These resources are discussed in the following sections.

Examining the SAS Log

The primary source of information for solving problems that occur within the SAS System is the SAS log. The log lists the SAS source statements along with notes about each step, warning messages, and error messages. Errors are flagged in the code, and a numbered error message is printed in the log. It is often easy to find the incorrect step or statement just by glancing at the SAS log.

Using SAS System Documentation

Sometimes information in the SAS log enables you to identify the source of the problem, but you cannot resolve the problem based on that information. In that case, the next step may be to read the documentation for the particular topic. The following books should be available at your site:

□ *SAS Language: Reference, Version 6, First Edition*

□ *SAS Procedures Guide, Version 6, Third Edition*

□ *SAS Language and Procedures: Usage, Version 6, First Edition.*

Each of these books contains not only syntax information but also detailed explanations of the various aspects of the SAS System. Examples are provided to illustrate specific tasks and usage areas. Most problems can be solved fairly quickly with this approach.

See the inside back cover of this book for a list of additional books that may be useful to you.

Using Online Help

In the SAS Display Manager windowing environment, extensive help is available through the online help facility. For host-specific features, use the HOST portion of online help. To invoke the host portion of the help facility, enter HELP HOST from the command line of any display manager window. Then make a selection from the menu of host-specific Help topics that appears.

DATA Step Debugger

The DATA step debugger is an interactive tool that helps you find logic errors, and sometimes data errors, in SAS DATA steps. By issuing commands, you can execute DATA step statements one by one or in groups, pausing at any point to display the resulting variable values in a window. You can also bypass the execution of one or more statements.

For complete information about the DATA step debugger, see *What's New for the 6.09 Enhanced Release of SAS Software: Changes and Enhancements in TS450.*

Using SAS Statements and Procedures to Identify Problems

If you are having a problem with the logic of your program, there might be no error messages or warning messages to help you. You might not get the results or output that you expect. Using the PUT statement to write messages to the SAS log or to dump the values of all or some of your variables might help. Using PUT statements enables you to follow the flow of the problem and to see what is going on at strategic places in your program.

Some problems may be data related; these can be very hard to trace. Notes that appear in the SAS log following the step that reads and manipulates the data might be very helpful. These notes provide information such as the number of variables and observations that were created. You can also use the CONTENTS and PRINT procedures to look at the data definitions as the SAS System recorded them or to actually look at all or parts of the data in question.

Host-System Subgroup Error Messages

See Appendix 3 for brief explanations of many of the host-system subgroup error messages that you might encounter during a SAS session.

Chapter 12 Optimizing Performance

Introduction 151

Collecting Performance Statistics 152
Use SAS system options to monitor the performance of your programs 152

Optimizing I/O 152
Put catalogs and data sets into separate libraries, using the optimal block size for each 152
Use the optimal buffer size and buffer number for your data 153
Determine whether you should compress your data 153
 Consider using SAS software compression in addition to hardware compression 154
Consider placing SAS data libraries in hiperspaces 155
 Examples of Using the HIPERSPACE Engine Option 155
 Controlling the Size of a Hiperspace Library 155
 Hiperspace Libraries and DIV Data Sets 156
 Performance Considerations for Hiperspace SAS Data Sets 156
Consider designating temporary SAS libraries as virtual I/O data sets 156

Efficient Sorting 157
Consider changing the values of SORTPGM= and SORTCUTP= 157
Take advantage of the DFSORT performance booster 157

Some SAS System Options That Can Affect Performance 157
MAUTOSOURCE and IMPLMAC 157
REXXMAC 158
SPOOL/NOSPOOL 158
VECTOR/NOVECTOR 158

Managing Memory 158
Specify a value for the MEMSIZE= system option when you invoke SAS 158
Consider using superblocking options to control memory fragmentation 159
Use SYSLEAVE= and PROCLEAVE= to handle out-of-memory conditions 159

Loading SAS Modules Efficiently 159
Use a bundled configuration of SAS 159

Other Considerations for Improving Performance 160
Leave AUTOSCROLL 0 in effect for the LOG and OUTPUT windows 160
Use the EM3179 device driver when appropriate 160
Consider using the direct log-on procedure to invoke SAS 161

Introduction

The SAS System includes many features that can help you manage CPU, memory and I/O resources effectively. This chapter describes features that are either MVS-specific or that have MVS-specific characteristics. The information in this chapter is applicable to your site whether you run SAS interactively or in batch.

For additional information about optimizing SAS performance under MVS, see *Tuning SAS Applications in the MVS Environment*, by Michael Raithel (available through SAS Institute as part of the Books by Users program).

For information about optimizing SAS performance on any host operating system, see *SAS Programming Tips: A Guide to Efficient SAS Processing*.

Collecting Performance Statistics

Use SAS system options to monitor the performance of your programs

Several SAS system options provide information that can help you optimize your SAS programs. Under MVS, the following options are enabled by default:

STIMER   specifies that timing statistics such as CPU time, elapsed time, and EXCP count* should be collected and maintained throughout the SAS session.

MEMRPT   performs a similar function for memory usage statistics.

STATS   causes SAS to write the STIMER and MEMRPT statistics to the SAS log.

In addition, two MVS-specific options can provide you with additional information:

FULLSTATS   causes the following additional statistics to be reported in the log: vector affinity time, vector usage time (see "VECTOR/NOVECTOR" on page 158), and RSM hiperspace time. As with STIMER and MEMRPT, the STATS option must be in effect in order for the FULLSTATS statistics to be written to the SAS log.

SMF   causes an SMF record to be generated for each DATA step and procedure. The STATS option must be in effect in order for the SMF statistics to be written to the system SMF log. This option gives you an alternative to extracting performance data from individual SAS logs. The SMF records contain the same statistics as those that are reported by the FULLSTATS option. For more information about the SMF option, see *Installation Instructions and System Manager's Guide*.

Optimizing I/O

Put catalogs and data sets into separate libraries, using the optimal block size for each

The physical block size (BLKSIZE=) of a SAS data library determines both the minimum page size and the minimum unit of space allocation for the library. The 6K default is relatively efficient across a range of device types, and it leads to lower memory requirements for catalog buffers. However, when you use the 6K default, more DASD space

---

*   The EXCP (execute channel program) count is the number of I/O operations that were required for a task.

is needed to hold a given amount of data, because smaller blocks lead to capacity losses. In one test case on a 3380, an MXG daily PDB required 8% more tracks when it was stored in 6K physical blocks instead of in half-track blocks.

Because the optimal block sizes for SAS catalogs and SAS data sets are not necessarily the same, consider putting catalogs and data sets into separate libraries. For catalog libraries, 6K is a good general physical block size on any device. For data sets, choose either a full-track or half-track block size, depending on whether the data library is stored on a device that supports full-track blocks.

Use the optimal buffer size and buffer number for your data

For sequential data sets, the values of the SAS system options BUFSIZE= and BUFNO= are the primary factors that affect I/O performance. When a SAS data library is processed sequentially, the unit of I/O transfer, in bytes, is equal to BUFSIZE*BUFNO.

BUFSIZE is the page size for the data set. You specify BUFSIZE only when you are creating an output data set; it then becomes a permanent attribute of the data set. BUFNO is the number of page buffers to allocate for the data set. For random access, BUFNO page buffers form a least-recently-used buffer pool that can significantly reduce physical I/O depending on the data-access pattern. Of course, the greater the number of page buffers, the more memory is required. Page buffers are stored above the 16M line.

Note that the product of BUFNO and BUFSIZE is the important factor in sequential I/O performance rather than the specific value of either option. As BUFNO is increased, there is a marked reduction in I/O time and I/O count, although the cost of buffer storage increases. As a result, elapsed times can be significantly reduced. For example, when BUFNO=16 and BUFSIZE=6144, the results are very similar to BUFNO=4, BUFSIZE=23040. Moreover, when BLKSIZE=6144, specifying BUFSIZE=24K yields performance results that are very close to those of BLKSIZE=23040 and BUFSIZE=23040.

Here are some guidelines for determining the optimal BUFSIZE and BUFNO values for your data:

□ When BLKSIZE is set to a full- or half-track value, let BUFSIZE = BLKSIZE.

□ Set BUFNO to at least 2.

□ Do not allow BUFNO*BUFSIZE to exceed 135K (three 3380 tracks). Exceeding that value can be detrimental to other users of the system, because long channel programs can monopolize devices and channels. Moreover, beyond that limit, further reductions in elapsed time are negligible.

Determine whether you should compress your data

Compressing data reduces I/O and disk space but increases CPU time. Therefore, whether or not data compression is worthwhile to you depends on the resource cost-allocation policy in your data center. Often your decision must be based on which resource is more valuable or more limited, DASD space or CPU time.

You can use the portable SAS system option COMPRESS= to compress all data sets that are created during a SAS session. Or, use the SAS data set option COMPRESS= to compress an individual data set. Data sets that contain many long character variables generally are excellent candidates for compression.

The following tables illustrate the results of compressing SAS data sets under MVS. In both cases, PROC COPY was used to copy data from an uncompressed source data set into uncompressed and compressed result data sets, using the system option values COMPRESS=NO and COMPRESS=YES, respectively.* In Table 12.1 and Table 12.2, the CPU row shows how much time was used by an IBM 3090-400S to copy the data, and the SPACE values show how much storage (in megabytes) was used.

For Table 12.1, the source data set was a problem-tracking data set. This data set contained mostly long, character data values, which often contained many trailing blanks.

Table 12.1
Compression of
Character Data

Resource	Uncompressed	Compressed	Change
CPU	13.7 sec	84.3 sec	+70.6 sec
SPACE	362.0 MB	56.5 MB	-305.5 MB

CPU Cost/MB: 0.2 sec

For Table 12.2, the source data set contained mostly numeric data from a MICS performance database. The results were again good, although not as good as when mostly character data were compressed.

Table 12.2
Compression of
Numeric Data

Resource	Uncompressed	Compressed	Change
CPU	2.4 sec	25.2 sec	+22.8 sec
SPACE	44.4 MB	23.5 MB	-20.9 MB

CPU Cost/MB: 0.5 sec

For more information about the pros and cons of compressing SAS data, see *SAS Programming Tips: A Guide to Efficient SAS Processing.*

Consider using SAS software compression in addition to hardware compression

Some storage devices such as Storage Technology's Iceberg system perform hardware data compression dynamically. Because this hardware compression is always performed, you may decide not to enable the SAS COMPRESS option when you are using these devices. However, if DASD space charges are a significant portion of your total bill for information services, you might benefit by using SAS software compression in addition to hardware compression. The hardware compression is transparent to the operating system; this means that if you use hardware compression only, space charges are assessed for uncompressed storage.

---

* When you use PROC COPY to compress a data set, you must include the NOCLONE option on your PROC statement. Otherwise, PROC COPY propagates all the attributes of the source data set, including its compression status.

Consider placing SAS data libraries in hiperspaces

One effective method of avoiding I/O operations is to use the SAS System's HIPERSPACE engine option. This MVS-specific option enables you to place a SAS data library in a hiperspace instead of on disk.

A hiperspace overrides the specified physical data library. This means that the physical data library on disk is neither opened nor closed, and data are neither written to nor read from the data library. All data access is done in the hiperspace.

Because the specified data library is not written to, it should be a temporary data set. The only time the specified data library is used is when it is a DIV (Data-In-Virtual) data set, as explained in "Hiperspace Libraries and DIV Data Sets" on page 156.

The HIPERSPACE option is processed after the normal allocation processing is complete. The requested data set is allocated first, as it is with any LIBNAME statement. It is deallocated when you issue a LIBNAME CLEAR statement or when you terminate the SAS session. The hiperspace, in effect, overrides the data set.

Examples of Using the HIPERSPACE Engine Option

Here is an example of using the HIPERSPACE engine option to place a data library in a hiperspace:

```
libname mylib '&templib' hip;
```

(HIP is an alias for the HIPERSPACE option.)

For a data library that was allocated externally with a DD statement or a TSO ALLOCATE command, specify a null data set name in quotes. For example, the following LIBNAME statement places a library that was allocated with the DDname "X" in a hiperspace:

```
libname x '' hip;
```

To place the WORK data library in a hiperspace, specify the HSWORK SAS system option when you invoke SAS. See "HSWORK" on page 335 for a description of the HSWORK option.

Controlling the Size of a Hiperspace Library

Just as you use the SPACE=, DISP=, and BLKSIZE= engine options to allocate a physical data set, you use the HSLXTNTS=, HSMAXPGS=, and HSMAXSPC= SAS system options to control the size of hiperspace libraries. These options are described in Chapter 20, "System Options."

The CONTENTS procedure reports all hiperspace libraries as residing on a 3380 device with a block size of 4096. These attributes may differ from the attributes of the physical data set.

Hiperspace Libraries and DIV Data Sets

The only time the allocated physical data set is actually used with the HIPERSPACE option is if the data set is a Data-In-Virtual (DIV) data set.[*] An empty DIV data set can be initialized by allocating it to a hiperspace library. An existing DIV data set that contains data can be read or updated, or both.

You can use the HSSAVE SAS system option to control whether the DIV pages are updated each time your application writes to the hiperspace or only when the data library is closed. See "HSSAVE" on page 334 for more information about this option.

Performance Considerations for Hiperspace SAS Data Sets

The major factor that affects hiperspace performance is the amount of expanded storage on your system. The best candidates for using hiperspace are jobs that execute on a system that has plenty of expanded storage. If expanded storage on your system is constrained, the hiperspaces are moved to auxiliary storage. This eliminates much of the potential benefit of using the hiperspaces.

For more information about using hiperspaces under MVS, see the *MVS/ESA Initialization and Tuning Guide.* Also see Chapter 11, "Exploiting Hiperspaces" in *Tuning SAS Applications in the MVS Environment*, by Michael Raithel.

Consider designating temporary SAS libraries as virtual I/O data sets

Treating data libraries as "virtual I/O" data sets is another effective method of avoiding I/O operations. This method works well with any temporary SAS data library—especially WORK. To use this method, specify UNIT=VIO as an engine option on the LIBNAME statement.

The VIO method is always effective for small libraries (<10 cylinders). If your installation has set up your system to allow VIO to go to expanded storage, then VIO can also be effective for large temporary libraries (up to several hundred cylinders). Using VIO is most practical during evening and night shifts when the demands on expanded storage and on the paging subsystem are typically light.

The VIO method can also save disk space, because it is an effective way of putting large paging data sets to double use. During the day, these data sets can be used for their normal function of paging and swapping back storage; during the night, they become a form of temporary scratch space.

---

[*]   DIV data sets are also referred to as VSAM linear data sets.

Efficient Sorting

Consider changing the values of SORTPGM= and SORTCUTP=

The SAS System includes an internal sort program that is often more efficient than host sort programs for sorting small volumes of data. Host sort programs are generally more efficient when the data volume is too high to perform the sort entirely in memory.

Under MVS, the default value of the SAS system option SORTPGM= is BEST. This value causes SAS to use the SAS sort program for less than 4M of data; for more than 4M of data, SAS uses the host sort program. You use the SORTNAME= system option to specify the name of the host sort program.

The 4M limit is the default value that is specified by the MVS-specific SORTCUTP= system option. You may want to change the value of this option in order to optimize sorting for your particular applications.

Take advantage of the DFSORT performance booster

If your installation uses Release 13 or later of IBM's DFSORT as its host sort utility for large sorts, then you can take advantage of a DFSORT "performance booster." To do so, specify SORTANOM=512 on an OPTIONS statement, in the OPTIONS parameter list of the SAS cataloged procedure, or in a configuration file.

SORTANOM=512 causes SAS to work in conjunction with DFSORT to process your SAS sorting applications faster. SAS applications that use either PROC SORT or PROC SQL for sorting can take advantage of this "performance booster." For large sorts of approximately 100,000 observations or more, CPU usage may be reduced by up to 25%.

Some SAS System Options That Can Affect Performance

MAUTOSOURCE and IMPLMAC

These two SAS system options affect the operation of the SAS autocall macro facility, and they interact in a way that you should be aware of.

Specifying IMPLMAC enables you to use statement-style macros in your SAS programs. With IMPLMAC in effect, each SAS statement is potentially a macro, and the first word (token) in each statement must be checked to determine whether it is a macro call.

When IMPLMAC is in effect without MAUTOSOURCE, no special checking takes place until the first statement-style macro is compiled. When both IMPLMAC and MAUTOSOURCE are in effect, however, this checking is done unconditionally. The initial occurrence of a word as the first token of a SAS statement results in a search of the autocall library. There can be a significant number of directory searches, especially when a large DATA step is compiled, in addition to the CPU time that is consumed by maintaining and searching the symbol table.

The combination of MAUTOSOURCE and IMPLMAC can add 20% to CPU time and 5% to I/O for a non-trivial job. Therefore, for best performance, leave NOIMPLMAC as the installation default.

REXXMAC

When SAS encounters an apparent SAS statement that it does not recognize, it typically generates a "statement is not valid" error message in the SAS log. However, when the REXXMAC system option is in effect, SAS passes the first word in the apparent statement to the MVS REXX processor, which looks for a member by that name in the SASREXX library. Hence, a mistyped statement could have unintended results and could have a negative impact on performance. For more information, see "REXXMAC" on page 366 and "REXXLOC=" on page 365.

SPOOL/NOSPOOL

The SPOOL system option is appropriate when you are running SAS interactively without the SAS display manager system. When SPOOL is in effect, SAS input statements are stored in a WORK library utility file; they are retrieved later by %INCLUDE and %LIST commands. SAS is shipped with SPOOL as the default setting for interactive sessions, but you may want to consider resetting it to NOSPOOL for batch jobs. In a batch job that has a large number of input lines, NOSPOOL can reduce I/O by as much as 9%.

VECTOR/NOVECTOR

The SAS system option VECTOR enables you to use the IBM 3090 Vector Facility for certain SAS procedures—most notably, PROC GLM. This option is in effect in both of the configuration files that are shipped with the SAS System. However, your site administrator may have reset this option to NOVECTOR if your data center limits the use of the vector facility. Therefore, you should check with your site administrator before enabling this option.

Managing Memory

Specify a value for the MEMSIZE= system option when you invoke SAS

For most programs and data, SAS uses memory (storage) above the 16MB line. This is sometimes referred to as 31-bit addressing. The few exceptions include data areas that require 24-bit addressability, and a small part of the host supervisor. Because the MVS JCL parameter REGION is ineffective at controlling 31-bit memory usage, the SAS MEMSIZE= option has been implemented for this purpose.

In order to limit the amount of virtual memory that SAS can use, you should specify a value for the MEMSIZE= system option when you invoke SAS. Under MVS, MEMSIZE= has a default value of 0, which means that SAS can use memory up to the maximum amount that is available. For example, once SAS programs are loaded into memory, they are not deleted until that memory is needed for another purpose. This enables you to invoke multiple procedures consecutively without reloading the program each time. However, if there is no upper limit on virtual memory usage, then memory is not freed for reuse even when the programs that are stored there are no longer needed.

For most batch applications, 8M is a reasonable value for MEMSIZE=, and it is the default setting for this option in the configuration files that are supplied with SAS. For interactive applications that use multiple SAS System components such as SAS/AF and SAS/GRAPH, specify MEMSIZE=16M.

Consider using superblocking options to control memory fragmentation

Superblocking options are SAS system options that set aside large blocks of memory for different classes of use. The default values for these options are set in the configuration files that are shipped with SAS. In most cases, these values are appropriate and should not be altered. However, if you receive a superblock-overflow warning message in the SAS log, you may want to use these options to adjust the memory allocation for your job.

For complete information about these options, see *Installation Instructions and System Manager's Guide.*

Use SYSLEAVE= and PROCLEAVE= to handle out-of-memory conditions

Sometimes a job runs out of memory in spite of additional memory allocations. To ensure that the job ends "gracefully" under that condition, you may want to increase the values of the SAS system options SYSLEAVE= and PROCLEAVE=.*

□ The SYSLEAVE= option reserves a specified amount of memory to ensure that, when a SAS System task ends, enough memory is available to close data sets and to "clean up" other resources. Under MVS, the default value for this option is 100K.

□ The PROCLEAVE= option serves a similar function for SAS procedures. For example, some procedures are designed to use memory until no more is available; they then continue by opening and using work files. PROCLEAVE ensures that there will be enough memory left to open these work files and to allocate I/O buffers for them so that the procedure can continue. Under MVS, the default value for this option is 100K.

Loading SAS Modules Efficiently

Use a bundled configuration of SAS

The SAS System has three possible program configurations:

□ unbundled

□ bundled (LPA/ELPA version).

□ bundled (non-LPA version)

---

* These options are portable, but their default values are host-specific.

In an unbundled configuration, all modules are loaded individually from the SAS System load library. Running in this manner is not generally recommended, because it significantly increases library-directory searches and I/O. However, SAS is shipped with this setting by default, because some of the installation tasks must invoke SAS before the installer has had the opportunity to select a bundled version.

In the two bundled configurations of SAS, many individual modules are combined into one large executable file. Invoking a bundled version of SAS eliminates both wasted space between modules and the overhead of loading each module individually. Performance is also improved slightly.

In a multi-user SAS environment, the most effective way to reduce memory requirements is to use the LPA/ELPA bundled configuration. This configuration dramatically reduces each user's working-set size. *

The non-LPA bundled configuration is intended for sites that do not want to place SAS modules in the Link Pack Area. In this configuration, the bundle is loaded into each user's address space. Although this decreases library-directory searches and I/O, it has the unfortunate side-effect of increasing individual working-set sizes. Therefore, this method is not recommended if you have many SAS users at your site.

For detailed information about the bundled configurations and how to install them, see *Installation Instructions and System Manager's Guide.*

Other Considerations for Improving Performance

Leave AUTOSCROLL 0 in effect for the LOG and OUTPUT windows

The AUTOSCROLL command controls how information is scrolled as it is written to the LOG and OUTPUT windows. Specifying small scrolling increments is very expensive in terms of response time, network data traffic, and CPU time.

Under MVS, AUTOSCROLL is preset to 0 for the LOG window. AUTOSCROLL 0 suppresses automatic scrolling and positions the LOG window at the bottom of the most recent output when a DATA step or procedure is completed. At that time, of course, you can scroll up to view the contents of the log.

To see the effect of this command, enter AUTOSCROLL 1 on the command line of the LOG window and then run PROC OPTIONS. Then enter AUTOSCROLL 0 and run PROC OPTIONS again. The CPU time ratio is more than 30 to 1.

---

*   Working-set size is the amount of real system memory that is required to contain a) the programs that consume most of system execution time, and b) the data areas that these programs reference.

Use the EM3179 device driver when appropriate

If you are running Attachmate or any other full-functioned 3270 emulator over a slow connection, specify the SAS system option FSDEVICE=EM3179 when you invoke SAS. Menus in applications such as SAS/ASSIST are then displayed as text menus instead of icon menus. The text menus require much less network data transfer and are considerably faster across slow lines.

Consider using the direct log-on procedure to invoke SAS

When you use the direct log-on procedure to invoke SAS instead of the TSO log-on procedure, SAS acts as your terminal monitor program. The direct log-on procedure has three potential advantages for your installation:

□   It eliminates the need for SAS users to know anything about TSO.

□   It saves a small amount of memory—approximately 50K per user in working-set size.

□   If you license TSO/E as a measured usage product, then you may be able to reduce your TSO charges significantly, because CPU time for SAS applications will no longer be accumulated as TSO/E usage.

For a sample log-on procedure and other information about configuring it into the environment at your site, see *Installation Instructions and System Manager's Guide.*

Part 3

Host-Specific Features of the SAS® Language

Chapter 13	CALL Routines
Chapter 14	Data Set Options
Chapter 15	Functions
Chapter 16	Informats and Formats
Chapter 17	Macro Facility
Chapter 18	Procedures
Chapter 19	Statements
Chapter 20	System Options
Chapter 21	Windows and Window Features

Chapter **13** CALL Routines

Portable CALL routines are documented in *SAS Language: Reference* and in the *Changes and Enhancements* technical reports that are listed on the inside back cover. The SYSTEM and TSO CALL routines are the only SAS CALL routines that are MVS-specific or that have MVS-specific aspects.

SYSTEM

Issues an operating system command during a SAS session

MVS specifics: issues a TSO command or invokes a CLIST or a REXX exec

Syntax

CALL SYSTEM(*command*);

MVS Specifics

The CALL SYSTEM routine is similar to the X (or TSO) statement, the X (or TSO) command, the SYSTEM (or TSO) function, and the %SYSEXEC (or %TSO) macro statement. It accepts the following argument:

command
    can be a system command enclosed in quotes, an expression whose value is a system command, or the name of a character variable whose value is a system command. Under MVS, "system command" includes TSO commands, CLISTs, and REXX execs.

In most cases, the X statement, the X command, or the %SYSEXEC macro statement are preferable because they require less overhead. However, the CALL SYSTEM routine can be useful in certain situations because it is executable, and because it accepts expressions as arguments. For example, the following DATA step executes one of three CLISTs depending on the value of a variable named ACTION that is stored in an external file named USERID.TRANS.PROG.

```
data _null_;
   infile 'userid.trans.prog';
   input action; /* action is assumed to have a value of 1, 2, or 3 */
    /* create and initialize a 3-element array: */
   array programs{3} $ 11 c1-c3
      ("exec clist1" "exec clist2" "exec clist3");
   call system(programs{action});
run;
```

In this example, the array elements are initialized with character strings that consist of TSO commands for executing the three CLISTs. In the CALL SYSTEM statement, an expression is used to pass one of these character strings to the CALL SYSTEM routine. For example, if

---

SYSTEM *continued*

action equals **2**, then `programs{2}`, which contains the EXEC CLIST2 command, is passed to the CALL SYSTEM routine.

Under MVS, CALL TSO is an alias for the CALL SYSTEM routine.

See Also

□ TSO statement on page 296 and X statement on page 297

□ SYSTEM function on page 171 and TSO function on page 172

□ TSO command on page 422 and X command on page 423

□ "Macro Statements" on page 193

TSO

Issues a TSO command or invokes a CLIST or a REXX exec during a SAS session

MVS specifics: all

Syntax

CALL TSO(*command*);

Description

The TSO and SYSTEM CALL routines are identical, with one exception: under an operating system other than MVS, the TSO CALL routine has no effect, whereas the SYSTEM CALL routine is always processed. See "SYSTEM" on page 165 for more information.

Chapter **14** Data Set Options

Summary of SAS Data Set Options **168**

Portable data set options are documented in *SAS Language: Reference* and in the *Changes and Enhancements* technical reports that are listed on the inside back cover. This chapter includes detailed information about only MVS-specific data set options. However, Table 14.1 on page 169 includes all SAS data set options that are available under MVS.

BLKSIZE=

Specifies the block size for a Version 5 SAS data set

MVS specifics: all

Engines: V5, V5SEQ

Default: for V5, the value of the BLKSIZE= system option; for V5SEQ, the block size in the data set label

Syntax

BLKSIZE=*block-size*

Description

Use this option only when you are creating a Version 5 SAS data set.

block-size
>   is the block size that you specify. For the V5 engine, valid values are between 1012 and 32760. For the V5SEQ engine, valid values are between 1024 and 32767.

If you specify a block size that is too small to contain one observation, SAS uses a value that is large enough to contain one observation. Also, the value must be at least four plus a multiple of the logical record length; otherwise, SAS uses the following formula to compute the block size:

$$(FLOOR(block\text{-}size/lrecl) * lrecl) + 4$$

FLOOR
>   is a SAS function that returns the largest integer that is less than or equal to the argument.

block-size
>   is the value that you specified for BLKSIZE=.

lrecl
>   is the observation length plus four.

FILEDISP=

Specifies the initial disposition for a sequential-format SAS data library

MVS specifics: all

Engines: V6SEQ, V5SEQ

Default: OLD

Syntax

FILEDISP=NEW | OLD

Description

This data set option tells SAS whether it should regard a SAS data library as having existing members. Use this option only when you are creating a SAS data set.

NEW
> specifies that the sequential data library is to be considered empty. SAS therefore does not look for previously written SAS data sets, even when DISP=OLD was specified in the JCL for an existing library.

OLD
> specifies that the sequential data library is not initially empty. SAS therefore begins writing at the end of the library. If the SAS data set that is being written has the same name as an existing member of the library, then SAS writes the new data set on top of the existing data set, and any existing members that follow the overwritten member are lost.

Summary of SAS Data Set Options

Table 14.1 lists both the MVS-specific data set options and the portable data set options. It gives a brief description of each option and tells whether the option can be used for a data set that has been opened for input, output, or update. The See column tells you where to look for more detailed information about an option, based on the following legend:

COMP   See the description of the data set option in this chapter.

LR   See *SAS Language: Reference*

P-222   See SAS Technical Report P-222, *Changes and Enhancements to Base SAS Software, Release 6.07*

P-242   See SAS Technical Report P-242, *SAS Software: Changes and Enhancements, Release 6.08*

6.09E   See *What's New for the 6.09 Enhanced Release of SAS Software: Changes and Enhancements in TS450.*

The last column lists the engines with which the option is valid.

Table 14.1 *Summary Table of SAS Data Set Options*

Data Set Option	Description	Where Used	See	Engines
ALTER=	assigns an alter password to a SAS file	output update	P-222	all
BLKSIZE=	specifies the block size for a SAS data set	output	COMP	V5 V5SEQ
BUFNO=	specifies the number of buffers for processing a SAS data set	input output update	LR	V6 V6SEQ
BUFSIZE=	specifies a permanent page size for output SAS data sets	output	LR	V6 V6SEQ
CNTLLEV=	specifies the level at which shared update access to a SAS data set is denied	input output update	LR	all
COMPRESS=	compresses observations in an output SAS data set	output	LR	V6
DROP=	excludes variables from processing or from output SAS data sets	input output update	LR	all
FILECLOSE=	specifies how to position a tape volume when a SAS file on the tape is closed	input output	LR	all
FILEDISP=	specifies the initial disposition for a sequential-format SAS data library	input output	COMP	V6SEQ V5SEQ
FILEFMT=	specifies the format of a SAS data set	output	P-222	V6
FIRSTOBS=	causes processing to begin at a specified observation	input	LR	all
INDEX=	defines one or more indexes for a new data set	output	P-242	V6
KEEP=	specifies variables for processing or for writing to output SAS data sets	input output update	LR	all
LABEL=	specifies a label for the SAS data set	input output update	LR	all
OBS=	specifies the last observation of the data set to process	input	LR	all
PW=	assigns a read, write, and alter password to a SAS file	input output update	P-222	all

(continued)

Table 14.1 *(continued)*

Data Set Option	Description	Where Used	See	Engines
PWREQ=	specifies whether to display a requestor window if a password has not been supplied	input output update	6.09E	all
READ=	assigns a read password to a SAS file	input update	P-222	all
RENAME=	changes the name of a variable	input output update	LR	all
REPLACE=	overrides the REPLACE= system option	output	LR	all
REUSE=	specifies whether SAS appends new observations to a compressed data set or inserts them in freed space	output	LR	V6
SORTEDBY=	specifies how the data set is currently sorted	input output update	P-222	all
TYPE=	specifies the data set type for data that are used by some SAS/STAT procedures	input output update	LR	all
WHERE=	selects observations that meet the specified condition	input update	LR, P-222	all
WRITE=	assigns a write password to a SAS file	output update	P-222	V6, V6SEQ

Chapter **15** Functions

Portable functions are documented in *SAS Language: Reference* and in the *Changes and Enhancements* technical reports that are listed on the inside back cover. The SYSTEM and TSO functions are the only SAS functions that are MVS-specific or that have MVS-specific aspects.

SYSTEM

Issues an operating system command during a SAS session

MVS specifics: issues a TSO command or invokes a CLIST or a REXX exec

Syntax

SYSTEM(*command*)

MVS Specifics

The SYSTEM function is similar to the X (or TSO) statement, the X (or TSO) command, the CALL SYSTEM (or CALL TSO) routine, and the %SYSEXEC (or %TSO) macro statement. In most cases, the X statement, the X command, or the %SYSEXEC macro statement are preferable because they require less overhead.

   This function returns the operating system return code after the command, CLIST, or REXX exec is executed.

   The SYSTEM function accepts the following argument:

command
       can be a system command enclosed in quotes, an expression whose value is a system command, or the name of a character variable whose value is a system command. Under MVS, "system command" includes TSO commands, CLISTs, and REXX execs.

SAS executes the SYSTEM function immediately. Under MVS, TSO is an alias for the SYSTEM function. On other operating systems, the TSO function has no effect, whereas the SYSTEM function is always processed.

   You can use the SYSTEM function to issue most TSO commands or to execute CLISTs or REXX execs. However, you cannot issue the TSO commands LOGON and LOGOFF, and you cannot execute CLISTs that include the TSO ATTN statement.

   In the following example, the SYSTEM function is used to allocate an external file:

```
data _null_;
   rc=system('alloc f(study) da(my.library)');
run;
```

SYSTEM *continued*

For a fully qualified data set name, use the following statements:

```
data _null_;
   rc=system("alloc f(study) da('userid.my.library')");
run;
```

In the second example, notice that the command is enclosed in double quotes. When the TSO command includes quotes, it is best to enclose the command in double quotes instead of single quotes. If you choose to use single quotes, then double each quote in the TSO command:

```
data _null_;
   rc=system('alloc f(study) da(''userid.my.library'')');
run;
```

See Also

□ TSO statement on page 296 and X statement on page 297

□ SYSTEM CALL routine on page 165 and TSO CALL routine on page 166

□ TSO command on page 422 and X command on page 423

□ "Macro Statements" on page 193

TSO

Issues a TSO command or invokes a CLIST or a REXX exec during a SAS session

MVS specifics: all

Syntax

TSO(*command*)

Description

The SYSTEM and TSO functions are identical, with one exception: under an operating system other than MVS, the TSO function has no effect, whereas the SYSTEM function is always processed. See "SYSTEM" on page 171 for more information.

Chapter **16** Informats and Formats

Considerations for Using Informats and Formats under MVS 173
EBCDIC and Character Data 173
Floating-Point Number Format and Portability 174
Reading and Writing Binary Data 174
Date and Time Informats 175

Numeric Informats 175

Numeric Formats 182

In general, informats and formats are completely portable. Only the informats and formats that have host-specific aspects are documented in this chapter.

All of these informats and formats are described in *SAS Language: Reference*; that information is not repeated here. Instead, there is an "MVS Specifics" section that tells how the informat or format behaves under MVS, and then you are referred to *SAS Language: Reference*.

Considerations for Using Informats and Formats under MVS

EBCDIC and Character Data

The following character informats and formats produce different results on different computing platforms, depending on which character-encoding system the platform uses. Because MVS uses the EBCDIC character-encoding system, all of the following informats and formats convert data to or from EBCDIC.

These informats and formats are not discussed in detail in this chapter because the EBCDIC character-encoding system is their only host-specific aspect.

$ASCIIw.	converts ASCII character data to EBCDIC character data and vice versa.
$BINARYw.	converts binary values to EBCDIC character data and vice versa.
$CHARZBw. (informat only)	reads character data and converts any byte that contains a binary zero to a blank.
$EBCDICw.	converts character data to EBCDIC and vice versa. Under MVS, $EBCDICw. and $CHARw. are equivalent.
$HEXw.	converts hexadecimal data to EBCDIC character data and vice versa.
$OCTALw.	converts octal data to EBCDIC character data and vice versa.
$PHEXw. (informat only)	converts packed hexadecimal data to EBCDIC character data.
w.d informat	reads standard numeric data.

All the information that you need in order to use these informats and formats under MVS is in *SAS Language: Reference*.

Floating-Point Number Format and Portability

The manner in which MVS stores floating-point numbers can affect your data. See "Representation of Floating-Point Numbers" on page 141 for details.

Reading and Writing Binary Data

If a SAS program that reads and writes binary data is run on only one type of machine, you can use the following native-mode* informats and formats:

IB*w.d*	reads or writes integer binary (fixed-point) values, including negative values, that are represented in two's complement notation
PD*w.d*	reads or writes data that are stored in IBM packed decimal format
PIB*w.d*	reads or writes positive integer binary (fixed-point) values
RB*w.d*	reads or writes real binary (floating-point) data

If you want to write SAS programs that can be run on multiple machines that use different byte-storage systems, use the following IBM 370 formats and informats:

S370FF*w.d*	is used on other computer systems to read EBCDIC data from IBM mainframe files
S370FIB*w.d*	reads or writes integer binary data in IBM mainframe format
S370FIBU*w.d*	reads or writes unsigned integer binary data in IBM mainframe format
S370FPD*w.d*	reads or writes packed decimal data in IBM mainframe format
S370FPDU*w.d*	reads or writes unsigned packed decimal data in IBM mainframe format
S370FPIB*w.d*	reads or writes positive integer binary data in IBM mainframe format
S370FRB*w.d*	reads or writes real binary data in IBM mainframe format
S370FZD*w.d*	reads or writes zoned decimal data in IBM mainframe format
S370FZDL*w.d*	reads or writes zoned decimal leading sign data in IBM mainframe format
S370FZDS*w.d*	reads or writes zoned decimal separate leading sign data in IBM mainframe format
S370FZDT*w.d*	reads or writes zoned decimal separate trailing sign data in IBM mainframe format
S370FZDU*w.d*	reads or writes unsigned zoned decimal data in IBM mainframe format

---

* Native mode means that these informats and formats use the byte-ordering system that is standard for the machine.

These IBM 370 informats and formats enable you to write SAS programs that can be run in any SAS environment, regardless of the standard for storing numeric data. They also enhance your ability to port raw data between host operating systems.

For more information about the IBM 370 informats and formats, see *SAS Language: Reference* and SAS Technical Report P-242, *SAS Software: Changes and Enhancements, Release 6.08.*

Date and Time Informats

Several informats are designed to read time and date stamps that have been written by the System Management Facility (SMF), or by the Resource Measurement Facility (RMF). SMF and RMF are standard features of the MVS operating system. They record information about each job that is processed. The following informats are used to read time and date stamps that are generated by SMF and RMF:

PDTIME*w*.   reads the packed decimal time of SMF and RMF records.

RMFDUR.   reads the duration values of RMF records.

RMFSTAMP*w*.   reads the time and date fields of RMF records.

SMFSTAMP*w*.   reads the time and date of SMF records.

TODSTAMP.   reads the 8-byte time-of-day stamp.

TU*w*.   reads the Timer Unit.

In order to facilitate the portability of SAS programs, these informats may be used with any operating system that is supported by the SAS System; therefore, they are documented in *SAS Language: Reference.*

Numeric Informats

Ew.d informat

Reads numeric values that are stored in scientific notation

Width range: 7- 32

Default width: 12

Decimal range: 0-31

MVS specifics: interprets input as EBCDIC, minimum and maximum values

MVS Specifics

Numbers are interpreted using the EBCDIC character-encoding system, with one digit per byte. The range of the magnitude of acceptable values is from 5.4×10^{-79} to 7.2×10^{75}. Any number outside this range causes an overflow error.

The following examples illustrate the use of E*w.d*.

Ew.d informat *continued*

Data Line	Informat	Numeric Value
----+----1----+----2		
1.230E+02	e10.	123
-1.230E+02	e10.	-123
1.230E+01	e10.	12.3
1.235E+08	e10.	123,500,000

Note: In these examples, **Data Line** shows what the input looks like when viewed from a text editor. **Numeric Value** is the number that is used by SAS after the data pattern has been read using the corresponding informat.

See Also

□ Ew.d informat in *SAS Language: Reference*

□ Ew. format on page 183

HEXw. informat

Converts hexadecimal positive binary values to either integer (fixed-point) or real (floating-point) binary values

Width range: 1-16

Default width: 8

MVS specifics: interprets input as EBCDIC, IBM floating-point format

MVS Specifics

Under MVS, each hexadecimal digit that is read by the HEXw. informat must be represented using the EBCDIC code, with one digit per byte. For example, the hexadecimal number '3B'x is actually stored in the external file as the bit pattern represented by 'F3C2'x, which is the EBCDIC code for 3B. (See Table 10.2 on page 144 for a table of commonly used EBCDIC characters.)

The format of floating-point numbers is host-specific. See "Representation of Floating-Point Numbers" on page 141 for a description of the IBM floating-point format that is used under MVS.

The w value of the HEXw. informat specifies the field width of the input value. It also specifies whether the final value is an integer binary (fixed-point) value or a real binary (floating-point) value. When you specify a width value of 1 through 15, the input hexadecimal number represents an integer binary number. When you specify a width of 16, SAS interprets the input hexadecimal number as a representation of a floating-point number.

The following examples illustrate the use of HEXw. under MVS.

Data Line	Informat	Numeric Value	Notes
----+----1----+----2			
433E800000000000	HEX16.	1000	input is interpreted as floating point
000100	HEX6.	256	input is interpreted as integer
C1A0000000000000	HEX16.	-10	input is interpreted as floating point

Note: In these examples, **Data Line** shows what the input looks like when viewed from a text editor. **Numeric Value** is the number that is used by SAS after the data pattern has been read using the corresponding informat.

See Also

□ HEX*w.d* informat in *SAS Language: Reference*

□ HEX*w.* format on page 184

□ "Representation of Numeric Variables" on page 141

IB*w.d* informat

Reads integer binary (fixed-point) values, including negative values

Width range: 1-8

Default width: 4

Decimal range: 0-10

MVS specifics: two's complement notation

MVS Specifics

On an IBM mainframe system, values are represented in two's complement notation. If the informat specification includes a *d* value, the number is divided by 10^d.

Here are several examples of the IB*w.d* informat:

Data Line (Hex)	Informat	Numeric Value
000004D2	ib4.	1234
FFFFFB2E	ib4.	-1234
000000003034	ib6.2	123.4
00000001E208	ib6.2	1234

IB*w.d* informat   *continued*

Note: In these examples, **Data Line** represents the bit pattern stored, which is the value you see if you view it in a text editor that displays values in hexadecimal representation. **Numeric Value** is the number that is used by SAS after the data pattern has been read using the corresponding informat.

See Also

□   IB*w.d* informat in *SAS Language: Reference*

□   IB*w.d* format on page 185

□   S370FIB*w.d* informat in *SAS Language: Reference*

□   S370FPIB*w.d* informat in *SAS Language: Reference*

PD*w.d* informat

Reads data that are stored in IBM packed decimal format

Width range: 1-16

Default width: 1

Decimal range: 0-31

MVS specifics: IBM packed decimal format

MVS Specifics

The *w* value specifies the number of bytes, not the number of digits. If the informat specification includes a *d* value, the number is divided by 10^d.

In packed decimal format, each byte except for the last byte represents two decimal digits. (The last byte represents one digit and the sign.) An IBM packed decimal number consists of a sign and up to 31 digits, thus giving a range from $10^{31} - 1$ to $-10^{31} + 1$. The sign is written in the rightmost nibble. (A nibble is 4 bits, or half a byte.) A hexadecimal C indicates a plus sign and a hexadecimal D indicates a minus sign. The rest of the nibbles to the left of the sign nibble represent decimal digits. The hexadecimal values of these digit nibbles correspond to decimal values; therefore, only values between '0'x and '9'x can be used in the digit positions.

Here are several examples of how data are read using the PD*w.d* informat:

Data Line (Hex)	Informat	Numeric Value	Notes
01234C	pd3.	1234	
01234D	pd3.	-1234	
0123400C	pd4.2	1234	the *d* value of 2 causes the number to be divided by 10^2

Note: In these examples, **Data Line** represents the bit pattern stored, which is the value you see if you view it in a text editor that displays values in hexadecimal representation. **Numeric Value** is the number that is used by SAS after the data pattern has been read using the corresponding informat.

See Also

□ PD*w.d* informat in *SAS Language: Reference*

□ PD*w.d* format on page 186

□ S370FPD*w.d* informat in *SAS Language: Reference*

RB*w.d* informat

Reads numeric data that are stored in real binary (floating-point) notation

Width range: 2- 8

Default width: 4

Decimal range: 0-10

MVS specifics: IBM floating-point format

MVS Specifics

The *w* value specifies the number of bytes, not the number of digits. If the informat specification includes a *d* value, the number is divided by 10^d .

The format of floating-point numbers is host-specific. See "Representation of Floating-Point Numbers" on page 141 for a description of the IBM floating-point format that is used under MVS.

The following examples show how data that represent decimal numbers are read as floating-point numbers using the RB*w.d* format.

Data Line (Hex)	Informat	Numeric Value
437B000000000000	rb8.	123
434CE00000000000	rb8.1	123
44300C0000000000	rb8.2	123
C27B000000000000	rb8.	-123
434D200000000000	rb8.	1234
41C4000000000000	rb8.	12.25

Note: In these examples, **Data Line** represents the bit pattern stored, which is the value you see if you view it in a text editor that displays values in hexadecimal representation. **Numeric Value** is the number that is used by SAS after the data pattern has been read using the corresponding informat.

RB*w.d* informat *continued*

See Also

□ RB*w.d* informat in *SAS Language: Reference*

□ S370FRB*w.d* informat in *SAS Language: Reference*

□ RB*w.d* format on page 187

□ "Representation of Numeric Variables" on page 141

ZD*w.d* informat

Reads zoned decimal data

Width range: 1-32

Decimal range: 0-32

MVS specifics: IBM zoned decimal format

MVS Specifics

Like numbers that are stored in standard format, zoned decimal digits are represented in EBCDIC code. Each digit requires one byte of storage space. The low-order, or rightmost, byte represents both the least significant digit and the sign of the number. Digits to the left of the least significant digit are represented in EBCDIC code as 'F0'x through 'F9'x. The character that is printed for the least significant digit depends on the sign of the number. In EBCDIC code, negative numbers are represented as 'D0'x through 'D9'x in the least significant digit position; positive numbers are represented as 'C0'x through 'C9'x.

The following examples illustrate the use of the ZD*w.d* informat.

Data Line (Hex)	Informat	Numeric Value
F0F0F0F0F0F1F2C3	zd8.	123
F0F0F0F1F2F3F0C0	zd8.2	123
F0F0F0F0F0F1F2D3	zd8.	-123
F0F0F0F0F1F2F3C0	zd8.6	0.00123
F0F0F0F0F0F0F0C1	zd8.6	1E-6

Note: In these examples, **Data Line** represents the bit pattern stored, which is the value you see if you view it in a text editor that displays values in hexadecimal representation. **Numeric Value** is the number that is used by SAS after the data pattern has been read using the corresponding informat. See Table 10.2 on page 144 for a table of commonly used EBCDIC characters.

See Also

- □ ZD*w.d* and S370FZD*w.d* informats in *SAS Language: Reference*

- □ ZD*w.d* format on page 189

- □ ZDB*w.* informat on page 181

- □ S370FZDL*w.d*, S370FZDS*w.d*, S370FZDT*w.d*, and S370FZDU*w.d* informats in SAS Technical Report P-242, *SAS Software: Changes and Enhancements, Release 6.08*

ZDB*w.* informat

Reads zoned decimal data in which zeros have been left blank

Width range: 1-32
Decimal range: 0-32
MVS specifics: used on IBM 1410, 1401, and 1620

MVS Specifics

As previously described for the ZD*w.* informat, each digit is represented as an EBCDIC character, and the low-order, or rightmost, byte represents both the sign and the least significant digit. The only difference between the two informats is the way in which zeros are represented. The ZDB*w.* informat treats EBCDIC blanks ('40'x) as zeros. (EBCDIC zeros are also read as zeros.)

The following examples show how the ZDB*w.* informat reads data.

Data Line (Hex)	Informat	Numeric Value
40404040F14040C0	zdb8.	1000
4040404040F1F2D3	zdb8.	-123
4040404040F1F2C3	zdb8.	123

Note: In these examples, the **Data Line** column represents the bit pattern stored, which is the value you see if you view it in a text editor that displays values in hexadecimal representation. The **Numeric Value** is the number that is used by SAS after the data pattern has been read using the corresponding informat. See Table 10.2 on page 144 for a table of commonly used EBCDIC characters.

See Also

- □ ZDB*w.* informat in *SAS Language: Reference*

- □ ZD*w.d* informat on page 180

- □ ZD*w.d* format on page 189

Numeric Formats

BESTw. format

SAS System chooses the best notation

Width range: 1-32

Default width: 12

MVS specifics: writes output as EBCDIC, minimum and maximum values

MVS Specifics

Numbers are written using EBCDIC code with one digit per byte. Because the value is output as EBCDIC text characters, you can print it without further formatting.

The range of the magnitude of numbers is from 5.4×10^{-79} to 7.2×10^{75}. Any number outside this range causes an overflow error. All numeric variables that are represented by the SAS System are within this range.

The following examples illustrate the use of BESTw. under MVS.

Numeric Value	Format	Results	Notes
		----+----1----+----2	
1234	best6.	1234	
-1234	best6.	-1234	
12.34	best6.	12.34	
123456789	best8.	1.2346E8	the number is truncated and rounded

Note: In these examples, the **Numeric Value** column represents the value of the SAS numeric variable. The **Results** column shows what the numeric output looks like when viewed from a text editor. See Table 10.2 on page 144 for a table of commonly used EBCDIC characters.

See Also

□   BESTw. format in *SAS Language: Reference*

E*w.* format

Writes numeric values in scientific notation

Width range: 7- 32

Default width: 12

MVS specifics: writes output as EBCDIC, minimum and maximum values

MVS Specifics

Numbers are represented using the EBCDIC code, with one digit per byte. Because the values are stored in EBCDIC, they can be printed without further formatting.

The range of the magnitude of numbers is from 5.4×10^{-79} to 7.2×10^{75}. Any number outside of this range causes an overflow error. All numeric variables that are represented by the SAS System are within this range.

The following examples illustrate the use of E*w.* under MVS.

Numeric Value	Format	Results	Notes
		----+----1----+----2	
123	e10.	1.230E+02	
-123	e10.	-1.230E+02	
12.3	e10.	1.230E+01	
123456789	e10.	1.235E+08	the number is truncated and rounded

Note: In these examples, the **Numeric Value** column represents the value of the SAS numeric variable. The **Results** column shows what the numeric value looks like when viewed from a text editor. See Table 10.2 on page 144 for a table of commonly used EBCDIC characters.

See Also

□   E*w.* format in *SAS Language: Reference*

□   E*w.d* informat on page 175

HEXw. format

Converts real binary (floating-point) values to hexadecimal representation

Width range: 1-16

Default width: 8

MVS specifics: writes output as EBCDIC, IBM floating-point format

MVS Specifics

Each hexadecimal digit is written using the EBCDIC code, which requires one byte per digit. See Table 10.2 on page 144 for a table of commonly used EBCDIC characters.

The format of floating-point numbers is host-specific. See "Representation of Floating-Point Numbers" on page 141 for a description of the IBM floating-point format that is used under MVS.

The w value of the HEXw. format determines whether the number is written as a floating-point number or an integer. When you specify a width value of 1 through 15, the real binary numbers are truncated to fixed-point integers before being converted to hexadecimal representation. When you specify 16 for the width, the floating point values are used, and the numbers are not truncated.

The following examples illustrate the use of HEXw. under MVS.

Numeric Value	Format	Results	Notes
		`----+----1----+----2`	
31.5	hex16.	`421F800000000000`	floating-point number
31.5	hex15.	`00000000000001F`	integer
-31.5	hex16.	`C21F800000000000`	floating-point number
-31.5	hex15.	`FFFFFFFFFFFFFE1`	integer

Note: In these examples, the **Numeric Value** column represents the value of the SAS numeric variable. The **Results** column shows what the numeric value looks like when viewed from a text editor.

See Also

□   HEXw. format in *SAS Language: Reference*

□   HEXw. informat on page 176

□   "Representation of Numeric Variables" on page 141

IB*w.d* format

Writes numbers in integer binary (fixed-point) format

Width range: 1-8

Default width: 4

Decimal range: 0-10

MVS specifics: two's complement notation

MVS Specifics

On an IBM mainframe system, values are stored in two's complement notation.

If an overflow occurs, the value written is the largest value that fits into the output field; the value will be positive, negative, or unsigned, as appropriate. If the informat includes a *d* value, the number is multiplied by 10^d.

Here are some examples of the IB*w.d* format:

Numeric Value	Format	Results (Hex)	Notes
1234	ib4.	000004D2	
-1234	ib4.	FFFFFB2E	
12.34	ib4.	0000000C	
123456789	ib4.	075BCD15	
1234	ib6.2	00000001E208	the *d* value of 2 causes the number to be multipled by 10^2
-1234	ib6.2	FFFFFFFE1DF8	the *d* value of 2 causes the number to be multipled by 10^2
1234	ib1.	7F	overflow occurred
-1234	ib1.	80	overflow occurred

Note: In these examples, the **Numeric Value** column represents the value of the numeric variable. The **Results** column shows a hexadecimal representation of the bit pattern written by the corresponding format. (You cannot view these data in a text editor, unless you can view them in their hexadecimal representations.)

See Also

□   IB*w.d* format in *SAS Language: Reference*

□   IB*w.d* informat on page 177

□   S370FIB*w.d* format in *SAS Language: Reference*

□   S370FPIB*w.d* format in *SAS Language: Reference*

PDw.d format

Writes values in IBM packed decimal format

Width range: 1-16

Default width: 1

Decimal range: 0-31

MVS specifics: IBM packed decimal format

MVS Specifics

In packed decimal format, each byte represents two decimal digits. An IBM packed decimal number consists of a sign and up to 31 digits, thus giving a range of $10^{31} - 1$ to $-10^{31} + 1$. The sign is written in the rightmost nibble. (A nibble is 4 bits, or half a byte.) A 'C'x indicates a plus sign and a 'D'x indicates a minus sign. The rest of the nibbles to the left of the sign nibble represent decimal digits. The hexadecimal values of these digit nibbles correspond to decimal values; therefore, only values between '0'x and '9'x can be used in the digit positions.

If an overflow occurs, the value written is the largest value that fits into the output field; the value will be positive, negative, or unsigned, as appropriate.

Here are several examples of packed decimal format:

Numeric Value	Format	Results (Hex)	Notes
1234	pd3.	01234C	
-1234	pd3.	01234D	
1234	pd2.	999C	overflow occurred
1234	pd4.	0001234C	
1234	pd4.2	0123400C	the *d* value of 2 causes the number to be multiplied by 10^2

Note: In these examples, the **Numeric Value** column represents the value of the data, and the **Results** column shows a hexadecimal representation of the bit pattern written by the corresponding format. (You cannot view these data in a text editor, unless you can view them in their hexadecimal representations.)

See Also

□   PDw.d format in *SAS Language: Reference*

□   PDw.d informat on page 178

□   S370FPDw.d format in *SAS Language: Reference*

RB*w.d* format

Writes numeric data in real binary (floating-point) notation

Width range: 2-8

Default width: 4

Decimal range: 0-10

MVS specifics: IBM floating-point format

MVS Specifics

The format of floating-point numbers is host-specific. See "Representation of Floating-Point Numbers" on page 141 for a description of the format used to store floating-point numbers under MVS.

Here are some examples of how decimal numbers are written as floating-point numbers using the RB*w.d* format:

Numeric Value	Format	Results (Hex)	Notes
123	rb8.	427B000000000000	
123	rb8.1	434CE00000000000	
123	rb8.2	44300C0000000000	
-123	rb8.	C27B000000000000	
1234	rb8.	434D200000000000	
1234	rb2.	434D	truncation occurred
12.25	rb8.	41C4000000000000	

Note: In these examples, the **Numeric Value** column represents the value of the data, and the **Results** column shows a hexadecimal representation of the bit pattern written by the corresponding format. (You cannot view these data in a text editor, unless you can view them in their hexadecimal representations.)

See Also

□   RB*w.d* format in *SAS Language: Reference*

□   RB*w.d* informat on page 179

□   S370FRB*w.d* format in *SAS Language: Reference*

w.d format

Writes numeric data

Width range: 1-32

Default width: 12

Decimal range: *d<w*

MVS specifics: writes output as EBCDIC, minimum and maximum values

MVS Specifics

The *w.d* format writes numeric values one digit per byte using EBCDIC code. Because the values are stored in EBCDIC, they can be printed without further formatting.

Numbers written with the *w.d* format are rounded to the nearest number that can be represented in the output field. If the number is too large to fit, the BEST*w.* format is used. Under MVS, the range of the magnitude of numbers that can be written with the BEST*w.d* format is from 5.4×10^{-79} to 7.2×10^{75}.

The following examples illustrate the use of the *w.d* format:

Numeric Value	Format	Results
		----+----1----+----2
1234	4.	1234
1234	5.	1234
12345	4.	12E3
123.4	6.2	123.40
-1234	6.	-1234

Note: In these examples, the **Numeric Value** column represents the value of the data, and the **Results** column shows what the numeric value looks like when viewed from a text editor. See Table 10.2 on page 144 for a table of commonly used EBCDIC characters.

See Also

□   *w.d* format in *SAS Language: Reference*

ZD*w.d* format

Writes zoned decimal data

Width range: 1-32

Default width: 1

Decimal range: 0-32

MVS specifics: IBM zoned decimal format

MVS Specifics

Like standard format, zoned decimal digits are represented as EBCDIC characters. Each digit requires one byte. The rightmost byte represents both the least significant digit and the sign of the number. Digits to the left of the least significant digit are written as the EBCDIC characters 0 through 9. The character written for the least significant digit depends on the sign of the number. Negative numbers are represented as the EBCDIC printable characters 'D0'x through 'D9'x in the least significant digit position, and positive numbers are represented as 'C0'x through 'C9'x.

If an overflow occurs, the value written is the largest value that fits into the output field; the value will be positive, negative, or unsigned, as appropriate.

The following examples illustrate the use of the zoned decimal format.

Numeric Value	Format	Results (Hex)	Notes
123	zd8.	F0F0F0F0F0F1F2C3	
1234	zd8.	F0F0F0F0F1F2F3C4	
123	zd8.1	F0F0F0F0F1F2F3C0	
123	zd8.2	F0F0F0F1F2F3F0C0	
-123	zd8.	F0F0F0F0F0F1F2D3	
0.000123	zd8.6	F0F0F0F0F0F1F2C3	
0.00123	zd8.6	F0F0F0F0F1F2F3C0	
1E-6	zd8.6	F9F9F9F9F9F9F9C9	overflow occurred

Note: In these examples, the **Numeric Value** column represents the value of the data, and the **Results** column shows a hexadecimal representation of the bit pattern that is written by the corresponding format. See Table 10.2 on page 144 for a table of commonly used EBCDIC characters.

See Also

□ ZDw.d format in *SAS Language: Reference*

□ ZDw.d informat on page 180

□ ZDBw. informat on page 181

□ S370FZDw.d informat in *SAS Language: Reference*

□ S370FZDLw.d, S370FZDSw.d, S370FZDTw.d, and S370FZDUw.d formats in SAS Technical Report P-242, *SAS Software: Changes and Enhancements, Release 6.08*

Chapter **17** Macro Facility

Macro Variables   191
Portable Automatic Macro Variables That Have Host-Specific Values   191
MVS-Specific Macro Variables   192

Macro Statements   193

Macro Functions   194

Autocall Libraries   194
Specifying a User Autocall Library   194
    Example: Specifying an Autocall Library in Batch Mode   194
    Example: Specifying an Autocall Library under TSO   195
Creating an Autocall Macro   195

Stored Compiled Macro Facility   196
Accessing Stored Compiled Macros   197

Other Host-Specific Aspects of the Macro Facility   197
Collating Sequence for Evaluating Macro Characters   197
SAS System Options Used by the Macro Facility   197

Additional Sources of Information   198

Most features of the SAS macro facility are portable. They are documented in the *SAS Guide to Macro Processing, Version 6, Second Edition*. This section discusses only those components of the macro facility that have MVS-specific aspects.

Macro Variables

Portable Automatic Macro Variables That Have Host-Specific Values

The following automatic macro variables are portable, but their values are host-specific:

SYSDEVIC
    contains the name of the current graphics device. The current graphics device is determined by the SAS system option DEVICE=. (See "DEVICE=" on page 314.) Ask your SAS Software Consultant which graphics devices are available at your site.

SYSENV
    is provided for compatibility with the SAS System on other operating systems. Under MVS, its value is FORE if you are running SAS under TSO; otherwise, its value is BACK.

SYSJOBID
    contains the job name of the batch job that is currently executing, or the user ID that is associated with the current SAS session. SAS obtains this value from the TIOCNJOB field of the TIOT control block, except in the case of SAS/SESSION. With

SAS/SESSION, SAS obtains the value from the User_id field that is returned by the Get_TP_Properties service of APPC/MVS. You cannot change the value of this variable.

SYSRC

contains the return code from the most recent operating system command that was issued from within a SAS session. The default value is 0.

SYSSCP

contains the operating system abbreviation OS. You cannot change the value of this variable.

SYSSCPL

contains the operating system abbreviation MVS. You cannot change the value of this variable.

MVS-Specific Macro Variables

The following macro variables are available only under MVS:

SYSDEXST

contains the value that is returned by the DSNEXST statement. (See "DSNEXST" on page 263.) SYSDEXST has a value of 1 if the data set specified in the DSNEXST statement exists, or a value of 0 if the data set does not exist.

SYSJCTID

contains the value of the JCTUSER field of the JCT control block as mapped by the IEFAJCTB macro. It is a 7-byte character value.

SYSJMRID

contains the value of the JMRUSEID field of the JCT control block as mapped by the IEFAJMR macro. It is a 7-byte character value.

SYSUID

contains the value of the TSO user ID that is associated with the SAS session, regardless of whether the session is a batch job, a remote connect session, a SAS/SESSION connection, or a TSO session. SAS obtains this value from the ACEEUSRI field of the ACEE control block.

Four additional automatic macro variables that are available only under MVS can be used to help diagnose failures in dynamic allocation. Their values are updated each time SAS does a dynamic allocation as a result of a FILENAME or LIBNAME statement (or equivalent SCL functions). They are undefined until the first dynamic allocation is performed. These macro variables are:

SYS99ERR

contains the error reason code that was returned in the SVC 99 request block.

SYS99INF

contains the information reason code that was returned in the SVC 99 request block.

SYS99MSG

contains the text of the message that is associated with the reason code.

SYS99R15

contains the return code that was returned in R15 from SVC 99.

Macro Statements

The following macro statements have MVS-specific aspects:

%KEYDEF
> is analogous to the display manager's KEYDEF command. It enables you to define function keys. The form of this statement is

> %KEYDEF <'>*key-name*<'> <'*definition*'>;

> The number of keys available depends on your terminal. Most terminals that are used under the MVS operating system have either 12 or 24 function keys. To define a key, specify the *key-name* (F1 through F24) of the key and the new *definition*.
>
> If you omit the definition, SAS prints a message in the log showing the current definition of the key; otherwise, the key's definition is changed to whatever you specified.

%TSO
> executes TSO commands during an interactive SAS session. It is similar to the TSO statement, which is described on page 296. The %TSO statement enables you to execute TSO commands immediately. It places the operating system return code in the automatic variable SYSRC. You can use the %TSO statement either inside or outside a macro. The form of the statement is

> %TSO <*command*>;

> You can use any TSO command or any sequence of macro operations that generate a TSO command. If you omit the *command*, your SAS session is suspended and your MVS session is placed in TSO submode. To return to the SAS session, enter either RETURN or END.
>
> If you execute a %TSO statement on an operating system other than MVS, the statement is treated as a comment.

%SYSEXEC
> executes TSO commands during an interactive SAS session. The form of the statement is

> %SYSEXEC <*command*>;

> Under MVS, the %SYSEXEC statement works exactly like the %TSO statement. The two statements are different only if you transport your SAS program to a different operating system. Because %SYSEXEC statements are recognized on multiple operating systems, each operating system expects commands that are appropriate for that operating system.

Macro Functions

The following macro functions have MVS-specific aspects:

%SCAN
> under MVS and other systems that use the EBCDIC collating sequence, if you specify
> no delimiters, SAS treats all of the following characters as delimiters:

> blank . < (+ | & ! $ *) ; ¬ − / , % ¦ ¢

%SYSGET
> has no effect under MVS except to generate the following message:

```
WARNING: The argument to macro function %SYSGET is not defined as
         a system variable.
```

Autocall Libraries

An autocall library contains files that define SAS macros. Under MVS, an autocall library is
a partitioned data set. SAS Institute supplies some autocall macros in the system autocall
library; you can also define autocall macros yourself in a user autocall library. In order to
use the autocall facility, the SAS system option MAUTOSOURCE must be in effect. (See
SAS Language: Reference for details about MAUTOSOURCE.)

Specifying a User Autocall Library

You can designate an operating system data set, or a concatenation of operating system data
sets, as your user-written autocall library in any of the following ways:

□ with the SASAUTOS= system option. You can designate one or more filerefs or data
   set names as your autocall library. See "SASAUTOS=" on page 367 for more
   information.

□ with the SASAUTOS parameter of the SAS CLIST (under TSO). In this case, SAS
   concatenates the user autocall library to the beginning of the system autocall library,
   which is specified by the CLIST parameter MAUTS.

□ with the SASAUTO= parameter of the SAS cataloged procedure.

Example: Specifying an Autocall Library in Batch Mode

In batch mode, you could use the following JCL statements to specify an autocall library:

single autocall library:

```
//MYJOB    JOB account. ...
//         EXEC SAS,OPTIONS='MAUTOSOURCE'
//SASAUTOS DD DSN=MY.MACROS,DISP=SHR
```

concatenated autocall library:

```
//MYJOB    JOB account ...
//         EXEC SAS,OPTIONS='MAUTOSOURCE'
//SASAUTOS DD DSN=MY.MACROS1,DISP=SHR
//         DD DSN=MY.MACROS2,DISP=SHR
//         DD DSN=default.autocall.library,DISP=SHR
```

Example: Specifying an Autocall Library under TSO

Under TSO, you can specify an autocall library either when you invoke SAS, or during a SAS session.

When you invoke SAS:

single autocall library:

```
sas options('mautosource sasautos="myid.macros"')
```

concatenated autocall library:

```
sas options('mautosource
    sasautos=("myid.macros1","myid.macros2",sasautos)')
```

During a SAS session:

single autocall library:

```
options mautosource sasautos='myid.macros';
```

concatenated autocall library:

```
options mautosource sasautos=('myid.macros1','myid.macros2',sasautos);
```

Creating an Autocall Macro

To create an autocall macro, do the following:

1. Create a partitioned data set to function as an autocall library, or use an existing autocall library.

2. In the autocall library, create a member that contains the source statements for the macro. The member name must be the same as the name of the macro.

Note: The SAS macro facility allows you to include the underscore character in macro names; however, MVS does not allow the underscore character in partitioned data set member names. To create an autocall member for a macro name that contains an underscore, use a pound sign (#) in place of the underscore in the member name. For example, to create an autocall member for a macro named _SETUP_, name the member #SETUP#. However, invoke the macro by the macro name, as follows:

```
%_setup_
```

Stored Compiled Macro Facility

The stored compiled macro facility gives you access to permanent SAS catalogs that contain compiled macros. In order for SAS to use stored compiled macros, the SAS system option MSTORED must be in effect. In addition, you use the SAS system option SASMSTORE= to specify the libref of a SAS data library that contains a catalog of stored compiled SAS macros. For more information about these options, see SAS Technical Report P-222, *Changes and Enhancements to Base SAS Software, Release 6.07.*

Using stored compiled macros offers the following advantages over other methods of making macros available to your session:

□   SAS does not have to compile a macro definition when a macro call is made.

□   Session-compiled macros and the autocall facility are also available in the same session.

Because you cannot re-create the source statements from a compiled macro, you must save the original macro source statements.

Note: Catalogs of stored compiled macros cannot be concatenated.

If you don't want to use the stored compiled macro facility, you can make macros accessible to your SAS session or job by doing the following:

□   placing all macro definitions in the program before calling them

□   using a %INCLUDE statement to bring macro definitions into the program from external files*

□   using the autocall facility to search predefined source libraries for macro definitions

Your most efficient choice may be to use the stored compiled macro facility.

---

*   The %INCLUDE statement takes as arguments the same types of file specifications as the INCLUDE display manager command. See "INCLUDE" on page 421 for examples of MVS file specifications.

Accessing Stored Compiled Macros

The following example illustrates how to create a stored compiled macro in one session and then use the macro in a later session.

```
/*  Create a Stored Compiled Macro in One Session    */
libname mylib 'u.macro.mysecret' disp=old;
options mstored sasmstore=mylib;

%macro myfiles / store;
  filename file1 'mylib.first';
   filename file2 'mylib.second';
%mend;

/*  Use the Stored Compiled Macro in a Later Session */
libname mylib 'u.macro.mysecret' disp=shr;
options mstored sasmstore=mylib;

%myfiles
data _null_;
   infile file1;
      *statements that read input file FILE1;
   file file2;
      *statements that write to output file FILE2;
run;
```

Other Host-Specific Aspects of the Macro Facility

Collating Sequence for Evaluating Macro Characters

Under MVS, the macro facility uses the EBCDIC collating sequence for %EVAL and for implicit evaluation of macro characters.

SAS System Options Used by the Macro Facility

Table 17.1 lists the SAS system options that are used by the macro facility and that have host-specific characteristics. It also tells you where to look for more information about these system options.

Table 17.1 *SAS System Options Used by the Macro Facility That Have Host-Specific Aspects*

System Option	Description	See ...
MSYMTABMAX=	specifies the maximum amount of memory available to all symbol tables (global and local combined). Under MVS, the default value for this option is 1,048,576 bytes.	"MSYMTABMAX=" on page 357 and SAS Technical Report P-222, *Changes and Enhancements to Base SAS Software, Release 6.07*
MVARSIZE=	specifies the maximum number of bytes for any macro variable stored in memory (0 <= n <= 32768). Under MVS, the default setting for this option is 8,192.	"MVARSIZE=" on page 357 and SAS Technical Report P-222, *Changes and Enhancements to Base SAS Software, Release 6.07*
SASAUTOS=	specifies the autocall library	"Specifying a User Autocall Library" on page 194 and "SASAUTOS=" on page 367

Additional Sources of Information

For more information about the SAS macro facility, see the following documents:

□ *SAS Guide to Macro Processing, Version 6, Second Edition*

□ *SAS Macro Facility Tips and Techniques, Version 6, First Edition*

□ the following chapters of SAS Technical Report P-222, *Changes and Enhancements to Base SAS Software, Release 6.07*:

   □ Chapter 41, "Macro Language Features"

   □ Chapter 42, "The Autocall Facility"

   □ Chapter 43, "The Stored Compiled Macro Facility"

□ the online help for the macro facility. Enter **HELP MACRO** from the command line of any display manager window.

Chapter **18** Procedures

Portable procedures are documented in the *SAS Procedures Guide.* Only the procedures that are MVS-specific or that have MVS-specific aspects are documented in this chapter.

If the SAS procedure is also described in the *SAS Procedures Guide*, that information is not repeated here. Instead, there is an "MVS Specifics" section that explains how the procedure works under MVS, and then you are referred to the *SAS Procedures Guide.* For procedures that are entirely MVS-specific, a full description is given.

BMDP

Calls any BMDP program to analyze data in a SAS data set

MVS Specifics: all

Syntax

PROC BMDP *<options>*;
    VAR *variable-list*;
    BY *variable-list*;
    PARMCARDS ;
    BMDP control statements
    ;

Description

BMDP is a library of statistical analysis programs that were originally developed at the UCLA Health Sciences Computing Facility. Use the BMDP procedure in SAS programs to

☐   call a BMDP program to analyze data in a SAS data set

☐   convert a SAS data set to a BMDP "save" file.

In order to use the BMDP procedure in a SAS session, the JCL EXEC statement must request the cataloged procedure SASBMDP rather than the usual cataloged procedure SAS. If the SASBMDP cataloged procedure is not available on your computer system, or if it has a different name, ask your computing center staff to help you set it up. Your SAS Software Representative has the SAS System installation instructions, which include directions for setting up the procedure.

You can use BMDP programs to analyze SAS data sets by invoking this procedure. To analyze BMDP data with the SAS System, create a BMDP "save" file in a BMDP program, and then use the SAS CONVERT procedure or the BMDP engine to convert the "save" file to a SAS data set. (See Chapter 4, "Accessing BMDP, SPSS, and OSIRIS Files," for more information about the BMDP engine.) You can use the BMDP procedure any number of times in a SAS job to invoke BMDP.

BMDP   *continued*

To use the BMDP procedure, first specify the name of the BMDP program you want to invoke in the PROC BMDP statement. The VAR and BY statements can follow, but they are optional. The BMDP control statements follow the PARMCARDS statement.

PROC BMDP Statement

PROC BMDP *<options>*;

The following options can be used in the PROC BMDP statement:

CODE=*save-file*
    assigns a name to the BMDP "save" file that the BMDP procedure creates from a SAS data set. The *save-file* corresponds to the CODE sentence in the BMDP INPUT paragraph. For example, you can use the following statement:

```
proc bmdp prog=bmdp3s code=judges;
```

Then, the BMDP INPUT paragraph must contain the following sentence:

```
CODE='JUDGES'
```

CODE= usually is not necessary in the PROC BMDP statement. When CODE= is not specified, the name of the BMDP "save" file is the SAS data set name.
    If you are converting a SAS data set to a BMDP "save" file, include the CODE sentence in the BMDP INPUT paragraph to name the "save" file. To use the name of the SAS data set, specify that name in the BMDP INPUT paragraph. If you use a different name, it must match the name that is supplied in the CODE= option.

CONTENT=DATA | CORR | MEAN | FREQ
    tells BMDP whether your SAS data set is a standard SAS data set (CONTENT=DATA) or whether it contains a correlation matrix (CORR), variable means (MEAN), or frequency counts (FREQ). You do not need to specify the CONTENT= option for specially structured SAS data sets that were created by other SAS procedures. If you omit the CONTENT= option, the data set's TYPE value is used.
    Note: BMDP may use a structure for special data sets (for example, a correlation matrix) that is different from the SAS structure. Ensure that the input SAS data set is in the form that BMDP expects.

DATA=*SAS-data-set*
    specifies the SAS data set that you want the BMDP program to process. If you do not specify the DATA= option, PROC BMDP uses the most recently created SAS data set.

LABEL=*variable*
    specifies a variable whose values are to be used as case labels for BMDP. Only the first four characters of the values are used. The LABEL= variable must also be included in the VAR statement if you use one.

LABEL2=*variable*
    specifies a variable whose values are to be used as second case labels for BMDP. As with the LABEL= option, only the first four characters are used, and the LABEL2= variable must also be given in the VAR statement if you use one.

NOMISS
> specifies that you want the BMDP program or "save" file to exclude observations that contain missing values.

PROG=BMDP*nn*
> specifies the BMDP program that you want to run. For example, the following PROC BMDP statement runs the BMDP3S program:

```
proc bmdp prog=bmdp3s;
```

> **Note:**   If you want only to convert a SAS data set to a BMDP "save" file and do not want to run a BMDP program, omit the PROG= option and include the UNIT= option, which is described next.

UNIT=*n*
> specifies the FORTRAN logical unit number for the BMDP "save" file that the BMDP procedure creates. The value you specify for *n* must correspond to the UNIT= value that is specified in the INPUT paragraph of the BMDP control language.
>
> If you omit this option, *n* defaults to 3 and FT03F001 is used as the fileref for the "save" file. The following message is also printed:

```
Note: The UNIT= option was not specified. Unlike Version 5,
the UNIT= option is required. Therefore, UNIT=3 is assumed.
Ensure that the INPUT paragraph uses a UNIT of 3, or explicitly
specify the correct UNIT value.
```

WRKSPCE=*nn* | PARM=*nn*
> controls the allocation of a workspace in BMDP. The WRKSPCE= or PARM= value is passed as a parameter to BMDP programs and corresponds to the WRKSPCE= feature in BMDP MVS cataloged procedures. The default value for *nn* is 30. If *nn* is less than 100, then its value represents kilobytes. If it is greater than 100, then its value represents bytes.

VAR Statement

VAR *variable-list*;

The VAR statement specifies which variables to use in the BMDP program. When you do not include a VAR statement, the BMDP program uses all the numeric variables in the SAS data set.

BY Statement

BY *variable-list*;

Use the BY statement with the BMDP procedure to obtain separate analyses of observations in groups. The groups are defined with the BY variables. When you use a BY statement, the procedure expects the input data set to be sorted in order of the BY variables or to have an

BMDP   *continued*

appropriate index. If your input data set is not sorted in ascending order, you can do the following:

□   use the SORT procedure with a similar BY statement to sort the data.

□   if appropriate, use the BY statement options NOTSORTED or DESCENDING.

□   create an index on the BY variables that you want to use. For more information about creating indexes and about using the BY statement with indexed data sets, see "The DATASETS Procedure" in the *SAS Procedures Guide.*

If a BY statement is used, it is included in the BMDP printed output to distinguish the BY group output.

For more information about the BY statement, see *SAS Language: Reference.*

PARMCARDS Statement

PARMCARDS;

The PARMCARDS statement indicates that the BMDP control language follows.

BMDP Control Statements

Put your BMDP control language statements after the PARMCARDS statement. These statements are similar for all BMDP programs; see the most current BMDP manual for information about their forms and functions.

The BMDP INPUT paragraph must include UNIT and CODE sentences. The values of these sentences must match the UNIT= and CODE= values that are given in the PROC BMDP statement. (If the PROC BMDP statement does not specify a UNIT= value, then use 3 as the UNIT= value in the BMDP statements.) Use the SAS data set name as the CODE value unless you have used the CODE= option in the PROC BMDP statement to specify a different name. Omit the VARIABLES paragraph from the BMDP statements, because it is not needed when your input is a "save" file.

How Missing Values Are Handled

Before the BMDP procedure sends data to BMDP, it converts missing SAS values to the standard BMDP missing value. When you use the NOMISS option in the PROC BMDP statement, observations that contain missing values are excluded from the data set that is sent to the BMDP program.

Invoking BMDP Programs that Need FORTRAN Routines

Some BMDP programs, such as the programs for nonlinear regression, need to invoke the FORTRAN compiler and linkage editor before executing. All BMDP compilation and link editing must be completed before you use PROC BMDP.

Example of Creating and Converting a BMDP Save File

Here is an example of creating and converting a BMDP "save" file.

❶
```
data temp;
    input x y z;
    cards;
    1 2 3 4 5 6 7 8 9 10 11 12
run;
```

❷
```
proc contents;
    title 'CONTENTS OF SAS DATA SET TO BE RUN THROUGH BMDP1D';
run;
```

❸
```
proc bmdp prog=bmdp1d unit=3;
    parmcards;
    /input unit=3. code='TEMP'.
    /print min.
    /save unit=4. code='NEW'. NEW.
    /end
    /finish
run;
```

❹
```
libname ft04f001 bmdp;
```
❺
```
data _null_;
    set ft04f001.new;
    put _all_;
run;
```

❻
```
proc contents data=ft04f001._all_;
run;
```

❼
```
proc convert bmdp=ft04f001 out=xyz;
```

The numbered lines of code are explained here:

❶ This DATA step creates a SAS data set called TEMP.

❷ The CONTENTS procedure shows the descriptive information for the data set TEMP.

❸ PROC BMDP calls the BMDP program BMDP1D to analyze the data set TEMP.

Note the BMDP program statements UNIT=3. and CODE='TEMP'. The results are stored in the BMDP "save" file, NEW.

The word NEW must be in the SAVE paragraph. UNIT=*nn* should refer to the FT*nn*F001 fileref that was defined in your data definition statement.

❹ The LIBNAME statement associates the libref FT04F001 with the BMDP engine so that SAS knows which engine to use to access the data.

❺ The DATA step reads the BMDP "save" file NEW, which was created in the previous PROC BMDP step. It uses the two-level name FT04F001.NEW to reference the file.

BMDP   *continued*

❻ The CONTENTS procedure prints the information regarding all members that reside in the FT04F001 file. The _ALL_ member name is a special member name for the BMDP engine; it causes PROC CONTENTS to process all BMDP members in the file.

❼ The CONVERT procedure converts the BMDP "save" file NEW to a SAS data set named XYZ. The NEW "save" file is on UNIT 4, that is, FT04F001.

The output from this SAS program is shown in Output 18.1.

Output 18.1
NEW Save File
Created from Data
Set TEMP and
Converted to SAS
Data Set XYZ

```
                    CONTENTS OF SAS DATA SET TO BE RUN THROUGH BMDP1D

                                   CONTENTS PROCEDURE
          .
          .
          .

                   -----Alphabetic List of Variables and Attributes-----

                      #    Variable   Type   Len   Pos
                      ---------------------------------
                      1    X          Num     8     0
                      2    Y          Num     8     8
                      3    Z          Num     8    16


      PAGE   1   1D


      BMDP1D - SIMPLE DATA DESCRIPTION
      COPYRIGHT 1977, 1979, 1981, 1982, 1983, 1985, 1987, 1988, 1990
                       BY BMDP STATISTICAL SOFTWARE, INC.


             BMDP STATISTICAL SOFTWARE, INC.| BMDP STATISTICAL SOFTWARE
             1440 SEPULVEDA BLVD            | CORK TECHNOLOGY PARK, MODEL FARM RD
             LOS ANGELES, CA 90025 USA      | CORK, IRELAND
                 PHONE  (213) 479-7799      |     PHONE +353 21 542722
                 FAX    (213) 312-0161      |     FAX   +353 21 542822
                 TELEX 4972934 BMDP UI      |     TELEX 75659 SSWL EI


      VERSION: 1990   (IBM/OS)          DATE: FEBRUARY 21, 1996  AT 14:27:43
       MANUAL: BMDP MANUAL VOL. 1 AND VOL. 2.
       DIGEST: BMDP USER'S DIGEST.
      UPDATES: STATE NEWS. IN THE PRINT PARAGRAPH FOR SUMMARY OF NEW FEATURES.


      PROGRAM INSTRUCTIONS

      /INPUT UNIT=3. CODE='TEMP'.
      /PRINT MIN.
      /SAVE UNIT=4. CODE='NEW'. NEW.
      /END


      PROBLEM TITLE IS

      NUMBER OF VARIABLES TO READ . . . . . . . . . .       3
      NUMBER OF VARIABLES ADDED BY TRANSFORMATIONS. .       0
      TOTAL NUMBER OF VARIABLES . . . . . . . . . . .       3
      CASE FREQUENCY VARIABLE . . . . . . . . . . . .
      CASE WEIGHT VARIABLE. . . . . . . . . . . . . .
      CASE LABELING VARIABLES . . . . . . . . . . . .
      NUMBER OF CASES TO READ . . . . . . . . . . . . TO END
      MISSING VALUES CHECKED BEFORE OR AFTER TRANS. . NEITHER
      BLANKS IN THE DATA ARE TREATED AS   . . . . . . MISSING
      INPUT UNIT NUMBER . . . . . . . . . . . . . .         3
      REWIND INPUT UNIT PRIOR TO READING. . DATA. . .     YES
      NUMBER OF INTEGER WORDS OF MEMORY FOR STORAGE . 1249790
```

```
INPUT BMDP FILE
CODE. . . IS      TEMP
CONTENT . IS      DATA
LABEL . . IS

VARIABLES
    1 X          2 Y          3 Z

VARIABLES TO BE USED
    1 X          2 Y          3 Z


   PRINT CASES CONTAINING VALUES LESS THAN THE STATED MINIMA.



-------------------------------------------
BMDP FILE IS BEING WRITTEN ON UNIT       4
CODE. . . IS      NEW
CONTENT . IS      DATA
LABEL . . IS       FEBRUARY 21, 1996      14:27:43

PAGE   2  1D  FEBRUARY 21, 1996      14:27:43

VARIABLES ARE
    1 X          2 Y          3 Z


BMDP    FILE ON UNIT  4 HAS BEEN COMPLETED.


-------------------------------------------
NUMBER OF CASES WRITTEN TO FILE          4

NUMBER OF CASES READ. . . . . . . . . . . . .       4
```

VARIABLE		TOTAL		STANDARD	ST.ERR	COEFF. OF	S M A
L L E S T		L A R G E S T					
NO. NAME		FREQUENCY	MEAN	DEVIATION	OF MEAN	VARIATION	VALUE
Z-SCORE	VALUE	Z-SCORE	RANGE				
1 X		4	5.5000	3.8730	1.9365	.70418	1.0000
-1.16	10.000	1.16	9.0000				
2 Y		4	6.5000	3.8730	1.9365	.59584	2.0000
-1.16	11.000	1.16	9.0000				
3 Z		4	7.5000	3.8730	1.9365	.51640	3.0000
-1.16	12.000	1.16	9.0000				

```
NUMBER OF INTEGER WORDS USED IN PRECEDING    PROBLEM    530
CPU TIME USED      0.084 SECONDS

PAGE   3  1D

BMDP1D - SIMPLE DATA DESCRIPTION
COPYRIGHT 1977, 1979, 1981, 1982, 1983, 1985, 1987, 1988, 1990
              BY BMDP STATISTICAL SOFTWARE, INC.

       BMDP STATISTICAL SOFTWARE, INC.| BMDP STATISTICAL SOFTWARE
       1440 SEPULVEDA BLVD            | CORK TECHNOLOGY PARK, MODEL FARM RD
       LOS ANGELES, CA 90025 USA      | CORK, IRELAND
           PHONE (213) 479-7799       |    PHONE +353 21 542722
           FAX   (213) 312-0161       |    FAX   +353 21 542822
           TELEX 4972934 BMDP UI      |    TELEX 75659 SSWL EI

VERSION: 1990   (IBM/OS)        DATE: FEBRUARY 21, 1996  AT 14:27:44

PROGRAM INSTRUCTIONS

/FINISH

NO MORE CONTROL LANGUAGE.

PROGRAM TERMINATED
```

BMDP   *continued*

```
                 SAS DATA SET CONVERTED FROM BMDP SAVE FILE

     Data Set Name: FT04F001.NEW              Observations:           .
     Member Type:   DATA                      Variables:              4
     Engine:        BMDP                       Indexes:                0
     Created:       14:27 Wednesday, February 21, 1996   Observation Length:   16
     Last Modified: 14:27 Wednesday, February 21, 1996   Deleted Observations: 0
     Protection:                              Compressed:            NO
     Data Set Type:                           Sorted:                NO
     Label:         FEBRUARY 21, 1996      14:27:43

                    -----Engine/Host Dependent Information-----

            -----Alphabetic List of Variables and Attributes-----

                 #    Variable   Type   Len   Pos
                 ------------------------------------
                 4    USE        Num     4    12
                 1    X          Num     4     0
                 2    Y          Num     4     4
                 3    Z          Num     4     8
```

CATALOG

Manages SAS catalogs

MVS Specifics: FILE= option

MVS Specifics

The FILE= option in the CONTENTS statement of the CATALOG procedure is the only portion of this procedure that is host-specific. Under MVS, if the value that you specify in the FILE= option has not been previously defined as a fileref (using a FILENAME statement, TSO ALLOCATE command, or JCL DD statement), then SAS uses the value to construct the operating system data set name.

In the following example, if the SAS system option FILEPROMPT is in effect, a requestor window asks whether you want to allocate the external file whose fileref is SAMPLE. If you reply **Yes**, then SAS attempts to locate the external file. If the file was not previously allocated, then SAS allocates it. To construct the data set name, SAS inserts the value of the SYSPREF= system option in front of the FILE= value (in this case, SAMPLE), and it appends the name LIST to it. In this example, if the value of SYSPREF= is SASDEMO.V6, then SAS allocates an operating system data set named SASDEMO.V6.SAMPLE.LIST.

```
proc catalog catalog=profile;
   contents file=sample;
run;
```

See Also

□   *SAS Procedures Guide*

CIMPORT

Restores a transport file that was created by the CPORT procedure

MVS Specifics: options

MVS Specifics

In addition to the options listed in the *SAS Procedures Guide*, the following options are available under MVS:

CBTCOLOR=*color*
> specifies the background color for the CBT entries that the CIMPORT procedure creates. This option is effective only when you are importing Version 5 SAS catalogs. Valid colors are

> | | |
> |---|---|
> | BLACK | PINK |
> | BLUE | RED |
> | CYAN | WHITE |
> | GREEN | YELLOW |

> The default color is BLACK.

HELPCOLOR=*color*
> specifies the background color for the HELP entries that PROC CIMPORT creates. This option is effective only when you are importing Version 5 SAS catalogs. For a list of valid colors, see the CBTCOLOR= option. The default color is BLACK.

MENUCOLOR=*color*
> specifies the background color for the MENU entries that PROC CIMPORT creates. This option is effective only when you are importing Version 5 SAS catalogs. For a list of valid colors, see the CBTCOLOR= option. The default color is BLACK.

PROGRAMCOLOR=*color*
> specifies the background color for the PROGRAM entries that PROC CIMPORT creates. This option is effective only when you are importing Version 5 SAS catalogs. For a list of valid colors, see the CBTCOLOR= option. The default color is BLACK.

The DISK option is the default for the CIMPORT procedure. Therefore, PROC CIMPORT defaults to reading from a file on disk instead of from a tape. If you want to read a file from tape, then specify the TAPE option.

When writing and reading files to and from tapes, you are not required to specify the DCB attributes in a SAS FILENAME statement. However, it is recommended that you specify BLKSIZE=8000.

Here is an example that uses PROC CIMPORT to import a transport file from disk. The transport file was created from a SAS data library on another operating system by PROC CPORT. Note that the FILENAME statement specifies BLKSIZE=8000.

CIMPORT *continued*

```
libname newlib 'SAS-data-library';
filename tranfile 'transport-file-name' blksize=8000;
proc cimport library=newlib infile=tranfile;
run;
```

PROC CIMPORT reads from disk the transport file TRANFILE that PROC CPORT created from a SAS data library. It imports the transport file to the SAS data library that is identified by the libref NEWLIB.

See Also

□ "Transporting SAS Catalogs" on page 134

□ *SAS Procedures Guide*

□ SAS Technical Report P-195, *Transporting SAS Files between Host Systems*

CONTENTS

Prints descriptions of the contents of one or more files from a SAS data library

MVS Specifics: engine/host-dependent information, directory information

MVS Specifics

Although most of the output that this procedure generates is the same on all operating systems, the Engine/Host Dependent Information is system-dependent and engine-dependent. Output 18.2 shows sample PROC CONTENTS output, including the information that is specific to MVS for the BASE engine.

Output 18.2 CONTENTS Procedure Output, Including Engine/Host Dependent Information

```
                               CONTENTS PROCEDURE

      Data Set Name: WORK.ORANGES              Observations:        4
      Member Type:   DATA                      Variables:           5
      Engine:        V609                      Indexes:             0
      Created:       15:56 Monday, February 19, 1996   Observation Length:  40
      Last Modified: 15:56 Monday, February 19, 1996   Deleted Observations: 0
      Protection:                              Compressed:          NO
      Data Set Type:                           Sorted:              YES
      Label:


                       -----Engine/Host Dependent Information-----

          Data Set Page Size:     6144
          Number of Data Set Pages: 1
          File Format:            607
          First Data Page:        1
          Max Obs per Page:       152
          Obs in First Data Page: 4
          Physical Name:          SYS96050.T153830.RA000.USERID.R0000004
          Release Created:        6.090450
          Release Last Modified:  6.090450
          Created by:             USERID
          Last Modified by:       USERID
          Subextents:             1
          Total Blocks Used:      1
```

```
                    Taste Test Results For Oranges

                           CONTENTS PROCEDURE

        -----Alphabetic List of Variables and Attributes-----

              #    Variable   Type    Len    Pos
              ------------------------------------
              2    FLAVOR     Num      8      8
              4    LOOKS      Num      8     24
              3    TEXTURE    Num      8     16
              5    TOTAL      Num      8     32
              1    VARIETY    Char     8      0
```

The procedure output provides values for the physical characteristics of the SAS data set WORK.ORANGES. Important values follow:

Observations
   is the number of nondeleted records in the data set.

Observation Length
   is the maximum record size in bytes.

Compressed
   has the value NO if records are not compressed; it has the value YES if records are compressed.

Data Set Page Size
   is the size of pages in the data set.

Number of Data Set Pages
   is the total number of pages in the data set.

First Data Page
   is the number of the page that contains the first data record; header records are stored in front of data records.

Max Obs per Page
   is the maximum number of records a page can hold.

Obs in First Data Page
   is the number of data records in the first data page.

   The DIRECTORY option lists several host-specific data library attributes at the beginning of PROC CONTENTS output. Output 18.3 shows the directory information that is listed by the following code:

```
proc contents data=test._all_ directory;
run;
```

CONTENTS *continued*

Output 18.3
Engine/Host
Dependent
Information

```
                        CONTENTS PROCEDURE

                       -----Directory-----

          Libref:                TEST
          Engine:                V609
          Physical Name:         USERID.TEST.TESTLIB
          Unit:                  DISK
          Volume:                SCR810
          Disposition:           OLD
          Device:                3380
          Blocksize:             6144
          Blocks per Track:      7
          Total Library Blocks:  105
          Total Used Blocks:     28
          Total Free Blocks:     77
          Highest Used Block:    28
          Highest Formatted Block: 35
          Members:               0
```

The following list explains these data library attributes:

Total Library Blocks

is the total number of blocks that are currently allocated to the data library. This value equals the sum of Total Used Blocks and Total Free Blocks. It also equals Blocks per Track multiplied by the number of tracks that are currently allocated to the data library. The current number of allocated cylinders or tracks can be found in the DSINFO window, or in ISPF panel 3.2. These windows show what the allocation was the last time the data library was closed.

Total Used Blocks

is the total number of library blocks that currently contain valid data. It equals the sum of the directory blocks and all the data blocks that are associated with existing members.

Total Free Blocks

is the total number of currently allocated library blocks that are available for use by members or as extra directory blocks. This count includes any data blocks that were previously associated with members that have been deleted.

Highest Used Block

is the number of the highest relative block in the data library that currently contains either directory information or data for an existing member.

Highest Formatted Block

is the number of the highest relative block in the data library that has been internally formatted for use. Blocks are internally formatted before they are used, and they are formatted in full track increments. Therefore, the highest formatted block is equal to the Blocks per Track multiplied by the number of tracks that are currently used by the data library. The number of currently used cylinders or tracks can be found in the DSINFO window or in ISPF panel 3.2. These windows show what the allocation was the last time the data library was closed. This number is also the true End Of File marker. It corresponds to the DS1LSTAR field in the DSCB in the VTOC, which is the MVS operating system's EOF flag.

Note: The same directory information that is generated by the DIRECTORY option in the PROC CONTENTS statement is also generated by the LIST option in the LIBNAME statement.

See Also

□ *SAS Language and Procedures*

□ *SAS Procedures Guide*

CONVERT

Converts BMDP, OSIRIS, and SPSS system files to SAS data sets

MVS Specifics: all

Syntax

PROC CONVERT *<options>*;

Description

PROC CONVERT produces one output SAS data set, but no printed output. The new SAS data set contains the same information as the input system file; exceptions are noted in "How Variable Names Are Assigned" on page 213.

The procedure converts system files from these software packages:

□ BMDP "save" files up to and including the most recent version of BMDP

□ SPSS "save" files up to and including Release 9, along with SPSS-X and the SPSS Portable File Format

□ OSIRIS files up to and including OSIRIS IV (hierarchical file structures are not supported).

These software packages are products of other organizations. Therefore, changes may be made that make the system files incompatible with the current version of PROC CONVERT. SAS Institute cannot be responsible for upgrading PROC CONVERT to support changes to other vendors' software packages; however, attempts to do so are made when necessary with each new version of the SAS System.

Information associated with each software package is given in Chapter 4, "Accessing BMDP, SPSS, and OSIRIS Files."

PROC CONVERT Statement

PROC CONVERT *<options>*;

options can be from the following list. Only one of the options that specify a system file (BMDP, OSIRIS, or SPSS) can be included. Usually only the PROC CONVERT statement is used, although data set attributes can be controlled by specifying the DROP=, KEEP=, or RENAME= data set options with the OUT= option of this procedure. See *SAS Language:*

CONVERT   *continued*

Reference for more information about these data set options. You can also use LABEL and FORMAT statements following the PROC statement.

BMDP=*fileref* | *libref*<(CODE=*code-id* | CONTENT=*content-type*)>
specifies the fileref or libref of a BMDP "save" file. The first "save" file in the operating system data set is converted. If you have more than one "save" file in the data set, then you can use two additional options in parentheses after the libref or fileref. The CODE= option lets you specify the code of the "save" file you want, and the CONTENT= option lets you give the "save" file's content. For example, if a file CODE=JUDGES has a CONTENT of DATA, you can use this statement:

```
proc convert bmdp=bmdpfile(code=judges content=data);
```

DICT=*fileref* | *libref*
specifies the fileref or libref of an operating system data set that contains the dictionary file for the OSIRIS data set. The DICT= option is required if you use the OSIRIS= option.

FIRSTOBS=*n*
gives the number of the observation at which the conversion is to begin. This enables you to skip over observations at the beginning of the BMDP, OSIRIS, or SPSS file.

OBS=*n*
specifies the number of the last observation to be converted. This enables you to exclude observations at the end of the file.

OSIRIS=*fileref* | *libref*
specifies a fileref or libref for an operating system data set that contains an OSIRIS file. The DICT= option is required when you use the OSIRIS= option.

OUT=*SAS-data-set*
names the SAS data set that will be created to hold the converted data. If OUT= is omitted, SAS still creates a data set and automatically names it DATA*n*, just as if you omitted a data set name in a DATA statement. That is, if it is the first such data set in a job or session, then SAS names it DATA1; the second is DATA2, and so on. If you omit the OUT= option, or if you do not specify a two-level name in the OUT= option, then the converted data set is not permanently saved.

SPSS=*fileref* | *libref*
specifies a libref or fileref for an operating system data set that contains an SPSS file. The SPSS file can be in any of three formats: SPSS Release 9 (or prior), SPSS-X format (whose originating operating system is MVS, CMS, or VSE), or the portable file format from any operating system.

How Missing Values Are Handled

If a numeric variable in the input data set has no value or has a system missing value, PROC CONVERT assigns a missing value to it.

How Variable Names Are Assigned

The following sections explain how names are assigned to the SAS variables that are created by the CONVERT procedure.

▶ *Caution* . . . . *Because some translation of variable names can occur (as indicated in the following sections), ensure that the translated names will be unique.*

Variable Names in BMDP Output

Variable names from the BMDP "save" file are used in the SAS data set, except that nontrailing blanks and all special characters are converted to underscores in the SAS variable names. The subscript in BMDP variable names, such as x(1), becomes part of the SAS variable name, with the parentheses omitted: X1. Alphabetic BMDP variables become SAS character variables of length 4. Category records from BMDP are not accepted.

Variable Names in OSIRIS Output

For single-response variables, the V1 through V9999 name becomes the SAS variable name. For multiple-response variables, the suffix Rn is added to the variable name, when n is the response. For example, V25R1 would be the first response of the multiple-response V25. If the variable after or including V1000 has 100 or more responses, then responses above 99 are eliminated. Numeric variables that OSIRIS stores in character, fixed-point binary, or floating-point binary mode become SAS numeric variables. Alphabetic variables become SAS character variables; any alphabetic variable whose length is greater than 200 is truncated to 200. The OSIRIS variable description becomes a SAS variable label, and OSIRIS print format information is translated to the appropriate SAS format specification.

Variable Names in SPSS Output

SPSS variable names and labels become variable names and labels without change. SPSS alphabetic variables become SAS character variables of length 4. SPSS blank values are converted to SAS missing values. SPSS print formats become SAS formats, and the SPSS default precision of no decimal places becomes part of the variables' formats. The SPSS DOCUMENT data are copied so that the CONTENTS procedure can display them. SPSS value labels are not copied.

Example of Converting a BMDP Save File

The following statements convert a BMDP "save" file and produce the temporary SAS data set TEMP, which contains the converted data. The PROC CONTENTS output would be similar to that shown in Output 18.1 on page 204.

```
filename ft04f001 'userid.bmdp.savefile';

proc convert bmdp=ft04f001 out=temp;
run;

title 'BMDP CONVERT Example';

proc contents;
run;
```

CONVERT *continued*

Example of Converting an OSIRIS File

The following statements convert an OSIRIS file and produce the temporary SAS data set TEMP, which contains the converted data. Output 18.4 shows the attributes of TEMP.

```
filename osiris 'userid.misc.cntl(osirdata)';
filename dict 'userid.misc.cntl(osirdict)';

proc convert osiris=osiris dict=dict out=temp;
run;

title 'OSIRIS CONVERT Example';

proc contents;
run;
```

Output 18.4
Converting an
OSIRIS File

```
                        OSIRIS CONVERT Example

                        CONTENTS PROCEDURE

Data Set Name: WORK.TEMP                    Observations:          20
Member Type:   DATA                         Variables:              9
Engine:        V609                         Indexes:                0
Created:       9:46 Wednesday, February 21, 1996   Observation Length:    36
Last Modified: 9:46 Wednesday, February 21, 1996   Deleted Observations:   0
Protection:                                 Compressed:            NO
Data Set Type: DATA                         Sorted:                NO
Label:

                 -----Engine/Host Dependent Information-----

        Data Set Page Size:        6144
        Number of Data Set Pages:  1
        File Format:               607
        First Data Page:           1
        Max Obs per Page:          169
        Obs in First Data Page:    20
        Physical Name:             SYS96052.T094503.RA000.USERID.R0000040
        Release Created:           6.090450
        Release Last Modified:     6.090450
        Created by:                USERID
        Last Modified by:          USERID
        Subextents:                1
        Total Blocks Used:         1

            -----Alphabetic List of Variables and Attributes-----

    #  Variable  Type  Len  Pos  Format  Label
    ------------------------------------------------------------------------
    1  V1        Num    4    0            INTERVIEW NUMBER       REF=   1 ID=
    2  V2        Num    4    4            INTERVIEWER NUMBER     REF=   2 ID=
    3  V3        Num    4    8            PRIMARY SAMPLING UNIT  REF=   3 ID=
    4  V4        Num    4   12            REGION                 REF=   4 ID=
    5  V5        Num    4   16            CHUNK AND SEGMENT      REF=   5 ID=
    6  V6        Num    4   20            LANGUAGE OF INTERVIEW  REF=   6 ID=
    7  V7        Num    4   24            LANGUAGE OF INTERVIEW  REF=1621 ID=
    8  V8        Num    4   28            LNGTH OF INTERVIEW     REF=1620 ID=
    9  V9        Num    4   32   12.4     WEIGHT                 REF=1700 ID=
```

Example of Converting an SPSS File

The following statements convert an SPSS Release 9 file and produce the temporary SAS data set TEMP, which contains the converted data. PROC CONTENTS shows the attributes of TEMP in Output 18.5.

```
filename spss 'userid.spssfile.num1';

proc convert spss=spss out=temp;
run;

title 'SPSSR9 CONVERT Example';

proc contents;
run;
```

Output 18.5
Converting an SPSS
Release 9 File

```
                          SPSSR9 CONVERT Example

                            CONTENTS PROCEDURE

Data Set Name: WORK.TEMP                    Observations:          91
Member Type:   DATA                         Variables:             7
Engine:        V609                         Indexes:               0
Created:       9:55 Wednesday, February 21, 1996   Observation Length:  32
Last Modified: 9:55 Wednesday, February 21, 1996   Deleted Observations: 0
Protection:                                 Compressed:            NO
Data Set Type: DATA                         Sorted:                NO
Label:

                    -----Engine/Host Dependent Information-----

        Data Set Page Size:      6144
        Number of Data Set Pages: 1
        File Format:             137
        First Data Page:         1
        Max Obs per Page:        190
        Obs in First Data Page:  91
        Physical Name:           SYS96052.T095451.RA000.USERID.R0000081
        Release Created:         6.090450
        Release Last Modified:   6.090450
        Created by:              USERID
        Last Modified by:        USERID
        Subextents:              1
        Total Blocks Used:       1

            -----Alphabetic List of Variables and Attributes-----

    #   Variable   Type   Len   Pos   Format  Label
    ----------------------------------------------------------------
    5   AREA       Num    4     20    11
    3   CASWGT     Num    4     12    11.4    WEIGHT OF SPSS CASE
    6   PERIM      Num    4     24    11.
    7   RATIO      Num    4     28    11.
    1   SEQNUM     Num    4     0     6.      SEQUENCE NUMBER SPSS CASE
    4   SPECIES    Num    4     16    11.
    2   SUBFILE    Char   8     4             NAME OF SPSS SUBFILE
```

CONVERT *continued*

See Also

□   Chapter 4, "Accessing BMDP, SPSS, and OSIRIS Files"

CPORT

Writes SAS data sets and catalogs into a special format in a transport file

MVS Specifics: specification of transport file

MVS Specifics

The DISK option is the default for the CPORT procedure; therefore, CPORT defaults to writing to a file on disk instead of on a tape. If you want to write to a file on tape, specify the TAPE option or assign SASCAT to a tape.

You are not required to define the logical name SASCAT to your tape, and you are not required to specify the full DCB attributes. However, the BLKSIZE= value must be an integral multiple of 80; a value of 8000 is recommended.

Here is an example of exporting all the SAS data sets and catalogs in a SAS data library to a transport file on disk. Note that the FILENAME statement specifies BLKSIZE=8000.

```
libname oldlib 'SAS-data-library';
filename tranfile 'transport-file-name' blksize=8000 disp=(new,catlg);
proc cport library=oldlib file=tranfile;
run;
```

PROC CPORT writes a transport file to the operating system data set that is referenced by TRANFILE. The file contains all the data sets and catalogs in the SAS data library OLDLIB.

See Also

□   "Transporting SAS Catalogs" on page 134

□   *SAS Procedures Guide*

□   SAS Technical Report P-195, *Transporting SAS Files between Host Systems*

DATASETS

Lists, copies, renames, and deletes SAS files; manages indexes for and appends SAS data sets in a SAS data library

MVS Specifics: output generated by CONTENTS statement

MVS Specifics

Part of the DATASETS procedure output is system-dependent. The SAS data library information that is displayed in the SAS log depends on the operating system and the engine. In Output 18.6, the SAS log shows the information that is generated by the DATASETS procedure for the V6 (BASE) engine under MVS.

    Note: The information produced for other engines varies slightly. See "Accessing V6 and V6SEQ SAS Data Libraries" on page 43 and "Accessing V5 and V5SEQ SAS Data Libraries" on page 431 for information about other engines.

Output 18.6
SAS Data Library Information from the DATASETS Procedure

```
                              -----Directory-----
          Libref:              WORK
          Engine:              V609
          Physical Name:       SYS96053.T145204.RA000.USERID.R0000128
          Unit:                DISK
          Volume:              ANYVOL
          Disposition:         NEW
          Device:              3380
          Blocksize:           6144
          Blocks per Track:    7
          Total Library Blocks: 105
          Total Used Blocks:   31
          Total Free Blocks:   74
          Highest Used Block:  44
          Highest Formatted Block: 49
          Members:             1

                    #  Name     Memtype  Indexes
                    ---------------------------
                    1  ORANGES  DATA
                    2  PROFILE  CATALOG
```

For explanations of the fields in Output 18.6, see "CONTENTS" on page 208.

See Also

□ CONTENTS procedure earlier in this chapter

□ *SAS Language and Procedures*

□ *SAS Procedures Guide*

FORMAT

Creates user-defined formats and informats

MVS Specifics: LIBRARY= option in the PROC FORMAT statement

FORMAT *continued*

MVS Specifics

If the value of the LIBRARY= option in the PROC FORMAT statement is a DDname that points to a load library, then formats are written out to the load library in Version 5 style format. If the value of the LIBRARY= option is a libref, then the formats are written in Version 6 format to the FORMATS catalog. The FORMATS catalog is stored in the Version 6 SAS data library that is identified by the LIBRARY= option.

The following format and informat features cannot be used when you are creating a Version 5-style load module:

□ the ROUND option in the PICTURE statement

□ the NOTSORTED option in the PROC FORMAT statement

□ numeric ranges in numeric informats

□ label lengths over 40 characters

□ range lengths over 16 characters

□ format or informat names that are used as labels.

If your program uses any of these features and you use the LIBRARY= option to create a Version 5-style load module from that program, then a message informs you that you cannot write such formats or informats.

For information about converting your Version 5 formats that are stored in load libraries to Version 6 formats, see "The V5TOV6 Procedure" in the *SAS Procedures Guide.* For information about accessing Version 5 style formats under Version 6, see SAS Technical Report P-195, *Transporting Files between Host Systems.*

See Also

□ *SAS Language and Procedures*

□ *SAS Procedures Guide*

OPTIONS

Lists the current values of all system options in the SAS log

MVS Specifics: host options displayed

MVS Specifics

The portable options that this procedure displays are the same for every operating system. However, the host options that are displayed under the heading "Host Options" are host-specific. Output 18.7 shows a partial listing of the host options that are displayed under MVS.

Output 18.7
Host Options
Displayed by the
OPTIONS
Procedure

```
HOST OPTIONS :

ALTLOG=            Fileref for alternate log file
ALTPRINT=          Fileref for alternate print file
AUTHENCR=OPTIONAL  Is encryption of authorization information by TCP
                   clients OPTIONAL or REQUIRED
AUTOEXEC=          Fileref containing SAS statements which will be
                   automatically executed whenever the SAS System is invoked
NOBLKALLOC         BLKSIZE and LRECL for new SAS Data Libraries will be
                   defaulted at library open time
BLKSIZE=0          Default block size for V6 SAS data libraries and V5 SAS
                   data sets
BMPREAD=N          Read only flag for BMP regions
BNDLSUFX=          One-character suffix for bundle load modules
NOCAPSOUT          Output is not to be uppercased
CHARTYPE=0         Character set to use for device
NOCLIST            SAS System will obtain its input from the terminal
CODEPASS=1         Number of passes during code generation
CODEPCT=0          Code generation storage allocation overhead percentage
COMAMID=XMS        Default communications access method
   .
   .
   .
```

Under MVS, the OPTIONS procedure accepts the following system-dependent options:

ADB   lists options that are specific to the SAS/ACCESS interface to ADABAS.

APF   lists options that are intended for system administrators.

DB2   lists options that are specific to the SAS/ACCESS interface to DB2.

DDB   lists options that are specific to the SAS/ACCESS interface to CA-DATACOM/DB.

IDM   lists options that are specific to the SAS/ACCESS interface to CA-IDMS.

IMS   lists options that are specific to the SAS/ACCESS interface to IMS-DL/I.

ISP   lists options that are specific to the SAS interface to ISPF (see "SAS Interface to ISPF" on page 106).

For more information about SAS system options that are associated with a particular SAS/ACCESS interface, see the documentation for that SAS/ACCESS interface.

See Also

□ "Displaying System Option Settings" on page 12

□ Chapter 20, "System Options"

□ *SAS Language and Procedures*

□ *SAS Procedures Guide*

PDS

Lists, deletes, or renames members of a partitioned data set

MVS Specifics: all

Syntax

PROC PDS DDNAME=*file-specification* *<options>*;
    DELETE *member-1* < . . . *member-n*>;
    CHANGE *old-name-1=new-name-1* < . . . *old-name-n=new-name-n*>;
    EXCHANGE *name-1=other-name-1* < . . . *name-n=other-name-n*>;

Description

Partitioned data sets are libraries that contain files called members. There are two kinds of partitioned data sets. One can contain source code, macros, cataloged procedures, and other data. The other, called a load library, can contain only load modules.

    PROC PDS operates on the directory of a partitioned data set to list, delete, and rename members and aliases. (Partitioned data sets are not the same as SAS data libraries.) When members are deleted or renamed, PROC PDS updates the directory of the partitioned data set. Also, unless NOLIST is specified, PROC PDS writes an updated listing of the PDS member names to the SAS log.

PROC PDS Statement

PROC PDS DDNAME=*file-specification* *<options>*;

DDNAME=*file-specification*
    specifies the operating system data set name (enclosed in quotes) or the fileref that is associated with the partitioned data set that you want to process. A fileref must have been previously assigned with a FILENAME statement, a JCL DD statement, or a TSO ALLOCATE command. The DDNAME= argument is required.

The following options can appear in the PROC PDS statement:

NOLIST
    suppresses the listing of the member names and aliases in the directory of the partitioned data set.

KILL
    deletes all the members of the partitioned data set that is specified by DDNAME=.

REFRESH | NOREFRESH
    specifies whether to update the directory information of the file that is being processed after each operation. The default, REFRESH, updates the directory information after each operation. Unless the operations that are being performed by PROC PDS are dependent on each other, specify NOREFRESH for better performance.

STRICT

> causes error messages to be generated and sets the return code to 8 if no members match the selection criteria. The default behavior is for note messages to be generated and for the return code to be set to 0 if no members match the selection criteria.

DELETE Statement

DELETE *member-1* < ... *member-n*>;

If you want to delete a member or members from the PDS, specify the member names in a DELETE statement.

When a specification in the DELETE statement is followed by a colon (:), all members whose names begin with the characters preceding the colon are deleted. For example, when the following statement is executed, PROC PDS deletes all members whose names begin with the characters PRGM:

```
delete prgm:;
```

CHANGE Statement

CHANGE *old-name-1=new-name-1* < ... *old-name-n=new-name-n*>;

If you want to rename a member or members of the PDS, use the CHANGE statement. Specify the old name on the left side of the equal sign, and specify the new name on the right. For example, the following statements change the name of member TESTPGM to PRODPGM:

```
filename loadlib 'partitioned-data-set ';
proc pds ddname=loadlib;
   change testpgm=prodpgm;
run;
```

If multiple members have names that begin with the same sequence of characters and you want to change all of the names so that they begin with a different sequence, use a colon (:) after *old-name* and *new-name*. Here is an example:

```
change exam:=test:;
```

All of the members whose names began with the characters EXAM will subsequently have names beginning with the characters TEST.

Note: If changing the name of a member would make the name the same as that of an existing member, then the member is not renamed and a note is written to the SAS log.

It is not necessary for the lengths of the character sequences that precede the colon to match. For example, the following statement is valid:

```
change am:=morn:;
```

However, if a new name is too long, then a note is written to the SAS log and no change is made.

PDS *continued*

EXCHANGE Statement

EXCHANGE *name-1=other-name-1* < . . . *name-n=other-name-n*>;

Use the EXCHANGE statement to switch the names of members of the partitioned data set. For example, after the following statements are executed, the member originally called A will be member Z, and the member originally called Z will be member A.

```
proc pds ddname='partitioned-data-set';
   exchange a=z;
run;
```

If multiple members have names that begin with the same sequence of characters and you want to exchange that sequence with the sequence from another group of data sets, use a colon (:) after *name* and *other-name*. For example, after the following statement is executed, all data sets whose names began with ABC will begin with DEFG. In addition, all of the data sets whose names began with DEFG will begin with ABC.

```
exchange abc:=defg:;
```

It is not necessary for the lengths of the sequences of characters that precede the colons to match. However, if a new name is too long, then a note is written to the SAS log and no change is made.

Usage Note

Unlike other SAS procedures that deal with partitioned data sets (for example, PROC PDSCOPY and PROC SOURCE), PROC PDS does not make any distinction between a member name and an alias, other than to report which names in the PDS directory are aliases for which members. If an alias is renamed, it is still an alias. PROC PDS allows you to delete a member that has aliases in the PDS directory, but then other procedures (PROC PDSCOPY, for example) cannot process the aliases.

Example of Deleting and Renaming Members with the PDS Procedure

This example writes the names of the members of USERID.MVS.OUTPUT to the SAS log and then generates a second listing showing the member changes and deletions that are specified by the second PROC step. The results are shown in Output 18.8.

```
filename pdstest 'userid.mvs.output';

proc pds ddname=pdstest;
run;

proc pds ddname=pdstest;
   delete tempout tempout2;
   change mem=out1603;
run;
```

Output 18.8
Deleting and
Renaming Members
with the PDS
Procedure

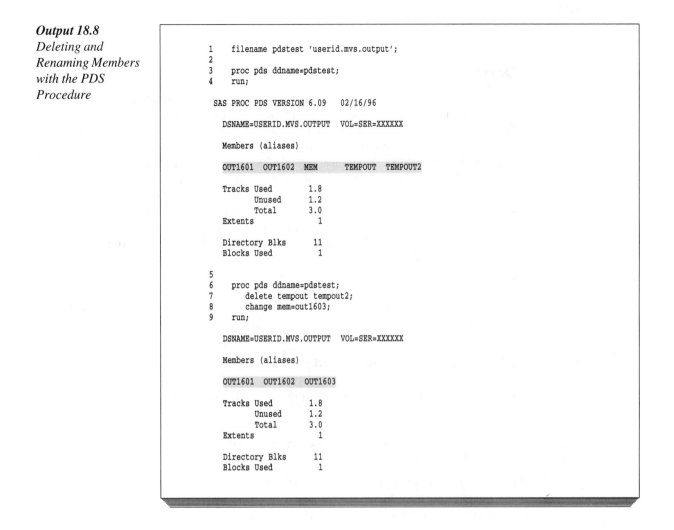

```
   1    filename pdstest 'userid.mvs.output';
   2
   3    proc pds ddname=pdstest;
   4    run;

    SAS PROC PDS VERSION 6.09   02/16/96

     DSNAME=USERID.MVS.OUTPUT   VOL=SER=XXXXXX

     Members (aliases)

     OUT1601  OUT1602  MEM      TEMPOUT  TEMPOUT2

     Tracks Used       1.8
            Unused     1.2
            Total      3.0
     Extents             1

     Directory Blks     11
     Blocks Used         1

   5
   6    proc pds ddname=pdstest;
   7       delete tempout tempout2;
   8       change mem=out1603;
   9    run;

     DSNAME=USERID.MVS.OUTPUT   VOL=SER=XXXXXX

     Members (aliases)

     OUT1601  OUT1602  OUT1603

     Tracks Used       1.8
            Unused     1.2
            Total      3.0
     Extents             1

     Directory Blks     11
     Blocks Used         1
```

PDSCOPY

Copies partitioned data sets from disk to disk, disk to tape, tape to tape, or tape to disk

MVS Specifics: all

Syntax

PROC PDSCOPY INDD=*file-specification* OUTDD=*file-specification* <*options*>;
    EXCLUDE *member-name-1* < ... *member-name-n*>;
    SELECT *member-name-1* < ... *member-name-n*>;

PDSCOPY   *continued*

Description

The PDSCOPY procedure can be used to copy an entire partitioned data set, or you can specify which members you want to copy. PROC PDSCOPY is useful for backing up source libraries and load module libraries to tape. If you use PROC PDSCOPY to copy a PDS to tape, then you must also use it if you want to copy that PDS back to *disk*. However, you can use either PROC PDSCOPY or other copy utilities to copy that tape to another *tape*.

When libraries are moved between disks that have different optimal block sizes, PROC PDSCOPY can be used to reblock the libraries. PROC PDSCOPY handles overlay programs and alias names. It also sets up the RLD count fields that are used by the FETCH program.

When a PDS contains load modules, it generally requires 13% to 18% less disk space after being copied by PROC PDSCOPY, because PROC PDSCOPY uses free space on a partially filled track to store records. The linkage editor constructs records that do not fit on a partially used track.

The PDSCOPY procedure does not copy scatter-loaded modules.

If errors are encountered during PDSCOPY processing, the return code for the job step is set to 8.

PROC PDSCOPY Statement

PROC PDSCOPY INDD=*file-specification* OUTDD=*file-specification* <*options*>;

INDD=*file-specification*
  specifies either the fileref or the operating system data set name (enclosed in quotes) of the library to copy. INDD= is required.

OUTDD=*file-specification*
  specifies either the fileref or the operating system data set name (enclosed in quotes) of the output partitioned data set. OUTDD= is required.

Options
Some of the options that can appear in the PROC PDSCOPY statement apply to both source libraries and load module libraries. Others apply only to load module libraries. The following options apply to both source libraries and load module libraries:

ALIASMATCH=TTR	NEWMOD	OUTTAPE
BLKSIZE=	NOALIAS	SHAREINPUT
INTAPE	NOREPLACE	

The following options apply only to load module libraries:

ALIASMATCH=BOTH|EITHER|NAME	MAXBLOCK=
DC	NE
DCBS|NODCBS	NOTEST

All the options that can appear in the PROC PDSCOPY statement are discussed in this section. In the discussion, the term *member* refers to both source library members and to load modules. The term *module* refers only to load modules.

ALIASMATCH=BOTH | EITHER | NAME | TTR

specifies how to match aliases with main members to determine whether they represent the same member.

BOTH

specifies that both the TTR (relative track and record) values and the names must match in order for a main module to be considered a match.

EITHER

specifies that a match for either the TTR value or the name is sufficient to identify the main module that corresponds to an alias. If more than one main module directory entry matches, it is impossible to predict which one will be used.

NAME

specifies that the main module name in the directory entry for the alias (at offset 36) is compared with main module names to find a match. The alias is assumed to represent the same module as the main module that has the matching name. When you specify ALIASMATCH=NAME, the TTR values do not need to match.

A situation in which names match even though TTR values do not match occurs when the main module is originally link edited specifying the alias names, and then link edited again without specifying them. In this case, the directory entries for the aliases still point to the old version of the module (that is, to a back-level version). Because of this, you should consider carefully whether to use the ALIASMATCH=NAME option or the NEWMOD option. ALIASMATCH=NAME updates the aliases to point to the current version of the main module rather than to the back-level version. The NEWMOD option causes the older version of the module to copy. Another alternative is to use TTR matching and not to copy the aliases when they are, in fact, obsolete names.

TTR

specifies that TTR values are compared. TTR is the default. An alias is assumed to represent the main member that has the same TTR value. If the TTR values match, then the directory entry for the main member and the alias currently point to the same place in the data set.

For load modules, the most common situation in which TTR values might match, but names may not match, occurs when the main module was renamed (for example, by using ISPF option 3.1) after the aliases were created. The alias directory entries may still contain the old main module name.

Whichever method you use, unmatched aliases are not copied to the output file unless you specify the NEWMOD option (described later in this section). Matched aliases in the output file always point to the main module to which they were matched (that is, they have the same TTR values), even if the TTR values were different in the input file (which might occur if ALIASMATCH=NAME or ALIASMATCH=EITHER was used). When modules are matched using the TTR values (that is, when TTR or EITHER was specified), the main module name in alias directory entries is changed in the output file.

BLKSIZE=*block-size*

specifies the maximum block size to use for reblocking the copied load modules on the output device. If the BLKSIZE= option is omitted, the default depends on the type of the output device and on the data set type:

PDSCOPY *continued*

□   If output is to tape, the default is 32,760.

□   If output is in tape (sequential) format on disk (that is, when the OUTTAPE option is used), the default is either the device track size or 32,760, whichever is less.

□   If output is to disk, the default depends on the device type. However, it is never greater than 18K unless you use the MAXBLOCK= option (described later in this section). In addition, the default cannot exceed the device track size or 32,760, whichever is less.

□   Unless the NODCBS option (described later) is specified and the output data set is a partitioned data set on disk, the default value is reduced to the data set control block (DSCB) block size of the partitioned data set, if that is smaller.

For tape (sequential) format output, the specified block size cannot be less than 1.125 times the maximum input device block size, nor greater than 32,760. For disk output, the specified block size cannot be less than 1,024.

DC

specifies that load modules that are marked downward compatible (that is, modules that can be processed by linkage editors that were used before MVS) are eligible for processing. After they are copied by PROC PDSCOPY, the load modules are not marked DC in their directory entry, because PROC PDSCOPY does not produce downward compatible load modules nor does it preserve their attributes. If you do not specify the DC option and you attempt to copy load modules marked DC, PROC PDSCOPY issues an error message.

DCBS | NODCBS

tells SAS whether to preserve the data control block (DCB) characteristics of the output partitioned data set on disk. If NODCBS is specified, the data control block (DCB) characteristics of the output partitioned data set on disk can be overridden. The default value is DCBS.

If the NODCBS option is specified, PROC PDSCOPY changes the DSCB (data set control block) block size of the output partitioned data set to the maximum permissible block size for the device. Otherwise, the maximum permissible value of the BLKSIZE= option is the current block size value from the DSCB, and the DSCB block size is not changed.

Using the NODCBS option may enable PROC PDSCOPY to block output load modules more efficiently. However, changing the DSCB block size could cause problems when the data set is moved, copied, or backed up by a program other than PROC PDSCOPY, particularly if your installation has more than one type of disk drive. Consult your systems staff before specifying NODCBS.

INTAPE

specifies that the INDD= library is in tape (sequential) format. The INTAPE option is assumed if a tape drive is allocated to the input data set.

MAXBLOCK=*block-size* | MAXBLK=*block-size*

enables you to override the limitation of 18K on the block size of text records in the output library. (The value of BLKSIZE must be greater than or equal to the value of MAXBLOCK in order to get text records at MAXBLOCK size.) If the value of MAXBLOCK is not specified, then the maximum block size for text records is 18K; this is the largest text block that can be handled by the FETCH program on many MVS systems. You can specify a block size greater than 18K for text records, but doing so may cause copied modules to ABEND with an ABEND code of 0C4 or 106-E when they are executed. You should use this parameter only if you are sure that your operating system (or TP monitor) FETCH program supports text blocks that are larger than 18K. CICS and MVS/XA FETCH programs, for example, support text blocks that are larger than 18K.

NE

specifies that the output library should not contain records that are used in the link editing process. Although programs in the output library are executable, they cannot be reprocessed by the linkage editor, nor can they be modified by the AMASPZAP program. Using the NE option can reduce the amount of disk space that is required for the output library.

NEWMOD

specifies that aliases that do not match a main member are to be copied as main members rather than being marked as aliases in the output file. The directory entry in the output file is reformatted to main member format. See the ALIASMATCH option for a description of how aliases are matched with main members. If you do not specify the NEWMOD option, unmatched aliases are not copied to the output file.

NOALIAS | NOA

prevents automatic copying of all aliases of each member that you have selected for copying. Any aliases that you want to copy must be named in the SELECT statement. If you select only an alias of a member, the member (that is, the main member name) is still automatically copied, along with the selected alias.

NOREPLACE | NOR

copies only members in the INDD= library that are not found in the OUTDD= library; that is, members or aliases that have the same name are not replaced.

NOTEST

deletes the symbol records produced by the assembler TEST option from the copied load modules. Using the NOTEST option can reduce the amount of disk space that is required for the output library by 10% to 20%.

OUTTAPE

specifies that the OUTDD= library is to be in tape (sequential) format. The OUTTAPE option is assumed if a tape drive is allocated to the output data set.

SHAREINPUT | SHAREIN

specifies that the INDD= library is to be shared with other jobs and TSO users. SHAREINPUT is the default for PDSCOPY when the INDD= library is enqueued for shared control (DISP=SHR). This means that the INDD= library is shared with ISPF and the linkage editor rather than being enqueued exclusively. This makes it possible for more than one person to use an INDD= library simultaneously. (The OUTDD= library is always enqueued for exclusive control against ISPF and the linkage editor; therefore, it cannot be changed while PROC PDSCOPY is processing it.)

EXCLUDE Statement

EXCLUDE *member-name-1 <. . . member-name-n>*;

Use this statement if you want to exclude certain members from the copying operation. The EXCLUDE statement is useful if you want to copy more members than you want to exclude. All members that are not listed in EXCLUDE statements are copied. You can specify as many EXCLUDE statements as necessary.

PDSCOPY *continued*

If you follow a specification in the EXCLUDE statement with a colon (:), then all members whose names begin with the characters preceding the colon are excluded.

Note: You cannot use both the SELECT statement and the EXCLUDE statement in one PROC PDSCOPY step.

SELECT Statement

SELECT *member-name-1 <. . . member-name-n>*;

Use this statement to specify the names of members to copy if you do not want to copy the entire library. You can specify as many SELECT statements as necessary.

If you follow a specification in the SELECT statement with a colon (:), then all members whose names begin with the characters preceding the colon are copied. In the following example all members whose names begin with the characters FCS are copied:

```
select fcs:;
```

Note: You cannot use both the SELECT statement and the EXCLUDE statement in one PROC PDSCOPY step.

Output Data Set

The PDSCOPY procedure produces an output partitioned data set on disk or on tape. The output data set contains copies of the requested members of the input partitioned data set.

If you use PROC PDSCOPY to copy partitioned data sets that contain source members, then the RECFM and LRECL of the output data set must match those of the input data set. If they differ, an error message is displayed. The BLKSIZE values for the input and output data sets do not have to be the same, however.

Usage Notes

If a member that you specified in a SELECT statement does not exist, PROC PDSCOPY issues a warning message and continues processing.

PROC PDSCOPY enqueues the input and output data sets using the SPFEDIT and SPFDSN QNAMEs.

Output

The PDSCOPY procedure writes the following information to the SAS log:

□ INPUT and OUTPUT, the data set names and volume serials of the input and output libraries

□ MEMBER, a list of the members copied

□ ALIAS, the members' aliases, if any

□ whether the copied members replaced others members of the same name

□ whether a selected member or alias was not copied and a note explaining why not.

If the output device is a disk, PROC PDSCOPY also writes the following information next to each member name:

□   TRACKS, the size of the member, in tenths of tracks

□   SIZE, the number of bytes in the member that was copied (in decimal notation).

Example of Copying Members Using the PDSCOPY Procedure

The following example copies all members and aliases that start with the letters OUT. In this example, the alias must match the main member both by name and by TTR in order for the alias to be copied.

```
filename old 'userid.mvs.output' disp=shr;
filename new 'userid.mvs.output2' disp=old;

proc pdscopy indd=old outdd=new aliasmatch=both shareinput;
   select out:;
run;
```

Output 18.9 shows the results.

Output 18.9
PDSCOPY
Procedure Example

```
1    filename old 'userid.mvs.output' disp=shr;
2    filename new 'userid.mvs.output2' disp=shr;
3
4    proc pdscopy indd=old outdd=new aliasmatch=both shareinput;
5       select out:;
6    run;

     SAS PROC PDSCOPY VERSION 6.09    02/16/96

     INPUT   DSNAME=USERID.MVS.OUTPUT    VOL=SER=XXXXXX
     OUTPUT  DSNAME=USERID.MVS.OUTPUT2   VOL=SER=XXXXXX

     MEMBER      TRACKS       SIZE
       ALIAS

     OUT1601      0.1        1600 replaced
     OUT1602      0.5       20560 replaced
     OUT1603      0.3       12720 replaced

     TRACKS USED      0.9
            UNUSED    1.1
             TOTAL    2.0
     EXTENTS          1
```

PMENU

Defines PMENU facilities for user-defined windows

MVS Specifics: Some statements are ignored.

MVS Specifics

The following statements and options are accepted without generating errors, but *with current device drivers* they have no effect under MVS:

□   SEPARATOR statement

□   ACCELERATE= option in the ITEM statement

□   MNEMONIC= option in the ITEM statement

□   HELP= option in the DIALOG statement.

See Also

□   *SAS Procedures Guide*

PRINTTO

Defines destinations for SAS procedure output and for the SAS log

MVS Specifics: UNIT= option; output destination

MVS Specifics

In the SAS CLIST and the SAS cataloged procedure that are supplied by SAS Institute, no filerefs of the form FT*nn*F001 are predefined for the UNIT= option. Ask your SAS Software Representative whether your site has predefined DDnames of the form FT*nn*F001.

Under MVS, the destination of the procedure output or the SAS log can be specified by either of the following:

fileref
sends the log or procedure output to a sequential data set or member of a partitioned data set that is identified by the fileref.

'*OS-data-set-name*'
sends the log or procedure output to a sequential data set or to a member of a partitioned data set.

The following restrictions apply to PROC PRINTTO under MVS:

□   When writing log or procedure output files to a *partitioned* data set member, you must specify the NEW option; you cannot append data to a partitioned data set member.

□   If you create a file to be used with the PRINTTO procedure and specify a record format that has no carriage control characters, the PROC PRINTTO output will not include carriage control characters.

□ In order to simultaneously route both the SAS log and procedure output files to partitioned data set members, the members must be in different partitioned data sets. SAS does not allow you to write to two members of one partitioned data set at the same time.

See Also

□ "Routing to External Files with the PRINTTO Procedure" on page 95

□ "Using the PRINTTO Procedure" on page 98

□ "Routing Output to a Remote Destination" on page 101

□ *SAS Language and Procedures*

□ *SAS Procedures Guide*

RELEASE

Releases unused space at the end of a disk data set

MVS Specifics: all

Syntax

PROC RELEASE   DDNAME=*file-specification* *<options>*;

Description

PROC RELEASE can be used with most sequential or partitioned data sets, not just with a SAS data library that contains SAS data sets. However, it cannot be used to release unused space from the SAS WORK data library, from ISAM or VSAM data sets, nor from multivolume disk-format SAS data libraries.

If you delete some members from a SAS data library (using the DATASETS procedure, for example), you can use the RELEASE procedure to release the unused space at the end of the last member. You cannot use RELEASE to release embedded space. That is, you can release only unused space that follows the highest track or block that is currently in use, as indicated by the CONTENTS or DATASETS procedure.

In order to use PROC RELEASE on a SAS data library, the data library must be closed. If the library is open, SAS generates an error message. If you have assigned a libref to the data library and have used some members of that library in your SAS session, the library will be open. To close it, issue a LIBNAME statement of the following form:

  LIBNAME *libref* CLEAR;

Then issue a new LIBNAME statement for the data library and immediately run PROC RELEASE. As an alternative to issuing a second LIBNAME statement, you can simply specify the data library's name (enclosed in quotes) as the value of the DDNAME= option in the PROC RELEASE statement, instead of using a libref.

RELEASE *continued*

In the control language, you can release unused space by using specifications such as SPACE=(,,RLSE) in the DD statement (in batch mode), or you can use the RELEASE operand of the TSO ALLOCATE command. However, releasing unused space with PROC RELEASE offers several advantages over methods provided by the operating system. For example, with PROC RELEASE, the user, not the operating system, controls when unused space is released. This advantage is especially applicable to TSO users.

Another advantage of PROC RELEASE is that you can use PROC RELEASE options to specify exactly how many tracks you want to keep or release. There is no danger of erasing all or part of a data set, because PROC RELEASE frees only unused space. PROC RELEASE returns unused space to the pool of available space on the disk volume. Once released, the space is still available for allocation to the data set, provided a secondary space allocation is given for the data set in the control language or SAS statement, and provided all free space on the volume is not subsequently allocated to other data sets.

PROC RELEASE Statement

PROC RELEASE DDNAME=*file-specification* *<options>*;

DDNAME=*file-specification*
    specifies either an operating system data set name (enclosed in quotes) or a fileref that refers to the operating system data set from which to release unused space. DDNAME= is required.

options
    specify how much unused space to keep or release and specify the unit boundary on which the data set should end.

□   Use one of the following options to specify how much space to keep in or to release from the data set:

TOTAL=*number* | TRACKS=*number*
    specifies the total number of tracks that the data set should contain after unused space is released, that is, after PROC RELEASE has executed. For example, the following statement releases all but ten tracks for the data set that is referenced by the fileref SURVEY:

```
proc release ddname=survey total=10;
```

The procedure calculates the amount of space to release as follows:

amount of space allocated − (value of TOTAL= option) =
    amount of unused space released

If the value that you specify is smaller than the amount of used space in the data set, then SAS releases only the unused space at the end of the data set.

UNUSED=*number*
    specifies the number of tracks of unused space that the data set should contain after PROC RELEASE has executed. The procedure calculates the amount of unused space to release as follows:

amount of space allocated − (used space + value of UNUSED= option) = amount of unused space released

If the value that you specify is greater than the amount of unused space at the end of the data set, then no space is released at the end of the data set.

RELEASE=*number*
specifies how many tracks of unused space to release. If the value that you specify is greater than the amount of unused space at the end of the data set, then SAS releases all the unused space at the end of the data set.

EXTENTS | EXTENT | EX
tells SAS to release only the space that is allocated to completely unused secondary extents. After the procedure releases unused space from the data set, the size of the data set is the sum of the primary extent plus all used secondary extents.

If you do not specify one of these options in the PROC RELEASE statement, then all unused space at the end of the data set is released.

□ Use the following option to specify the unit boundary on which the data set should end:

BOUNDARY=*type* **| TYPE=***type*
specifies whether the data set will end on a track boundary or on a cylinder boundary.
After the total amount of space to be retained is calculated, this amount is rounded up to the next unit boundary. Any remaining space is then released. Remember that the total amount of space will include the space that is actually used and may also include unused space that was requested with other options. BOUNDARY=*type* then will increase the amount of unused space that is retained in the data set by the portion of the unit that is needed in order to reach (or round up to) the next boundary. *Type* can be one of the following:

DATASET | DSCB
specifies that the data set will end on the next track or cylinder boundary depending on how space is currently allocated. If allocated in tracks, the total amount of space to be retained is calculated, and remaining unused tracks are released. If allocated in cylinders, the space to be retained is rounded up to the next cylinder boundary, and remaining unused space is released. This is the default boundary type.

CYLINDERS | CYLINDER | CYLS | CYL
specifies that space to be retained is rounded to the next cylinder boundary before remaining unused space is released. This specification is effective only if the data set is currently allocated in multiples of cylinders.

TRACKS | TRACK | TRKS | TRK
specifies that unused tracks are to be released. Because the minimum unit of space that can be released is a track, the space to be retained is not rounded up.

ALLOC | DD | JCL
specifies that space to be retained is rounded to the next unit boundary (tracks or cylinders) depending on the allocation unit that was specified in the JCL statement, TSO ALLOCATE command, or FILENAME or

RELEASE *continued*

LIBNAME statement. For example, the following, in combination with BOUNDARY=DD, is equivalent to specifying BOUNDARY=CYL:

```
//DD2 DD DISP=OLD,DSN=MY.DATA,SPACE=(CYL,2)
```

Usage Notes

If the messages in the SAS log indicate that no space was released from the data set, check to see whether the data set is allocated to another job or to another user. When PROC RELEASE is invoked, the operating system's disk space management function (DADSM) must be able to obtain exclusive control of the data set. If it cannot, then no indication that DADSM does not have control is passed to the SAS System, no space is released from the data set, and no error message is issued by the SAS System.

Output

PROC RELEASE writes the following information to the SAS log:

□ how many tracks were allocated to the data set before and after the procedure was executed

□ how many tracks were used

□ how many extents were used.

Example

The following example releases the unused secondary extents for an operating system data set that is referenced by the fileref THISFILE:

```
filename thisfile 'OS-data-set-name';

proc release ddname=thisfile extents;
run;
```

References

□ IBM's *MVS JCL Reference, MVS/ESA JCL Reference,* and *MVS/XA JCL Reference*

SORT

Sorts observations in a SAS data set according to the values of one or more variables

MVS Specifics: available MVS sort utilities and SORT procedure statement options; MVS system options

MVS Specifics

You can direct the SORT procedure to use either the SAS sort program, which is available under MVS and under all other operating systems, or a sort utility that is specific to MVS. You can also use the SORTPGM= system option to tell SAS to choose the best sort program to use. (See "SORTPGM=" on page 379.)

The following SAS system options also affect any sorting that is done by the SAS System:

DYNALLOC	SORTLIST	SORTSIZE=
FILSZ	SORTMSG	SORTSUMF
SORT=	SORTMSG=	SORTUNIT=
SORTANOM=	SORTNAME=	SORTWKDD=
SORTCUTP=	SORTOPTS	SORTWKNO=
SORTDEV=	SORTPARM=	SORT31PL
SORTEQOP	SORTPGM=	
SORTLIB=	SORTSHRB	

SORT Procedure Statement Options

The following host-specific sort options are available in the PROC SORT statement under MVS in addition to the sort options that are available under all host operating systems. The list includes the portable EQUALS option because it has aspects that are specific to MVS.

DIAG
    passes the DIAG parameter to the sort utility. If the utility supports this option, then it will produce additional diagnostic information if the sort fails.

EQUALS
    passes the EQUALS parameter to the sort utility program whether or not the sort utility supports it. The SAS System defaults to EQUALS by passing the parameter to the utility if the SAS system option SORTEQOP is in effect.

LEAVE=*n*
    specifies how many bytes to leave unallocated in the region. Occasionally, the SORT procedure runs out of main storage. If this happens, rerun the job and increase the LEAVE= value (which has a default value of 16000) by 30000.

LIST | L
    provides additional information about the system sort. Not all sort utilities support the specification of the LIST option; they may require that it be specified when the sort utility is generated or installed. This option is the default action if the SAS system option SORTLIST is in effect. Also, this option overrides NOSORTLIST if it is in effect.

MESSAGE | M
    prints a summary of the system sort utility's actions. This option is the default action if the SAS system option SORTMSG is in effect. Also, this option overrides NOSORTMSG if it is in effect. MESSAGE is useful if you run PROC SORT and the SAS log prints a message indicating that the sort did not work properly. Explanations of the message can be found in the IBM or vendor reference manual that describes your system sort utility.

SORT *continued*

SORTSIZE=*n* | *n*K | MAX | SIZE
SIZE=*n* | *n*K | MAX | SIZE
    specifies the maximum virtual storage that can be used by the system sort utility. If not specified, the default is given by the SAS system option SORTSIZE=.

SORTWKNO=*n*
    specifies how many sort work areas PROC SORT allocates. If not specified, the default is given by the SAS system option SORTWKNO=.

TECHNIQUE=*xxxx* | T=*xxxx*
    specifies a four-character sort technique to be passed to the system sort utility. SAS does not check the validity of the specified value, so you must ensure that it is correct.

See Also

□ Chapter 20, "System Options," for descriptions of system options

□ "Efficient Sorting" on page 157

□ *SAS Language and Procedures*

□ *SAS Procedures Guide*

SOURCE

Provides an easy way to back up and process source library data sets

MVS Specifics: all

Syntax

PROC SOURCE *<options>*;
    SELECT *member-1 <...member-n>*;
    EXCLUDE *member-1 <...member-n>*;
    FIRST *'model-control-statement'*;
    LAST *'model-control-statement'*;
    BEFORE *'model-control-statement'* *<options>*;
    AFTER *'model-control-statement'* *<options>*;

Description

You can use the SOURCE procedure to

□ write the contents of an entire library to the SAS log.

□ process only the directory of a library in order to produce input for the SAS System, for a utility, or for other programs.

□ route the members of a library to other programs for processing. By default, PROC SOURCE generates records for the IBM utility, IEBUPDTE, which reloads an unloaded data set.

□   create a sequential, or unloaded, version of the library's directory records.

□   construct an unloaded data set from a library. The unloaded data set is suitable for reloading by IEBUPDTE or other source library maintenance utilities, including the ability to recognize and properly handle aliases.

Using the SOURCE procedure, a source library can be copied into a sequential tape or disk data set to create either a backup or a manually transportable copy of the source data. This copy is called an *unloaded data set*; it consists of 80-byte records that contain the source data and the control information that are needed to restore the source to its original organization. When an unloaded data set is restored by the proper utility to a device that will support the data in their original form, the data are reconstructed, or *loaded*.

An advantage of having an unloaded data set is that one or more members can be retrieved without reloading the entire library.

PROC SOURCE has several advantages over IBM's IEBPTPCH utility. With PROC SOURCE you can

□   list members in alphabetical order

□   select members by specifying a wildcard or range

□   list the number of records in each member

□   list each member on a new page

□   produce an unloaded version of the library that can be ported to some other host systems.

The *model-control-statements* in the FIRST, LAST, BEFORE, and AFTER statements are usually either utility or job control statements, depending on the destination given by the OUTDD= option in the PROC SOURCE statement.

PROC SOURCE Statement

PROC SOURCE *<options>*;

The following options are used in the PROC SOURCE statement:

DIRDD=*file-specification*
>   specifies either the fileref or operating system data set name of the output data set to which PROC SOURCE writes a sequential, unloaded form of the PDS directory. Each directory record is written into one 80-byte record. Records are left-aligned and padded on the right with blanks. If specified, the fileref must match the reference name that was used in the FILENAME statement, JCL DD statement, or TSO ALLOCATE command that allocated the output data set.
>
>   **Note:**   The SELECT and EXCLUDE statements have no effect when the DIRDD= option is specified.

INDD=*file-specification*
>   specifies the fileref or the operating system data set name of an input PDS. The fileref, if specified, must match the reference name that was specified in the FILENAME statement, JCL DD statement, or TSO ALLOCATE command that allocated the input library. If the INDD= option is not specified, the default fileref is SOURCE.

SOURCE   *continued*

If OUTDD is specified, then the RECFM of the INDD file must be either F or FB. The fileref may not refer to a concatenation of data sets. If it does, then an error message is generated. If the member names in the INDD file are nonstandard, then specify FILEEXT=ASIS in an OPTIONS statement.

MAXIOERROR=*n*

specifies the maximum number of I/O errors to allow before terminating. Normally, PROC SOURCE detects, issues a warning message about, and then ignores I/O errors that occur while reading the library members. When the number of errors specified by MAXIOERROR= has occurred, however, PROC SOURCE assumes that the library is unreadable and stops. The default MAXIOERROR= value is 50.

NOALIAS

treats aliases as main member names. Therefore, PROC SOURCE does not generate . / ALIAS cards or alias BEFORE and AFTER cards.

NODATA

specifies that you do not want to read the members in the input library. In other words, PROC SOURCE produces only control statements and a list of the member names; it does not produce the member source records. The list of member names includes any aliases. NODATA is particularly useful when you want to process only the directory of a library.

NOPRINT

specifies that you do not want to generate the list of member names and record counts. (These listings are produced even when the PRINT option is not specified.) The NOPRINT option is ignored when PRINT is specified.

NOSUMMARY

specifies that you do not want to generate the member summary. The NOSUMMARY option is ignored when the NODATA, NOPRINT, or PRINT option is specified.

NOTSORTED

causes PROC SOURCE to process library members in the order in which they either appear (in SELECT statements) or remain (after EXCLUDE statements). Normally, PROC SOURCE processes (that is, unloads, writes to the SAS log, and so on) the library members in alphabetical order by member name.

NULL

specifies that null members (library members that contain no records, just an immediate end-of-file) should be processed. Such members occasionally appear in source libraries, but they are not normally unloaded because IEBUPDTE and most other source library maintenance utilities do not create null members. If you are using a source library maintenance utility that can properly recognize and create a null member, then specify this option and provide the appropriate BEFORE (and possibly, AFTER) statements.

OUTDD=*file-specification*

specifies the fileref or the operating system data set name of the output file to which PROC SOURCE writes the unloaded (sequential) form of the input library and any records that FIRST, LAST, BEFORE and AFTER statements generate. If specified, the fileref must match the reference name used in the FILENAME statement, JCL DD statement, or TSO ALLOCATE command that allocated the data set. This option cannot be used when the INDD file contains variable-length records.

PAGE
   begins the listing of each member on a new page.

PRINT
   lists the entire library. The PRINT option is ignored when NODATA is specified.

SELECT Statement

SELECT *member-1 < . . . member-n>*;

When you use the SELECT statement, only the members that you specify are processed. You can use any number of SELECT statements.
   Use a colon (:) to indicate that you want to select all members whose names begin with the characters that precede the colon. (See the second example below.)
   You can include an alphabetic range of names in the SELECT statement by joining two names with a hyphen (-). The two hyphenated members and all members in between are processed. For example, if a library contains members called BROWN, GRAY, GREEN, RED, and YELLOW, and you want to process the first four members, use this SELECT statement:

```
select brown-red;
```

The colon (:) and hyphen (-) notation can be used together. For example, the following statement produces the same results as the previous SELECT statement:

```
select br:-gr: red;
```

EXCLUDE Statement

EXCLUDE *member-1 < . . . member-n>*;

When you use the EXCLUDE statement, all members except those that you specify are processed. You can use any number of EXCLUDE statements.
   Use a colon (:) to indicate that you want to exclude all members whose names begin with the characters that precede the colon.
   You can include an alphabetic range of names in the EXCLUDE statement by joining two names with a hyphen. The two hyphenated members and all members in between are excluded from processing. (See the SELECT examples in the SELECT statement description.)
   The colon and hyphen notation can be used together. (See the second SELECT statement example.)
   Note: Sometimes it is convenient to use SELECT and EXCLUDE statements together. For example, you can use the colon or hyphen notation in a SELECT statement to select many members, then use the EXCLUDE statement to exclude a few of the selected members. Suppose there are 200 members called SMC1 through SMC200, and you want to copy all of them except SMC30 through SMC34. You could use these statements:

```
select smc:;
exclude smc30-smc34;
```

SOURCE *continued*

When you use both EXCLUDE and SELECT statements, the EXCLUDE statements should specify only members that are specified by the SELECT statements. However, excluding unselected members has no effect other than to generate warning messages.

FIRST Statement

FIRST '*model-control-statement*';

The FIRST statement generates initial control statements that invoke a utility program or that are needed only once. The specified *model-control-statement* is reproduced, left-aligned, on a record that precedes all members in the unloaded data set. You can use any number of FIRST statements. One FIRST statement can specify one model control statement. Each model control statement generates a record.

LAST Statement

LAST '*model-control-statement*';

The LAST statement generates final control statements that terminate a utility program or that are needed only once. The specified *model-control-statement* is reproduced, left-aligned, on a record that follows all members in the unloaded data set. You can use any number of LAST statements. One LAST statement can specify one model control statement. Each model control statement generates a record.

BEFORE Statement

BEFORE '*model-control-statement*' <*options*>;

The BEFORE statement generates a utility control statement before each member. You can use any number of BEFORE statements. One BEFORE statement can specify one model control statement. Each *model-control-statement* that you specify is reproduced, left-aligned, on a record that precedes each member in the unloaded data set.

By default, PROC SOURCE generates control statements for the IBM IEBUPDTE utility program before each member of an unloaded data set. You can use the BEFORE and AFTER statements to override the default and generate control statements for other utility programs. To prevent PROC SOURCE from generating these statements, use the BEFORE statement with no parameters.

Options for the BEFORE and AFTER statements are the same. A list of these options follows the description of the AFTER statement.

AFTER Statement

AFTER '*model-control-statement*' <*options*>;

The AFTER statement generates a utility control statement after each member. You can use any number of AFTER statements. One AFTER statement can specify one model control statement. Each *model-control-statement* that you specify is reproduced, left-aligned, on a record that follows each member in the unloaded data set.

By default, PROC SOURCE generates control statements for the IBM IEBUPDTE utility program after each member of an unloaded data set. You can use the AFTER statement to override the default and generate control statements for other utility programs.

The following options are used in the BEFORE and AFTER statements:

ALIAS
>   tells SAS to produce a record containing the *model-control-statement* only for each defined alias. (The alias is placed into the record at the specified column, if any.)

column number
>   tells SAS to substitute the member name in records that are generated by BEFORE and AFTER statements in an 8 byte field beginning in this column. The beginning column can be any column from 1 to 73. Aliases, as well as main member names, are substituted. The name is left-aligned in the field unless the RIGHT option is specified, and it is padded on the right with blanks unless the NOBLANK option is specified.

NOBLANK
>   is meaningful only if *column number* is specified. When the member name is substituted in records that are generated by the BEFORE and AFTER statements, NOBLANK eliminates blanks between the end of the member and any text that follows. In the following record, a member name precedes the text; NOBLANK has *not* been specified:

```
name ,text text text
```

>   When NOBLANK is specified, the same record looks like this:

```
name,text text text
```

RIGHT
>   is meaningful only if *column number* is specified. When the member name is substituted in records that are generated by the BEFORE and AFTER statements, RIGHT causes the member name to be right-aligned in the specified field. By default, the name is left-aligned in an eight-column field.

Output

PROC SOURCE writes the following information to the SAS log:

□   the entire library, if the PRINT option is specified

□   a listing of the member names in the library (unless you specify NOPRINT)

□   the number of records for each member (unless you specify NOPRINT or NODATA)

□   a summary of the attributes and contents of the library.

SOURCE   *continued*

Even when PRINT is not specified, some records may still be written to the log. The signal NAME: or ENTRY: or AUTHOR: beginning in column 5 of a record in the library starts the listing; the signal END beginning in column 5 stops it. If you do not want SAS to list this subset of records, specify the NOSUMMARY option.

Example of Printing Selected Members from a PDS

The following example writes to the SAS log the member ORANGES4 from the source library USERID.TASTE.TEST:

```
proc source indd='userid.taste.test' print;
   select oranges4;
run;
```

The log is shown in Output 18.10.

Output 18.10
Selecting a Member
from a Source
Statement Library

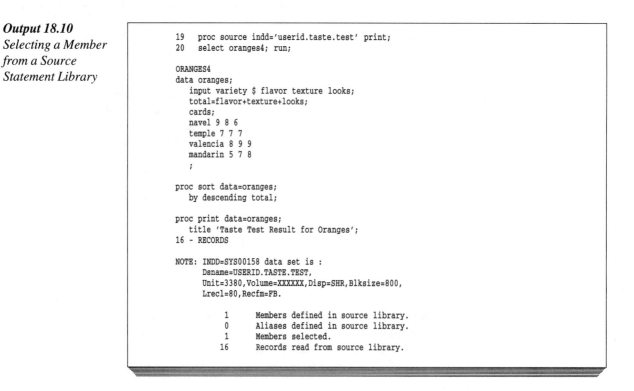

```
19   proc source indd='userid.taste.test' print;
20   select oranges4; run;

ORANGES4
data oranges;
   input variety $ flavor texture looks;
   total=flavor+texture+looks;
   cards;
   navel 9 8 6
   temple 7 7 7
   valencia 8 9 9
   mandarin 5 7 8
   ;

proc sort data=oranges;
   by descending total;

proc print data=oranges;
   title 'Taste Test Result for Oranges';
16 - RECORDS

NOTE: INDD=SYS00158 data set is :
      Dsname=USERID.TASTE.TEST,
      Unit=3380,Volume=XXXXXX,Disp=SHR,Blksize=800,
      Lrecl=80,Recfm=FB.

         1      Members defined in source library.
         0      Aliases defined in source library.
         1      Members selected.
        16      Records read from source library.
```

Example of Building and Submitting a Job to Assemble Programs

The following PROC SOURCE program builds and submits a job to compile assembler programs. It writes the output directly to the internal reader so that the compile job can be executed.

```
filename out sysout=a pgm=intrdr lrecl=80 recfm=f;
proc source indd='userid.asm.src' nodata outdd=out;
    first '//COMPILE JOB (0,ROOM),''DUMMY'',';
    first '// NOTIFY=,REGION=4M,TYPRUN=HOLD';
    first '/*JOBPARM FETCH';
    last  '//';
    before '//XXXXXXXX EXEC ASMHCL,MAC2=''XXX.MACLIB'' ' 3;
    before '//SYSIN DD DSN=USERID.ASM.SRC(XXXXXXXX),DISP=SHR' 31 NOBLANK;
run;
```

The output that is written to the internal reader is shown in Output 18.11. Note that this output shows only the statements that are generated by PROC SOURCE, before they are executed.

Output 18.11
Building and
Submitting a Job to
Assemble Programs

```
//COMPILE JOB (0,ROOM),'DUMMY',
// NOTIFY=,REGION=4M,TYPRUN=HOLD
/*JOBPARM FETCH
//OUT1601  EXEC ASMHCL,MAC2='XXX.MACLIB'
//SYSIN DD DSN=USERID.ASM.SRC(OUT1601),DISP=SHR
//OUT1602  EXEC ASMHCL,MAC2='XXX.MACLIB'
//SYSIN DD DSN=USERID.ASM.SRC(OUT1602),DISP=SHR
//OUT1603  EXEC ASMHCL,MAC2='XXX.MACLIB'
//SYSIN DD DSN=USERID.ASM.SRC(OUT1603),DISP=SHR
//
```

Example of Producing Directory Records

The following PROC SOURCE program produces directory records. The subsequent DATA step extracts the ISPF statistics, if any are present.

```
filename indd 'userid.sas.src' disp=shr;
filename out  '&temp';

/* Build directory records. */
proc source indd=indd nodata noprint dirdd=out;

/* Read directory records and extract ISPF statistics. */
data test;
infile out;
file print header=h;
input member $8. ttr pib3. ind pib1. @;
datalen = 2*mod(ind,32);
if (datalen = 30)
then do;
   input ver pib1. mod pib1. blank pib2. create pd4.
        changed pd4. hh pk1. mm pk1. size pib2. init pib2.
        modl pib2. userid $8.;
   jcreate = datejul(create);
   jchange = datejul(changed);
```

SOURCE *continued*

```
/* Print the results. */
  put @4 member $8.
      @15 jcreate yymmdd8.
      @25 jchange yymmdd8.
      @35 hh 2. ':' mm 2.
      @44 userid;
end;
return;
h:
put @4 'NAME '
    @15 'CREATED'
    @25 'CHANGED'
    @35 'TIME'
    @44 ' ID ';
put;
return;
run;
```

Output 18.12 shows the results.

Output 18.12
Producing Directory
Records

```
                          The SAS System

   NAME      CREATED   CHANGED   TIME     ID

   OUT1601   96-02-20  96-02-20  10:50    USERID
   OUT1602   96-02-20  96-02-20  10:54    USERID
   OUT1603   96-02-20  96-02-20  10:59    USERID
```

Example of Generating Control Cards for IEBCOPY

This example first produces control statements for the IBM utility program, IEBCOPY.
Then IEBCOPY executes, copying selected members.

```
//IEBPDS JOB (0,ROOM),'USERID',
//  NOTIFY=,REGION=4096K
/*JOBPARM FETCH
//    EXEC SAS
//IN DD DSN=XXX.SUBLIB,DISP=SHR
//OUT DD DSN=&&TEMP,SPACE=(CYL,(1,2)),DISP=(,PASS),UNIT=DISK
//SYSIN DD *
  proc source indd=in outdd=out nodata  noprint;
  select hc:;
  select lm:;
  select sasextrn;
  first ' COPY INDD=IN,OUTDD=NEWPDS';
  before '  SELECT MEMBER=XXXXXXXX -----------' 17;
  before '      S      M=XXXXXXXX ***ALIAS***' 17 ALIAS;
```

```
//S1     EXEC PGM=IEBCOPY
//SYSPRINT DD SYSOUT=A
//IN       DD DSN=XXX.SUBLIB,DISP=SHR
//NEWPDS DD DSN=&&NEW,SPACE=(CYL,(20,10,20)),UNIT=DISK
//SYSUT1 DD UNIT=DISK,SPACE=(CYL,(2,3))
//SYSUT2 DD UNIT=DISK,SPACE=(CYL,(2,3))
//SYSUT3 DD UNIT=DISK,SPACE=(CYL,(2,3))
//SYSIN  DD DSN=&&TEMP,DISP=(OLD,DELETE)
```

Output 18.13 shows what is written to the SAS log after PROC SOURCE is run. Output 18.14 shows the IEBCOPY output.

Output 18.13
Producing Control
Statements for the
IEBCOPY Utility

```
1              proc source indd=in outdd=out nodata  noprint;
2              select hc:;
3              select lm:;
4              select sasextrn;
5              first ' COPY INDD=IN,OUTDD=NEWPDS';
6              before '  SELECT MEMBER=XXXXXXXX -----------' 17;
7              before '        S    M=XXXXXXXX ***ALIAS***' 17 ALIAS;

NOTE: INDD=IN data set is :
      Dsname=USERID.DATASET,
      Unit=3380,Volume=XXXXXX,Disp=SHR,Blksize=6160,
      Lrecl=80,Recfm=FB.

NOTE: OUTDD=OUT data set is :
      Dsname=SYS96052.T131013.RA000.IEBPDS.TEMP,
      Unit=3390,Volume=,Disp=NEW,Blksize=27920,
      Lrecl=80,Recfm=FB.

      9      Members defined in source library.
      0      Aliases defined in source library.
      6      Members selected.
      0      Records read from source library.
```

Output 18.14
IEBCOPY Output:
Selected Members
Copied

```
                    IEBCOPY MESSAGES AND CONTROL STATEMENTS
     COPY INDD=IN,OUTDD=NEWPDS
      SELECT MEMBER=HCMEM1  -----------
      SELECT MEMBER=HCMEM2  -----------
      SELECT MEMBER=HCMEM3  -----------
      SELECT MEMBER=LMMEM1  -----------
      SELECT MEMBER=LMMEM2  -----------
      SELECT MEMBER=SASEXTRN -----------
                        .
                        .
                        .
IEB167I FOLLOWING MEMBER(S) COPIED FROM INPUT DATA SET REFERENCED BY IN
IEB154I HCMEM1   HAS BEEN SUCCESSFULLY COPIED
IEB154I HCMEM2   HAS BEEN SUCCESSFULLY COPIED
IEB154I HCMEM3   HAS BEEN SUCCESSFULLY COPIED
IEB154I LMMEM1   HAS BEEN SUCCESSFULLY COPIED
IEB154I LMMEM2   HAS BEEN SUCCESSFULLY COPIED
IEB154I SASEXTRN HAS BEEN SUCCESSFULLY COPIED
IEB144I THERE ARE 239 UNUSED TRACKS IN OUTPUT DATA SET REFERENCED BY NEWPDS
IEB149I THERE ARE 8 UNUSED DIRECTORY BLOCKS IN OUTPUT DIRECTORY
IEB147I END OF JOB - 0 WAS HIGHEST SEVERITY CODE
```

SOURCE *continued*

References

□ IBM's *MVS/ESA Data Administration: Utilities* and *MVS/XA Data Administration: Utilities*

TAPECOPY

Copies an entire tape volume (tape), or files from one or several tape volumes, to one output tape volume

MVS Specifics: all

Syntax

PROC TAPECOPY *options*;
   INVOL *options*;
   FILES *file-numbers*;

Description

PROC TAPECOPY always begins writing at the beginning of the output tape volume; any files that previously existed on the output tape are destroyed. See "Examples" on page 251 for examples of using PROC TAPECOPY.

   Note: PROC TAPECOPY copies to a *single* output tape volume.

   The TAPECOPY procedure can copy either standard labeled or nonlabeled 9-track tapes. You can specify, within limits, whether the output tape is standard labeled (SL) or nonlabeled (NL). You cannot create an SL tape using an NL input tape, because TAPECOPY cannot manufacture tape labels. Also, if LABEL=(,SL) was specified in a DD statement for an output tape volume, you cannot change that tape into a nonlabeled tape. PROC TAPECOPY does allow you to write over an existing volume label on a standard labeled tape if you specify LABEL=(,BLP) in the DD statement. (The BLP value indicates bypass label processing.)

   The JCL DD statement parameter LABEL=(,BLP) must be authorized specifically by each computing installation. If your installation allows the BLP specification, then ANSI-labeled, non-standard labeled, and standard user-labeled tapes can be treated as nonlabeled tape volumes. If the BLP specification is not authorized at your installation, then LABEL=(,BLP) is treated as LABEL=(,NL). PROC TAPECOPY will work as you expect if your tape is in fact nonlabeled; otherwise, the operating system does not allow TAPECOPY to use the tape, thus preserving the label.

   Throughout this description, references to specifying LABEL=(,BLP) assume that LABEL=(,BLP) is a valid specification at your installation.

▶ *Caution* . . . . *Record lengths cannot exceed 32K bytes.*
PROC TAPECOPY copies up to 32K bytes of data per record, even if the length of the record exceeds 32K. No error message is generated. ▲

Input Tape DD Statement Requirements

In the DD statement that describes an input tape, you need to specify the UNIT, VOL=SER, DISP parameters, and usually either the LABEL or DSN parameter.

VOL=SER gives the volume serial of the first input tape. You can omit VOL=SER if the UNIT parameter specifies deferred mounting—for example, UNIT=(*tape*,,DEFER). If you specify deferred mounting, remember to use the INVOL= option in the PROC TAPECOPY statement or in an INVOL statement to specify the volume serial of the input tape.

For a nonlabeled input tape, you must specify either LABEL=(,NL) or LABEL=(,BLP) in the DD statement. If you are unsure whether the input tape volume is labeled or nonlabeled, specify LABEL=(,BLP) in the input tape DD statement, if your installation allows it.

For a standard labeled input tape at an installation that does not allow LABEL=(,BLP), specify LABEL=(,SL) and the DSN parameter, giving the DSNAME of the first data set on the tape.

Output Tape DD Statement Requirements

In the DD statement that describes the output tape, you usually need to specify only the UNIT, VOL=SER, and DISP parameters, and possibly the LABEL or DSN parameters.

VOL=SER gives the volume serial of the output tape. You can omit VOL=SER if the UNIT parameter specifies deferred mounting—for example, UNIT=(*tape*,,DEFER). If you specify deferred mounting, use the OUTVOL= option in the PROC TAPECOPY statement to specify the volume serial of the output tape.

You should usually specify DISP=(NEW,KEEP) for the output tape in the DD statement. At some installations it may be necessary to specify DISP=(OLD,KEEP) along with the DSN parameter, giving the DSNAME of the first data set on the tape volume. The LABEL parameter should give the tape's label type as it is before the TAPECOPY procedure is executed, regardless of its label type after the copying operation.

Output

The TAPECOPY procedure writes to the SAS log a listing of the input and output tape characteristics plus a summary of the files that were copied.

PROC TAPECOPY Statement

PROC TAPECOPY *options*;

The following options can appear in the PROC TAPECOPY statement. The options are listed alphabetically.

COPYVOLSER

specifies that the output tape should have a standard label with the same volume serial as the first input tape. COPYVOLSER is effective only when both of the following conditions are true:

□ the output tape volume is to be standard labeled—that is, LABEL=SL

□ the output tape DD statement specifies LABEL=(,NL) or LABEL=(,BLP).

If you specify COPYVOLSER and these conditions are not true, PROC TAPECOPY stops processing.

TAPECOPY *continued*

DEN=*density*

specifies the density of the output tape. If the DEN= option appears in the PROC TAPECOPY statement, it overrides any DCB=DEN specification in the DD statement for the output tape volume. If you do not specify a density in the PROC TAPECOPY statement or in the DD statement, the operating system writes the tape at its default density. The default density is usually the highest density at which the unit allocated to the output tape volume can record.

Valid density values are:

Tape Density Value	Tape Volume Type
DEN=2 DEN=800	800 bpi
DEN=3 DEN=1600	1600 bpi
DEN=4 DEN=6250	6250 bpi

INDD=*fileref*

specifies the fileref that is referenced in the JCL DD statement for the first input tape volume. The default INDD= option value is VOLIN.

INVOL=*volume-serial*

specifies the volume serial of the first input tape when deferred mounting is specified in the DD statement for the first input tape. The INVOL= option specification overrides the volume serial, if any, that was specified in the DD statement for the tape.

Specify the INVOL= option only if you are using deferred mounting.

LABEL=SL | NL

specifies whether the output tape volume is to be standard labeled (LABEL=SL) or nonlabeled (LABEL=NL).

Note: Be careful not to confuse the LABEL= option on the PROC TAPECOPY statement with the DD statement parameter LABEL=(, *specification*). The PROC TAPECOPY statement LABEL= option specifies whether the output tape is standard labeled or nonlabeled *after* the copy operation. The output tape volume's DD statement LABEL= parameter specifies what the output tape's label status is *before* the copy operation.

The DD statement for nonlabeled output tapes must specify either LABEL=(,NL) or LABEL=(,BLP). If the output tape has an existing label (before the copy operation) and the output tape is to be nonlabeled (after the copy operation), then the DD statement must specify LABEL=(,BLP).

The default LABEL= option value is NL when multiple input volumes are used and when the DD statements for any of them specify LABEL=(,NL). If there are multiple input tapes and LABEL=(,NL) is not specified for any of them, and if the first input tape volume is actually standard labeled, then the default LABEL= option value is SL. This is true even if the DD statement specifies LABEL=(,BLP) for the first tape; in this case, PROC TAPECOPY reads the tape volume's first record to determine the actual label type.

NEWVOLSER=*new-volume-serial*

specifies a new volume serial for the output tape. NEWVOLSER is effective only if the output tape is standard labeled. If the output tape has an existing label, then the DD statement for the output tape must specify LABEL=(,BLP); otherwise, PROC TAPECOPY stops processing and does not write over the label.

NOFSNRESEQ

specifies that file sequence numbers in the file labels should not be resequenced when a standard labeled output tape volume is being produced. PROC TAPECOPY usually resequences these numbers and updates the label in order to reflect both the ordinal position of the file on the output tape as it is copied and the actual density at which the output tape is written. NFR is an alias for the NOFSNRESEQ option.

NOLIST

tells SAS not to write the tape characteristics and the summary of copied files to the SAS log. Even when you specify NOLIST, the SAS log contains a brief summary of PROC TAPECOPY's action; this summary is usually enough to verify proper functioning of PROC TAPECOPY if you are familiar with the contents of the input tape(s).

NORER

tells SAS not to specify the "reduced error recovery for tape devices" feature of the operating system for each input tape volume. When NORER is specified, some tapes of marginal quality can be read successfully by PROC TAPECOPY, because the error recovery procedures are more extensive.

OUTDD=*fileref*

specifies the fileref that is referenced in the JCL DD statement for the output tape. The default OUTDD= option value is VOLOUT.

OUTVOL=*volume-serial*

specifies the volume serial of the output tape when deferred mounting is specified in the DD statement for the output tape. The OUTVOL= option specification overrides the volume serial, if any, that was specified in the DD statement for the tape.

Specify the OUTVOL= option only if you are using deferred mounting.

INVOL Statement

INVOL *options*;

The INVOL statement defines an input tape volume from which some or all files are to be copied to the output tape volume. The INVOL statement is not necessary if you are using only one input tape nor for the first of several input tapes. (Use the INDD= and INVOL= options of the PROC TAPECOPY statement instead.) When you are using several input tapes, use an INVOL statement for each tape after the first input tape.

The following options can appear in the INVOL statement. The options are listed alphabetically.

DSNAME='*data-set-name*'

specifies the data set name of the first file on the current input tape. You must use this option when both of the following conditions are true:

□   The data set name specified in the DD statement is incorrect or missing.

TAPECOPY *continued*

(DSNAME='data-set-name' continued)

□ LABEL=(,SL) is specified (or implied by default) on the input tape volume DD statement.

You typically use this option when one of the following conditions is true:

□ The DD statement for the input tape specifies deferred mounting.

□ You are reusing a DD statement (and tape drive); that is, when the fileref is the same but you want another standard labeled tape volume on the same unit. LABEL=(,SL) should be specified or implied by default, and the data set name cannot be the same as that on the previous tape that was used with this fileref.

DSN= is an alias for the DSNAME= option.

INDD=*fileref*
specifies the fileref that is referenced in the JCL DD statement for the current input tape. The default INDD= option value is the fileref that is already in effect for the previous input tape volume, as specified in the PROC TAPECOPY statement or in the last INVOL statement.

INVOL=*volume-serial*
specifies the volume serial of the current input tape. Use the INVOL= option when the JCL DD statement for the input tape specifies deferred mounting (as described in "PROC TAPECOPY Statement" on page 247), or when you are reusing a DD statement (and tape drive); that is, when the fileref is the same, but you want a different tape volume on the same unit.

NL
specifies that the input tape is nonlabeled; if LABEL=(,SL) or LABEL=(,BLP) has been specified in the DD statement for the input tape and the tape is actually standard labeled, specifying the NL option causes the tape to be treated as if it were nonlabeled. In this case, any file numbers that are specified in FILES statements must be physical file numbers, not logical file numbers.

NORER
tells SAS not to specify the "reduced error recovery for tape devices" feature of the operating system for the input tape volume. When this option is specified, some tapes of marginal quality can be read successfully by PROC TAPECOPY, because the error recovery procedures are more extensive. If NORER is specified in the PROC TAPECOPY statement, then NORER is in effect for all input tape volumes and INVOL statements.

SL
specifies that the input tape is standard labeled. If you specify LABEL=(,BLP) in the DD statement for the input tape and specify SL in the INVOL statement, PROC TAPECOPY verifies that the tape is standard labeled. Do not specify SL unless the tape is actually standard labeled.

Note: If you do not specify NL or SL in the INVOL statement, the actual input tape label type determines whether PROC TAPECOPY treats the tape as nonlabeled or standard labeled, even when LABEL=(,BLP) is specified in the DD statement.

FILES Statement

FILES *file-numbers*;

When you want to copy particular files from an input tape, use the FILES statement to specify which files you want to copy. Use as many FILES statements as you want. Give the physical file numbers for nonlabeled tapes or for labeled tapes that are being treated as nonlabeled. Give the logical file numbers for standard labeled tapes that are not being treated as nonlabeled, even when the output tape volume is to be nonlabeled (LABEL=NL). FILE is an alias for the FILES statement.

If you are using only one input tape, the FILES statement(s) can directly follow the PROC TAPECOPY statement. When you use several input tape volumes, follow each INVOL statement with the associated FILES statement or statements.

Specifying Individual Files
File numbers in a FILES statement can be specified in any order. For example, you might want to copy file 5 and then file 2 and then file 1, as in the following example:

```
proc tapecopy;
   files 5 2;
   files 1;
run;
```

Specifying a Range
You can specify a range of files by putting a dash between two file numbers, as in the following example:

```
proc tapecopy;
   files 1-7;
run;
```

In a range, the second number must be greater than the first. The keyword EOV (end of volume) can be used as the second file in a range; PROC TAPECOPY copies all files on the input tape until the end of the volume (in most cases, a double tapemark). On a nonlabeled tape, you can copy files beyond the double tapemark by specifying the physical file number, counting tapemarks as usual. If another double tapemark exists on the input tape volume, you can then specify EOV in another range.

Examples

Copying Standard Labeled to Standard Labeled
The following job copies a standard labeled tape (volume serial XXXXXX) to another standard labeled tape (volume serial YYYYYY).

```
//jobname  JOB account,name
//  EXEC SAS
//VOLIN DD UNIT=TAPE,DISP=OLD,
//  VOL=SER=XXXXXX,LABEL=(,SL),DSN=first-dsname-on-tape
//VOLOUT DD UNIT=TAPE,DISP=(,KEEP),
//  VOL=SER=YYYYYY,LABEL=(,SL)
```

TAPECOPY *continued*

```
//SYSIN DD *
   proc tapecopy;
   run;
/*
//
```

After PROC TAPECOPY executes, the output tape volume is labeled YYYYYY.

If LABEL=(,BLP) had been specified in the input tape DD statement (VOLIN), then it would not have been necessary to use the DSN= option. Because some installations do not permit the BLP label type specification, and because no volume label checking is performed when it is specified, it is recommended that you specify (or allow to default) LABEL=(,SL).

The specification of LABEL=(,SL) in the output tape DD statement (VOLOUT) causes the operating system to check the volume label when a tape volume is mounted on the tape drive. The operating system ensures that a tape with volume serial YYYYYY is mounted. However, if the tape with external volume label YYYYYY were, in fact, internally labeled something other than YYYYYY, PROC TAPECOPY would fail. In this case, you would have to specify LABEL=(,BLP) or else give the actual internal volume serial in the output tape DD statement. If the output tape is not labeled internally, you can specify LABEL=(,NL) or LABEL=(,BLP).

Copying Standard Labeled to Nonlabeled

The next job copies a standard labeled tape with volume serial TAPEIN to a nonlabeled tape, FCSTP1. After the job is executed, the output tape volume is still a nonlabeled tape, presumably with only an external volume label of FCSTP1. You must specify LABEL=NL in the PROC TAPECOPY statement; otherwise, the procedure defaults to LABEL=SL, because the first (and only) input tape volume is standard labeled.

```
//jobname  JOB account,name
//  EXEC SAS
//VOLIN DD UNIT=TAPE,DISP=OLD,VOL=SER=TAPEIN,LABEL=(,BLP)
//VOLOUT DD UNIT=TAPE,DISP=(,KEEP),VOL=SER=FCSTP1,LABEL=(,NL)
//SYSIN DD *
   proc tapecopy label=nl;
   run;
/*
//
```

Copying Nonlabeled to Nonlabeled

The following job copies a nonlabeled tape with volume serial QDR123 to a nonlabeled, 1600 bpi tape, SLXATK:

```
//jobname  JOB account,name
//  EXEC SAS
//INTAPE DD UNIT=TAPE,DISP=OLD,VOL=SER=QDR123,LABEL=(,NL)
//OUTTAPE DD UNIT=2927-3,DISP=(,KEEP),VOL=SER=SLXATK,LABEL=(,NL)
//SYSIN DD *
   proc tapecopy indd=intape outdd=outtape den=1600;
   run;
/*
//
```

Copying Multiple Files from One Input Tape

This next job copies the first seven files from the standard labeled input tape U02746 plus four files from the standard labeled input tape T13794 to an initially nonlabeled output tape with volume serial MINI01. After the procedure is executed, the output tape is standard labeled and has a volume serial of U02746.

```
//jobname  JOB account,name
//  EXEC SAS
//TAPI1 DD DISP=SHR,UNIT=TAPE,
//    VOL=SER=U02746,LABEL=(,SL),DSN=first-file-dsname
//TAPI2 DD UNIT=(TAPE,,DEFER)
//OUTDDN DD DISP=(,KEEP),UNIT=TAPE,VOL=SER=MINI01,LABEL=(,NL)
//SYSIN DD *
   proc tapecopy outdd=outddn indd=tapi1 copyvolser;
       files 3 2 1;
       invol indd=tapi2 invol=t13794 dsn='first-dsname-on-this-tape ';
       file 3;
       invol indd=tapi1;
       files 5-7 4;
       invol indd=tapi2;
       files 2 4 1;
   run;
/*
//
```

Copying Multiple Files from Multiple Input Tapes

The next job copies several files from several input tape volumes to one output tape volume:

```
//REARRNGE JOB account,name
//  EXEC SAS
//DEN2IN DD UNIT=(2927-4,,DEFER),LABEL=(,BLP)
//DEN3IN DD UNIT=(2927-3,,DEFER),LABEL=(,SL)
//TAPE1 DD UNIT=TAPE,DISP=SHR,VOL=SER=XR8475,LABEL=(,BLP)
//TAPE2 DD UNIT=TAPE,DISP=OLD,VOL=SER=BKT023,
//  DSN=first-file-dsname
//OUTPUT DD UNIT=(3400-5,,DEFER),DISP=(,KEEP)
//SYSIN DD *
   proc tapecopy label=sl den=6250 nolist outdd=output outvol=histpe;
       invol indd=den2in invol=ptftp0;
       files 2-4 8-eov 7 6;
       invol indd=tape1;
       files 5 7 9-eov;
       invol indd=tape2;
       files 4 5 1;
       invol indd=den3in invol=s03768 dsn='xrt.bkt120.g0081v00';
       files 1-6 22-34;
       invol invol=so3760 dsn='t.bkt120.g0023v00';
       files 4 5 6 9;
       invol indd=tape2;
       files 7-eov;
   run;
/*
//
```

TAPELABEL

Writes the label information of an IBM standard-labeled tape volume to the SAS procedure output file

MVS Specifics: all

Syntax

PROC TAPELABEL *<options>*;

Description

Only one volume per job control statement or command is processed; however, multiple job control statements or commands can be used in one job to process more than one tape volume. At some installations, you may need to specify the data set name of the first file on the tape volume in the job control statements that describe the volumes to be processed. *

The procedure writes information from the tape label, including the data set name, DCB information, and data set history, to the SAS procedure output file.

PROC TAPELABEL Statement

PROC TAPELABEL *<options>*;

The following options can be specified in the PROC TAPELABEL statement:

DCBDEVT=128
    enables PROC TAPELABEL to process Fujitsu F6470 tape cartridges.

DDNAME=(*fileref-1 . . . fileref-n*)
    specifies the *fileref* of the tape volume that you want to process. More than one fileref can be specified. If you specify only one fileref, you can omit the parentheses.
        If DDNAME= is omitted, the default fileref is TAPE.

NOTRAP813
    tells the TAPELABEL procedure not to trap 813-04 abends. When you use LABEL=(,SL) to access an IBM standard labeled tape, this option prevents you from reading the tape unless you specify the data set name of the first file on the tape volume.

PAGE
    begins the output for each tape volume on a new page.

---

*   This applies only if you cannot use LABEL=(,BLP), which is restricted at many sites.

Output

For each file on a tape volume, TAPELABEL generates the following information:

- □ FILE NUMBER, the file sequence number
- □ DSNAME, the data set name
- □ RECFM, the record format
- □ LRECL, the logical record length
- □ BLKSIZE, the block size
- □ BLOCK COUNT, the number of blocks in the file (from the trailer label)
- □ EST FEET, the *estimated* length of the file in feet (assumes all blocks=BLKSIZE)
- □ CREATED, the file creation date
- □ EXPIRES, the file expiration date
- □ CREATED BY JOB NAME STEPNAME, the job and step names of the job that created the file
- □ TRTCH, the track recording technique
- □ DEN, the file recording density code
- □ PSWD, the file protection indicator
- □ UHL, the number of user header labels
- □ UTL, the number of user trailer labels.

TAPELABEL also lists the sum of the estimated file lengths.

Note: On an IBM standard tape label, only 17 characters are available for the data set name. If a longer name is specified in the JCL when the data set is created, only the rightmost 17 characters are used. PROC TAPELABEL displays what is stored in the tape's header label. Some tape management systems catalog data sets by the full name specified in the JCL and therefore require you to specify the full name when you access the data set.

Example

The following job generates the label information for all files on tape volumes that are referenced by the fileref OURTAPE:

```
//jobname JOB acct,name
/*JOBPARM FETCH
//TLABEL   EXEC SAS
//OURTAPE  DD   UNIT=TAPE,DISP=OLD,VOL=SER=MVSV6
//SYSIN DD *
   proc tapelabel ddname=ourtape;
   run;
/*
//
```

Output 18.15 shows the results.

TAPELABEL   *continued*

Output 18.15   *Output from the TAPELABEL Procedure*

```
                                    The SAS System

                              TAPE LIST FOR DDNAME -  OURTAPE
     CONTENTS OF TAPE VOLUME -  MVS609E                                      OWNER -

     FILE                             BLOCK  EST                   CREATED BY
     NUMBER DSNAME     RECFM LRECL BLKSIZE COUNT FEET  CREATED  EXPIRES  JOB NAME STEPNAME  TRTCH DEN PSWD UHL UTL

        1   USERID.V6FILE  FB   6144   6144   35  14.2 20FEB1996 0000000  V6BATCH /SDSSAS       3  NO   0   0
        2   USERID.SASDAT  FB    132   1320    1   1.1 20FEB1996 0000000  V6BATCH /SDSSAS       3  NO   0   0
                                                ------
                                                 15.3
```

V5TOV6

Converts either members of a SAS data library or formats in a load library from Version 5 format to Version 6 format

MVS Specifics: FORMAT= option

MVS Specifics

The FORMAT= argument is host-specific. See the *SAS Procedures Guide* for details.

To convert files of type GCAT, use the following statement if you are converting a catalog that contains dependent or independent pictures for IBM32*xx* devices and you are not using an IBM32*xx* terminal of the same type:

```
goptions nodisplay;
```

See Also

□   *SAS Procedures Guide*

□   SAS Technical Report P-195, *Transporting SAS Files between Host Systems*

XCOPY

Exports or imports one or more SAS data sets

MVS Specifics: all

Syntax

PROC XCOPY IN=*libref* OUT=*fileref* EXPORT;
PROC XCOPY IN=*fileref* OUT=*libref* IMPORT;
  SELECT *SAS-data-set-1* < ... *SAS-data-set-n*>;
  EXCLUDE *SAS-data-set-1* < ... *SAS-data-set-n*>;

Description

The XCOPY procedure is a SAS System Version 5 tool that is still available in Version 6. Although PROC XCOPY is still available, other tools are available in Version 6 for transporting SAS data sets: the XPORT engine, and the CPORT and CIMPORT procedures. With the XPORT engine, a SAS data set in transport format can be used as input in a DATA step or processed by SAS procedures, including the COPY procedure. (See "Transporting SAS Data Sets" on page 132 for more information.) The CPORT and CIMPORT procedures are intended primarily for transporting SAS catalogs, but they can be used to transport SAS data sets as well. (See "Transporting SAS Catalogs" on page 134 for more information.)

The XCOPY procedure can perform only two operations on SAS data sets. With the EXPORT option, PROC XCOPY writes SAS data sets in transport format. With the IMPORT option, it reads SAS data sets in transport format. The transport format that PROC XCOPY reads and writes is the same as the transport format that is read and written by the XPORT engine.

PROC XCOPY performs operations only on SAS data sets. If the SAS data library contains other types of files, XCOPY ignores them. XCOPY processes all the SAS data sets in the SAS data library during one XCOPY operation, or you can select the data sets to be processed from the library.

When you write one or more SAS data sets in transport format, you create a *transport file.* Use the XCOPY procedure to create a transport file that can be moved to the SAS System on another operating system. Also, use the XCOPY procedure to read a transport file that was created by the SAS System on another operating system.

XCOPY cannot process SAS data sets that contain nonstandard characters, such as those produced by nonstandard hexadecimal literals.

Comparison with the Version 6 CPORT and CIMPORT Procedures

The XCOPY procedure and the XPORT engine write a transport file that can be processed by each other. The transport file that is produced by the CPORT procedure, however, is in a different format and cannot be processed by PROC XCOPY nor by the XPORT engine. Similarly, the transport file that is produced by PROC XCOPY or by the XPORT engine cannot be processed by the CIMPORT procedure.

PROC XCOPY Statement

PROC XCOPY IN=*libref* OUT=*fileref* EXPORT;
PROC XCOPY IN=*fileref* OUT=*libref* IMPORT;

Both IN= and OUT= are required arguments, and either EXPORT or IMPORT must be specified.

XCOPY *continued*

IN=*libref* | *fileref*
> specifies the *libref* (if EXPORT is specified) or the *fileref* (if IMPORT is specified) to use as the source for the copy operation.

OUT=*fileref* | *libref*
> specifies the *fileref* (if EXPORT is specified) or *libref* (if IMPORT is specified) to use as the destination for the copy operation.

EXPORT
> specifies that the input (IN=) is a SAS data library that is to be copied to a transport file.

IMPORT
> specifies that the input (IN=) is a transport file that is to be copied to a SAS data library.

SELECT Statement

SELECT *SAS-data-set-1* < . . . *SAS-data-set-n*>;

Use the SELECT statement to specify the names of one or more SAS data sets in the input library that you want to write to the destination. You can use it both when exporting data sets and when importing data sets from a transport file. All selected data sets must belong to the library that you referenced in the IN= option.

In all of the following examples, SAS data sets are selected from the SAS data library referenced by the libref INPUT, and written to the transport file referenced by the fileref TRANFILE.

There are several ways to specify the SELECT statement:

□ You can select a single SAS data set to be copied as follows:

```
libname input 'my.sasdata.library';

filename tranfile 'my.tran.file' disp=(new,catlg) space=(cyl,(1,1))
                  recfm=fb lrecl=80 blksize=8000;

proc xcopy in=input out=tranfile export;
   select test;
run;
```

□ You can select more than one data set by listing the name of each:

```
proc xcopy in=input out=tranfile export;
   select test test2;
run;
```

□ You can select a range of data sets. The following statements select DATA1, DATA2, and DATA3:

```
proc xcopy in=input out=tranfile export;
   select data1-data3;
run;
```

□ Specify one or more characters followed by a colon (:) to select all data sets whose names begin with those characters. For example, the following statements write to a transport file the SAS data set TEST plus all SAS data sets whose names begin with AB:

```
proc xcopy in=input out=tranfile export;
   select test ab:;
run;
```

Note: You cannot use a SELECT statement and an EXCLUDE statement in the same PROC step.

EXCLUDE Statement

EXCLUDE *SAS-data-set-1* < . . . *SAS-data-set-n*>;

Use the EXCLUDE statement to specify the names of one or more SAS data sets that you want to exclude from the destination. You can use it both when exporting data sets and when importing data sets from a transport file. The data sets that you specify are not copied.

To specify SAS data set names in the EXCLUDE statement, use the same syntax shown for the SELECT statement examples. As shown in the following example, you can specify single data set names, a range of data sets, and a group of SAS data sets:

```
filename tranfile 'my.tran.file';

libname output 'my.sasdata.library';

proc xcopy in=tranfile out=output import;
   exclude ds1 stat4-stat6 xyz:;
run;
```

When this program executes, all data sets in the TRANFILE transport file are copied, except DS1, STAT4, STAT5, STAT6, and data sets whose names begin with the letters XYZ.

Note: You cannot use a SELECT statement and an EXCLUDE statement in the same PROC step.

Input Data Set

When you write one or more SAS data sets in transport format, you are *exporting* the SAS data sets. The libref that you specify in the IN= option refers to a SAS data library, and you must specify the EXPORT option.

If you are reading a transport file, then you are *importing* a transport file. The fileref that you specify in the IN= option refers to a transport file, and you must specify the IMPORT option.

The input can be located on either disk or tape.

XCOPY *continued*

Output Data Set

When you write one or more SAS data sets in transport format, you are *exporting* SAS data sets. The fileref that you specify in the OUT= option refers to a transport file, and you must specify the EXPORT option.

If you are reading a transport file, then you are *importing* a transport file. The fileref that you specify in the OUT= option refers to a SAS data library, and you must specify the IMPORT option.

The output data library can be located on either disk or tape.

Output

A message is written to the SAS log for each SAS data set that is copied. No other output is produced.

See Also

□ CPORT and CIMPORT procedures earlier in this chapter

□ Chapter 9, "Transporting SAS Files to and from MVS"

□ *SAS Procedures Guide*

□ SAS Technical Report P-195, *Transporting SAS Files between Host Systems*

Chapter **19** Statements

Portable statements are documented in *SAS Language: Reference*. Only the statements that are MVS-specific or that have MVS-specific aspects are documented in this chapter.

If the SAS statement is also described in *SAS Language: Reference*, that information is not repeated here. Instead, there is an "MVS Specifics" section that explains how the statement works under MVS, and then you are referred to *SAS Language: Reference*. For the DSNEXST and TSO statements, which are entirely MVS-specific, a full description is given.

The "Valid:" information that follows the short description of each statement indicates whether the statement is valid only in a DATA step, or anywhere in a SAS program.

ABORT

Stops the execution of the current DATA step, SAS job, or SAS session

Valid: in a DATA step

MVS specifics: action of ABEND and RETURN, maximum value of n

---

Syntax

ABORT <ABEND | RETURN> <*n*>;

MVS Specifics

The following options are used primarily in batch processing, although they can be used with any method of running SAS. These options have host-specific characteristics.

ABEND
>   causes abnormal termination of the current SAS job or session. This also terminates the step in your MVS job stream that was used to execute your SAS job. Because the step terminates abnormally, the operating system data sets that were allocated to the step are handled as specified by the abnormal-termination condition of the DISP= parameter for those data sets. (The DISP= parameter is specified in the JCL DD statement or the TSO ALLOCATE command, or in the SAS FILENAME or LIBNAME statement.)

RETURN
>   causes an immediate normal termination of the SAS job or session. The step return code (condition code) should be used to indicate the error. To pass the specific return code back to the operating system, use the *n* option. You can then use this return code in your JCL to conditionally execute later steps in your MVS job stream.

n
>   enables you to specify an abend code or a condition code that SAS returns to the operating system when it stops executing. The value of *n* must be an integer. Under MVS, the range of acceptable values is from 1 to 4095. If you do not specify a value for

---

ABORT *continued*

n, an ABORT ABEND statement returns a user abend 999; an ABORT RETURN statement returns condition code 20.

You can use the ABORT statement to control the conditional execution of MVS job steps. For example, depending on the result of the MVS job step that executes your SAS program, you may need to either bypass or execute later steps. To do this you can establish a variable in your SAS DATA step program that is set to a particular value whenever an error occurs; in the following example, we use a variable named ERRCODE that is set to 16 if an error occurs in the DATA step. You can choose any variable name and value that are required by your program. Then, use the following ABORT statement, coded in the THEN clause of an IF statement, to cause the MVS job step to ABEND if ERRCODE=16:

```
if errcode=16 then abort abend;
```

When the MVS job step that is used to execute your SAS job ends (either normally or abnormally) the next MVS job step is processed. You could then use the following EXEC statement to conditionally execute that job step if an ABEND occurs. If ERRCODE is not set to 16, then the ABORT statement is not executed, and because an ABEND did not occur, the job step is bypassed.

```
//stepname EXEC PGM=your-program,COND=ONLY
```

See Also

□   *SAS Language: Reference*

□   *MVS/XA JCL Reference* or *MVS/ESA JCL Reference*

ATTRIB

Associates a format, informat, label, length, or any combination of these attributes, with one or more variables

Valid: in a DATA step

MVS specifics: LENGTH= specification in *attribute-list*

Syntax

ATTRIB *variable-list-1 attribute-list-1* < . . . *variable-list-n attribute-list-n*>;

MVS Specifics

LENGTH=<$> *length* is one of the attributes that may be specified in the *attribute-list*. The LENGTH= attribute specifies the length of variables in the *variable-list*. Character variables can range from 1 to 200 bytes in length and, under MVS, numeric variables can range from 2 to 8 bytes in length.

See Also

□ *SAS Language: Reference*

DSNEXST

Checks to see whether the specified operating system data set exists

Valid: anywhere

MVS specifics: all

Syntax

DSNEXST *<'>OS-data-set-name<'>*;

Description

DSNEXST is a global statement. The first time the statement is issued, it creates the macro variable &SYSDEXST and assigns a value of 1 to it if the data set exists or a value of 0 if the data set does not exist.

OS-data-set-name
    is the name of an operating system data set. Quotation marks around the name are optional; however, the data set name must always be fully qualified.

Examples

The following example allocates a data set differently depending on whether the data set already exists or not.

```
%macro mydsn;
   dsnexst 'my.data.set';
   filename myds 'my.data.set'

%if &sysdexst %then %do;
   disp=old;
   %end;

%else %do;
   disp=(new,catlg) space=(cyl,(1,1)) blksize=6160
      dsorg=ps recfm=fb lrecl=80 unit=disk volser='MYVOL';
   %end;
```

DSNEXST *continued*

```
%mend mydsn;

%mydsn
```

The next example shows how you can submit some SAS statements if a data set already exists and bypass them if it does not.

```
%macro copylib;
    dsnexst 'my.data.library';

%if &sysdexst %then %do;
    libname mylib 'my.data.library' disp=shr;
    proc copy in=mylib out=work;
    run;
    %end;

%mend;

%copylib
```

See Also

□ *SAS Guide to Macro Processing, Version 6, Second Edition*

□ *SAS Macro Facility Tips and Techniques, Version 6, First Edition*

FILE

Specifies the current output file for PUT statements

Valid: in a DATA step

MVS specifics: *file-specification, type, host-options*

Syntax

FILE *file-specification* *<type>* *<options>* *<host-options>*;

MVS Specifics

You can use the following arguments with the FILE statement:

file-specification

identifies the file and can have any of the following forms:

fileref

directs output to the assigned fileref or the allocated DDname. A fileref must conform to the rules for DDnames. That is, it can consist of one to eight letters,

numbers, or the national characters $, @, and #. The first character must be either a
letter or a national character.

fileref(member)
    directs output to a member in a partitioned data set, where the PDS is specified by
    the assigned fileref or allocated DDname.

'OS-data-set-name'
    directs output to an operating system data set that SAS will dynamically allocate
    for this FILE statement.

LOG
    directs output to the SAS log file.

PRINT
    directs output to the SAS procedure output file.

type
    specifies the type of file. When you omit *type*, the default is a standard external file.
    Nonstandard (host-specific) file types that you can specify for MVS are:

DLI	for IMS-DL/I databases. For information about IMS-DL/I options for the FILE statement, see *SAS/ACCESS Interface to IMS-DL/I: Usage and Reference, Version 6, Second Edition*.
HFS and PIPE	for files in the Hierarchical File System (see "Accessing OpenEdition MVS Hierarchical File System Files" on page 84)
VSAM	for VSAM files (see "Accessing VSAM Data Sets" on page 83).

options
    are portable options that can be specified in the FILE statement. See *SAS Language:
    Reference* for information about these options.

host-options
    are host-specific options that can be specified in the FILE statement. You can specify
    portable options and *host-options* in any order. When specifying more than one option,
    use a blank space to separate each option. The *host-options* that you can specify depend
    on what type of file you are accessing. See the following sections for details:

    □ "Standard Options for the FILE Statement under MVS" on page 266

    □ "Options for Retrieving Information about Data Sets" on page 267

    □ "Host-Specific Options for HFS Files" on page 88

    □ "Options That Specify SMS Keywords" on page 279

    □ "VSAM Options for the FILE and INFILE Statements under MVS" on page 268.

FILE *continued*

Standard Options for the FILE Statement under MVS

The following standard options can be used with all standard external files under MVS.

BLKSIZE=*value* | BLK=*value*
  specifies the block size of the file. Block size is discussed in more detail in "DCB Option Descriptions" on page 275 and in "Overview of DCB Attributes" on page 277.

CLOSE=*keyword*
  indicates how a tape volume is to be positioned at the end of the DATA step. Values for *keyword* can be

REREAD	positions the tape at the logical beginning of the data set.
LEAVE	positions the tape at the logical end of the data set.
REWIND	rewinds the tape to the physical beginning of the volume.
FREE	dynamically deallocates the tape volume.
DISP	is implied by the control language.

CSRC
  specifies that you want to use the CSRCESRV services (available with MVS/ESA) to compress data on output. For example:

```
data _null_;
   file myfile csrc;
      put ... ;
   run;
```

  You cannot use this option with a data set that has a fixed-length record format.

DCB=*fileref*
  gives the fileref of an external file that was referenced in an earlier FILE or INFILE statement in the same DATA step. SAS uses that file's RECFM=, LRECL=, and BLKSIZE= information for the current file.

LRECL=*value*
  specifies the logical record length of the file. For more information, see the discussion of LRECL= in "DCB Option Descriptions" on page 275.

MOD
  writes the output lines following any existing lines in the file. This option overrides a disposition that was specified in JCL or under TSO. It is not valid if the specified file is a member of a partitioned data set (PDS).

NOPROMPT
  specifies that if the file that you reference in the FILE statement is unavailable, a requestor window is not displayed.

OLD

> writes the output lines at the beginning of the file, causing any existing data in the file to be overwritten. This option overrides a disposition that was specified in JCL or under TSO, and it is the default if no disposition is specified. Using OLD is necessary only if you used MOD for the file in an earlier FILE statement and you want to overwrite the file.

RECFM=*record-format*

> specifies the record format of the file. Valid values are:

F	fixed length records, unblocked.
V	variable length records, unblocked.
FB	fixed length records, blocked.
VB	variable length records, blocked.
U	undefined length records, unblocked.

> The following values can be appended to the values above:

A	the first byte of each record is an ANSI printer-control character.
S	if appended to V, the file contains spanned records; if appended to F, the file contains standard blocks.

> The following value stands alone; no other values can be appended:

N	a format specific to SAS; this format indicates that the file can be processed as a stream of bytes with no record boundaries.

Options for Retrieving Information about Data Sets

The following options retrieve information about a data set from the operating system control blocks. SAS assigns values to the variables that are defined by these options when it opens the data set. It updates the values every time it opens a new data set in a concatenation. These options can be used with all standard external files under MVS.

DEVTYPE=*variable*

> defines a character variable (minimum length 24) that SAS sets to the device type. SAS obtains the device type by using the MVS operating system DEVTYPE macro. For more information, see the IBM documentation for your system.

DSCB=*variable*

> defines a character variable (minimum length 96) that SAS sets to the Data Set Control Block (DSCB) information from a non-VSAM data set. For more information, see the IBM documentation for your system.

JFCB=*variable*

> defines a character variable (minimum length 176) that SAS sets to the Job File Control Block (JFCB). For more information, see the IBM documentation for your system.

FILE *continued*

UCBNAME=*variable*
> defines a character variable (minimum length 3) that SAS sets to the unit name (device address), which is derived from information in the unit control block (UCB).

VOLUME=*variable* | VOLUMES=*variable*
> defines a character variable (minimum length 6) that SAS sets to the disk volume serial number, which is taken from the JFCB. The JFCB lists only the first five volume serial numbers, so in the case of a multivolume file, the VOLUME= variable contains the concatenated volume serial numbers (up to five volumes).

VSAM Options for the FILE and INFILE Statements under MVS

The following options can be used for VSAM files in the FILE statement, the INFILE statement, or both. (Unless otherwise indicated, the option can be used in both.)

BACKWARD | BKWD
> tells SAS to read the VSAM data set backwards. (INFILE only)

BUFND=*value*
> indicates how many data buffers to use for the VSAM data set.

BUFNI=*value*
> indicates how many index buffers to use for the VSAM data set.

CONTROLINTERVAL | CTLINTV | CNV
> indicates that you want to read physical VSAM control interval records rather than logical records. This is typically used for diagnostic purposes. (INFILE only)

ERASE=*variable*
> defines a numeric SAS variable that you must set to 1 when you want to erase a VSAM record. (INFILE only)

FEEDBACK=*variable* | FDBK=*variable*
> defines a numeric variable that SAS will set to the VSAM logical error code. This is similar to the _FDBK_ automatic variable. When SAS sets the FEEDBACK variable, you must set it to 0 to continue.

GENKEY
> causes SAS to use the KEY= variable as the leading portion of a record's key. VSAM retrieves the first record whose key matches the generic key. (INFILE only)

KEY=*variable* | KEY=(*variable1 variable2 . . .*)
> indicates that direct keyed access is being used to read records either from a KSDS, or from an ESDS via an alternate index. The maximum length of the variable is 256 characters. (INFILE only)

KEYGE
> is used in conjunction with the KEY= option. KEYGE indicates that, when KEY= is used in a retrieval request, SAS should retrieve any record whose key is equal to or greater than the specified key. This is useful when the exact key is not known. (INFILE only)

KEYLEN=*variable*
> specifies a numeric SAS variable that, when used with GENKEY, specifies the length of the key that is to be compared to the keys in the file.

KEYPOS=*variable*
> indicates the numeric variable that SAS sets to the position of the VSAM key field. This option enables you to read keys without knowing the key position in advance. This variable is set to the column number (starting from 1).

PASSWD=*value*
> gives the appropriate password for a VSAM data set that has password protection.

RBA=*variable*
> specifies a numeric variable that you set to the relative byte address (RBA) of the data record that you want to read. The RBA= option indicates that addressed direct access is being used; it is appropriate for KSDS and ESDS. If the CNV option is specified, the RBA= option can be used to access control records in an RRDS. (INFILE only)

RC4STOP
> stops the DATA step from executing if, when the VSAM data set is opened, a return code greater than 4 is returned by the system.

RECORDS=*variable*
> defines a numeric variable that SAS sets to the number of logical records in a VSAM data set that has been opened for input.

RECORG=*record-organization*
> specifies the organization of records in a new VSAM data set. Use this option only if SMS is active. Valid values are:
>
> KS   VSAM key-sequenced data set
>
> ES   VSAM entry-sequenced data set
>
> RR   VSAM relative-record data set
>
> LS   VSAM linear-space data set

RESET
> indicates that the VSAM file is to be reset to empty (no records) when it is opened. This option applies only to loading a VSAM data set that has been marked REUSE. This option cannot be used if the data set contains an alternate index.

RRN=*variable*
> defines a numeric variable that you set to the relative record number (RRN) of the record that you want to read or write. This option indicates that keyed direct access is being used; it is appropriate for RRDS only.

SEQUENTIAL
> specifies sequential VSAM record retrieval when either the RBA= (for an ESDS) or the RRN= option (for an RRDS) is specified. (INFILE only)

SKIP
> indicates skip-sequential processing of VSAM files. Skip-sequential processing finds the first record whose value is the same as the value specified by the KEY= option; records are read sequentially from that point on. (INFILE only)

FILE *continued*

UPDATE=*variable*
defines a numeric SAS variable that tells SAS that not every record that it reads is to be updated. This option is used when you are updating records in a VSAM data set. (INFILE only)

Options for HFS Files and Pipes

Several options can be specified in the FILE statement for files and pipes that are in the Hierarchical File System of OpenEdition MVS. For information about these options, see "Host-Specific Options for HFS Files" on page 88.

See Also

□ "Writing to External Files" on page 70

□ "Using the FILE Statement to Specify Data Set Attributes" on page 74

□ *SAS Language: Reference*

FILENAME

Associates a SAS fileref with an external file

Valid: anywhere

MVS specifics: *fileref, device-type, OS-data-set-name, host-options*

Syntax

FILENAME *fileref* <*device-type*> '*OS-data-set-name*' <*host-options*>;
FILENAME *fileref* <*device-type*> ('*OS-data-set-name-1*'...'*OS-data-set-name-n*')
       <*host-options*>;
FILENAME *fileref* | _ALL_ CLEAR;
FILENAME *fileref* | _ALL_ LIST;

MVS Specifics

You can use the following arguments with the FILENAME statement:

fileref
is used to identify the external file. The *fileref* must conform to the rules for DDnames. That is, it can consist of one to eight letters, numbers, or the national characters $, @, and #. The first character must be either a letter or one of the national characters.

device-type
specifies a device type for the output. It can be one of the following:

CART   send the output to a tape cartridge.

DISK   sends the output to a disk drive.

DUMMY   specifies a null output device. This value is especially useful in testing situations.

PLOTTER   sends the output to the default system plotter.

PRINTER   sends the output to the default system printer.

TAPE   sends the output to a tape drive.

TERMINAL   sends the output to your terminal.

You can specify *device-type* in two ways: either specify it between the fileref and the data set name in the FILENAME statement, or use the standard file option UNIT= to specify it. (See the following section, "Standard File Options for the FILENAME Statement.") If you specify *device-type* in both ways, the UNIT= option takes priority. If you do not specify a device type or UNIT value for a new file, SAS uses the current value of the SAS system option FILEDEV=.

'OS-data-set-name'

specifies the operating system data set name of an external file. In a concatenation, each data set name must be enclosed in quotes, and the entire group of concatenated file specifications must also be enclosed in parentheses. *'OS-data-set-name'* must be enclosed in quotes and must refer to one of the following:

☐ a fully qualified data set name. For example: `'myid.raw.datax'`.

☐ a fully qualified data set name with a member in parentheses. For example: `'sas.raw.data(mem1)'`.

☐ a partially qualified data set name with a period preceding. For example: `'.raw.data'`.

☐ a partially qualified data set name with a period preceding and a member name in parentheses. For example: `'.raw.data(mem1)'`.

☐ a temporary data set name. For example: `'&mytemp'`.

See "Specifying Operating System Data Sets" on page 13 for more information about partially qualified data set names.

host-options

are host-specific options that may be specified in the FILENAME statement. These options can be categorized into several groups. For details, see the following sections:

☐ "Standard File Options for the FILENAME Statement" on page 272

☐ "DCB Attribute Options" on page 275

☐ "SYSOUT Data Set Options for the FILENAME Statement" on page 280

☐ "Subsystem Options for the FILENAME Statement" on page 281

☐ "Options That Specify SMS Keywords" on page 279

☐ "Host-Specific Options for HFS Files" on page 88.

You can specify these options in any order following *'OS-data-set-name'*. When specifying more than one option, use a blank space to separate each option. Values for options may be specified with or without quotes. However, if a value contains one of the supported national characters ($, #, or @), the quotes are required.

FILENAME *continued*

Standard File Options for the FILENAME Statement

Standard file options provide information about a data set's disposition and physical attributes. The following standard options can be used with all external files under MVS except for files that are in the Hierarchical File System of OpenEdition MVS. (See "Host-Specific Options for HFS Files" on page 88.)

DISP=*status* | (*status*,*<normal-termination-disp>*,*<abnormal-termination-disp>*)
> specifies the status of the operating system data set at the beginning and ending of a job, as well as what to do if the job step terminates abnormally. If you are specifying only *status*, you can omit the parentheses.

> *status*
>> specifies the status of the data set at the beginning of a job. Valid values are:

>> NEW   a new data set is to be created.

>> OLD   the data set exists and is not to be shared.

>> SHR   the data set exists and may be shared.

>> MOD   if the data set exists, new records are to be added to the end; if the data set does not exist, a new data set is to be created. MOD cannot be specified for a partitioned data set.

> The default is SHR.
>> **Note:** You can also supply any of these values for status as a separate, individual keyword on the FILENAME statement rather than as a subparameter of the DISP= option.

> *normal-termination-disp*
>> specifies what to do with the data set if the job step that was using the data set terminates normally. Valid values are:

>> DELETE   deletes the data set at the end of the step.

>> KEEP   keeps the data set.

>> CATLG   places the entry in the system catalog or user catalog.

>> UNCATLG   deletes the entry from the system catalog or user catalog.

> For a new data set, the default is CATLG. For an existing data set, the default is KEEP.

> *abnormal-termination-disp*
>> specifies what to do if the job step terminates abnormally. The default is to take the action that is specified or implied by *normal-termination-disp*. Valid values are:

>> DELETE   indicates that the data set is to be deleted at the end of a job step.

>> KEEP   indicates that the data set is to be kept.

>> CATLG   indicates that the system should place an entry in the system or user catalog.

UNCATLG   indicates that the system is to delete the entry in the system or user catalog.

Here are some examples of the DISP parameter:

```
DISP=SHR

DISP=(NEW,CATLG)

DISP=(OLD,UNCATLG,DELETE)
```

SPACE=(*unit*,(*primary,secondary,directory*), RLSE,*type*,ROUND)
is the amount of disk space to be provided for a data set that is being created.

unit
may be any of the following:

TRK   specifies that the space is to be allocated in tracks.

CYL   specifies that the space is to be allocated in cylinders.

blklen   specifies that the space is to be allocated in blocks whose block length is *blklen* bytes. The system computes how many tracks are allocated.

primary
specifies how many tracks, cylinders, or blocks to allocate.

secondary
specifies how many additional tracks, cylinders, or blocks to allocate if more space is needed. The system does not allocate additional space until it is needed.

directory
specifies how many 256-byte records are needed for the directory of a partitioned data set.

RLSE
causes unused space that was allocated to an output data set to be released when the data set is closed. Unused space is released only if the data set is opened for output and if the last operation was a write operation.

type
can be any of the following:

CONTIG   means that the allocated space must be contiguous.

MXIG   means that the maximum contiguous space is required.

ALX   means that different areas of contiguous space are needed.

Note: You can also specify MXIG or ALX as a separate, individual keyword on the FILENAME statement rather than as a subparameter of the SPACE= option.

ROUND
specifies that the allocated space must be equal to an integral number of cylinders when the *unit* specified was a block length. If *unit* was specified as TRK or CYL, the system ignores ROUND.

Here are some examples of the SPACE parameter:

FILENAME *continued*

```
SPACE=(CYL,10) or SPACE=(CYL,(10,,10),,CONTIG)
```

```
SPACE=(1024,(100,50,20),RLSE,MXIG,ROUND)
```

If SPACE is not specified, its values are taken from the SAS system options
FILEUNIT=, FILESPPRI=, FILESPSEC=, and FILEDIRBLK=, in the following form:

```
SPACE=(FILEUNIT,(FILESPPRI,FILESPSEC,FILEDIRBLK))
```

The default specifications are as follows:

for partitioned data sets:
    SPACE=(CYL,(1,1,6))

for sequential data sets:
    SPACE=(CYL,(1,1))

See your *IBM MVS/ESA JCL Reference* for complete information about how to use the
SPACE= option.

VOLSER=*value* | VOL=*value*
    specifies the disk or tape volume serial number.
        If VOLSER= is not specified, its value is taken from the SAS system option
FILEVOL=.

UNIT=*value*
    can name one of several different devices. Some valid values follow. Ask your system
administrator whether additional valid values have been defined at your site.

□ CART

□ DISK

□ DUMMY

□ PLOTTER

□ PRINTER

□ TAPE

□ TERMINAL

The default for UNIT= is DISK.

LABEL=(*subparameter-list*)
    enables you to specify the type and contents of the label of either a tape data set or a
disk data set, as well as other information such as the retention period or expiration date
for the data set. It is identical to the JCL LABEL= parameter. Here is a simple example:

```
label=(3,SL,,,EXPDT=1998/123)
```

This label specification indicates that the data set sequence number is 3, that it uses
standard labels, and that it expires on the 123rd day of 1998. See your *IBM MVS/ESA
JCL Reference* for complete information about how to use the LABEL= option,
including which subparameters you can specify in *subparameter-list*.

NOMOUNT
>specifies that the mount message is not to be issued for a volume that is not already online. The default action is to issue the mount message.

NOPROMPT
>specifies that if the file that you reference in the FILENAME statement is unavailable, a requestor window is not displayed.

REUSE
>indicates that the file that you reference in the FILENAME statement is to be freed and reallocated if it is currently in use. By default, SAS does not free and reallocate a file that is currently in use.

WAIT=n
>controls how many minutes SAS waits if the file that you reference in the FILENAME statement is unavailable. SAS tries to reacquire the reserved data set every 15 seconds. The value *n* specifies a length of time in clock minutes.

DCB Attribute Options

The following section describes DCB options that can be used in the FILENAME statement. For additional information about DCB characteristics, see "Overview of DCB Attributes" on page 277.

DCB Option Descriptions

The following DCB options can be used in the FILENAME statement for all types of external files under MVS, except for files that are in the Hierarchical File System (HFS) of OpenEdition MVS. (For information about options that are available for HFS files, see "Host-Specific Options for HFS Files" on page 88.) These options correspond to the DCB parameters that you would specify in a JCL DD statement.

BLKSIZE=value
>specifies the number of bytes in a block of records. A block is a group of records that SAS and the operating system move as a unit when reading or writing an external file. The term also refers to the space allowed for each group of records. You seldom need to calculate block size when you write an external file because SAS automatically selects the block size.
>
>The values of the FILEBLKSIZE(*device-type*)= system option contain, for each model of disk that is currently available, the block size that your installation considers best for external, nonprint data sets on that type of disk. Some installations may provide different FILEBLKSIZE default values for batch processing than they do for interactive processing. Therefore, to see the values for the FILEBLKSIZE(*device-type*)= option, run the OPTIONS procedure both in a batch job and in a SAS session under TSO.
>
>For print data sets, which by default have variable-length records, SAS uses a default block size of 264, with one record per block.
>
>You can use the OPT value of the FILEBLKSIZE(*device-type*)= option to tell SAS to calculate the optimal block size for nonprint files. (See "FILEBLKSIZE()=" on page 317.) Or you can calculate the block size yourself:
>
>□ To calculate a block size for fixed-length records, multiply the LRECL= value by the number of records you want to put into the block.
>
>□ For variable-length records, multiply the LRECL= value by the number of records per block and add 4 bytes.

FILENAME *continued*

(BLKSIZE=value continued)

In each case, if you are writing the data set to disk, compare the block size to the track size for the disk. A block cannot be longer than one track of the disk device on which it is stored, and the operating system does not split a block between tracks. The maximum block size for a data set on tape is 32760. Make sure that the block size does not leave a large portion of the track unused. (If you are not sure, consult your computing center staff.) See "Optimizing I/O" on page 152 for information about determining the optimal block size for your data.

BUFNO=*value*

specifies how many memory buffers to allocate for reading and writing. If BUFNO= is not specified, the default is BUFNO=5. See "Optimizing I/O" on page 152 for information about determining the optimal BUFNO= value for your data.

DSORG=*organization*

The following types of organization can be specified:

□ DA (direct access)

□ PO (partitioned)

□ PS (sequential).

The following types of organization, used to refer to operating system data sets that contain location-dependent information, are also valid: DAU, POU, PSU.

You do not need to include the DSORG= value when you create an external file of type PS or PO. This is because the operating system identifies a partitioned data set by the presence of a directory allocation in the SPACE= parameter. And when you use a FILE statement to write data, SAS identifies a partitioned data set by the presence of a member name in the FILE statement. If no member name is present, SAS assumes that the data set is sequential.

LRECL=*value*

specifies the logical record length (that is, the number of bytes in a record). SAS defaults to the size that is needed (for either print or nonprint files) when a file is opened.

Logical record length is affected by the record format (see RECFM=). When the record format is fixed (indicated by an F as part of the RECFM= value), all records have the same length, and that length is the value of the LRECL= value.

When the record format is variable (indicated by a V as part of the RECFM= value), records may have different lengths, and each record contains 4 bytes of length information in addition to its other data. Therefore, you must specify an LRECL= value that is 4 bytes longer than the longest record you expect to write. If you do not know the length of the longest record to be put into a variable-format data set, choose a maximum value and add 4 to it to create an LRECL= value.

OPTCD=*value*

specifies the optional services to be performed by the operating system. For example, specifying W requests a validity check for write operations on direct-access devices. For more information, see the appropriate IBM MVS JCL manual for your system.

Valid values are R, J, T, Z, A, Q, F, H, O, C, E, B, U, and W. You can specify more than one code by listing them with no blanks or commas between them (as with RECFM). A maximum of four characters is allowed.

RECFM=*record-format*
    specifies the record format of the file. Valid values are:

F	fixed length records, unblocked.
V	variable length records, unblocked.
FB	fixed length records, blocked.
VB	variable length records, blocked.
U	undefined length records, unblocked.

The following values can be appended to the RECFM= values:

A	specifies that the first byte of each record is an ANSI-printer control character.
M	specifies that the file is a machine control character file. SAS does not interpret machine-code control characters nor does it create them in output files. See your *IBM MVS/ESA JCL Reference* for more information.
S	specifies that the file contains spanned records (when appended to V), or that the file contains standard blocks (when appended to F).

The next format stands alone; no other values may be appended.

N	indicates that the file is in binary format. The file is treated as a byte stream; that is, line boundaries are not recognized. This record format is specific to the SAS System.

Overview of DCB Attributes

DCB attributes and options are relevant to INFILE and FILE statements as well as to the FILENAME statement. This section provides some background information about DCB characteristics.

DCB attributes are those data set characteristics that describe the organization and format of the data set records. If you do not specify these attributes, the SAS System uses default values for them. This section discusses how and under what circumstances these attributes are changed or default values are used.

The discussion focuses on the RECFM, LRECL, and BLKSIZE file attributes. For more information, see the appropriate *MVS Data Administration Guide* for your system.

Values for these attributes are kept in each of the following operating system control blocks:

Data Set Control Block (DSCB)	is the description found in the VTOC of the disk device that the operating system data set resides on. These are the permanent characteristics of the data set. For tape devices, the data set label in the header of SL tapes contains this information.
Job File Control Block (JFCB)	maps a physical operating system data set on a device to a logical name (DDname). Contains information from a JCL DD statement, TSO ALLOCATE command, or SAS FILENAME statement. These attributes are either temporary (for the duration of the allocation) or new (to be made permanent).

FILENAME *continued*

Data Control
Block (DCB)
describes the current state of an open data set. MVS and its access methods (BSAM for the SAS System) use the DCB to control how data are read or written. These attributes are temporary for input, but they become permanent for output.

For existing data sets, DCB attributes are almost always used unchanged from the DSCB. These attributes may be overridden by a DD statement or TSO ALLOCATE command or by SAS FILENAME, FILE, or INFILE options. If an option is specified in both places, the FILENAME, FILE, or INFILE option takes precedence.

When a data set is opened, MVS merges information from the DSCB (or data set label) and the JFCB to obtain the current DCB characteristics before entering the DCB open exit. SAS then merges its own information (FILENAME/FILE/INFILE statement options, data set device type, requested data set type, requested linesize from LS=) and inspects the resulting DCB attributes. If the result is invalid for some reason, SAS terminates the open operation and issues an appropriate message. Attributes may be considered invalid for any of the following reasons:

□ For RECFM=V or VB, BLKSIZE is not at least 4 bytes greater than LRECL.

□ For RECFM=F, LRECL equals neither 0 nor BLKSIZE.

□ For RECFM=FB, BLKSIZE is not a multiple of LRECL.

□ BLKSIZE or LRECL is greater than the MVS maximum (32,760).

□ LRECL is greater than BLKSIZE (except RECFM=VBS).

□ RECFM is not consistent with the requested data set type.

□ The requested data length cannot be contained in LRECL.

For any unspecified attributes, SAS takes default values that seem to fit existing attributes. This may cause unexpected combinations of attributes to be set, so be wary of specifying an incomplete set of attributes for a data set.

If no permanent attributes are present (as is possible with a new data set), and if none are given by FILENAME/FILE/INFILE options, then SAS uses default values that are based on the device type and data set type. The following table summarizes these default values.

Attribute	DISK	TAPE	PRINT/ SYSOUT	TERMINAL	DUMMY
RECFM	FB	FB	VBA	V	FB
LRECL	80	80	260	261	80
BLKSIZE	D*	T**	264	265	D*

* The smaller of the SAS system option FILEBLKSIZE(*device-type*)= value and the output device maximum, rounded down to a multiple of the LRECL.

** The smaller of the SAS system option FILEBLKSIZE(*device-type*)= value and 32,760, rounded down to a multiple of the LRECL.

If a linesize (LS=) parameter is given, SAS uses this value to compute the LRECL, and the BLKSIZE is computed accordingly.

If permanent attributes are overridden on input, these values are used only for the duration of the INFILE processing; the permanent attributes of the data set are not changed. However, if attributes are overridden on output, the specified attributes become permanent for the data set, even if no records are physically written.

Options That Specify SMS Keywords

Several options that specify SMS keywords can be specified in the FILENAME or FILE statement when you create an external file. All of these options are ignored for existing data sets; they apply only when you are creating a data set. If you do not specify any of these options when you create an SMS data set, the system defaults are used. The default values are site-dependent; see your system administrator for details. For more information about SMS data sets, see your *IBM MVS/ESA JCL Reference.*

DATACLAS=*data-class-name*
> specifies the data class for an SMS-managed data set. The name can have up to 8 characters. This option applies only to new data sets; it is ignored for existing data sets. The data class is predefined and controls the DCB attributes for a data set.
>
> The implementation of the DATACLAS= option is compatible with the SMS DATACLAS= JCL parameter. For complete information about this parameter, see your *IBM MVS/ESA JCL Reference.* Ask your system administrator for the data-class names that are used at your site.

DSNTYPE=LIBRARY | PDS
> specifies the data set name type.

LIBRARY	indicates that the data set is a PDSE.
PDS	indicates that the data set is a PDS.

LIKE=*data-set-name*
> enables you to allocate an external file that has the same attributes as an existing file. See your *IBM MVS/ESA JCL Reference* for more information.

MGMTCLAS=*management-class-name*
> specifies a management class for an SMS data set. The name can have up to 8 characters. This option applies only to new data sets; it is ignored for existing data sets. The management class is predefined and controls how your data set is managed, such as how often it is backed up and how it is migrated.
>
> The implementation of the MGMTCLAS= option is compatible with the SMS MGMTCLAS= JCL parameter. For complete information about this parameter, see your *IBM MVS/ESA JCL Reference.* Ask your system administrator for the management class names that are used at your site.

RECORG=*record-organization*
> specifies the organization of records in a new VSAM data set. Use this option only if SMS is active. Valid values are:

KS	VSAM key-sequenced data set
ES	VSAM entry-sequenced data set
RR	VSAM relative-record data set
LS	VSAM linear-space data set

FILENAME *continued*

STORCLAS=*storage-class-name*
> specifies a storage class for an SMS data set. The name can have up to 8 characters. This option applies only to new data sets; it is ignored for existing data sets. The storage class is predefined and controls which device your SMS data set is stored on, such as disk or tape.
>
> The implementation of the STORCLAS= option is compatible with the SMS STORCLAS= JCL parameter. For full details on this parameter, refer to your *IBM MVS/ESA JCL Reference*. See your system administrator for storage class names at your site.

SYSOUT Data Set Options for the FILENAME Statement

The following options apply to data sets that are sent to a system output device (usually a printer). The default value is usually the value that was specified by your site as the installation default. See Chapter 6, as well as your IBM JCL reference, for more information about print data sets.

ALIGN	asks the operator to check the alignment of the printer forms before printing the data set.
BURST	tells the operator that the printed output is to go to a burster-trimmer-stacker machine, to be burst into separate sheets.
CHAR1=*value*	specifies a one- to four-character name for character-arrangement table #1 (used in conjunction with the 3800 Printing Subsystem).
CHAR2=*value*	specifies a one- to four-character name for character-arrangement table #2 (used in conjunction with the 3800 Printing Subsystem).
CHAR3=*value*	specifies a one- to four-character name for character-arrangement table #3 (used in conjunction with the 3800 Printing Subsystem).
CHAR4=*value*	specifies a one- to four-character name for character-arrangement table #4 (used in conjunction with the 3800 Printing Subsystem).
CLOSE	tells the operating system to deallocate the data set when the DCB is closed.
COPIES=*value*	specifies how many copies of the SYSOUT data set to print. The default is COPIES=1.
DEST=*dest-name*	specifies a destination for the SYSOUT data set. If DEST is not defined, its value is taken from the SAS system option FILEDEST=.
FCB=*fcb-image*	specifies the forms control buffer image that JES should use to control the printing of the SYSOUT data set.
FLASH=*value*	specifies which forms overlay frame to use when printing the data set on a 3800 Printing Subsystem.
FLASHC=*value*	specifies the number of copies on which to print the forms overlay frame.

FOLD	requests that the print chain or print train for the universal character set be loaded in fold mode.
FORMDEF=*member*	identifies a member that contains statements that tell the Print Services Facility how to print the SYSOUT data set on a page-mode printer.
FORMS=*form-num*	specifies the form number. If FORMS is not defined, its value is taken from the SAS system option FILEFORMS=.
HOLD	tells the system to hold the SYSOUT data set when it is deallocated until it is released by the system operator.
ID=*dest-userid*	specifies the user ID for the SYSOUT destination.
MODIFY=*value*	specifies a copy-modification module that tells JES how to print the SYSOUT data set on a 3800 Printing Subsystem.
MODIFYT=*value*	specifies which of the CHAR*n* tables to use. For example, if *value* equals 1, then the character-arrangement table that is identified by the CHAR1= option is used.
OUTDES=*value*	specifies the output descriptor.
OUTLIM=*value*	specifies a limit for the number of logical records in the SYSOUT data set.
PAGEDEF=*member*	identifies a member that contains statements that tell the Print Services Facility how to format the page on a page-mode printer.
PGM=*pgm-name*	specifies the SYSOUT program name.
PRMODE=*value*	specifies which process mode is required for printing the SYSOUT data set.
SYSOUT=*value*	specifies the output class for the SYSOUT data set. If SYSOUT is not defined, its value is taken from the SAS system option FILESYSOUT=.
UCS=	specifies the universal character set.
UCSVER	tells the operator to visually verify that the character set image is for the correct print chain or print train. The character set image is displayed on the printer before the data set is printed.
VERIFY	tells the operator to verify that the image displayed on the printer is for the correct FCB image.

Subsystem Options for the FILENAME Statement

The following subsystem data set options are also available. For more information about subsystem data sets, see the appropriate IBM MVS JCL manual for your site.

SUBSYS=*value*	specifies the name of the subsystem (from 1 to 4 characters).
PARM1=*value*	specifies a subsystem parameter (up to 67 characters).
PARM2=*value*	specifies a subsystem parameter (up to 67 characters).

FILENAME *continued*

PARM3=*value*	specifies a subsystem parameter (up to 67 characters).
PARM4=*value*	specifies a subsystem parameter (up to 67 characters).
PARM5=*value*	specifies a subsystem parameter (up to 67 characters).

Options for HFS Files and Pipes

Several options can be specified in the FILENAME statement for files and pipes that are in the Hierarchical File System of OpenEdition MVS. For information about these options, see "Host-Specific Options for HFS Files" on page 88.

See Also

□   *SAS Language: Reference*

FOOTNOTE

Prints up to ten lines at the bottom of the procedure output

Valid: anywhere

MVS specifics: maximum length of footnote

Syntax

FOOTNOTE *<n> <'text'* | *"text">;*

MVS Specifics

Under MVS, the maximum length of footnotes is 200 characters. If you specify a footnote length that is greater than the value of the LINESIZE= system option, the footnote is truncated to the line size.

See Also

□   *SAS Language: Reference*

%INCLUDE

Includes SAS statements and data lines

Valid: anywhere

MVS specifics: *file-specification*, JCLEXCL, HFS options

Syntax

%INCLUDE *source-1* < . . *source-n*>
        </<SOURCE2> <S2=*length*> <JCLEXCL> <*HFS-options*>>;

MVS Specifics

The following list explains some of the components of the %INCLUDE statement. See *SAS Language: Reference* for the complete syntax information.

source
> describes the location of the information you want to access with the %INCLUDE statement. The three possible sources follow:

> *file-specification*
>> Under MVS, this can be a fileref, or an operating system data set name enclosed in quotes.

> *internal-lines*
>> You can access lines that were entered earlier in the same SAS job or session. In order to use this technique in a line mode session, the SAS system option SPOOL must be in effect.

> *keyboard-entry*
>> You can enter the statements or data lines directly from the terminal. Use an asterisk (*) to indicate that the statements are to come from the terminal.

SOURCE2
> causes the SAS log to show the source statements that are being included in your SAS program. In other words, this option has the same effect as the SAS system option SOURCE2, except that it applies only to the records that you are currently including. Specifying SOURCE2 in the %INCLUDE statement works even if the NOSOURCE2 system option is in effect.

S2=*length*
> specifies the length of the record to be used for input. Possible values are:

> S   sets S2 equal to the current setting of the SAS system option S=.

> 0   tells SAS to use the setting of the SAS system option SEQ= to determine whether the line contains a sequence field. If the line does contain a sequence field, SAS determines the line length by excluding the sequence field from the total length.

%INCLUDE *continued*

> *n*
> indicates which columns SAS should scan and which columns, if any, contain sequence numbers that should be ignored. *n* specifies the column in which to start scanning (for variable-length records) or stop scanning (for fixed-length records).
>
> If the source lines in an external file that you are including contain sequence numbers, then either delete them before including the SAS program in your SAS session, or specify S2=0.

JCLEXCL
ignores any lines of JCL in the included source.

HFS-options
are options that you can specify for files that are in the Hierarchical File System of OpenEdition MVS. See "Host-Specific Options for HFS Files" on page 88 for details.

See Also

□ *SAS Language: Reference*

INFILE

Specifies an external file to read with an INPUT statement

Valid: in a DATA step

MVS specifics: *file-specification, type, host-options*

Syntax

INFILE *file-specification <type> <options> <host-options>*;

MVS Specifics

You can use the following arguments with the INFILE statement:

file-specification
identifies the file that you want to read and can have any of the following forms:

> *fileref*
> specifies the assigned fileref or allocated DDname of the file. The fileref must conform to the rules for DDnames. That is, it can consist of one to eight letters, numbers, or national characters ($, @, #); the first character must be a letter or a national character.

fileref(member)
> specifies the assigned fileref or allocated DDname and the name of a member in a partitioned data set.

'OS-data-set-name'
> specifies the name of the operating system data set to be dynamically allocated by the SAS System for this INFILE statement.

CARDS
> specifies that input data immediately follow a CARDS statement in your SAS program.

type
> specifies the type of file. When you omit *type*, the default is a standard external file. Nonstandard (host-specific) file types that you can specify for MVS are:

> DLI
>> specifies that the file is an IMS-DL/I file. For information about IMS-DL/I options for the INFILE statement, see *SAS/ACCESS Interface to IMS-DL/I: Usage and Reference, Version 6, Second Edition.*

> IDMS
>> specifies that the file is a CA-IDMS file. For information about CA-IDMS options for the INFILE statement, see SAS Technical Report P-269, *SAS/ACCESS Interface to CA-IDMS: DATA Step Interface, 6.09 Enhanced Release.*

> ISAM
>> specifies that the file is an ISAM file. See "Accessing ISAM Files" on page 83.

> VSAM
>> specifies that the file is a VSAM file. See "Accessing VSAM Data Sets" on page 83.

> VTOC
>> specifies that the Volume Table of Contents (VTOC) is to be accessed.

options
> are portable options that can be specified in the INFILE statement. See *SAS Language: Reference* for information about these options.

host-options
> are host-specific options that can be specified in the INFILE statement. You can specify portable options and *host-options* in any order. When specifying more than one option, use a blank space to separate each option.
>
> The *host-options* that you can specify depend on which type of external file is being accessed. See the following sections for details:
>
> □ "Standard Options for the INFILE Statement under MVS" on page 286
>
> □ "Options for Retrieving Information about Data Sets" on page 287
>
> □ "VSAM Options for the FILE and INFILE Statements under MVS" on page 268
>
> □ "VTOC Options for the INFILE Statement under MVS" on page 288
>
> □ "Host-Specific Options for HFS Files" on page 88

INFILE *continued*

Standard Options for the INFILE Statement under MVS

The following standard options can be used with all standard external files under MVS.

BLKSIZE=*value* | BLK=*value*
 specifies the block size of the file. Block size is discussed in more detail in "DCB Attribute Options" on page 275.

CCHHR=*variable*
 specifies a character variable to which the physical address (cylinder head record) of a record is returned. This applies to files on CKD disks only.

CLOSE=*keyword*
 indicates how a tape volume is to be positioned at the end of the DATA step. Values for *keyword* are:

REREAD positions the tape at the logical beginning of the data set.

LEAVE positions the tape at the logical end of the data set.

REWIND rewinds the tape to the physical beginning of the volume.

FREE dynamically deallocates the tape volume.

DISP is implied by the control language.

CSRC
 specifies that you want to use the CSRCESRV services that are available with MVS/ESA to decompress data on input. The following example illustrates the use of this option:

```
data;
   infile myfile csrc;
   input;
run;
```

DCB=*fileref*
 gives the fileref of an external file that was referenced in an earlier FILE or INFILE statement in the same DATA step. SAS uses that file's RECFM=, LRECL=, and BLKSIZE= information for the current file.

LRECL=*value*
 specifies the logical record length of the file. For more information, see the description of LRECL= in "DCB Option Descriptions" on page 275.

RECFM=*record-format*
 specifies the record format of the file. Valid values are:

F fixed length records, unblocked.

V variable length records, unblocked.

FB fixed length records, blocked.

VB variable length records, blocked.

U   undefined length records, unblocked.

The following values can be appended to the RECFM= values:

A   the first byte of each record is an ANSI printer control character.

M   specifies that the file is a machine control character file. SAS does not interpret machine-code control characters nor does it create them in output files. See your *IBM MVS/ESA JCL Reference* for more information.

S   the file contains spanned records (V), or the file contains standard blocks (F).

The following value stands alone; no other values can be appended:

N   indicates that the file is in binary format. The file is treated as a byte stream; that is, line boundaries are not recognized. This record format is specific to the SAS System.

Options for Retrieving Information about Data Sets

The following options enable you to retrieve information about a data set from the operating system control blocks. SAS assigns values to the variables that are defined by these options when it opens the data set. It updates the values every time it opens a new data set in a concatenation. These options can be used with all standard external files under MVS.

DEVTYPE=*variable*
  defines a character variable (minimum length 24) that the SAS System sets to the device type from information in the MVS operating system DEVTYPE macro. You can use DEVTYPE= to access the information both initially and when opening a new data set in a concatenation. See the IBM documentation for your system for more details.

DSCB=*variable*
  defines a character variable (minimum length 96) that the SAS System sets to the Data Set Control Block (DSCB) information from a non-VSAM data set. You can use DSCB= to access the information both initially and when opening a new data set in a concatenation. See the IBM documentation for your system for more details.

JFCB=*variable*
  defines a character variable (minimum length 176) that the SAS System sets to the Job File Control Block (JFCB). You can use JFCB= to access the information both initially and when opening a new data set in a concatenation. See the IBM documentation for your system for more details.

UCBNAME=*variable*
  defines a character variable (minimum length 3) that SAS sets to the unit name (device address), which is taken from information in the unit control block (UCB).

VOLUME=*variable* | VOLUMES=*variable*
  defines a character variable (minimum length 6) that SAS sets to the disk volume serial number, which is taken from the JFCB. The JFCB lists only the first five volume serial numbers, so for a multivolume file the value of VOLUME= is the concatenated volume serial numbers (up to five volumes). You can use VOLUME= to access the information both initially and when opening a new data set in a concatenation.

INFILE   *continued*

VTOC Options for the INFILE Statement under MVS

The following options are used only in INFILE statements that involve VTOC (Volume Table of Contents) access:

CCHHR=*variable*
>   defines a SAS character variable of length 5 whose value is set to the CCHHR of the last VTOC record that was read by SAS. The returned value is in hexadecimal format; it can be printed by using the $HEX10. SAS format.

CVAF
>   tells SAS to use the Common VTOC Access Facility (CVAF) of the IBM program product Data Facility/Device Support (DF/DS) for indexed VTOCs. If the VTOC is not indexed, or if your installation does not have CVAF, this option is ignored.
>
>   **Note:**   When you use CVAF and CCHHR=, values that are returned for Format-5 DSCB records are not valid, because indexed VTOCs do not have Format-5 DSCB records.

Options for HFS Files and Pipes

Several options can be specified in the INFILE statement for files and pipes that are in the Hierarchical File System of OpenEdition MVS. For information about these options, see "Host-Specific Options for HFS Files" on page 88.

See Also

□   "Reading from External Files" on page 78

□   *SAS Language: Reference*

LENGTH

Specifies how many bytes SAS uses to store a variable's value

Valid: in a DATA step

MVS specifics: length of numeric variables

Syntax

LENGTH *variables* <$> *length* . . . <DEFAULT=*n*>;

>   **Note:**   This is a simplified version of the LENGTH statement syntax; see *SAS Language: Reference* for the complete syntax and its explanation.

MVS Specifics

length   can range from 2 to 8 for numeric variables and from 1 to 200 for character variables.

n   changes from 8 to *n* the default number of bytes that SAS uses for storing the values of newly created numeric variables. Under MVS, *n* can range from 2 to 8.

See Also

□   "Using the LENGTH Statement to Save Storage Space" on page 143

□   *SAS Language: Reference*

LIBNAME

Assigns a SAS libref and an engine to a SAS data library

Valid: anywhere

MVS specifics: *libref, engine, OS-data-set-name, engine/host-options*

Syntax

LIBNAME *libref* *<engine>* *<'OS-data-set-name'>* *<engine/host-options>*;
LIBNAME *libref* | _ALL_ CLEAR;
LIBNAME *libref* | _ALL_ LIST;

MVS Specifics

The LIBNAME statement assigns a libref to a SAS data library.

Note: The LIBNAME statement is also used to list the attributes of a SAS data library and to clear a libref. For more information, see "Listing Your Current Librefs" on page 39 and "Deallocating SAS Data Libraries" on page 38.

Assigning Librefs

Assigning a libref associates a SAS data library with an engine and with engine/host options. Use the following form of the LIBNAME statement to assign a libref.

LIBNAME *libref* *<engine>* *<'OS-data-set-name'>* *<engine/host-options>*;

You can use this form to assign a libref to either a permanent SAS data library or a temporary one. The following statement allocates a temporary SAS data library, assigns the libref ABC to it, and associates it with the V6 engine:

```
libname abc v6 '&mytemp' disp=new;
```

The operating system data set name for this temporary SAS data library is a specially formatted name chosen by the operating system; it includes your user prefix and the temporary name that you specify (MYTEMP in this example). You can view the operating system data set name in the LIBNAME window by typing **LIBNAME** on the command line of

LIBNAME *continued*

any display manager window.

You can use the following arguments with this form of the LIBNAME statement:

libref

is a one- to eight-character name that conforms to the rules for both SAS names and DDnames. That is, the first character must be a letter; subsequent characters can be either letters or numbers.

Note: Unlike filerefs, librefs cannot include the national characters $, @, and #.

engine

specifies which engine to use to access the SAS data library. The following engines can be specified in the LIBNAME statement under MVS:

V6	specifies the engine for accessing Version 6 SAS files in disk format. BASE, V609, V608, V607, and V606 are aliases for the V6 engine.
V6SEQ	specifies the engine for accessing Version 6 SAS files in sequential format, either on tape or on disk. TAPE is an alias for this engine.
V5	specifies the engine for accessing Version 5 SAS files on disk.
V5SEQ	specifies the engine for accessing Version 5 SAS files in sequential format, either on tape or on disk.
XPORT	specifies the engine for accessing SAS files in transport format.
BMDP	specifies the engine for (read-only) access to BMDP files.
OSIRIS	specifies the engine for (read-only) access to OSIRIS files.
REMOTE	specifies the engine that SAS/CONNECT and SAS/SHARE use to access remote files.
SPSS | SPSSX	specifies the engine for (read-only) access to SPSS files.

If you do not specify an engine, SAS attempts to assign an engine according to the rules described in "How SAS Assigns an Engine When No Engine Is Specified" on page 32. See the discussion of engines in *SAS Language: Reference* for more information about the library engines.

'OS-data-set-name'

is the operating system data set name of a SAS data library, enclosed in quotes. Under MVS, it may be either a fully qualified data set name, or a partially qualified data set name that is preceded by a period. If you use a partially qualified data set name, then SAS constructs a fully qualified data set name by appending the partially qualified name to the prefix that is established by the SAS system option SYSPREF=. For example, if the option SYSPREF=MY.SASLIB has been processed, you can use the partially qualified data set name '.DATA', instead of the fully qualified data set name 'MY.SASLIB.DATA'.

For some engines, the *OS-data-set-name* may begin with a single or double ampersand (& or &&), followed by a one- to eight-character value. Such engines are those that can cause an operating system data set to be created by way of a LIBNAME statement and include the V6, V5, and V6SEQ engines. The first character after the & must be alphabetic; others may be alphanumeric or the national characters $, #, or @. If the *OS-data-set-name* begins with &, a temporary operating system data set is allocated.

The *OS-data-set-name* argument is optional. If you specify it, it must follow the engine name. If you did not specify an engine, then it must follow the libref.

engine/host-options

are host-specific options that apply to the SAS data library. Each option is identified by a keyword, and most keywords assign a specific value to that option. You may specify one or more of these options using the following forms:

keyword=value | *keyword*

When you specify more than one option, use a blank space to separate each option. The specific options that are available depend on which engine you have specified. See Chapter 3, "Accessing V6 and V6SEQ SAS Data Libraries," and Appendix 1, "Accessing V5 and V5SEQ SAS Data Libraries," for details about specific *engine/host-options*, and about the values that you specify with the various engines.

The complete list of options is presented here:

BLKSIZE=*value*

specifies the number of bytes in a block of records. See "DCB Option Descriptions" on page 275 for more information about BLKSIZE=.

DATACLAS=*data-class-name*

specifies the data class for an SMS-managed data set. The name can have up to 8 characters. This option applies only to new data sets; it is ignored for existing data sets. The data class is predefined and controls the DCB attributes for a data set.

The implementation of the DATACLAS= option is compatible with the SMS DATACLAS= JCL parameter. For complete information about this parameter, see your *IBM MVS/ESA JCL Reference.* Ask your system administrator which data-class names are used for SAS data libraries at your site.

DISP= *status* | (< *status* >,< *normal-termination-disp* >,< *abnormal-termination-disp* >)

specifies the status of the data set at the beginning and ending of a job, as well as what to do if the job step terminates abnormally. If you are specifying only *status*, you can omit the parentheses.

status

specifies the status of the operating system data set at the beginning of a job. Valid values are:

NEW   a new data set is to be created.

OLD   the data set exists and is not to be shared.

SHR   the data set exists and may be shared.

The default for *status* is OLD.

normal-termination-disp

specifies disposition for the data set if the job using the data set terminates normally. If you omit the normal termination disposition value, the default is CATLG for new data sets or KEEP for existing data sets. Valid values are:

DELETE   the data set is deleted at the end of the step.

KEEP   the data set is to be kept.

LIBNAME *continued*

CATLG	the system should place an entry in the system catalog or user catalog.
UNCATLG	the system is to delete the entry in the system catalog or user catalog.

abnormal-termination-disp

specifies what to do if the job step terminates abnormally. The default is to take the action that is specified or implied by *normal-termination-disp*. Valid values are:

DELETE	the data set is deleted at the end of the step.
KEEP	the data set is to be kept.
CATLG	the system should place an entry in the system catalog or user catalog.
UNCATLG	the system is to delete the entry in the system catalog or user catalog.

HIPERSPACE

specifies that the SAS data library be placed in a hiperspace rather than on disk. HIP is an alias for the HIPERSPACE option. For more information about this option, see "Consider placing SAS data libraries in hiperspaces" on page 155.

LABEL=(*subparameter-list*)

enables you to specify for a tape or direct access data set the type and contents of the label of the tape or disk data set, as well as other information such as the retention period or expiration date for the data set.

The LABEL= option is identical to the JCL LABEL= parameter. Here is a simple example:

```
label=(3,SL,,,EXPDT=1998/123)
```

This label specification indicates the data set sequence number is 3, that it uses standard labels, and that it expires on the 123rd day of 1998. See your *IBM MVS/ESA JCL Reference* for complete information about how to use the LABEL= option, including which subparameters you can specify in *subparameter-list*.

MGMTCLAS=management-class-name

specifies a management class for an SMS data set. The name can have up to 8 characters. This option applies only to new data sets; it is ignored for existing data sets. The management class is predefined and controls how your data set is managed, such as how often it is backed up and how it is migrated.

The implementation of the MGMTCLAS= option is compatible with the SMS MGMTCLAS= JCL parameter. For complete information about this parameter, see your *IBM MVS/ESA JCL Reference*. Ask your system administrator which management class names are used at your site.

SPACE=(*unit*,(*primary*<,*secondary*>), <RLSE>,<*type*>, <ROUND>)

specifies how much disk space to provide for a data set that is being created. The space can be requested in terms of tracks, cylinders, or blocks, as follows:

unit
 may be any of the following:

  TRK specifies that the space is to be allocated in tracks.

  CYL specifies that the space is to be allocated in cylinders.

  blklen specifies that the space is to be allocated in blocks whose block length is *blklen* bytes. The system computes how many tracks are allocated.

primary
 specifies how many tracks, cylinders, or blocks to allocate.

secondary
 specifies how many additional tracks, cylinders, or blocks to allocate if more space is needed. The system does not allocate additional space until it is needed.

RLSE
 causes unused space that was allocated to an output data set to be released when the data set is closed. Unused space is released only if the data set is opened for output and if the last operation was a write operation.

type
 can be any of the following:

  CONTIG means that the space to be allocated must be contiguous.

  MXIG means that the maximum contiguous space is required.

  ALX means that different areas of contiguous space are needed.

ROUND
 specifies that the allocated space must be equal to an integral number of cylinders when the *unit* specified was a block length. If *unit* was specified as TRK or CYL, the system ignores ROUND.

If SPACE is not defined, its values are taken from the SAS system options FILEUNIT=, FILESPPRI=, and FILESPSEC=, in the following form:

```
SPACE=(FILEUNIT,(FILESPPRI,FILESPSEC))
```

The default specifications are as follows:

```
SPACE=(CYL,(1,1))
```

UNIT=*value*
 can name one of several different devices. Some likely values are DISK and SYSDA. Additional valid values may be defined at your site.

LIBNAME *continued*

VOLSER=*value*

defines a character value (maximum length 6) that SAS uses for a disk volume serial number.

If VOLSER= is not specified, its value is taken from the SAS system option FILEVOL=.

STORCLAS=*storage-class-name*

specifies a storage class for an SMS data set. The name can have up to 8 characters. This option applies only to new data sets; it is ignored for existing data sets. The storage class is predefined and controls which device your SMS data set is stored on, such as disk or tape.

The implementation of the STORCLAS= option is compatible with the SMS STORCLAS= JCL parameter. For full details on this parameter, refer to your *IBM MVS/ESA JCL Reference*. Ask your system administrator which storage class names are used at your site.

WAIT=*n*

specifies how long the SAS System waits for a data set that is held by another job or user before the LIBNAME statement fails. The value *n* specifies a length of time in clock minutes. If the data set becomes free before *n* minutes expire, then the LIBNAME statement is processed as usual. The dynamic allocation request is retried internally every 15 seconds.

When you use the WAIT= option, you must also specify the engine name in the LIBNAME statement if you are accessing uncataloged data libraries or libraries that do not reside on disk. Otherwise, you do not have to specify the engine name.

See Also

□ "Allocating SAS Data Libraries Internally" on page 28

□ "Listing Your Current Librefs" on page 39

□ "LIBNAME Window" on page 414

□ *SAS Language: Reference*

OPTIONS

Changes the value of one or more SAS system options

Valid: anywhere

MVS specifics: *options*

Syntax

OPTIONS *options-1* < . . . *option-n*>;

MVS Specifics

Some of the options that you can specify are host-specific. Chapter 20, "System Options," describes the host-specific system options as well as the portable system options that have host-specific aspects. You may also use the portable system options that are described in *SAS Language: Reference.*

Some system options can be changed only when you invoke SAS, not in an OPTIONS statement. Table 20.1 on page 398 tells where each system option can be specified.

See Also

□ "SAS System Options" on page 11

□ *SAS Language: Reference*

TITLE

Specifies title lines for SAS output

Valid: anywhere
MVS specifics: maximum length of title

Syntax

TITLE <*n*> <*'text'* | *"text"*>;

MVS Specifics

Under MVS, the maximum title length is 200 characters. If you specify a title length that is greater than the value of the LINESIZE= system option, the title is truncated.

See Also

□ *SAS Language: Reference*

TSO

Issues a TSO command or invokes a CLIST or a REXX exec during a SAS session

Valid: anywhere
MVS specifics: all

TSO *continued*

Syntax

TSO *<command>*;

Description

The TSO statement is similar to the TSO (or SYSTEM) CALL routines, the TSO (or X) command, the TSO (or SYSTEM) function, and the %TSO (or %SYSEXEC) macro statement. It accepts the following argument:

command
> can be a system command enclosed in quotes, an expression whose value is a system command, or the name of a character variable whose value is a system command. Under MVS, "system command" includes TSO commands, CLISTs, and REXX execs.

> SAS executes the TSO statement immediately. Under MVS, TSO is an alias for the X statement. On other operating systems, the TSO statement has no effect, whereas the X statement is always processed.
> You can use the TSO statement to issue most TSO commands or to execute CLISTs or REXX execs. However, you cannot issue the TSO commands LOGON and LOGOFF, and you cannot execute CLISTs that include the TSO ATTN statement.
> **Note:** You cannot use the TSO statement in a batch job.

TSOEXEC
TSOEXEC is a TSO command that is used to invoke authorized commands. At MVS sites that run under later releases of TSO/E, you can invoke authorized commands such as RACF commands by submitting the following statement:

```
tso tsoexec authorized-command ;
```

For more information, see the IBM document *TSO Extensions Command Reference.*

Entering TSO Submode
You can also use the TSO statement to go into TSO submode during a SAS session.
> To start the submode, place the TSO statement in your program without specifying any options. (In a display manager session, enter TSO submode by issuing **TSO** as a command-line command. See "TSO" on page 422.) When the statement is executed, SAS goes into TSO submode and prompts you for TSO commands. Any commands that you enter in TSO submode are processed by TSO; they are not processed as SAS statements. They can be any length; however, if the command is longer than one line, you must enter a TSO continuation symbol.
> To return to the SAS session, enter **RETURN**, **END**, or **EXIT**. Any characters that follow the RETURN, END, or EXIT subcommand are ignored. An END command that occurs within a CLIST terminates the command procedure without ending the TSO submode.

See Also

☐   X statement in this chapter

☐   SYSTEM function on page 171 and TSO function on page 172

☐   SYSTEM CALL routine on page 165 and TSO CALL routine on page 166

☐   TSO command on page 422

☐   "SAS Interface to REXX" on page 122

X

Issues an operating system command during a SAS session

Valid: anywhere

MVS specifics: issues a TSO command or invokes a CLIST or a REXX exec

Syntax

X *<command>*;

MVS Specifics

Under MVS, the X and TSO statements are identical; on other operating systems, the TSO statement has no effect, whereas the X statement is always processed. See "TSO" on page 295 for more information.

298

Chapter **20** System Options

A Note about System Option Values   299

Summary Table of SAS System Options   396

Portable system options are documented in *SAS Language: Reference.* Only the system options that are MVS-specific or that have host-specific aspects are documented in this chapter. However, Table 20.1 on page 398 includes all SAS system options that are available under MVS.

For information about using SAS system options under MVS, see "SAS System Options" on page 11.

A Note about System Option Values

For each system option, one of the following types of values is listed:

Default Value
is the value that is listed when you run the OPTIONS procedure at the beginning of your SAS session, unless it has been overridden using one of the methods described in "Customizing Your SAS Session" on page 6.

Operational Value
is a value that SAS uses even though it does not actually assign that value to the option. For example, if you run PROC OPTIONS, the PFKEY= system option may appear not to have a default value. However, when no other value has been specified, SAS uses PRIMARY as the operational value.

Configuration-file Value
is a value specified in the system configuration file that is distributed with the SAS System. Options that have configuration-file values are of interest primarily to system administrators, and your system administrator may have changed the values of these options. Most of these options appear in PROC OPTIONS output only if you specify the APF option. (See "OPTIONS" on page 218.)

ALTLOG=

Specifies a destination for a copy of the SAS log

Default value: none

Valid as part of: configuration file, SAS invocation

ALTLOG= *continued*

Syntax

ALTLOG=*fileref*

MVS Specifics

The *fileref* identifies an external file. Under MVS, it can be any valid DDname. The fileref must have been previously associated with an external file using either a TSO ALLOCATE command or a JCL DD statement.

See Also

☐ Chapter 7, "Routing the SAS Log and SAS Procedure Output"

☐ *SAS Language: Reference*

ALTPRINT=

Specifies a fileref for a copy of the SAS procedure output file

Default value: none

Valid as part of: configuration file, SAS invocation

Syntax

ALTPRINT=*fileref*

MVS Specifics

The *fileref* identifies an external file. Under MVS, it can be any valid DDname. The fileref must have been previously associated with an external file using either a TSO ALLOCATE command or a JCL DD statement.

See also

☐ Chapter 7, "Routing the SAS Log and SAS Procedure Output"

☐ *SAS Language: Reference*

APPCSEC=

Controls how security is handled for the APPC communication protocol

Default value: none

Valid as part of: configuration file, SAS invocation, OPTIONS statement

Syntax

APPCSEC=<*user-ID.>password* | _SECURE_ | _NONE_ | _PROMPT_

Description

Advanced Program-to-Program Communication (APPC) is IBM's strategic enterprise connectivity solution. Based on Systems Network Architecture (SNA) logical unit type 6.2 (LU 6.2), APPC is the foundation for distributed processing within an SNA network.

The APPCSEC= option specifies how security is handled for SNA Type 6.2 APPC communication. The effect of this option depends on whether you specify it in the originating (user) session or in the destination (server) session. The following list explains the meanings of the various values that you can specify for this option.

<user-ID.>password

is valid only in the user session, and specifies a user ID and password to be passed to the remote host. It also enables security presentation. *Security presentation* means that you must supply a valid password and user ID combination from the user session in order to complete the communication link. Use this form of the APPCSEC= option when you are establishing a link between a local MVS host and a remote CMS, MVS, or OS/2 host.

Both the user ID and the password can be one to eight characters long. They can consist of letters, numbers, and the national characters #, $, or @. The first character must be either a letter or a national character. If the user ID and password are case-sensitive on the remote host, then specify their values in the appropriate case and enclose them in quotation marks.

The user ID is optional and is usually omitted when both the MVS and CMS host sessions have the same user ID. In that case, the MVS session derives the user ID from the appropriate Accessor Environment Element (ACEE).

If this option is used when connecting to an OS/2 host, then user ID/password profiles must already exist on the OS/2 host.

SECURE

is valid only in the server session, and enables security screening. *Security screening* means that the server session checks for a valid password and user ID combination.

NONE

disables the following:

□   security presentation, if specified in the user session.

□   security screening, if specified in the server session.

APPCSEC= *continued*

PROMPT
    causes a dialog window to be displayed so that the user can enter a user ID and password.

The following SAS system options are used in conjunction with the APPCSEC= option, to define APPC communication:

LUFIRST=	LUPOOL=	LU0MODE=
LULAST=	LUPREFIX=	LU62MODE=
LUNAME=	LUTYPE=	

The LU pooling options are used with SAS/CONNECT and SAS/SHARE software. A system administrator typically specifies the appropriate LU pooling options in your site's system configuration file.

APPCSEC can be specified in an OPTIONS statement; however, for security reasons its value is not displayed in PROC OPTIONS output.

See Also

You can ask your SAS Software Consultant for more information, or refer to the following documentation:

□   *SAS/CONNECT Software: Usage and Reference, Version 6, Second Edition*

□   the appendix "Post-Installation Setup for SAS/CONNECT Software" in *Installation Instructions and System Manager's Guide: The SAS System under MVS, 6.09 Enhanced Release*

□   SAS Technical Report P-260, *SAS/SHARE Software for the MVS Environment, Release 6.08.*

AUTHENCR=

Specifies whether encryption of authorization information is required or optional

Default value: OPTIONAL

Valid as part of: configuration file, SAS invocation, OPTIONS statement

---

Syntax

AUTHENCR=OPTIONAL | REQUIRED

Description

In the 6.09 Enhanced Release of the SAS System, this option indicates whether authorization information that is provided via the *username* and *password* in the TCP access method (for use by SAS/CONNECT and SAS/SHARE software) must be sent in encrypted form. The default, OPTIONAL, means that clients are not required to send authorization information in encrypted form. Thus, the 6.09E server will accept connections from clients that are running earlier versions of SAS that *are not* capable of encryption as well as from clients that *are* capable of encryption.

If you specify REQUIRED, then clients are required to send authorization information in encrypted form.

AUTOEXEC=

Specifies the fileref of the autoexec file to use when the SAS System is initialized

Operational value: SASEXEC

Valid as part of: configuration file, SAS invocation

Syntax

AUTOEXEC=*fileref*

MVS Specifics

The *fileref* identifies an external file. Under MVS, it can be any valid DDname. The fileref must have been previously associated with an external file using either a TSO ALLOCATE command or a JCL DD statement.

If you do not specify a value for AUTOEXEC=, then SAS checks to see whether the SASEXEC DDname has been allocated. If so, SAS sets the value of AUTOEXEC= to SASEXEC.

See also

□ "Autoexec Files" on page 8

□ *SAS Language: Reference*

BLKALLOC

Causes SAS to set LRECL and BLKSIZE values for a SAS data library when it is allocated rather than when it is first accessed

Default value: NOBLKALLOC

Valid as part of: configuration file, SAS invocation, OPTIONS statement

BLKALLOC   *continued*

Syntax

BLKALLOC | NOBLKALLOC

Description

If BLKALLOC is in effect, then SAS sets LRECL and BLKSIZE values for a SAS data library even if the data library is not opened during the SAS session in which it is allocated. Both LRECL and BLKSIZE are set to the value specified in the first of the following that has a value:

□   the SAS system option BLKSIZE=

□   the SAS system option BLKSIZE(OTHER)

□   6144

BLKSIZE=

Specifies the default block size for Version 5 SAS data sets and for Version 6 SAS data libraries

Default value: 0

Valid as part of: configuration file, SAS invocation, OPTIONS statement

Syntax

BLKSIZE=*number*

Description

The BLKSIZE= option has an effect when you are creating a Version 5 SAS data set or a Version 6 SAS data library. After the data set or library is created, the block size is set. Note that for Version 6 data libraries, this option sets the physical block size of the library.

number
> specifies the block size. Acceptable values for *number* are 0 or a number in the range 1024 to 32760. A 0 indicates that the value given by the BLKSIZE(*device-type*)= option is to be used for Version 6 SAS data libraries, and that the SAS System is to select the value for Version 5 SAS data sets.

> The BLKSIZE= data set option takes precedence over the BLKSIZE= system option. For Version 6 SAS data libraries, the BLKSIZE= system option takes precedence over the BLKSIZE(*device-type*)= system option.

BLKSIZE(*device-type*)=

Specifies the default block size for Version 6 SAS data libraries by *device-type*

Default value: varies by device type

Valid as part of: configuration file, SAS invocation, OPTIONS statement

Syntax

BLKSIZE(*device-type*)=*value*

Description

device-type
>   specifies any valid specific device number, as well as esoteric types such as DISK or DASD, and OTHER. DISK or DASD sets values for the device types 2301, 2303, 2305-1, 2305-2, 2311, 2314, 2321, 3330, 3330-1, 3340, 3350, 3375, 3380, 3390, and 9345.

>   OTHER
>>   specifies that SAS is not able to determine the exact device type.

value
>   specifies the default block size. Valid values are

>   *number*
>>   specifies the block size that SAS is to use for the device.

>   OPT
>>   specifies that SAS is to choose an optimum block size for the device.

>   MAX or FULL
>>   specifies that SAS is to use the maximum permitted block size for the device.

>   HALF, THIRD, FOURTH, or FIFTH
>>   specifies that SAS is to use the largest value that results in obtaining two, three, four, and five blocks per track, respectively (if a disk device), or the maximum permitted block size divided by two, three, four, and five, respectively (if not a disk device).

The following example tells the SAS System to choose optimum block size values for all disk devices except 3380s, for which one-third track blocking is requested, and to use the maximum permitted block size on all tape devices:

```
options blksize(disk)=opt
        blksize(3380)=third
        blksize(tape)=max;
```

BLKSIZE(*device-type*)= continued

See Also

□ "Optimizing I/O" on page 152

BUFSIZE=

Specifies the permanent buffer size for an output SAS data set

Default value: 0

Valid as part of: configuration file, SAS invocation, OPTIONS statement,
                              OPTIONS window

Syntax

BUFSIZE=*number-of-bytes*

MVS Specifics

Under MVS, *number-of-bytes* can range from 4096 to 16,777,216. The value of BUFSIZE= is always an integral multiple of the library block size. If you do not specify an integral multiple of the block size, SAS uses the next higher multiple. The value of BUFSIZE= must always be at least the length of one observation plus overhead. An observation cannot span a buffer.

You may want to vary the value of BUFSIZE= if you are trying to minimize memory usage or the number of observations per page.

See Also

□ "Optimizing I/O" on page 152

□ *SAS Language: Reference*

CAPSOUT

Specifies that all output to print files is to be converted to uppercase

Default value: NOCAPSOUT

Valid as part of: configuration file, SAS invocation, OPTIONS statement

Syntax

CAPSOUT | NOCAPSOUT

CHARTYPE=

Specifies a character set or screen size to use for a device

Default value: 0

Valid as part of: configuration file, SAS invocation

Syntax

CHARTYPE=*cell-size* | *screen-size*

Description

For an IBM 3290 terminal, the CHARTYPE= option specifies which character cell size to use. For other Extended-Data-Stream (EDS) terminals, it specifies which screen size to use. This option corresponds to the CHARTYPE option in SAS/GRAPH.

cell-size
   specifies the character set number for an IBM 3290 terminal. Values are 1 for a 6 x 12 cell and 2 for a 9 x 16 cell.

screen-size
   specifies the screen size for other (EDS) terminals. Values are 1 for a primary screen size and 2 for an alternate screen size.

   The default value, 0, indicates that the CHARTYPE= option is not applicable to the terminal you are using.

CLEANUP

Specifies how to handle an out-of-resource condition

Default value: CLEANUP

Valid as part of: configuration file, SAS invocation, OPTIONS statement,
                     OPTIONS window

Syntax

CLEANUP | NOCLEANUP

CLEANUP *continued*

MVS Specifics

This section describes a host-specific selection on the requestor window that appears if you run out of a resource:

Do nothing
> tells SAS to stop processing and to let the request fail. You may select this option at any time or after trying all other selections. This selection applies only for the current out-of-resource condition.

The requestor window is not displayed during a batch job. When a resource-critical situation arises, the SAS System performs automatic continuous cleanup. If not enough resources are recovered, SAS responds just as if you had specified NOCLEANUP.

See Also

□ *SAS Language: Reference*

CLIST

Specifies that SAS will obtain its input from a CLIST

Default value: NOCLIST

Valid as part of: configuration file, SAS invocation

Syntax

CLIST | NOCLIST

Description

The CLIST option controls whether SAS obtains its input from the terminal directly (NOCLIST specified) or indirectly (CLIST specified) when running interactively under TSO. When CLIST is specified, you can use TSO CLISTs that include SAS statements after the TSO command that invokes SAS. NODMS must be specified if SAS is to obtain its primary input from a CLIST; otherwise, only input from files that are allocated to the terminal will come from a CLIST.

CODEPASS=

Specifies whether SAS makes one pass or two passes during code generation

Default value: 1

Valid as part of: configuration file, SAS invocation, OPTIONS statement

---

Syntax

CODEPASS=1 | 2

Description

If you specify CODEPASS=2, the SAS System makes two passes during code generation. The first pass determines memory requirements and adjusts branch targets to the overall size requirements of the SAS program that is being generated. The second pass uses this information to generate the SAS program.

Do not change the value of the CODEPASS= option unless you get one or more of the following messages in your SAS log:

```
NOTE: Additional internal pass was required to compute
      correct code size.  Specifying OPTION CODEPCT=nnn  may
      reduce execution time.

NOTE: Additional internal pass was required to compute
      branch offsets.  Specifying OPTION CODEPASS=2 may
      reduce execution time.

NOTE: Additional pass was required.  Specifying OPTION
      CODEPASS=2 CODEPCT=nnn  may reduce execution time.
```

If one of these messages appears in your SAS log, using the CODEPASS= and CODEPCT= values (2 and *nnn*) suggested by the message may improve performance during subsequent invocations of the SAS program. Performance improves because the SAS System does not have to determine that two-pass code generation is required before using the two-pass process.

CODEPCT=

Specifies the value used to allocate extra memory for generating SAS program code

Operational value: 120

Valid as part of: configuration file, SAS invocation, OPTIONS statement

Syntax

CODEPCT=*n*

Description

The SAS System estimates how much memory it needs for a certain task. If that amount of memory is not sufficient, you can use the CODEPCT= option to allocate extra memory. Extra memory may be required to reach the data area or resolve program branch targets. The value of the CODEPCT= option represents a percentage. For example, if the value is 120, SAS allocates 20 percent more memory than it has already allocated.

The value of *n* can range from 100 to 200. If CODEPCT= is set to 0, SAS uses a value of 120.

CODEPCT=   *continued*

You should not change the value of the CODEPCT= option unless one of the following messages appears in the SAS log:

```
NOTE: Additional internal pass was required to compute correct code
      size.  Specifying OPTION CODEPCT=nnn  may reduce execution
      time.

NOTE: Additional pass was required.  Specifying OPTION
      CODEPASS=2 CODEPCT=nnn  may reduce execution time.
```

If one of these messages appears in your SAS log, using the CODEPCT= and CODEPASS= values (*nnn* and 2) suggested by the message may improve performance during subsequent invocations of the SAS System.

COMAMID=

Specifies which communications access method to use for SAS/SHARE and SAS/CONNECT software

Default value: none

Valid as part of: configuration file, SAS invocation, OPTIONS statement

Syntax

COMAMID=*access-method-id*

MVS Specifics

The *access-method-id* specifies the communications access method. The following access methods are valid:

APPC
:   specifies the VTAM LU 6.2 access method.

PCLINK
:   specifies the access method for a 3270 communication link.

RASYNC
:   specifies the access method for an asynchronous communication link.

RSASNORM
:   specifies the access method for an asynchronous communication link through the IBM 3708, which does not have a transparent mode capability.

RSASPSTD
:   specifies the access method for an asynchronous communication link through the PCI 1076, which uses hex code '70'x as the transparent mode introducer and assumes bidirectional ASCII data streams.

RSASPSTF

specifies the access method for an asynchronous communication link through the MICOM 7400 protocol converter that uses hex code '70'x as the transparent mode introducer and assumes ASCII outbound and ASCII-to-EBCDIC conversion inbound.

RSAS7171

specifies the access method for an asynchronous communication link through an IBM 7171 protocol converter or COMMTEX Cx-80.

TCP

specifies the TCP/IP access method.

VTAM

specifies the VTAM LU 0 access method.

XMS

specifies the cross-memory services access method.

See Also

□ *SAS/CONNECT Software: Usage and Reference*

□ *SAS Language: Reference*

COMAUX1=

Specifies the first auxiliary communication access method

Default value: none

Valid as part of: configuration file, SAS invocation

Syntax

COMAUX1=*name*

Description

The COMAUX1= option is used primarily with SAS/SHARE software.

The COMAUX1= option specifies the first auxiliary communication access method. For example, you may specify COMAMID=XMS and COMAUX1=VTAM. These specifications indicate that the primary method of communication is cross-memory services. If this access method is unable to establish a connection, VTAM communication is attempted.

If the COMAUX1= option is specified in a destination (server) session, it defines additional communication support to be initialized. In an originating (user) session, it specifies that the communication access method should try to connect to the destination session if the initial COMAMID-based attempt is unsuccessful.

COMAUX1= *continued*

See Also

□ SAS Technical Report P-260, *SAS/SHARE Software for the MVS Environment, Release 6.08*

COMAUX2=

Specifies the second auxiliary communication access method

Default value: none

Valid as part of: configuration file, SAS invocation

Syntax

COMAUX2=*name*

Description

The COMAUX2= option specifies the second auxiliary communication access method. This option works similarly to the COMAUX1= SAS system option. That is, if the COMAUX2= option is specified in a destination (server) session, it defines additional communication support to be initialized. In an originating (user) session, it specifies that the communication access method should try to connect to the destination session if the initial COMAMID-based attempt and the secondary COMAUX1-based attempt are unsuccessful.

You can use the COMAUX2= option only if you have also specified the COMAUX1= option.

See Also

□ SAS Technical Report P-260, *SAS/SHARE Software for the MVS Environment, Release 6.08*

CONFIG=

Specifies a fileref for the configuration file

Default value: CONFIG

Valid as part of: SAS invocation

Syntax

CONFIG=*fileref*

MVS Specifics

The configuration file can contain any SAS system options except CONFIG=. If this option appears in the configuration file, it is ignored.

   The *fileref* that you specify can be any valid DDname. The fileref must have been previously associated with an external file using either a TSO ALLOCATE command or a JCL DD statement.

See Also

□   "Configuration Files" on page 7

□   *SAS Language: Reference*

DBCSTYPE=

Specifies a double-byte character set (DBCS) encoding method

Default value: none

Valid as part of: configuration file, SAS invocation

Syntax

DBCSTYPE=*encoding-method*

MVS Specifics

The three valid values for *encoding-method* are

FACOM   specifies the Fujitsu encoding method (JEF code).

HITAC   specifies the Hitachi encoding method (KEIS code).

IBM   specifies the IBM host encoding method.

See Also

□   *SAS Language: Reference*

DEVICE=

Specifies a terminal device driver for SAS/GRAPH software

Default value: none

Valid as part of: configuration file, SAS invocation, OPTIONS statement,
                    OPTIONS window

Syntax

DEVICE=*device-driver-name*

MVS Specifics

To see a list of available device drivers, you can use the GDEVICE procedure. If you are
using display manager, submit the following statements:

```
proc gdevice catalog=sashelp.devices;
run;
```

If you are running in interactive line mode, noninteractive mode, or batch mode, use the
following statements:

```
proc gdevice catalog=sashelp.devices nofs;
list _all_;
run;
```

See Also

□   *SAS/GRAPH Software: Using Graphics Devices in the MVS Environment*

□   *SAS Language: Reference*

DLORGCK

**Controls whether SAS validates DCB attributes of a data set that was allocated with
the V5 engine**

Default value: NODLORGCK

Valid as part of: configuration file, SAS invocation, OPTIONS statement

Syntax

DLORGCK | NODLORGCK

Description

DLORGCK causes SAS to validate DCB attributes of a data set that was allocated with the V5 engine. If DLORGCK is specified and a data set that is not a Version 5 SAS data library is allocated with the V5 engine, the following message is produced:

```
ERROR: dataset ON volume IS NOT A VERSION 5 FORMAT SAS DATA LIBRARY
       (DSORG=DA,RECFM=U).
```

If NODLORGCK is specified, DCB attributes are not validated. Consequently, SAS overwrites the DCB attributes when it opens the data set, and the data set may be corrupted.

DSRESV

Requests exclusive use of shared disk volumes when accessing partitioned data sets on shared disk volumes

Default value: NODSRESV

Valid as part of: configuration file, SAS invocation, OPTIONS statement

Syntax

DSRESV | NODSRESV

Description

The DSRESV option controls whether certain SAS utility procedures, such as PDSCOPY, issue the RESERVE macro instruction when they access partitioned data sets on shared disk volumes. The DSRESV option has two forms:

DSRESV
    reserves the device, which prevents other processors from accessing the volume on which the partitioned data set resides.

NODSRESV
    enqueues the resources that are defined by the operating system.

DYNALLOC

Specifies whether SAS should allocate sort work data sets

Default value: NODYNALLOC

Valid as part of: configuration file, SAS invocation, OPTIONS statement

DYNALLOC   *continued*

Syntax

DYNALLOC | NODYNALLOC

Description

The DYNALLOC option controls whether the SAS System or the host sort utility allocates sort work files dynamically. The DYNALLOC option has two forms:

DYNALLOC
> specifies that the host sort utility supports dynamic allocation of any necessary work files. Therefore, SAS does not attempt to allocate them.

NODYNALLOC
> specifies that SAS will allocate sort work files. This may be necessary if the host sort utility does not support allocation. Some sort programs will not reallocate previously allocated work files even if the space requirements are greater.

See Also

□   SORT=, SORTDEV=, SORTUNIT=, SORTWKDD=, SORTWKNO= system options in this chapter

ENGINE=

Specifies the default access method for SAS data libraries

Default value: V609

Valid as part of: configuration file, SAS invocation

Syntax

ENGINE=*engine-name*

MVS Specifics

The ENGINE= system option specifies the default access method, or engine, for SAS data libraries. The valid values for the ENGINE= option are V609 (BASE), V608, V607, V606, V6, and V5. The use of the SPSS, OSIRIS, BMDP, and XPORT engines with the ENGINE= option is not recommended.

See Also

□ "SAS Library Engines" on page 26

□ "How SAS Assigns an Engine When No Engine Is Specified" on page 32

□ *SAS Language: Reference*

FILEBLKSIZE(*device-type*)=

Specifies the default maximum block size for external files

Default value: varies by device type

Valid as part of: configuration file, SAS invocation, OPTIONS statement

Syntax

FILEBLKSIZE(*device-type*)=*value*

Description

device-type
> specifies any valid specific device number, as well as esoteric types such as DISK or DASD, TAPE, and OTHER.

> DISK or DASD
>> sets values for the device types 2301, 2303, 2305-1, 2305-2, 2311, 2314, 2321, 3330, 3330-1, 3340, 3350, 3375, 3380, 3390, and 9345.

> SYSOUT
>> sets values for SYSOUT data sets.

> TAPE
>> sets values for the 2400, 3400, 3480, and 3490E device types.

> TERM
>> sets values for data sets directed to the terminal.

> OTHER
>> specifies the value that SAS uses when it is unable to determine the exact device type.

value
> specifies the default block size. Valid values are

> *number*
>> specifies the block size that SAS is to use for the device.

> OPT
>> tells SAS to choose an optimum block size for the device.

> MAX or FULL
>> tells SAS to use the maximum permitted block size for the device.

FILEBLKSIZE(*device-type*)= *continued*

HALF, THIRD, FOURTH, or FIFTH
> tells SAS to use the largest value that results in obtaining two, three, four, and five blocks per track, respectively, (if a disk device) or the maximum permitted block size divided by two, three, four, and five, respectively (if not a disk device).

FILECC

Specifies whether to treat data in column 1 of a printer file as carriage-control data when reading the file

Default value: NOFILECC

Valid as part of: configuration file, SAS invocation, OPTIONS statement

Syntax

FILECC | NOFILECC

Description

This option has two forms:

FILECC
> specifies that data in column 1 of a printer file should be treated as carriage-control data.

NOFILECC
> indicates that data in column 1 of a printer file should be treated as data.

FILEDEST=

Specifies the default printer destination

Default value: none

Valid as part of: configuration file, SAS invocation, OPTIONS statement

Syntax

FILEDEST=*printer-destination*

Description

The FILEDEST= system option specifies the default destination to be used for printer data sets when the DEST= option is omitted. This can occur when the FILENAME statement does not have a DEST= value or when the form being used does not have a DEST= value.

See Also

□ "SYSOUT Data Set Options for the FILENAME Statement" on page 280

FILEDEV=

Specifies the device name used for allocating new operating system data sets

Default value: SYSDA

Valid as part of: configuration file, SAS invocation, OPTIONS statement

Syntax

FILEDEV=*device-name*

Description

FILEDEV= specifies the device name to be used when dynamically allocating a new operating system data set if *device-type* or UNIT= is not specified in the FILENAME statement, or if UNIT= is not specified in the LIBNAME statement. Device names are site-specific.

FILEDIRBLK=

Specifies the default directory block allocation for new partitioned data sets

Default value: 6

Valid as part of: configuration file, SAS invocation, OPTIONS statement

Syntax

FILEDIRBLK=*n*

Description

The FILEDIRBLK= system option specifies how many directory blocks to allocate for a new partitioned data set when the SPACE= option is omitted from the FILENAME statement.

FILEDIRBLK=   *continued*

See Also

□   FILESPPRI=, FILESPSEC=, FILEUNIT= system options in this chapter

FILEEXT=

Specifies how to handle extensions in member names of partitioned data sets

Default value: VERIFY

Valid as part of: configuration file, SAS invocation, OPTIONS statement

Syntax

FILEEXT=VERIFY | IGNORE | INVALID | ASIS

Description

For compatibility with the SAS System on other platforms, the FILEEXT= system option enables you to specify how SAS should handle extensions in the member names of partitioned data sets. Usually, a member name is one to eight alphanumeric characters starting with a letter or with one of the following national characters: $, #, @. A member name extension is an optional part of the member name that follows a period. For example, in the member name QTR1.SAS, .SAS is the extension.

The FILEEXT= option accepts the following values:

VERIFY
verifies that the part of the member name after the period corresponds to the last level of the operating system data set name.

IGNORE
ignores the part of the member name after the period and specifies that only the part before the period is to be used.

INVALID
disallows any member name with an extension.

ASIS
accepts the member name as it is.

Examples

Example of FILEEXT=VERIFY
In this example, SAS verifies that the part of the member name that follows the period corresponds to the last level of the partitioned data set name. If it does not, an error message is written to the SAS log.

```
options fileext=verify;

filename out2 'myid.fileext.sas' disp=old;

data _null_;
   file out2(versas.sas);  /* the member name is 'versas'*/
   put 'text';
run;
```

Example of FILEEXT=IGNORE

Using the IGNORE value causes the extension, if present, to be ignored:

```
options fileext=ignore;

filename out2 'myid.fileext.testsrc' disp=old;

data _null_;
   file out2(dotnd.some);  /* the member name is 'dotnd' */
   put 'text';
run;
```

Example of FILEEXT=ASIS

With the ASIS parameter, the member name is accepted as is.

```
options fileext=asis;

filename out3 'myid.fileext.testsrc' disp=old;

data _null_;
   file out3(mem.as);  /* the member name is 'mem.as' */
   put 'text';
run;
```

FILEFORMS=

Specifies the default SYSOUT form number for a print file

Default value: none

Valid as part of: configuration file, SAS invocation, OPTIONS statement

Syntax

FILEFORMS=*operating-system-form*

FILEFORMS= *continued*

Description

The FILEFORMS= system option specifies the default operating system form. The default form is used when a printer file is dynamically allocated if FORMS= is not specified in the FILENAME statement.

Comparison

The FILEFORMS= option specifies operating system forms, whereas the portable FORMS= system option specifies the name of the default form that is used by the SAS FORM subsystem. For information about the FORM subsystem and about the FORMS= system option, see *SAS Language: Reference* and "Using the PRINT Command and the FORM Subsystem" on page 99.

FILEMOUNT

Specifies that an off-line volume is to be mounted

Default value: FILEMOUNT

Valid as part of: configuration file, SAS invocation, OPTIONS statement

---

Syntax

FILEMOUNT | NOFILEMOUNT

Description

This option applies to the allocation of external files. It tells SAS what to do when an attempt is made to allocate an operating system data set on a volume that is off-line.

If FILEMOUNT is in effect, a request is made to mount the volume. If NOFILEMOUNT is in effect, then the volume is not mounted and the allocation fails.

FILEMSGS

Controls whether you receive expanded dynamic allocation error messages when you are assigning a fileref or libref to an operating system data set

Default   NOFILEMSGS

Valid as part of: configuration file, SAS invocation, OPTIONS statement

---

Syntax

FILEMSGS | NOFILEMSGS

Description

The FILEMSGS option applies to operating system data sets that are referenced in either a FILENAME statement or a LIBNAME statement.

If FILEMSGS is in effect and you try to assign a fileref or a libref to a data set that is allocated to another user, SAS generates detailed error messages explaining why the allocation failed. Under TSO, the messages are written to the display. The display is cleared and the messages appear. You must press ENTER to return to your display manager session. In batch mode, the messages are written to the job log.

If NOFILEMSGS is in effect, you will still receive some error messages in your SAS log, but they may not be as detailed.

FILENULL

Specifies whether zero-length records are written to external files

Default value: FILENULL

Valid as part of: configuration file, SAS invocation, OPTIONS statement

Syntax

FILENULL | NOFILENULL

Description

FILENULL   allows zero-length records to be written to external files. This is the default value.

NOFILENULL   prevents zero-length records from being written to external files. This type of record is ignored.

If your file transfer program cannot handle zero-length records, you should specify NOFILENULL before you create the file that you want to transfer.

FILEPROMPT

Controls whether you are prompted if you reference a data set that does not exist

Default value: FILEPROMPT (interactive); NOFILEPROMPT (batch)

Valid as part of: configuration file, SAS invocation, OPTIONS statement

FILEPROMPT *continued*

Syntax

FILEPROMPT | NOFILEPROMPT

Description

The FILEPROMPT option controls whether you are prompted if the operating system data set that is referenced in a FILENAME or LIBNAME statement does not exist. The FILEPROMPT option is not valid for batch mode.

The FILEPROMPT option has two forms:

FILEPROMPT   specifies that you want to be prompted. The prompt allows you to create the data set dynamically, or to cancel the request. This is the default value.

NOFILEPROMPT   specifies that you do not want to be prompted. In this case, the data set is not created, and your LIBNAME or FILENAME statement fails.

The FILEPROMPT option applies to operating system data sets that are referenced in either a FILENAME statement or a LIBNAME statement.

FILEREUSE

Specifies whether to reuse an existing allocation for a file that is being allocated to a temporary DDname

Default value: NOFILEREUSE

Valid as part of: configuration file, SAS invocation, OPTIONS statement

Syntax

FILEREUSE | NOFILEREUSE

Description

If FILEREUSE is in effect, and there is a request to allocate a file that is already allocated, the existing allocation is used whenever the new allocation would cause a temporary DDname (of the form @SAS*nnnn*) to be generated.

FILESPPRI=

Specifies the default primary space allocation for new operating system data sets

Default value: 1

Valid as part of: configuration file, SAS invocation, OPTIONS statement

Syntax

FILESPPRI=*primary-space-size*

Description

The default primary space is allocated in units that are specified by the FILEUNIT= option. Use the FILESPSEC= option to specify secondary space allocation and the FILEDIRBLK= option to specify the number of directory blocks to be allocated.

   The value of this option is used if you omit the SPACE= option from the LIBNAME or FILENAME statements when creating a new operating system data set.

FILESPSEC=

Specifies the default secondary space allocation for new operating system data sets

Default value: 1

Valid as part of: configuration file, SAS invocation, OPTIONS statement

Syntax

FILESPSEC=*secondary-space-size*

Description

The default secondary space is allocated in units that are specified by the FILEUNIT= system option. Use the FILESPPRI= option to specify primary space allocation and the FILEDIRBLK= option to specify the number of directory blocks to allocate.

   The value of this option is used if you omit the SPACE= option in the LIBNAME or FILENAME statements when creating a new operating system data set.

FILESTAT

Specifies whether ISPF statistics will be written

Default value: NOFILESTAT

Valid as part of: configuration file, SAS invocation, OPTIONS statement

FILESTAT   *continued*

Syntax

FILESTAT | NOFILESTAT

Description

FILESTAT causes ISPF statistics to be written in the directory entry for a new member of a partitioned data set, or updated for an existing member that already contains ISPF statistics. NOFILESTAT suppresses ISPF statistics.

FILESYSOUT=

Specifies the default SYSOUT CLASS for a printer file

Default value: none

Valid as part of: configuration file, SAS invocation, OPTIONS statement

Syntax

FILESYSOUT=*sysout-class*

Description

The FILESYSOUT= option specifies the default SYSOUT CLASS that will be used when a printer file is allocated dynamically, and when the SYSOUT= option is omitted from the FILENAME statement.
     A valid *sysout-class* is a single character (number or letter only). Valid classes are site-dependent. At some sites, data center personnel may have set up a default class that cannot be overridden.

FILEUNIT=

Specifies the default unit of allocation for new operating system data sets

Default value: CYLS

Valid as part of: configuration file, SAS invocation, OPTIONS statement

Syntax

FILEUNIT=*unit-type*

Description

The FILEUNIT= option specifies the default unit of allocation that will be used for new operating system data sets if the SPACE= option is not specified in either the FILENAME statement or the LIBNAME statement.

unit-type
> specifies the unit of allocation. Valid values include TRKS, CYLS, or an integer. The default is CYLS. If an integer is specified, it is the block size that will be used for the allocation.

FILEVOL=

Specifies which VOLSER to use for allocation of new operating system data sets when the VOL= option is omitted from FILENAME or LIBNAME statements.

Default value: none

Valid as part of: configuration file, SAS invocation, OPTIONS statement

Syntax

FILEVOL=*volser*

Description

volser
> specifies any valid VOLSER (volume serial number). A VOLSER is a six-character name of an MVS DASD or tape volume. The name contains one to six alphanumeric or national characters. VOLSERs are site-specific.

FILSZ

Specifies that the host sort utility supports the FILSZ parameter

Default value: FILSZ

Valid as part of: configuration file, SAS invocation, OPTIONS statement

Syntax

FILSZ | NOFILSZ

FILSZ *continued*

Description

If a program product sort utility that supports the FILSZ parameter is installed, specifying the FILSZ option increases the sort efficiency. The FILSZ option has two forms:

FILSZ

specifies that the host sort utility supports the FILSZ parameter. SAS uses the FILSZ= option in the SORT control statement that it generates and passes to the sort program. FILSZ is more efficient than the SIZE parameter.

NOFILSZ

specifies that the host sort utility does not support the FILSZ parameter. SAS uses the SIZE= option in the SORT control statement that it generates and passes to the sort utility program.

Note: This option can be disabled by specifying SORTANOM=16. (See "SORTANOM=" on page 372.) Therefore, in order to determine whether FILSZ or NOFILSZ is in effect, you must check the value of the SORTANOM= option in PROC OPTIONS output.

See Also

□ your site's sort utility documentation

□ SORTANOM= system option in this chapter

FSBCOLOR

Specifies whether you can set background colors in SAS windows on vector graphics devices

Default value: NOFSBCOLOR

Valid as part of: configuration file, SAS invocation, OPTIONS statement

Syntax

FSBCOLOR | NOFSBCOLOR

Description

Non-graphics terminals and *program symbols* graphics terminals such as the IBM 3279, the PC 3270 emulators, and the Tektronix 4205 do not allow you to set the background color of individual windows; the background color is always black. *Vector* graphics terminals such as the IBM 3179G, 3192G, and 3472G allow you to set the background color.

The FSBCOLOR option has two forms:

FSBCOLOR
> enables you to set the background color in your SAS windows. For example, if you specify FSBCOLOR when you invoke the SAS System, you can issue commands like the following in any SAS window:

```
color back blue
```

> This command sets the background color to blue.
>   Use the FSBCOLOR option only on vector graphics devices. The FSBCOLOR system option is ignored if you specify it on a program symbols device, and you will receive an error message if you try to set the background color of a window.

NOFSBCOLOR
> specifies that no background colors are to be used. This is the default value on all devices.

FSBORDER=

Specifies what type of symbols are to be used in borders

Default value: BEST

Valid as part of: configuration file, SAS invocation

Syntax

FSBORDER=BEST | PS | APL | NONE

Description

The FSBORDER= system option specifies what type of symbols are to be used in window borders and other widgets. Valid values are

BEST
> tells SAS to choose the border symbols based on the type of terminal you are using.

PS
> tells SAS to use programmed symbols for border symbols in interactive display manager mode.

APL
> tells SAS to use APL symbols.

NONE
> indicates that no special border symbols are to be used (normal text is used).

FSDEVICE=

Specifies the terminal device driver

Default value:　none

Valid as part of:　configuration file, SAS invocation

Syntax

FSDEVICE=*device-name*

MVS Specifics

See "Display Manager Under MVS – Terminal Support" on page 424 for a list of all devices that are supported by the terminal-based interactive windowing SAS System under MVS.

See Also

□　*SAS Language: Reference*

FSMODE=

Specifies the full-screen data stream type

Default value:　IBM

Valid as part of:　configuration file, SAS invocation

Syntax

FSMODE=*data-stream-type*

Description

The FSMODE= system option specifies the type of IBM 3270 data stream for the terminal.

data-stream-type
　　is the name of an acceptable data stream type. Valid values are

IBM
　　is the default.

FACOM | FUJITSU
　　specifies the F6683 data stream, which can be used for F6683 and F6653 terminals.

HITAC | HITACHI
　　specifies the T560/20 data stream, which can be used for T560/20, H2020, and H2050 terminals.

An incorrect setting of this option can cause a 3270 data stream program check or a system abend.

FULLSTATS

Specifies whether full system performance statistics are to be written to the SAS log

Default value: NOFULLSTATS

Alias: FULLSTIMER

Valid as part of: configuration file, SAS invocation, OPTIONS statement

Syntax

FULLSTATS | NOFULLSTATS

MVS Specifics

If the system option STIMER is in effect, the FULLSTATS system option causes the following resource statistics to be written after each step:

□ CPU time

□ elapsed time

□ EXCP count.

If the MEMRPT system option is in effect, the FULLSTATS system option causes the following resource statistics to be written after each step:

□ task memory

□ total memory.

If NOFULLSTATS is in effect, only CPU time and total memory are reported, provided that STIMER and MEMRPT are in effect.

Under MVS, FULLSTIMER is an alias for the SAS system option FULLSTATS.

MVS Comparison

The STIMER system option specifies whether system timing statistics are to be maintained. The MEMRPT system option specifies whether memory usage statistics are to be written. The FULLSTATS system option specifies whether the statistics that are written are to be in an expanded or condensed format. The STATS system option indicates whether any statistics that are maintained are to be written.

FULLSTATS   *continued*

See Also

□   MEMRPT, STIMER, and STATS system options in this chapter

□   "Collecting Performance Statistics" on page 152

□   *SAS Language: Reference*

GHFONT=

Specifies the default graphic hardware font

Default value: none

Valid as part of: configuration file, SAS invocation

Syntax

GHFONT=*font-specification*

Description

The GHFONT= option specifies the default hardware font in graphics. It applies only to vector graphics devices that support stroke precision in the vector graphics symbol set (for example, IBM terminals such as 3179G, 3192G, and 3472G). Examples of values for *font-specification* are

F6X9   specifies characters that are 6 pixels wide and 9 high.

F9X12   specifies characters that are 9 pixels wide and 12 high.

I6X9   specifies an italic font with characters that are 6 pixels wide and 9 high.

See your system administrator for a complete list of fonts that are available to you.

    This option is used with SAS Software products such as SAS/INSIGHT software where you can specify a smaller font and display more information in the tables on the display.

HSLXTNTS=

Specifies the size of each physical hiperspace that is created for a SAS data library

Default value: 1,500

Valid as part of: configuration file, SAS invocation, OPTIONS statement

Syntax

HSLXTNTS=*value*

Description

The HSLXTNTS= option specifies the size, in pages, of each physical hiperspace that is created for a SAS data library with the HIPERSPACE option in the LIBNAME statement. These physical hiperspaces are analogous to physical data set extents in that when one is filled, another is obtained. They are logically combined internally to form a single logical hiperspace representing a library.

The value that you specify must be greater than 0. Check with your system administrator for any site-specific maximum number of pages you can have.

See Also

□ "Consider placing SAS data libraries in hiperspaces" on page 155

□ *Tuning SAS Applications in the MVS Environment*, by Michael Raithel.

HSMAXPGS=

Specifies the maximum number of hiperspace pages allowed in a SAS session

Default value: 75,000

Valid as part of: configuration file, SAS invocation, OPTIONS statement

Syntax

HSMAXPGS=*value*

Description

The HSMAXPGS= option specifies the maximum number of hiperspace pages that can be allocated in a single SAS session for all hiperspaces. The value of the HSMAXPGS= option is equal to the product of the values of the HSLXTNTS= and HSMAXSPC= options.

The value that you specify must be greater than 0. Check with your system administrator for any site-specific maximum number of pages you can have.

If you are responsible for controlling resource use at your site, and are concerned with hiperspace usage, you can use the IBM SMF installation exit, IEFUSI, to limit the hiperspace resources that are available to users.

See Also

□ "Consider placing SAS data libraries in hiperspaces" on page 155

□ *Tuning SAS Applications in the MVS Environment*, by Michael Raithel.

HSMAXSPC=

Specifies the maximum number of hiperspaces allowed in a SAS session

Default value: 50

Valid as part of: configuration file, SAS invocation, OPTIONS statement

Syntax

HSMAXSPC=*value*

Description

The HSMAXSPC= option specifies the maximum number of physical hiperspaces (each of which has the size specified by the HSLXTNTS= option) that can be allocated in a single SAS session.

The value that you specify must be greater than 0. Check with your system administrator for any site-specific maximum number of hiperspaces you can have.

See Also

□   "Consider placing SAS data libraries in hiperspaces" on page 155

□   *Tuning SAS Applications in the MVS Environment*, by Michael Raithel.

HSSAVE

Controls how often the DIV data set pages are updated when a DIV data set backs a hiperspace library

Default value: HSSAVE

Valid as part of: configuration file, SAS invocation, OPTIONS statement

Syntax

HSSAVE | NOHSSAVE

Description

The HSSAVE option has two forms:

HSSAVE
:   specifies that the DIV data set pages are updated every time SAS writes to the hiperspace.

NOHSSAVE
:   specifies that the DIV data set pages are updated only when the library is closed. A SAS data library is closed when you clear the libref, or when you end your SAS session.

Note: DIV data sets are also referred to as VSAM linear data sets.

HSSAVE is the default setting for this option, and this default is probably suitable for most of your programming needs. However, there may be times when you want to specify NOHSSAVE. For example, specifying NOHSSAVE may improve your program's performance significantly, because it decreases the number of I/O operations to the DIV data set. Also, if you are testing the output of a SAS program but have not fully developed the program to produce the output you want, specifying NOHSSAVE will prevent needless saves to the DIV data set.

▶ *Caution* . . . . *Specifying NOHSSAVE prevents the DIV data set from being updated until the library is closed.*

If your system crashes before the library is closed, then you may lose all your changes. ▲

See Also

□ "Consider placing SAS data libraries in hiperspaces" on page 155

□ *Tuning SAS Applications in the MVS Environment*, by Michael Raithel.

HSWORK

Tells SAS to place the WORK data library in a hiperspace

Default value: NOHSWORK

Valid as part of: configuration file, SAS invocation

Syntax

HSWORK | NOHSWORK

Description

The HSWORK option indicates that a hiperspace should be used for the WORK data library. Specifying NOHSWORK indicates that the WORK data library will not be a hiperspace.

NOHSWORK is the default setting for this option, and this default is probably suitable for most of your programming needs. However, there may be times when you want to place the WORK data library in a hiperspace. For example, the performance of programs (with regard to elapsed time) that perform only output operations to the WORK data library may improve significantly when the WORK data library is a hiperspace library. The performance of programs that perform a mixture of input, output, and update operations usually does not show a significant improvement in elapsed time.

Note: The effect on performance of using a hiperspace for WORK data sets is site-dependent. Your system administrator may want to make recommendations based on investigations of this issue for your site.

HSWORK   *continued*

See Also

□   "Consider placing SAS data libraries in hiperspaces" on page 155

□   *Tuning SAS Applications in the MVS Environment*, by Michael Raithel.

ICSRSLV=

Enables sites that use Interlink TCP/IP to specify when or if the ICS name resolver is called to translate an IP address to a name

Operational value: ONLY

Valid as part of: configuration file, SAS invocation

Syntax

ICSRSLV=ONLY | FIRST | LAST | NEVER

Description

The value specified for the ICSRSLV option is stored into the SAS/C environment variable ICS_RESOLVER. Valid values for this option are:

ONLY   only the ICS name resolver is called.

FIRST   the ICS name resolver is called first. If there is an error, the SAS/C resolver is called.

LAST   the SAS/C resolver is called first. If there is an error, the ICS name resolver is called.

NEVER   the ICS name resolver is never called. The SAS/C resolver is always called.

   If you do not specify a value for ICSRSLV=, then SAS acts as if ONLY had been specified.

ISPCAPS

Specifies whether to convert to uppercase all printable ISPF parameters (both variables and literals) that are used in CALL ISPEXEC and CALL ISPLINK

Default value: NOISPCAPS

Valid as part of: configuration file, SAS invocation, OPTIONS statement

Syntax

ISPCAPS | NOISPCAPS

Description

If ISPCAPS is in effect, the values of the variables or literals used as parameters will be in uppercase after the call completes.

If NOISPCAPS is specified, it is the caller's responsibility to ensure that the parameters are in the proper case. (The names of most ISPF parameters must be in upper case.)

The following example shows two ISPLINK calls. The first will be converted to uppercase and the second will not be changed.

```
DATA _NULL_;
   CALL ISPLINK('display', 'dmiem1');  /* this will not work */
   CALL ISPLINK('SAS','ISPCAPS');
   CALL ISPLINK('display', 'dmiem1');  /* this will work     */
   CALL ISPLINK('SAS','NOISPCAPS');
   RUN;
```

See Also

□   "SAS Interface to ISPF" on page 106

ISPCHARF

Specifies whether or not SAS character variables with explicit informats or formats have their values converted by the informats or formats each time they are used as ISPF variables

Default value: NOISPCHARF

Valid as part of: configuration file, SAS invocation, OPTIONS statement

---

Syntax

ISPCHARF | NOISPCHARF

Description

If ISPCHARF is specified, formats and informats are used for SAS character variables that have been defined to ISPF via the VDEFINE service. If NOISPCHARF is in effect, formats and informats are not used for these SAS character variables.

ISPCHARF *continued*

See Also

□ "SAS Interface to ISPF" on page 106

ISPCSR=

Specifies the name of the ISPF variable that is set by the SAS VDEFINE exit to contain the name of a variable whose value is found to be invalid

Default value: none

Valid as part of: configuration file, SAS invocation

Syntax

ISPCSR=*variable-name*

Description

The ISPF variables that are specified by both ISPCSR= and ISPMSG= are set by the VDEFINE exit whenever the exit finds an ISPF variable that has a zero length, or whenever the SAS informat that is associated with the variable finds the value invalid. SAS uses the VDEFINE service to define *variable-name* as a character variable of length 8, placing it in the explicit function pool.

See Also

□ "SAS Interface to ISPF" on page 106

ISPEXECV=

Specifies the name of an ISPF variable which, when set, passes its value to an ISPF service

Default value: none

Valid as part of: configuration file, SAS invocation

Syntax

ISPEXECV=*variable-name*

Description

When accessed, the variable contains the return code for the service request that it was used for. SAS uses the VDEFINE service to define *variable-name* as a character variable of length 2, placing it in the explicit function pool.

For example, if ISPEXECV = SASEXEC, then you could do the following from an ISPF panel:

&SASEXEC = 'DISPLAY PANEL (XXX)'
IF (&SASEXEC ¬= '00') ...

See Also

□   "SAS Interface to ISPF" on page 106

ISPMISS=

Specifies the value for VDEFINEd SAS character variables when the associated ISPF variable that is being changed has a length of zero

Default value: blank

Valid as part of: configuration file, SAS invocation, OPTIONS statement

Syntax

ISPMISS=*value*

Description

When the ISPF variable has a length of zero, the value of ISPMISS= is the value that will be assigned to VDEFINEd SAS character variables that have explicit formats or informats associated with them. The specified value must be one byte in length.

Note: The specified value is substituted only if the SAS system option ISPCHARF was in effect when the variable was VDEFINEd. (See "ISPCHARF" on page 337.)

See Also

□   "SAS Interface to ISPF" on page 106

ISPMSG=

Specifies the name of the ISPF variable that is set by the SAS VDEFINE exit to contain a message ID for a VDEFINEd variable with an invalid value

Default value: none

Valid as part of: configuration file, SAS invocation

ISPMSG= *continued*

Syntax

ISPMSG=*variable-name*

Description

The ISPF variables that are specified by both ISPMSG= and ISPCSR= are set by the VDEFINE exit whenever the exit finds an ISPF variable that has a zero length, or whenever the SAS informat that is associated with the variable finds the value invalid. SAS VDEFINEs *variable* as a character variable of length 8, placing it in the explicit function pool.

See Also

□ "SAS Interface to ISPF" on page 106

ISPNOTES

Specifies whether ISPF error messages are to be written to the SAS log

Default value: NOISPNOTES

Valid as part of: configuration file, SAS invocation, OPTIONS statement

Syntax

ISPNOTES | NOISPNOTES

Description

If ISPNOTES is specified, then ISPF error messages are written to the SAS log. If NOISPNOTES is in effect, then ISPF error messages are not written to the SAS log.

The ISPTRACE option overrides the NOISPNOTES option, so all messages are written to the SAS log when ISPTRACE is specified.

See Also

□ "SAS Interface to ISPF" on page 106

ISPNZTRC

Specifies whether non-zero ISPF service return codes are to be written to the SAS log

Default value: NOISPNZTRC

Valid as part of: configuration file, SAS invocation, OPTIONS statement

Syntax

ISPNZTRC | NOISPNZTRC

Description

If ISPNZTRC is specified, non-zero ISPF service return codes are written to the SAS log. If NOISPNZTRC is in effect, then non-zero ISPF service return codes are not written to the SAS log.

   To display *all* parameter lists and return codes in the SAS log, use the ISPTRACE option instead of ISPNZTRC.

See Also

□   "SAS Interface to ISPF" on page 106

ISPPT

Specifies whether ISPF parameter value pointers and lengths are to be written to the SAS log

Default value: NOISPPT

Valid as part of: configuration file, SAS invocation, OPTIONS statement

Syntax

ISPPT | NOISPPT

Description

The ISPPT option is used for debugging. If ISPPT is specified, then ISPF parameter value pointers and lengths are displayed. If NOISPPT is in effect, then ISPF parameter value pointers and lengths are not displayed.

ISPPT   *continued*

See Also

□   "SAS Interface to ISPF" on page 106

ISPTRACE

Specifies whether the parameter lists that are passed to ISPF and the service return codes are to be written to the SAS log

Default value: NOISPTRACE

Valid as part of: configuration file, SAS invocation, OPTIONS statement

Syntax

ISPTRACE | NOISPTRACE

Description

If ISPTRACE is specified, then all ISPF service calls and return codes are written to the SAS log. Fixed binary parameters are written to the SAS log, converted to decimal display. After a VDEFINE or VDELETE service request, the list of currently defined SAS variables is written to the SAS log.

If NOISPTRACE is in effect, then ISPF service calls and return codes are not written to the SAS log.

Note: The ISPTRACE option can be set based on the value of the ISPF variable named DMITRACE. In the following example, if the DMITRACE value is YES, then ISPTRACE will be in effect. If the DMITRACE value is NO, then NOISPTRACE will be in effect.

```
CALL ISPLINK('DMI','*ISPTRACE');
```

See Also

□   "SAS Interface to ISPF" on page 106

ISPVDEFA

Specifies whether all current SAS variables are to be VDEFINEd

Default value: NOISPVDEFA

Valid as part of: configuration file, SAS invocation, OPTIONS statement

Syntax

ISPVDEFA | NOISPVDEFA

Description

If ISPVDEFA is specified, then all current SAS variables are VDEFINEd. If an explicit VDEFINE service request is issued, then any variables that it specifies will be defined twice.

If NOISPVDEFA is in effect, then only those variables that are passed explicitly to the VDEFINE service will be defined.

See Also

□   "SAS Interface to ISPF" on page 106

ISPVDLT

Specifies whether a VDELETE is done before each SAS variable is VDEFINEd

Default value: NOISPVDLT

Valid as part of: configuration file, SAS invocation, OPTIONS statement

Syntax

ISPVDLT | NOISPVDLT

Description

If ISPVDLT is specified, then each SAS variable is VDELETEd before it is VDEFINEd. This prevents a SAS variable from being VDEFINEd more than once in any SAS DATA step.

If NOISPVDLT is in effect, then SAS variables are not VDELETEd before they are VDEFINEd. This may cause SAS variables to be VDEFINEd more than once in a SAS DATA step.

See Also

□   "SAS Interface to ISPF" on page 106

ISPVDTRC

Specifies whether to trace every VDEFINE for SAS variables.

Default value: NOISPVDTRC

Valid as part of: configuration file, SAS invocation, OPTIONS statement

ISPVDTRC *continued*

Syntax

ISPVDTRC | NOISPVDTRC

Description

Tracing means that as each SAS variable is VDEFINEd to ISPF, its name, its VDEFINE length, and any non-zero ISPF return codes are written to the SAS log.

If NOISPVDTRC is in effect, then no information is written to the SAS log when a SAS variable is VDEFINEd to ISPF. The NOISPVDTRC setting is useful when many variables are defined with one service request, because SAS actually issues multiple VDEFINE requests (one for each variable).

See Also

□   "SAS Interface to ISPF" on page 106

ISPVIMSG=

Specifies the ISPF message ID that is to be set by the SAS VDEFINE exit whenever the informat for a variable returns a non-zero return code

Default value: none

Valid as part of: configuration file, SAS invocation, OPTIONS statement

Syntax

ISPVIMSG=*message-id*

Description

The message ID is stored in the ISPF variable that is specified by the ISPMSG= option.

See Also

□   "SAS Interface to ISPF" on page 106

ISPVRMSG=

Specifies the ISPF message ID that is to be set by the SAS VDEFINE exit whenever a variable has a null value

Default value: none

Valid as part of: configuration file, SAS invocation, OPTIONS statement

Syntax

ISPVRMSG=*message-id*

Description

The message ID is stored in the ISPF variable that is specified by the ISPMSG= option.

See Also

□ "SAS Interface to ISPF" on page 106

ISPVTMSG=

Specifies the ISPF message ID that is to be displayed by the SAS VDEFINE exit whenever the ISPVTRAP option is in effect

Default value: none

Valid as part of: configuration file, SAS invocation, OPTIONS statement

---

Syntax

ISPVTMSG=*message-id*

See Also

□ "SAS Interface to ISPF" on page 106

ISPVTNAM=

Causes the information that is displayed by the ISPVTRAP option to be limited to information for the specified variable name only

Default value: none

Valid as part of: configuration file, SAS invocation, OPTIONS statement

---

Syntax

ISPVTNAM=*variable-name*

ISPVTNAM=   *continued*

See Also

□   "SAS Interface to ISPF" on page 106

ISPVTPNL=

Specifies the name of the ISPF panel that is to be displayed by the VDEFINE exit whenever the ISPVTRAP option is in effect

Default value: none

Valid as part of: configuration file, SAS invocation, OPTIONS statement

Syntax

ISPVTPNL=*panel*

See Also

□   "SAS Interface to ISPF" on page 106

ISPVTRAP

Specifies whether the SAS VDEFINE exit is to write information to the SAS log (for debugging purposes) each time it is entered

Default value: NOISPVTRAP

Valid as part of: configuration file, SAS invocation, OPTIONS statement

Syntax

ISPVTRAP | NOISPVTRAP

Description

If ISPVTRAP is specified, the VDEFINE exit writes a message to the SAS log each time it is entered. If the parameters for the ISPVTPNL, ISPVTVARS, and ISPVTMSG options are set, it sets the ISPVTVARS variables and displays the ISPVTPNL panel with the ISPVTMSG message on it. If you press the END key on the information display, the option is set to NOISPVTRAP.

    If NOISPVTRAP is in effect, the SAS VDEFINE exit does not write information to the SAS log each time it is entered.

See Also

□ "SAS Interface to ISPF" on page 106

ISPVTVARS=

Specifies the prefix for the ISPF variables to be set by the SAS VDEFINE exit whenever the ISPVTRAP option is in effect

Default value: none

Valid as part of: configuration file, SAS invocation, OPTIONS statement

Syntax

ISPVTVARS=*prefix*

Description

The numbers 0 through 5 are appended to this prefix to generate the ISPF variable names. These variables contain the following information:

prefix 0 =	whether the variable is being read or written
prefix 1 =	the name of the variable that is being updated
prefix 2 =	the address of the parameter list for the VDEFINE exit
prefix 3 =	the address of the variable that is being updated
prefix 4 =	the length of the variable that is being updated
prefix 5 =	the value of the variable that is being updated

For example, if ISPVTVARS=SASVT, then the variables SASVT0 - SASVT5 would be created. Possible values for these variables could be as follows:

SASVT0	READ (or WRITE)
SASVT1	MYVAR
SASVT2	083C1240
SASVT3	00450138
SASVT4	7
SASVT5	MYVALUE

See Also

□ "SAS Interface to ISPF" on page 106

LINESIZE=

Specifies the line size of SAS output

Default value: the terminal's width setting for interactive modes;
                          132 for noninteractive modes

Valid as part of: configuration file, SAS invocation, OPTIONS statement,
                               OPTIONS window

Syntax

LINESIZE=*width*

MVS Specifics

Under MVS, the default for interactive mode (display manager and interactive line mode) is the terminal's width setting. For noninteractive and batch mode, the default is 132.

See Also

□   *SAS Language: Reference*

LOG=

Specifies a fileref to which the SAS log is written when executing SAS programs in modes other than display manager

Default value: SASLOG

Valid as part of: configuration file, SAS invocation

Syntax

LOG=*fileref*

MVS Specifics

The *fileref* identifies an external file. It can be any valid DDname. The fileref must have been previously associated with an external file using either a TSO ALLOCATE command or a JCL DD statement.

See Also

□ Chapter 7, "Routing the SAS Log and SAS Procedure Output" on page 93

□ *SAS Language: Reference*

LUFIRST=

Defines the beginning numeric suffix to be applied to a pooled VTAM LU acquisition

Default value: 1

Valid as part of: configuration file, SAS invocation

Syntax

LUFIRST=*value*

Description

The LUFIRST= option specifies the beginning numeric suffix that is applied to build an LU acquisition request when LU pooling is enabled under the VTAM communication protocol.

All SAS system options that are associated with VTAM communication are typically set by the system administrator in the site's system configuration file. Do not use this option without consulting your system administrator. Refer to the description of the APPCSEC= SAS system option, earlier in this chapter, for a brief overview of APPC communication and a list of references.

LULAST=

Defines the ending numeric suffix to be applied to a pooled VTAM LU acquisition

Default value: 9

Valid as part of: configuration file; SAS invocation

Syntax

LULAST=*value*

Description

The LULAST= option specifies the ending numeric suffix that is applied to build an LU acquisition request when LU pooling is enabled under the VTAM communication protocol. The following equation defines the LU pool depth:

```
LULAST-LUFIRST+1
```

If an LU is not acquired after cycling from LUFIRST to LULAST, the request fails.

LULAST=   *continued*

All SAS system options that are associated with VTAM communication are typically set by the system administrator in the site's system configuration file. Do not use this option without consulting your system administrator. Refer to the description of the APPCSEC= SAS system option, earlier in this chapter, for a brief overview of APPC communication and a list of references.

LUNAME=

Specifies a VTAM communication LU name

Default value: none

Valid as part of: configuration file, SAS invocation

Syntax

LUNAME=*name*

Description

The LUNAME= option defines the LU to be used by VTAM to establish communication with a partner session. This name should be used to define a dedicated LU, in lieu of pooled acquisition. This option can be specified in both the local and remote sessions.

The name can be one to eight characters long, consisting of letters, numbers, and the national characters #, $, or @. The first character must be a letter or a national character, and the name must be defined to VTAM.

All SAS system options that are associated with VTAM communication are typically set by the system administrator in the site's system configuration file. Do not use this option without consulting your system administrator. Refer to the description of the APPCSEC= SAS system option, earlier in this chapter, for a brief overview of APPC communication and a list of references.

LUPOOL=

Specifies when the VTAM LU is to be acquired from a pool

Default value: USER

Valid as part of: configuration file, SAS invocation

Syntax

LUPOOL=USER | ALL

Description

The LUPOOL= option determines the environment in which the VTAM LU is acquired from a pool, according to the specifications of the system options LUPREFIX=, LUFIRST=, and LULAST=.

Here is an explanation of the values for the LUPOOL= option:

USER   enables VTAM LU pooling in originating (user) executions.

ALL   enables VTAM LU pooling in both originating (user) and destination (server) executions.

All SAS system options that are associated with VTAM communication are typically set by the system administrator in the site's system configuration file. Do not use this option without consulting your system administrator. Refer to the description of the APPCSEC= SAS system option, earlier in this chapter, for a brief overview of APPC communication and a list of references.

LUPREFIX=

Specifies the prefix that is applied to a pooled VTAM LU acquisition

Default value: none

Valid as part of: configuration file, SAS invocation

Syntax

LUPREFIX=*name*

Description

The LUPREFIX= option names the prefix that is applied to build an LU acquisition request when LU pooling is enabled.

All SAS system options that are associated with VTAM communication are typically set by the system administrator in the site's system configuration file. Do not use this option without consulting your system administrator. Refer to the description of the APPCSEC= SAS system option, earlier in this chapter, for a brief overview of APPC communication and a list of references.

LUTYPE=

Tells SAS which LU protocol to use when COMAMID=VTAM is in effect

Default value: SNA0

Valid as part of: configuration file, SAS invocation, OPTIONS statement

Syntax

LUTYPE=SNA0 | SNA62

Description

The LUTYPE= option tells SAS which LU protocol to use for initiating VTAM communications with a remote partner.

Here is an explanation of the values for this option:

SNA0   is the default, chosen for compatibility with Version 5 of the SAS System. It is limited to communication between two MVS partners, using an LU 0 protocol. When you specify LUTYPE=SNA0, use the LU0MODE= SAS system option to give the name of the VTAM session mode.

SNA62   is used to support SNA communication between heterogeneous host environments, using the LU 6.2 protocol. When you specify LUTYPE=SNA62, use the LU62MODE= SAS system option to give the name of the VTAM session mode. APPC is a synonym for the SNA62 value.

The LUTYPE= system option is used only in conjunction with a specification of COMAMID=VTAM. If you specify COMAMID=APPC, the LUTYPE= system option is ignored.

All SAS system options that are associated with VTAM communication are typically set by the system administrator in the site's system configuration file. Do not use this option without consulting your system administrator. Refer to the description of the APPCSEC= SAS system option, earlier in this chapter, for a brief overview of APPC communication and a list of references.

LU0MODE=

Specifies the VTAM session mode name to use for LU 0 connections

Default value: none

Valid as part of: configuration file, SAS invocation, OPTIONS statement

Syntax

LU0MODE=*name*

Description

The mode name must be defined to VTAM, and encodes attributes for the supporting SNA sessions. If you do not use this option, a hard-coded bind image is used. Use this option when you have specified LUTYPE=SNA0.

The name can be one to eight characters long, consisting of letters, numbers and national characters (#, $, or @). The first character must be a letter or national character.

All SAS system options that are associated with VTAM communication are typically set by the system administrator in the site's system configuration file. Do not use this option without consulting your system administrator. Refer to the description of the APPCSEC= SAS system option, earlier in this chapter, for a brief overview of APPC communication and a list of references.

LU0SEC=

Controls whether the VTAM LU 0 access method presents the user ID of a connecting user to a server as if it had been validated with a password

Default value: none

Valid as part of: configuration file, SAS invocation, OPTIONS statement

Syntax

LU0SEC=_TRUST_

Description

Specifying LU0SEC=_TRUST_ for a server's SAS execution causes the VTAM LU 0 access method to present the user ID of a connecting user to the server as if it had been validated with a password. If the user ID of a connecting user is defined to the security software on the server's system and belongs to that user, then any authorization checks for SAS libraries that are made by the server will be valid.

LU0SEC can be specified in an OPTIONS statement; however, for security reasons its value is not displayed in PROC OPTIONS output.

Note: Specifying LU0SEC=_TRUST_ preserves the behavior of the VTAM LU 0 access method and the server in previous releases of SAS/SHARE software.

All SAS system options that are associated with VTAM communication are typically set by the system administrator in the site's system configuration file. Do not use this option without consulting your system administrator. Refer to the description of the APPCSEC= SAS system option, earlier in this chapter, for a brief overview of APPC communication and a list of references.

LU62MODE=

Specifies the VTAM session mode name to use for LU6.2/APPC connections

Default value: none

Valid as part of: configuration file, SAS invocation, OPTIONS statement

Syntax

LU62MODE=*name*

Description

The mode name must be defined to VTAM, and encodes attributes for the supporting SNA sessions. Use this option when you have specified LUTYPE=SNA62.

The name can be one to eight characters long, consisting of letters, numbers and national characters (#, $, or @). The first character must be a letter or a national character.

All SAS system options that are associated with VTAM communication are typically set by the system administrator in the site's system configuration file. Do not use this option without consulting your system administrator. Refer to the description of the APPCSEC= SAS system option, earlier in this chapter, for a brief overview of APPC communication and a list of references.

MAPS=

Gives the location of the SAS data library that contains the SAS/GRAPH map data sets

Default value: MAPS

Valid as part of: configuration file, SAS invocation, OPTIONS statement, OPTIONS window

Syntax

MAPS=*library-specification*

Description

library-specification
> specifies either a libref that has been previously associated with the MAPS SAS data library, or the name of an operating system data set (enclosed in quotes) that comprises a SAS data library.

MEMRPT

Specifies whether memory usage statistics are to be written to the SAS log for each step

Default value: MEMRPT

Valid as part of: configuration file, SAS invocation, OPTIONS statement

Syntax

MEMRPT | NOMEMRPT

Description

MEMRPT
> writes memory usage statistics to the SAS log for each step.

NOMEMRPT
> suppresses the writing of memory usage statistics for each step.

Comparison

The STATS system option indicates whether any statistics that are maintained are to be written to the SAS log for each step. If both the STATS and MEMRPT options are in effect, then the memory statistics are reported.

> If the FULLSTATS option is in effect, then task memory and total memory are written. If NOFULLSTATS is in effect, only total memory is written.

See Also

□   "Collecting Performance Statistics" on page 152

MEMSIZE=

Specifies the limit on the total amount of memory that SAS can use

Configuration-file value: 8M

Alias: PROCSIZE=

Valid as part of: configuration file, SAS invocation, OPTIONS statement

Syntax

MEMSIZE=n | nK | nM

MEMSIZE= *continued*

Description

The MEMSIZE= option specifies a limit on the total amount of memory that SAS uses at any one time. The operating system may use additional amounts of memory.

You can use the following values with the MEMSIZE= option:

n specifies a number in the range 0 to 2,147,483,648. A value of 0 indicates that there is no limit except the operating system limit, which may be site-specific.

*n*K specifies the number of kilobytes, from 0 to 2,097,152.

*n*M specifies the number of megabytes, from 0 to 2048.

See Also

□ "Specify a value for the MEMSIZE= system option when you invoke SAS" on page 158

MINSTG

Tells SAS to minimize its use of storage

Default value: NOMINSTG

Valid as part of: configuration file, SAS invocation, OPTIONS statement

---

Syntax

MINSTG | NOMINSTG

Description

The MINSTG system option causes SAS to minimize its use of storage by returning unused storage and deleting unused load modules at the termination of steps and pop-up windows. This option should be used on memory-constrained systems or when sharing the address space with other applications, such as ISPF split-screen or multisession products.

The MINSTG option has two forms:

MINSTG
tells SAS to minimize storage in use.

NOMINSTG
tells SAS not to minimize storage in use.

MSYMTABMAX=

Specifies the maximum amount of memory available to the macro variable symbol table(s)

Default value: 1,048,576 bytes

Valid as part of: configuration file, SAS invocation, OPTIONS statement, OPTIONS window

Syntax

MSYMTABMAX=*n* | *n*K | *n*M | *n*G | MAX

MVS Specifics

Under MVS, the default value for this option is 1,048,576 bytes.

See Also

□ SAS Technical Report P-222, *Changes and Enhancements to Base SAS Software, Release 6.07*

MVARSIZE=

Specifies the maximum size for macro variables that are stored in memory

Default value: 8,192 bytes

Valid as part of: configuration file, SAS invocation, OPTIONS statement, OPTIONS window

Syntax

MVARSIZE=*n* | *n*K | *n*M | *n*G | MAX

MVS Specifics

Under MVS, the default value for this option is 8,192 bytes.

See Also

□ SAS Technical Report P-222, *Changes and Enhancements to Base SAS Software, Release 6.07*

NDSVOLS=

Specifies the VOLSER on which no SAS data library processing is to occur

Default value: none

Valid as part of: configuration file, SAS invocation, OPTIONS statement

Syntax

NDSVOLS=*volser*

Description

This option is used only for Version 5 SAS data libraries. With this option you can specify a volume serial that causes SAS to treat a data set reference to that volume as if you had specified _NULL_. This option is useful for production SAS jobs that, for example, need to initialize catalog generation data groups.

volser
> specifies any valid VOLSER (volume serial number). A VOLSER is a six-character name of an MVS DASD volume. The name contains one to six alphanumeric or national characters. Volume serial numbers are site-specific.

NEWS=

Specifies the location of a file that contains messages to be written to the SAS log at invocation time

Default value: none

Valid as part of: configuration file, SAS invocation

Syntax

NEWS=*file-specification* | NONEWS

MVS Specifics

file-specification
> specifies an external file. An acceptable value for the *file-specification* is any valid DDname or an operating system data set name (sequential data set or a member of a PDS).

NONEWS
> causes SAS to set the value of the NEWS= option to blanks and to display its value as blank in PROC OPTIONS output. NONEWS is supported for compatibility with Version 5 of the SAS System.

See Also

□ *SAS Language: Reference*

OBS=

Specifies which observation the SAS System processes last

Default value: MAX

Valid as part of: configuration file, SAS invocation, OPTIONS statement,
                     OPTIONS window

Syntax

OBS=*n* | MAX

MVS Specifics

The default value, MAX, is the largest signed 4-byte integer that is representable on a host. Under MVS, this value is 2,147,483,647.

See Also

□ *SAS Language: Reference*

OPLIST

Writes to the SAS log the settings of all SAS system options that you specified when you invoked SAS

Default value: NOOPLIST

Valid as part of: configuration file, SAS invocation

Syntax

OPLIST | NOOPLIST

MVS Specifics

On MVS, the OPLIST system option writes to the SAS log the settings of all options that were specified on the command line, up to 100 characters. It does not list the settings of system options that were specified in the configuration file. Contrast the OPLIST option with the VERBOSE system option, which is discussed later in this chapter.

OPLIST *continued*

See Also

□ *SAS Language: Reference*

PAGESIZE=

Specifies the page size of SAS output

Default value: terminal screen size for display manager; 21 for interactive line-mode; 60 for noninteractive modes

Valid as part of: configuration file, SAS invocation, OPTIONS statement, OPTIONS window

Syntax

PAGESIZE=*n*

MVS Specifics

Under MVS, display manager uses the terminal screen size to determine page size. The interactive line mode default is 21 (portable default). For noninteractive and batch modes, the default is 60. The value for this option can range from 15 to 32767.

See Also

□ *SAS Language: Reference*

PFKEY=

Specifies which set of function keys to designate as primary

Operational value: PRIMARY

Valid as part of: configuration file, SAS invocation

Syntax

PFKEY=*pfkey-set*

Description

The PFKEY= option allows you to specify which set of 12 programmed function keys is to be considered *primary*. Whichever set is designated as primary has settings that are equivalent to Version 5 settings, where appropriate.

pfkey-set
> specifies which set of function keys are the primary set. Acceptable values include the following:

> PRIMARY
>> specifies that the primary set be F13 through F24. Thus, F13 through F24 would have Version 5 settings; F1 through F12 would have Version 6 settings.

> ALTERNATE
>> specifies that the primary set be F1 through F12. Thus F1 through F12 would have Version 5 settings; F13 through F24 would have Version 6 settings.

> 12
>> specifies that F1 through F12 exactly match F13 through F24. Thus, both F1 through F12 and F13 through F24 would have Version 5 settings. As a result, the KEYS window displays only F1 through F12.

The following values are displayed in the KEYS window when you specify PFKEY=PRIMARY. F1 through F12 are Version 6 settings; F13 through F24 are Version 5 settings.

Key	Definition	Key	Definition
F1	mark	F13	help
F2	smark	F14	zoom
F3	unmark	F15	zoom off; submit
F4	cut	F16	pgm; recall
F5	paste	F17	rfind
F6	store	F18	rchange
F7	prevwind	F19	backward
F8	next	F20	forward
F9	pmenu	F21	output
F10	command	F22	left
F11	keys	F23	right
F12	undo	F24	home

If you do not specify a value for PFKEY=, then SAS acts as if PFKEY=PRIMARY were specified.

PFKEY= *continued*

See Also

□ *SAS Language: Reference*

PGMPARM=

Specifies the parameter that is passed to the external program specified by the SYSINP= option

Default value: none

Valid as part of: configuration file, SAS invocation

Syntax

PGMPARM='*string*'

Description

The PGMPARM= option specifies the parameter that is passed to the external program specified by the SYSINP= option (described later in this chapter).

The parameter string can be up to 255 characters long. If the parameter string contains blanks or special characters, enclose it in single quotation marks.

For more information about using the PGMPARM= and SYSINP= options, contact your SAS Software Consultant.

PRINT=

Specifies the fileref for the SAS output file when executing SAS programs in modes other than display manager

Default value: SASLIST

Valid as part of: configuration file, SAS invocation

Syntax

PRINT=*fileref*

MVS Specifics

The *fileref* identifies an external file. It can be any valid DDname. The fileref must have been previously associated with an external file using either a TSO ALLOCATE command or a JCL DD statement.

See Also

□ Chapter 7, "Routing the SAS Log and SAS Procedure Output"

□ *SAS Language: Reference*

PRINTINIT

Initializes the SAS print file

Default value: NOPRINTINIT

Valid as part of: configuration file, SAS invocation

Syntax

PRINTINIT | NOPRINTINIT

MVS Specifics

The PRINTINIT system option is provided for compatibility with Version 5 of the SAS System. This option initializes the SAS print file.

Under MVS, specifying PRINTINIT causes the SAS print file to become empty before SAS writes output to it. It also forces the file attributes to be correct for a print file. Specify NOPRINTINIT if a previous program or job step has already written output to the same file, and you want to preserve that output.

PROCLEAVE=

Specifies how much memory to leave unallocated for SAS procedures to use to complete critical functions during out-of-memory conditions

Default value: (0,102400)

Valid as part of: configuration file, SAS invocation, OPTIONS statement

Syntax

PROCLEAVE=nK | nM | (nK,nK) | (nM,nM)

PROCLEAVE= *continued*

MVS Specifics

You can use the following values with the PROCLEAVE= option:

*n*K

> specifies in kilobytes how much memory to leave unallocated above the 16-megabyte line. Valid values are any integer from 0 to the maximum amount of available memory.

*n*M

> specifies in megabytes how much memory to leave unallocated above the 16-megabyte line. Valid values are any integer from 0 to the maximum amount of available memory.

(*n*K,*n*K) | (*n*M,*n*M)

> specifies how much memory to reserve below the 16-megabyte line, followed by the amount of memory to reserve above the line.

See Also

□ "Use SYSLEAVE= and PROCLEAVE= to handle out-of-memory conditions" on page 159

□ *SAS Language: Reference*

PSUP=

Specifies the name of the SAS portable supervisor

Operational value: SASXKERN

Valid as part of: configuration file, SAS invocation

Syntax

PSUP=*load-module*

Description

The PSUP= option specifies the name of the load module to which the host supervisor passes control after the host supervisor is initialized.

This option is typically set in the system configuration file by the system administrator at your site. If no value is specified for PSUP=, then the value SASXKERN is used.

REMOTE=

Specifies the remote session ID used for SAS/CONNECT software

Default value: none

Valid as part of: configuration file, SAS invocation, OPTIONS statement,
OPTIONS window

Syntax

REMOTE=*session-id*

MVS Specifics

This option is not required under MVS.

See Also

□   *SAS/CONNECT Software: Usage and Reference*

□   *SAS Language: Reference*

REXXLOC=

Specifies the DDname of the REXX exec library to be searched when the REXXMAC option is in effect

Default value: SASREXX

Valid as part of: configuration file, SAS invocation

Syntax

REXXLOC=*DDname*

Description

The REXXLOC= option specifies the DDname of the REXX exec library to be searched for any SAS REXX execs, if the REXXMAC option is in effect.

See Also

□   "SAS Interface to REXX" on page 122

□   REXXMAC system option in this chapter

REXXMAC

Enables or disables the REXX interface

Default value: NOREXXMAC

Valid as part of: configuration file, SAS invocation, OPTIONS statement

Syntax

REXXMAC | NOREXXMAC

Description

If REXXMAC is in effect, then the REXX interface is enabled. This means that when SAS encounters an unrecognized statement, it searches for a REXX exec whose name matches the first word of the unrecognized statement. The REXXLOC= system option specifies the DDname of the REXX exec library to be searched.

If the default, NOREXXMAC, is in effect, the REXX interface is disabled. This means that when SAS encounters an unrecognized statement, a "statement is not valid" error occurs.

See Also

□   "SAS Interface to REXX" on page 122

□   REXXLOC= system option in this chapter

RSASUSER

Controls whether the SASUSER data library can be opened for read-only access or for update access

Default value: NORSASUSER

Valid as part of: configuration file, SAS invocation

Syntax

RSASUSER | NORSASUSER

MVS Specifics

This option has two forms:

RSASUSER   specifies that the SASUSER data library can be opened for read
                        access only. Under MVS, specifying RSASUSER is similar to
                        specifying DISP=SHR in a JCL DD statement or in a TSO
                        ALLOCATE command. See your IBM documentation for more
                        information about this topic.

NORSASUSER   is the default value, and allows the SASUSER data library to be opened for update access.

S=

For data lines that follow a CARDS statement and for SAS source statements, specifies which columns SAS should scan and which columns, if any, contain sequence numbers that should be ignored

Default value: 0

Valid as part of: configuration file, SAS invocation, OPTIONS statement, OPTIONS window

Syntax

S=*n*

MVS Specifics

Under MVS, *n* can range from 0 to 32760, which is the maximum length of records on MVS.

    Note: If *n* is 0, SAS uses the value of the SEQ= system option to determine whether the input contains sequence fields that should be ignored. Otherwise, SAS interprets *n* as the column in which to start scanning (for variable-length records) or stop scanning (for fixed-length records).

See Also

□   *SAS Language: Reference*

SASAUTOS=

Specifies the location of the autocall library

Default value: SASAUTOS

Valid as part of: configuration file, SAS invocation, OPTIONS statement, OPTIONS window

Syntax

SASAUTOS=*file-specification* | (*file-specification-1 . . . file-specification-n*)

SASAUTOS= *continued*

MVS Specifics

file-specification
> specifies the name of a partitioned data set that functions as an autocall library. Do not specify the member name with the SASAUTOS= system option. Each member is used to hold the source statements for one macro. Member names must be the same as the name of the macro.
>
> You can specify the partitioned data set in a number of ways: by enclosing the fully qualified data set name in quotes, by specifying a partially qualified data set name preceded by a period in quotes, or by using a fileref. Also, you can specify one or more autocall libraries at the same time. They will be searched in the order in which they are listed.

SAS looks for autocall members in partitioned data sets that are identified by the SAS system option SASAUTOS=. By default, SAS looks in the partitioned data set that is associated with the SASAUTOS fileref. Once you specify the SASAUTOS= system option, that specification replaces the default. SAS no longer searches the partitioned data set that is associated with the fileref SASAUTOS unless you include it in the new specification for SASAUTOS=. To add a partitioned data set to the list of partitioned data sets that SAS searches, issue the following statement:

```
options sasautos=('your.personal.autocall.lib' sasautos);
```

Then SAS searches your personal autocall library before it searches the partitioned data sets that are associated with the SASAUTOS fileref.

See Also

□ *SAS Language: Reference*

□ "Specifying a User Autocall Library" on page 194

SASHELP=

Specifies the location of the SASHELP SAS data library

Operational value: SASHELP

Valid as part of: configuration file, SAS invocation

Syntax

SASHELP=*libref*

MVS Specifics

If the SASHELP= option is not specified, then the value SASHELP is used. *libref* must have been previously associated with the SASHELP SAS data library.

See Also

□ *SAS Language: Reference*

SASLIB=

Specifies the DDname for an alternate load library

Default value: SASLIB

Valid as part of: configuration file, SAS invocation

Syntax

SASLIB=*fileref*

Description

The SASLIB= option specifies the DDname of a single load library or of a concatenation of load libraries that the SAS System is to search before it searches the standard libraries. The DDname must be allocated before SAS is invoked. The SASLIB= option can be used to specify a library that contains Version 5 formats, informats, and functions.

SASMSG=

Specifies the fileref of the partitioned data set that contains SAS messages

Operational value: SASMSG

Valid as part of: configuration file, SAS invocation

Syntax

SASMSG=*fileref*

MVS Specifics

Under MVS, the SASMSG= system option specifies the fileref of the partitioned data set that contains error, warning, and informational messages that are issued during a SAS session.

If this option is not specified, then the value SASMSG is used.

SASMSG= *continued*

See Also

□ *SAS Language: Reference*

SASUSER=

Specifies the location of the SAS data library that contains the user profile catalog

Operational value: SASUSER

Valid as part of: configuration file, SAS invocation

Syntax

SASUSER=*libref*

MVS Specifics

If the SASUSER= option is not specified, then the value SASUSER is used. *libref* must have been previously associated with the SASUSER SAS data library.

See Also

□ *SAS Language: Reference*

SEQENGINE=

Specifies the default engine for sequential SAS data libraries

Default value: SASV6SEQ

Valid as part of: configuration file, SAS invocation, OPTIONS statement

Syntax

SEQENGINE=*sequential-engine*

Description

The SEQENGINE= system option specifies the engine that SAS will use to access an existing sequential format data library when an engine name is not explicitly stated in the LIBNAME statement. *sequential-engine* can have the following values:

V5SEQ or SASV5SEQ
   specifies the engine for accessing sequential SAS data libraries in Version 5 tape format.

V6SEQ or SASV6SEQ
> specifies the engine for accessing sequential SAS data libraries in Version 6 tape format.

See Also

- "Using the V6SEQ Engine" on page 49
- "Using the V5SEQ Engine" on page 436

SITEINFO=

Specifies the location of the file that contains site information

Default value: none

Valid as part of: configuration file, SAS invocation

Syntax

SITEINFO=*file-specification*

MVS Specifics

file-specification can be either a fileref that was previously associated with an external file or the operating system data set name of the external file.

SORT=

Specifies the minimum size of all allocated sort work data sets

Default value: 0

Valid as part of: configuration file, SAS invocation, OPTIONS statement

Syntax

SORT=*n*

Description

The SORT= option specifies the minimum size of all sort work files that SAS allocates. The units are specified by the SORTUNIT= option. If the DYNALLOC system option is specified, then any value that you specify for the SORT= option is ignored.

SORT= *continued*

See Also

□ SORTUNIT= and DYNALLOC system options in this chapter

SORTANOM=

Specifies sort features that are not supported by your host sort utility

Default value: 0

Valid as part of: configuration file, SAS invocation, OPTIONS statement

Syntax

SORTANOM=*value*

Description

The SORTANOM= option specifies a number that represents a fullword of 32 bits. Each bit represents a particular host sort-utility anomaly. Currently, most host sort packages support a common set of features. This option allows you to specify any of these features that are not supported by your host sort utility. The one exception to this is bit 512 (see the explanation below).

The following list explains which bits of *value* are currently defined:

1	specifies that your sort utility does not support a 31-bit parameter list (equivalent to the NOSORT31PL option).
2	specifies that your host sort utility does not support the SUM FIELDS=NONE statement (equivalent to the NOSORTSUMF option).
4	specifies that your host sort utility does not support the EQUALS option (equivalent to the NOSORTEQOP option).
8	specifies that your host sort utility does not support the OPTIONS statement (equivalent to the NOSORTOPTS option).
16	specifies that your host sort utility does not support the FILSZ option (equivalent to the NOFILSZ option).
32	specifies that your host sort utility does not support passing a user address constant to E15/E35 exits. (An example of such a utility is FUJITSU.)
64	specifies that your host sort utility has alternate message flags. (An example of such a sort utility is FUJITSU.)
128	specifies that no warning will be issued if the SAS system option SORTDEV= specifies a generic or esoteric device type.
256	specifies that the host sort utility's output buffer will not be modified. Setting this bit may be required for the SYNCSORT utility.
512	See "Bit 512: Enabling Block-Mode Sorting" on page 373.

The default for all of the above bits is 0 (off). When a bit is off, it indicates that your sort utility supports that particular feature. If a bit is on, it indicates that your host utility does not support that particular feature. Therefore, if your host sort utility supports all the features that are represented by the SORTANOM= option, you do not have to do anything. Specify a nonzero value for SORTANOM= only if your host sort utility does not support a particular feature.

You can set multiple bits by specifying a number that is the sum of the corresponding bits. For example, if you want to set bits 1 and 2, specify the following:

```
sortanom=3
```

Alternatively, you can specify an expression in which each value is expressed with the current value in an OR or AND logical operation. Values can be decimal or numeric hexadecimal integers. If a value is preceded by a plus sign (+), then an OR operation is performed on that value and the current option value. If a value is preceded by a minus sign (-), then an AND operation is performed on the complement of that value and the current option value, effectively "turning off" those bits. If the first value is not preceded by a plus or minus sign, then its value replaces the current value. For example, the following specification sets the current value to 0. Then it performs an OR operation on the 1, 2, and 4 bits:

```
sortanom=0+1+2+4
```

As another example, the following specification performs an OR operation on the 4 bit and performs an AND operation on the 8 bit.

```
sortanom=+4-8
```

Bit 512: Enabling Block-Mode Sorting

Unlike other bits in the value of SORTANOM=, when bit 512 is on, it *enables* a feature rather than indicating that your host sort utility does not support the feature.

512   enables SAS support for block-mode sorting.

By default, SAS does not use block-mode sorting. Therefore, you must set this bit in order to use this feature. See "Take advantage of the DFSORT performance booster" on page 157 for more information about block-mode sorting.

SORTCUTP=

Specifies the number of bytes above which the host sort utility is used instead of the SAS sort program

Default value: 4M

Valid as part of: configuration file, SAS invocation, OPTIONS statement

SORTCUTP=   *continued*

Syntax

SORTCUTP=*value* | *value*K | *value*M

Description

The SORTCUTP= option specifies the number of bytes (or kilobytes or megabytes) above which the host sort (external) utility is used instead of the SAS sort (internal) program, if SORTPGM=BEST is in effect. *value* must be an integer less than or equal to 2,147,483,647 bytes.

The following equation computes the number of bytes to be sorted:

$$number\text{-}of\text{-}bytes=((length\text{-}of\text{-}obs)+(length\text{-}of\text{-}all\text{-}keys))*number\text{-}of\text{-}obs$$

See Also

□   "Efficient Sorting" on page 157

SORTDEV=

Specifies the device name used for allocated sort work data sets

Default value: SYSDA

Valid as part of: configuration file, SAS invocation, OPTIONS statement

Syntax

SORTDEV=*unit-device-name*

Description

The SORTDEV= option specifies the unit device name if SAS dynamically allocates the sort work file. (See the DYNALLOC option.) Use a generic device type unit name, such as 3380, rather than a group name, such as SYSDA. To determine the memory requirements, the SAS System must look up the device characteristics for the specified unit name. A group name might represent multiple device types, making it impossible to predict on which device type the sort work files will be allocated and, therefore, what the memory requirements will be.

For group names, the device characteristics of the WORK library are used, as in Version 5. This may result in a warning message, unless SORTANOM=128 is in effect. (See "SORTANOM=" on page 372.)

SORTEQOP

Specifies whether the host sort utility supports the EQUALS option

Default value: SORTEQOP

Valid as part of: configuration file, SAS invocation, OPTIONS statement

Syntax

SORTEQOP | NOSORTEQOP

Description

The SORTEQOP option specifies whether the host sort utility accepts the EQUALS option. (The EQUALS option sorts observations that have duplicate keys in the original order.) If the utitility does accept the EQUALS option, then SORTEQOP causes the EQUALS option to be passed to it unless you specify NOEQUALS in the PROC SORT statement. If NOSORTEQOP is in effect, then the EQUALS option is not passed to the host sort utility unless you explicitly specify the EQUALS option in the PROC SORT statement.

Note that equals processing is the default for PROC SORT. Therefore, if NOSORTEQOP is in effect, and if you did not explicitly specify EQUALS, then the host sort interface must do additional processing to ensure that observations with identical keys will remain in the original order. This may adversely affect performance.

Note: This option can be disabled by specifying SORTANOM=4. (See "SORTANOM=" on page 372.) Therefore, in order to determine whether SORTEQOP or NOSORTEQOP is in effect, you must check the value of the SORTANOM= option in PROC OPTIONS output.

SORTLIB=

Specifies the name of the sort library

Default value: SYS1.SORTLIB

Valid as part of: configuration file, SAS invocation, OPTIONS statement

Syntax

SORTLIB=*OS-data-set-name*

Description

The SORTLIB= option specifies the name of the partitioned data set in which the host sort utility (other than the main module specified by the SORTPGM= or SORTNAME= option) resides. This library is dynamically allocated to the DDname SORTLIB. If the sort resides in a link list library or if the sort library is part of the JOBLIB, STEPLIB, or TASKLIB libraries, then this option is unnecessary and should not be specified.

SORTLIB= *continued*

OS-data-set-name
> specifies the name of a partitioned data set.

SORTLIST

Controls whether the host sort utility lists control statements

Default value: NOSORTLIST

Valid as part of: configuration file, SAS invocation, OPTIONS statement

---

Syntax

SORTLIST | NOSORTLIST

Description

The SORTLIST option controls whether the LIST parameter is passed to the host sort utility. The SORTLIST option has two forms:

SORTLIST
> tells SAS to automatically pass the LIST parameter to the host sort utility when the SORT procedure is invoked. The host sort utility uses the LIST parameter to determine whether or not to list control statements.

NOSORTLIST
> tells SAS not to pass the LIST parameter to the host sort utility.

   Note: If the default for your sort utility is to print messages, then NOSORTLIST has no effect.

SORTMSG

Controls the class of messages to be written by the host sort utility

Default value: NOSORTMSG

Valid as part of: configuration file, SAS invocation, OPTIONS statement

---

Syntax

SORTMSG | NOSORTMSG

Description

The SORTMSG option has two forms:

SORTMSG
> tells SAS to pass the MSG=AP parameter to the sort utility.

NOSORTMSG
> tells SAS to pass the MSG=CP parameter to the sort utility, which means that only critical messages are written.

SORTMSG=

Specifies the fileref to be dynamically allocated for the message print file of the host sort utility

Default value: SYSOUT

Valid as part of: configuration file, SAS invocation, OPTIONS statement

Syntax

SORTMSG=*fileref*

Description

The SORTMSG= option specifies a fileref to be dynamically allocated to either a SYSOUT data set (with class *) or a terminal.

fileref
> can be any valid DDname or a null string. The DDname will be dynamically allocated to either a SYSOUT data set (with class *) under batch or a terminal under TSO, and the DDname passed to the host sort utility.

SORTNAME=

Specifies the name of the host sort utility

Default value: SORT

Valid as part of: configuration file, SAS invocation, OPTIONS statement

Syntax

SORTNAME=*host-sort-utility-name*

SORTNAME= *continued*

Description

The SORTNAME= option specifies the name of the host sort utility to be invoked if SORTPGM=HOST, or if SORTPGM=BEST and the host sort utility is chosen.

host-sort-utility-name
> is any valid operating system name. A valid operating system name can be up to eight characters, the first of which must be a letter or national character ($, #, or @). The remaining characters, following the first, can be any of the above, or digits.

SORTOPTS

Specifies whether the host sort utility supports the OPTIONS statement

Default value: SORTOPTS

Valid as part of: configuration file, SAS invocation, OPTIONS statement

Syntax

SORTOPTS | NOSORTOPTS

Description

The SORTOPTS option specifies whether the host sort utility accepts the OPTIONS statement. The OPTIONS statement is generated by the host sort interface only if the 31-bit extended parameter list is requested via the SORT31PL option.

If the SORT31PL and NOSORTOPTS options are both specified, then not all of the available sort options can be passed to the host sort utility. This may cause the sort to fail. In particular, the sort work areas may not be used because the SORT option cannot be passed the value of the SORTWKDD= option.

You should therefore specify the DYNALLOC option, even though this may cause problems with multiple sorts within a single job. Older releases of some vendors' sort utilities dynamically allocate sort work files only if they are not already allocated. As a result, subsequent sorts might fail if they require more sort work space than the first sort.

   Note: This option can be disabled by specifying SORTANOM=8. (See "SORTANOM=" on page 372.) Therefore, in order to determine whether SORTOPTS or NOSORTOPTS is in effect, you must check the value of the SORTANOM= option in PROC OPTIONS output.

SORTPARM=

Specifies a string of parameters to pass to your host sort utility

Default value: none

Valid as part of: configuration file, SAS invocation, OPTIONS statement

Syntax

SORTPARM='*string*'

Description

The string of parameters that you specify is appended to the OPTIONS statement that is generated by the SAS host sort interface. This enables you to specify options that are unique to the particular sort utility you are using. The sort utility must accept a 31-bit parameter list and an OPTIONS statement; otherwise, this option is ignored.

You can specify up to 255 characters for *string*.

SORTPGM=

Specifies which sort utility to use

Default value: BEST

Valid as part of: configuration file, SAS invocation, OPTIONS statement

Syntax

SORTPGM='*utility*' | BEST | HOST | SAS

MVS Specifics

The *utility* can be any valid operating system name that specifies the name of an accessible utility, except one of the three keywords for this option.

The host sort utility may be more suitable than the sort utility supplied by the SAS System for SAS data sets that contain a large number of observations. The name of the host sort utility is also given by the SORTNAME= system option.

See Also

□   "Efficient Sorting" on page 157

□   "SORTNAME=" on page 377

SORTSHRB

Specifies whether the host sort interface can modify data in buffers

Default value: SORTSHRB for all modes except batch; NOSORTSHRB for batch mode

Valid as part of: configuration file, SAS invocation, OPTIONS statement

SORTSHRB *continued*

Syntax

SORTSHRB | NOSORTSHRB

Description

SORTSHRB
> specifies that two or more tasks are likely to be sharing the data in buffers. If SORTSHRB is in effect, the host sort interface cannot modify data in buffers, but must move the data first. This could have a severe performance impact on your job, especially for large sorts.
>
> SORTSHRB is the default value for display manager mode, interactive line mode, and noninteractive mode, where it is quite likely that multiple tasks will be using the same data.

NOSORTSHRB
> specifies that no tasks will be sharing the data in buffers. If NOSORTSHRB is in effect, the host sort interface can modify data in buffers. NOSORTSHRB is the default value for batch mode, because it is unlikely that buffers will be shared during batch jobs, where larger sorts are usually run. If this is not suitable for your batch environment, be sure to specify SORTSHRB.

> SAS data sets can be opened for input by more than one SAS task (or window). When this happens, the buffers into which the data is read can be shared between the tasks. Because the host sort interface needs to modify the data before passing it to the host sort utility, and by default does this directly to the data in the buffers, data can be corrupted if more than one task is using the data in the buffers.

SORTSUMF

Specifies whether the host sort utility supports the SUM FIELDS=NONE control statement

Default value: SORTSUMF

Valid as part of: configuration file, SAS invocation, OPTIONS statement

Syntax

SORTSUMF | NOSORTSUMF

Description

If the NODUPKEY procedure option is specified when the SORT procedure is invoked, the SORTSUMF system option can be used to specify whether the host sort utility supports the SUM FIELDS=NONE control statement.

The SORTSUMF option has the following two forms:

SORTSUMF

specifies that the host sort utility supports the SUM FIELDS=NONE control card.

NOSORTSUMF

specifies that the host sort utility does not support the SUM FIELDS=NONE control card. IF NOSORTSUMF is in effect and the NODUPKEY option was specified when PROC SORT was invoked, then records that have duplicate keys are eliminated.

Note that duplicate keys are not the same as duplicate records. Duplicate keys can be eliminated with the NODUPKEY option, whereas duplicate records can be eliminated with the NODUP option in the PROC SORT statement.

Note: This option can be disabled by specifying SORTANOM=2. (See "SORTANOM=" on page 372.) Therefore, in order to determine whether SORTSUMF or NOSORTSUMF is in effect, you must check the value of the SORTANOM= option in PROC OPTIONS output.

SORTUNIT=

Specifies the allocation space units for sort work files

Default value: CYLS

Valid as part of: configuration file, SAS invocation, OPTIONS statement

Syntax

SORTUNIT=CYL<S> | TRK<S> | BLK<S> | *n*

Description

The SORTUNIT= option specifies the allocation space units to be used if the SAS System dynamically allocates the sort work files (see the DYNALLOC option).

You can use the following values with the SORTUNIT= option:

CYL<S>

specifies that the space units be cylinders. The space calculation for cylinder allocations requires that the characteristics of the device on which the allocations will be made need to be known. The device type is specified with the SORTDEV= option. The device type should be specified as generic, such as 3380, rather than esoteric, such as DISK. This is because when an esoteric name is specified, it is impossible to predict what device type will be used and thus the device characteristics.

TRK<S>

specifies that the space units be track(s). The space calculation for track allocations requires that the characteristics of the device on which the allocations will be made need

SORTUNIT= *continued*

to be known. The device type is specified with the SORTDEV= option. The device type should be specified as generic, such as 3380, rather than esoteric, such as DISK. This is because when an esoteric name is specified, it is impossible to predict what device type will be used and thus the device characteristics.

BLK<S>
specifies that the files will be allocated with an average block size equal to the record length rounded up to approximately 6K (6144). Therefore, if the input record length was 136, the average block size used for the allocation would be 6120.

n
is an integer that specifies the average block size.

SORTWKDD=

Specifies the prefix of sort work data sets

Default value: SASS

Valid as part of: configuration file, SAS invocation, OPTIONS statement

Syntax

SORTWKDD=*prefix*

Description

The SORTWKDD= option specifies the prefix to be used to generate the DDnames for the sort work files if the SAS System or the host sort utility dynamically allocates them (see the DYNALLOC option). The DDnames will be of the form *prefix*WK*nn*, where *nn* can be in the range 01 to the value of the SORTWKNO= option, which is usually 3.

prefix
is a four-character, valid operating system name.

SORTWKNO=

Specifies how many sort work data sets to allocate

Operational value: 3

Valid as part of: configuration file, SAS invocation, OPTIONS statement

Syntax

SORTWKNO=*n*

Description

The SORTWKNO= option specifies how many sort work files are to be allocated dynamically by either SAS or the SORT utility. (See "DYNALLOC" on page 315.)

n can be 0 through 6. If SORTWKNO=0 is specified, any existing sort work files are freed and none are allocated.

If you do not specify a value for SORTWKNO=, then SAS uses a value of 3.

SORT31PL

Controls what type of parameter list is used to invoke the host sort utility

Default value: SORT31PL

Valid as part of: configuration file, SAS invocation, OPTIONS statement

Syntax

SORT31PL | NOSORT31PL

Description

If SORT31PL is in effect, a 31-bit extended parameter list is used to invoke the host sort utility. If NOSORT31PL is in effect, a 24-bit parameter list is used.

If SORT31PL is specified, then the SORTOPTS system option should also be specified. Also, because sorts that currently support a 31-bit parameter list also support the EQUALS option, the SORTEQOP system option should be specified in order to maximize performance.

Note: This option can be disabled by specifying SORTANOM=1. (See "SORTANOM=" on page 372.) Therefore, in order to determine whether SORT31PL or NOSORT31PL is in effect, you must check the value of the SORTANOM= option in PROC OPTIONS output.

STAE

Enables a system ESTAE exit

Default value: STAE

Valid as part of: configuration file, SAS invocation, OPTIONS statement

---

STAE   *continued*

Syntax

STAE | NOSTAE

Description

The STAE option causes the SAS System's error trapping and handling to be activated by an ESTAE macro in the host supervisor.

STATS

Tells SAS to write resource usage statistics to the SAS log

Default value: STATS

Valid as part of: configuration file, SAS invocation, OPTIONS statement

---

Syntax

STATS | NOSTATS

Description

The STATS system option specifies whether the performance statistics that are maintained by the SAS System are written to the SAS log. The STATS option has two forms:

STATS
    tells SAS to write the available statistics to the SAS log for each step and for the entire SAS session.

NOSTATS
    tells SAS not to write the available statistics to the SAS log.

What the STATS system option writes to the SAS log depends on the setting of other host-specific options:

☐   If NOSTATS is in effect, no statistics are written to the SAS log.

☐   If the STATS and STIMER options are in effect, system timing statistics are written.

☐   If the STATS and MEMRPT options are in effect, then memory usage statistics are written.

☐   If the FULLSTATS option is in effect, an expanded list is written (containing both CPU and elapsed time, EXCP count, and task and system memory usage). Otherwise, a single line is written with just the CPU time and/or system memory usage.

See Also

□ FULLSTATS, MEMRPT, and STIMER system options in this chapter

STAX

Enables attention handling exit

Default value: STAX

Valid as part of: configuration file, SAS invocation

Syntax

STAX | NOSTAX

Description

The STAX option causes attention handling to be activated by a STAX macro in the host supervisor. Specifying NOSTAX causes the SAS session to end when the attention key is pressed.

STIMER

Tells SAS whether to maintain system performance statistics

Default value: STIMER

Valid as part of: configuration file, SAS invocation

Syntax

STIMER | NOSTIMER

MVS Specifics

STIMER
> tells SAS to maintain the statistics. When the STATS option is also in effect, the SAS System writes to the SAS log the statistics maintained for each step and the entire SAS session.

NOSTIMER
> tells SAS not to maintain the statistics. (Note that no SMF records are written if NOSTIMER is specified, even if the SMF option is in effect.)

STIMER   *continued*

See Also

□   FULLSTATS and STATS system options in this chapter

□   *SAS Language: Reference*

SUBSYSID=

Specifies the name used to anchor resource descriptors

Default value: SAS0

Valid as part of: configuration file, SAS invocation

Syntax

SUBSYSID=*name*

Description

The SUBSYSID= option tells the cross memory services communication facility to use the MVS subsystem ID that was chosen in the installation process to anchor its resource descriptors.

This option is used in conjunction with SAS/SHARE software. It is typically set in the system configuration file by the system administrator at your site.

SYNCHIO

Specifies whether synchronous I/O is enabled

Default value: SYNCHIO (for batch); NOSYNCHIO (for interactive)

Valid as part of: configuration file, SAS invocation

Syntax

SYNCHIO | NOSYNCHIO

Description

SYNCHIO
   causes WAIT macros to be issued immediately for SAS data set I/O, external data set I/O, and TGETs, thus putting the SAS System task in a wait state.

NOSYNCHIO
   allows other logical SAS tasks to execute (if any are ready) while the I/O is being done.

SYSIN=

Specifies the fileref for the primary SAS input data stream

Default value: none (interactive), SYSIN (batch)

Valid as part of: configuration file, SAS invocation

Syntax

SYSIN=*fileref*

MVS Specifics

This option is applicable when you run SAS programs in noninteractive or batch mode. *fileref* is any valid DDname that has been previously associated with an external file that contains SAS program statements.

See Also

□   *SAS Language: Reference*

SYSINP=

Specifies the name of an external program that provides SAS input statements

Default value: none

Valid as part of: configuration file, SAS invocation

Syntax

SYSINP=*external-program-name*

Description

SAS calls this external program every time it needs a new SAS input statement. The PGMPARM= option (described earlier in this chapter) enables you to pass a parameter to the program that you specify with the SYSINP= option. The SYSINP= option overrides the SYSIN= system option.

For more information about using the SYSINP= and PGMPARM= options, contact your SAS Software Consultant.

SYSLEAVE=

Specifies how much memory to leave unallocated to ensure that SAS System tasks will be able to terminate successfully

Default value: (0,102400)

Valid as part of: configuration file, SAS invocation, OPTIONS statement

Syntax

SYSLEAVE= *n*K | *n*M | (*n*K,*n*K) | (*n*M,*n*M)

MVS Specifics

You can use the following values with the SYSLEAVE= option:

*n*K

specifies in kilobytes how much space to leave unallocated above the 16-megabyte line. Valid values are any integer from 0 to the maximum amount of available space.

*n*M

specifies in megabytes how much space to leave unallocated above the 16-megabyte line. Valid values are any integer from 0 to the maximum amount of available space.

(*n*K,*n*K) | (*n*M,*n*M)

represents how much space to reserve below the 16-megabyte line and how much to reserve above the 16-megabyte line, respectively.

See Also

□   "Use SYSLEAVE= and PROCLEAVE= to handle out-of-memory conditions" on page 159

□   *SAS Language: Reference*

SYSPREF=

Specifies a prefix for partially-qualified operating system data set names

Operational value: user profile prefix for TSO; user ID for batch

Valid as part of: configuration file, SAS invocation, OPTIONS statement

Syntax

SYSPREF=*prefix*

Description

The SYSPREF= option specifies a prefix to be used in constructing a fully qualified operating system data set name from a partially qualified name. Wherever a physical name must be entered in quotation marks in SAS statements or in DMS commands, you may enter a data set name in the form '*.rest.of-name*', and SAS inserts the value of the SYSPREF= option in front of the first period.

Unlike the user profile prefix, the SYSPREF= option may have more than one qualifier in its name. If, for example, SYSPREF=SAS.TEST, then '.SASDATA' is interpreted as 'SAS.TEST.SASDATA'.

If no value is specified for SYSPREF=, then SAS uses the user profile prefix (under TSO) or the user ID (in batch).

SYSPRINT=

Specifies the handling of output that is directed to the default print file

Default value: none

Valid as part of: configuration file, SAS invocation, OPTIONS statement

Syntax

SYSPRINT= * | DUMMY | *DDname*

Description

You can use the following values with the SYSPRINT= option:

*   terminates redirection of output.

DUMMY   suppresses output to the default print file.

DDname   causes output to default print file to be redirected to specified DDname.

> **Note:** The default print file is designated by the PRINT= system option.

S99NOMIG

Tells SAS whether to recall a migrated data set

Default value: NOS99NOMIG

Valid as part of: configuration file, SAS invocation, OPTIONS statement

S99NOMIG *continued*

Syntax

S99NOMIG | NOS99NOMIG

Description

The S99NOMIG option tells SAS what to do when an operating system data set that you reference (in a FILENAME statement, LIBNAME statement, or INCLUDE command, for example) has been migrated. If S99NOMIG is in effect, then the data set is not recalled and the allocation fails. If NOS99NOMIG is in effect, the data set is recalled, and allocation proceeds as it would have if the data set had not been migrated.

TAPECLOSE=

Specifies the default CLOSE disposition for a SAS data library on a tape volume

Default value: REREAD

Valid as part of: configuration file, SAS invocation, OPTIONS statement, OPTIONS window

Syntax

TAPECLOSE=REREAD | REWIND | LEAVE | DISP | FREE

MVS Specifics

Under MVS, the default is REREAD.

See Also

□   *SAS Language: Reference*

TCPIPMCH=

Specifies which TCP/IP to use

Default value: none

Valid as part of: configuration file, SAS invocation

Syntax

TCPIPMCH=*started-task-name*

Description

If your site runs multiple instances of TCP/IP simultaneously, you can use this option to specify which TCP/IP to use. The value that you specify is the name of the started task for the TCP/IP that you want to use.

The value that you specify is stored into the SAS/C environment variable TCPIP_MACH. TCPIP_MACH defines the name of the address space that is running TCP/IP.

If the TCPIP_MACH environment variable is not defined, the value that SAS uses depends on which TCP/IP is used. If Interlink TCP/IP is used, then SAS uses the value ACSS; for all other TCP/IPs, SAS uses the value TCPIP.

TCPIPPRF=

Explicitly sets the TCP/IP prefix for a SAS session

Default value: none

Valid as part of: configuration file, SAS invocation

Syntax

TCPIPPRF=*configuration-file-prefix*

Description

This option provides additional flexibility when more than one set of TCP/IP configuration data sets is available at a site. Each SAS session that acts as a server or user employing the TCP/IP access method must set this option to the site value at initialization time.

See Also

□   the "Implementing SAS/SHARE Software" appendix in *Installation Instructions and System Manager's Guide: The SAS System under MVS, 6.09 Enhanced Release*

TCPSEC=

Controls how security is handled for TCP/IP communication

Default value: none

Valid as part of: configuration file, SAS invocation, OPTIONS statement

---

TCPSEC= *continued*

Syntax

TCPSEC=<*user-ID.*>*password* | _SECURE_ | _NONE_ | _PROMPT_

Description

The TCPSEC= option specifies how security is handled for SNA Type 6.2 TCP/IP communication. The effect of this option depends on whether you specify it in the originating (user) session or in the destination (server) session. The following list explains the meanings of the various values that you can specify for this option.

<*user-ID.*>*password*

is valid only in the user session, and specifies a user ID and password to be passed to the remote host. It also enables security presentation. *Security presentation* means that you must supply a valid password and user ID combination from the user session in order to complete the communication link. Use this form of the TCPSEC= option when you are establishing a link between a local MVS host and a remote CMS, MVS, or OS/2 host.

Both the user ID and the password can be one to eight characters long. They can consist of letters, numbers, and the national characters #, $, or @. The first character must be either a letter or a national character. If the user ID and password are case-sensitive on the remote host, then specify their values in the appropriate case and enclose them in quotation marks.

The user ID is optional and is usually omitted when both the MVS and CMS host sessions have the same user ID. In that case, the MVS session derives the user ID from the appropriate Accessor Environment Element (ACEE).

If this option is used when connecting to an OS/2 host, then user ID/password profiles must already exist on the OS/2 host.

SECURE

is valid only in the server session, and enables security screening. *Security screening* means that the server session checks for a valid password and user ID combination.

NONE

disables the following:

□   security presentation, if specified in the user session.

□   security screening, if specified in the server session.

PROMPT

causes a dialog window to be displayed so that the user can enter a user ID and password.

TCPSEC can be specified in an OPTIONS statement; however, for security reasons its value is not displayed in PROC OPTIONS output.

See Also

□ the "Implementing SAS/SHARE Software" appendix in *Installation Instructions and System Manager's Guide*

USER=

Specifies the location of the default SAS data library

Default value: none

Valid as part of: configuration file, SAS invocation, OPTIONS statement, OPTIONS window

Syntax

USER=*library-specification*

MVS Specifics

library-specification can be either a libref that was previously associated with a SAS data library, or the name of the operating system data set (enclosed in quotation marks) that comprises a SAS data library.

See Also

□ "Directing Temporary SAS Data Sets to the USER Library" on page 16

□ *SAS Language: Reference*

VECTOR

Specifies that vector facility instructions will be used if available

Configuration-file value: VECTOR

Valid as part of: configuration file, SAS invocation

Syntax

VECTOR | NOVECTOR

VECTOR   *continued*

Description

The VECTOR option specifies that vector facility instructions will be used if your system has the IBM 3090 vector facility installed.

VERBOSE

Writes the settings of SAS system options either to the terminal or to the batch job log

Default value: NOVERBOSE

Valid as part of: configuration file, SAS invocation

Syntax

VERBOSE | NOVERBOSE

MVS Specifics

If you specify the VERBOSE system option at SAS invocation, the settings of all SAS system options that were set at SAS invocation or in the configuration files will be displayed in the following order:

1.   settings in the system configuration file

2.   settings in the user configuration file, if you have one

3.   settings at SAS invocation.

If you specify the VERBOSE system option in a configuration file, only the options that are processed after VERBOSE is encountered are displayed. In other words, VERBOSE can appear in a configuration file, but the resulting options list then includes only those options that follow it in the configuration file.

If you invoke SAS at a terminal, the settings are displayed at the terminal. If you invoke SAS as part of a batch job, the settings are written to the batch job log.

VSAMLOAD

Enables you to load a VSAM data set

Default value: NOVSAMLOAD

Valid as part of: configuration file, SAS invocation, OPTIONS statement

Syntax

VSAMLOAD | NOVSAMLOAD

Description

The VSAMLOAD option must be specified in order to load an empty VSAM data set from a SAS DATA step.

See Also

□ *SAS Guide to VSAM Processing*

VSAMREAD

Enables the user to read a VSAM data set

Default value: VSAMREAD

Valid as part of: configuration file, SAS invocation, OPTIONS statement

Syntax

VSAMREAD | NOVSAMREAD

Description

The VSAMREAD option enables you to process VSAM data sets with a SAS DATA step.

See Also

□ *SAS Guide to VSAM Processing*

VSAMUPDATE

Enables you to update a VSAM data set

Default value: NOVSAMUPDATE

Valid as part of: configuration file, SAS invocation, OPTIONS statement

Syntax

VSAMUPDATE | NOVSAMUPDATE

VSAMUPDATE *continued*

Description

The VSAMUPDATE option must be specified in order to update VSAM data sets. Specifying VSAMUPDATE implies VSAMREAD.

See Also

□ *SAS Guide to VSAM Processing*

WORK=

Specifies the libref of the SAS WORK library

Operational value: WORK

Valid as part of: configuration file, SAS invocation

Syntax

WORK=*libref*

MVS Specifics

libref must have been previously associated with a SAS data library. If no value is specified for WORK=, then SAS uses the value WORK.

See Also

□ "WORK Library" on page 14

□ *SAS Language: Reference*

Summary Table of SAS System Options

The following table lists all the SAS system options that are available to MVS SAS users. The table gives you the following information about each SAS system option:

□ the option name

□ the default if you do not specify the option and if the option does not appear in the configuration file or in your site's default options table or restricted options table

□ where you can specify the option

□ where to look for more information about the option.

For example, find the CONFIG= system option in the table. You see that the default is CONFIG and that it can be specified only when you invoke SAS. Read across to the "See" column. COMP means that more information about this option is in the previous section of this chapter.

Here is the legend for the "See" column:

ADB *SAS/ACCESS Interface to ADABAS: Usage and Reference, Version 6, First Edition*

COMP the description of the system option earlier in this chapter of the *SAS Companion for the MVS Environment*

DB2 *SAS/ACCESS Software for Relational Databases: Reference — DB2 Chapter, Version 6, Second Edition*

DDB *SAS/ACCESS Interface to CA-DATACOM/DB: Usage and Reference, Version 6, First Edition*

HELP SAS System Help facility

IDMS *SAS/ACCESS Interface to CA-IDMS: Reference, Version 6, First Edition*

IMS *SAS/ACCESS Interface to IMS-DL/I: Usage and Reference, Version 6, Second Edition*

INST *Installation Instructions and System Manager's Guide: The SAS System under MVS, 6.09 Enhanced Release*

LR *SAS Language: Reference, Version 6, First Edition*

ORACLE *SAS/ACCESS Software for Relational Databases: Reference — ORACLE Chapter, Version 6, First Edition*

P-221 SAS Technical Report P-221, *SAS/ACCESS Software: Changes and Enhancements, Release 6.07*

P-222 SAS Technical Report P-222, *Changes and Enhancements to Base SAS Software, Release 6.07*

P-242 SAS Technical Report P-242, *SAS Software: Changes and Enhancements, Release 6.08*

P-252 SAS Technical Report P-252, *SAS Software: Changes and Enhancements, Release 6.09*

6.09E *What's New for the 6.09 Enhanced Release of SAS Software: Changes and Enhancements in TS450*

When two references are listed in the "See" column, the first reference is the primary source of information and should be consulted first.

Note: Some of the values in the "Default" column are designated as operational values or as configuration-file values. For definitions of these terms, see "A Note about System Option Values" on page 299.

Table 20.1 *Summary of All SAS System Options Available under MVS*

Option name	Default	SAS Invocation	CONFIG file	OPTIONS window	OPTIONS statement	See
			Specified in			
ADBBYMD=	R	X	X			ADB
ADBDBID=	0	X	X			ADB
ADBDBMD=	M	X	X			ADB
ADBDEFW=	0	X	X			ADB
ADBDEL=	N	X	X			ADB
ADBDELIM=	\ ('E0'x in hex)	X	X			ADB
ADBFMTL=	500	X	X			ADB
ADBISNL=	5,000	X	X			ADB
ADBL3=	N	X	X			HELP
ADBMAXM=	191	X	X			ADB
ADBMAXP=	9	X	X			ADB
ADBMINM=	1	X	X			ADB
ADBNATAP=	none	X	X			ADB
ADBNATPW=	none	X	X			ADB
ADBNATUS=	none	X	X			ADB
ADBRECL=	7,500	X	X			ADB
ADBSCHL=	500	X	X			ADB
ADBSECCC=	none	X	X			ADB
ADBSECDB=	0	X	X			ADB
ADBSECFL=	16	X	X			ADB
ADBSECPW=	none	X	X			ADB
ADBSPANS=	* (asterisk)	X	X			ADB
ADBSYSCC=	none	X	X			ADB
ADBSYSDB=	0	X	X			ADB
ADBSYSFL=	15	X	X			ADB
ADBSYSPW=	none	X	X			ADB
ADBTASK=	S	X	X			P-221
ADBUISN=	Y	X	X			ADB
ADBUPD=	Y	X	X			HELP

(continued)

Table 20.1 *(continued)*

Option name	Default	SAS Invocation	CONFIG file	OPTIONS window	OPTIONS statement	See
ADBVALL=	300	X	X			ADB
ALTLOG=	none	X	X			COMP, LR
ALTPRINT=	none	X	X			COMP, LR
APPCSEC=	none	X	X		X	COMP, INST
AUTHENCR	OPTIONAL	X	X		X	COMP
AUTOEXEC=	SASEXEC†	X	X			COMP, LR
BATCH	NOBATCH (interactive), BATCH (batch)	X	X			LR, P-252
BLKALLOC	NOBLKALLOC	X	X		X	COMP
BLKSIZE=	0	X	X		X	COMP
BLKSIZE()=	varies by device type	X	X		X	COMP
BMPREAD=	N	X	X			IMS
BNDLSUFX=	none	X	X			INST
BUFNO=	3‡	X	X	X	X	LR
BUFSIZE=	0	X	X	X	X	LR, COMP
BYERR	BYERR	X	X	X	X	P-222
BYLINE	BYLINE	X	X	X	X	P-222
CAPS	NOCAPS	X	X	X	X	LR
CAPSOUT	NOCAPSOUT	X	X		X	COMP
CARDIMAGE	CARDIMAGE	X	X	X	X	LR
CATCACHE=	0	X	X			LR
CBUFNO=	0	X	X	X	X	6.09E
CENTER	CENTER	X	X	X	X	LR
CHARCODE	NOCHARCODE	X	X	X	X	LR
CHARTYPE=	0	X	X			COMP
CLEANUP	CLEANUP	X	X	X	X	LR, COMP
CLIST	NOCLIST	X	X			COMP
CMDMAC	NOCMDMAC	X	X	X	X	P-222

(continued)

† operational value

‡ configuration-file value

Table 20.1 (*continued*)

Option name	Default	Specified in				See
		SAS Invocation	CONFIG file	OPTIONS window	OPTIONS statement	
CODEPASS=	1	X	X		X	COMP
CODEPCT=	120†	X	X		X	COMP
COMAMID=	none	X	X		X	LR, COMP, INST
COMAUX1=	none	X	X			COMP
COMAUX2=	none	X	X			COMP
COMPRESS=	NO	X	X	X	X	LR
CONFIG=	CONFIG	X				COMP, LR
CPUID	CPUID	X	X			P-222
DATE	DATE	X	X	X	X	LR
DBCS	NODBCS	X	X	X	X	LR
DBCSLANG=	none	X	X			LR
DBCSTYPE=	none	X	X			LR, COMP
DB2DECPT=	. (period)	X	X			DB2
DB2PKCHK=	N	X	X			DB2
DB2SSID=	DB2	X	X		X	DB2
DB2UPD=	Y	X	X			DDB, P-221
DDBDBN=	none	X	X			DDB
DDBDELIM=	\ ('E0'x in hex)	X	X			DDB
DDBLOAD=	0	X	X			DDB
DDBLOCK=	0	X	X			DDB
DDBMASK=	#	X	X			DDB
DDBMISS=	none	SAS	X			DDB
DDBPW=	none	X	X			DDB
DDBSPANS=	* (asterisk)	X	X			DDB
DDBSV=	PROD	X	X			DDB
DDBTASK=	2	X	X			DDB
DDBTRACE=	0	X	X			DDB
DDBUPD=	Y	X	X			DDB

(*continued*)

† operational value

Table 20.1 *(continued)*

Option name	Default	SAS Invocation	CONFIG file	OPTIONS window	OPTIONS statement	See
DDBURT=	none	X	X			DDB
DDBUSER=	none	X	X			DDB
DETAILS	NODETAILS	X	X	X	X	P-222
DEVICE=	none	X	X	X	X	LR, COMP
DKRICOND=	ERROR	X	X	X	X	P-222
DKROCOND=	WARN	X	X	X	X	P-222
DLIREAD=	N	X	X			IMS
DLORGCK	NODLORGCK	X	X		X	COMP
DMR	NODMR	X	X			LR
DMS	DMS (interactive), NODMS (batch and noninteractive)	X	X			LR
DMSBATCH	NODMSBATCH	X	X			P-252
DSNFERR	DSNFERR	X	X	X	X	LR
DSRESV	NODSRESV	X	X		X	COMP
DYNALLOC	NODYNALLOC	X	X		X	COMP
ECHOAUTO	NOECHOAUTO	X	X			LR
ENGINE=	V609	X	X			LR, COMP
ERRORABEND	NOERRORABEND	X	X	X	X	LR
ERRORCHECK=	NORMAL	X	X	X	X	P-242
ERRORS=	20	X	X	X	X	LR
FILEBLKSIZE()=	varies by device type	X	X		X	COMP
FILECC	NOFILECC	X	X		X	COMP
FILEDEST=	none	X	X		X	COMP
FILEDEV=	SYSDA	X	X		X	COMP
FILEDIRBLK=	6	X	X		X	COMP
FILEEXT=	VERIFY	X	X		X	COMP
FILEFORMS=	none	X	X		X	COMP
FILEMOUNT	FILEMOUNT	X	X		X	COMP
FILEMSGS	NOFILEMSGS	X	X		X	COMP

(continued)

Table 20.1 *(continued)*

Option name	Default	SAS Invocation	CONFIG file	OPTIONS window	OPTIONS statement	See
		Specified in				
FILENULL	FILENULL	X	X		X	COMP
FILEPROMPT	FILEPROMPT (interactive), NOFILEPROMPT (batch)	X	X		X	COMP
FILEREUSE	NOFILEREUSE	X	X		X	COMP
FILESPPRI=	1	X	X		X	COMP
FILESPSEC=	1	X	X		X	COMP
FILESTAT	NOFILESTAT	X	X		X	COMP
FILESYSOUT=	none	X	X		X	COMP
FILEUNIT=	CYLS	X	X		X	COMP
FILEVOL=	none	X	X		X	COMP
FILSZ	FILSZ	X	X		X	COMP
FIRSTOBS=	1	X	X	X	X	LR
FMTERR	FMTERR	X	X	X	X	LR
FMTSEARCH=	none	X	X	X	X	P-222
FORMCHAR=	|----|+|---+=|−∧<>*	X	X	X	X	LR
FORMDLIM=	none	X	X	X	X	LR
FORMS=	DEFAULT	X	X	X	X	LR
FSBCOLOR	NOFSBCOLOR	X	X		X	COMP
FSBORDER=	BEST	X	X			COMP
FSDEVICE=	none	X	X			LR, COMP
FSMODE=	IBM	X	X			COMP
FULLSTATS	NOFULLSTATS	X	X		X	COMP
FULLSTIMER	NOFULLSTIMER	X	X		X	LR
GHFONT=	none	X	X			COMP
GWINDOW	GWINDOW	X	X	X	X	LR
HSLXTNTS=	1,500	X	X		X	COMP
HSMAXPGS=	75,000	X	X		X	COMP
HSMAXSPC=	50	X	X		X	COMP
HSSAVE	HSSAVE	X	X		X	COMP
HSWORK	NOHSWORK	X	X			COMP

Table 20.1 (*continued*)

Option name	Default	SAS Invocation	CONFIG file	OPTIONS window	OPTIONS statement	See
ICSRSLV	ONLY†	X	X			COMP
IDMWHST=	I	X	X			IDMS
IMPLMAC	NOIMPLMAC	X	X	X	X	LR
IMSBPAGN=	* (asterisk)	X	X		X	IMS
IMSBPCPU=	0	X	X		X	IMS
IMSBPDCA=	0	X	X		X	IMS
IMSBPIN=	* (asterisk)	X	X		X	IMS
IMSBPNBA=	0	X	X		X	IMS
IMSBPOBA=	0	X	X		X	IMS
IMSBPOPT=	C	X	X		X	IMS
IMSBPOUT=	* (asterisk)	X	X		X	IMS
IMSBPPAR=	0	X	X		X	IMS
IMSBPSTI=	0	X	X		X	IMS
IMSBPSWP=	Y	X	X		X	IMS
IMSBPUPD=	Y	X	X			IMS
IMSDEBUG=	N	X	X		X	IMS
IMSDLBKO=	* (asterisk)	X	X		X	IMS
IMSDLBUF=	16	X	X		X	IMS
IMSDLDBR=	* (asterisk)	X	X		X	IMS
IMSDLEXC=	0	X	X		X	IMS
IMSDLFMT=	P	X	X		X	IMS
IMSDLIRL=	* (asterisk)	X	X		X	IMS
IMSDLIRN=	* (asterisk)	X	X		X	IMS
IMSDLLOG=	0	X	X		X	IMS
IMSDLMON=	N	X	X		X	IMS
IMSDLSRC=	0	X	X		X	IMS
IMSDLSWP=	* (asterisk)	X	X		X	IMS
IMSDLUPD=	Y	X	X			IMS
IMSID=	* (asterisk)	X	X			IMS

(*continued*)

† operational value

Table 20.1 *(continued)*

Option name	Default	SAS Invocation	CONFIG file	OPTIONS window	OPTIONS statement	See
IMSIOB=	* (asterisk)	X	X		X	IMS
IMSREGTP=	DLI	X	X			IMS
IMSSPIE=	0	X	X		X	IMS
IMSTEST=	0	X	X		X	IMS
IMSWHST=	N	X	X			IMS
INITSTMT=	none	X	X			LR
INVALIDDATA=	. (period)	X	X	X	X	LR
ISPCAPS	NOISPCAPS	X	X		X	COMP
ISPCHARF	NOISPCHARF	X	X		X	COMP
ISPCSR=	none	X	X			COMP
ISPEXECV=	none	X	X			COMP
ISPMISS=	none	X	X		X	COMP
ISPMSG=	none	X	X			COMP
ISPNOTES	NOISPNOTES	X	X		X	COMP
ISPNZTRC	NOISPNZTRC	X	X		X	COMP
ISPPT	NOISPPT	X	X		X	COMP
ISPTRACE	NOISPTRACE	X	X		X	COMP
ISPVDEFA	NOISPVDEFA	X	X		X	COMP
ISPVDLT	NOISPVDLT	X	X		X	COMP
ISPVDTRC	NOISPVDTRC	X	X		X	COMP
ISPVIMSG=	none	X	X		X	COMP
ISPVRMSG=	none	X	X		X	COMP
ISPVTMSG=	none	X	X		X	COMP
ISPVTNAM=	none	X	X		X	COMP
ISPVTPNL=	none	X	X		X	COMP
ISPVTRAP	NOISPVTRAP	X	X		X	COMP
ISPVTVARS=	none	X	X		X	COMP
LABEL	LABEL	X	X	X	X	LR
LAST=	_NULL_	X	X	X	X	LR

(continued)

Table 20.1   *(continued)*

Option name	Default	Specified in				See
		SAS Invocation	**CONFIG file**	**OPTIONS window**	**OPTIONS statement**	
LINESIZE=	width of terminal (interactive), 132 (batch, noninteractive)	X	X	X	X	LR, COMP
LOG=	SASLOG	X	X			COMP, LR
LUFIRST=	1	X	X			COMP, INST
LULAST=	9	X	X			COMP, INST
LUNAME=	none	X	X			COMP, INST
LUPOOL=	USER	X	X			COMP, INST
LUPREFIX=	none	X	X			COMP, INST
LUTYPE=	SNA0	X	X		X	COMP, INST
LU0MODE=	none	X	X		X	COMP, INST
LU0SEC=	none	X	X		X	COMP, INST
LU62MODE=	none	X	X		X	COMP, INST
MACRO	MACRO	X	X			LR
MAPS=	MAPS	X	X	X	X	COMP, P-222
MAUTOSOURCE	MAUTOSOURCE	X	X	X	X	LR
MEMRPT	MEMRPT	X	X		X	COMP
MEMSIZE=	8M‡	X	X		X	COMP
MERROR	MERROR	X	X	X	X	LR
MINSTG	NOMINSTG	X	X		X	COMP
MISSING=	. (period)	X	X	X	X	LR
MLOGIC	NOMLOGIC	X	X	X	X	LR
MPRINT	NOMPRINT	X	X	X	X	LR
MRECALL	NOMRECALL	X	X	X	X	LR
MSGCASE	NOMSGCASE	X	X			P-222
MSGLEVEL=	N	X	X	X	X	P-222
MSTORED	NOMSTORED	X	X	X	X	P-222
MSYMTABMAX=	1,048,576	X	X	X	X	P-222, COMP
MVARSIZE=	8,192	X	X	X	X	P-222, COMP
NDSVOLS=	none	X	X		X	COMP

(continued)

‡ configuration-file value

Table 20.1 *(continued)*

		Specified in				
Option name	Default	SAS Invocation	CONFIG file	OPTIONS window	OPTIONS statement	See
NEWS=	none	X	X			LR, COMP
NOTES	NOTES	X	X	X	X	LR
NUMBER	NUMBER	X	X	X	X	LR
OBS=	MAX	X	X	X	X	LR, COMP
OPLIST	NOOPLIST	X	X			COMP, LR
ORAVER	V7	X	X		X	HELP
OVP	NOOVP (interactive), OVP (batch)	X	X	X	X	LR
PAGENO=	1	X	X	X	X	LR
PAGESIZE=	size of terminal (display manager), 60 (batch, noninteractive), 21 (interactive line mode)	X	X	X	X	LR, COMP
PARM=	none	X	X	X	X	LR
PARMCARDS=	SASPARM	X	X	X	X	LR
PFKEY=	PRIMARY†	X	X			COMP
PGMPARM=	none	X	X			COMP
PRINT=	SASLIST	X	X			COMP, LR
PRINTINIT	NOPRINTINIT	X	X			COMP, P-252
PROBSIG=	0	X	X	X	X	LR
PROC	PROC	X	X	X	X	P-222
PROCLEAVE=	(0,102400)	X	X		X	COMP, LR
PSUP=	SASXKERN†	X	X			COMP
PSUPISA=	136K, or 170K (TSO)‡	X	X			INST
PSUPOSA=	4K, or 20K (TSO)‡	X	X			INST
REMOTE=	none	X	X	X	X	LR, COMP
REPLACE	REPLACE	X	X	X	X	LR
REUSE=	NO	X	X	X	X	LR
REXXLOC=	SASREXX	X	X			COMP
REXXMAC	NOREXXMAC	X	X		X	COMP

(continued)

† operational value

‡ configuration-file value

Table 20.1 (*continued*)

Option name	Default	SAS Invocation	CONFIG file	OPTIONS window	OPTIONS statement	See
RSASUSER	NORSASUSER	X	X			P-242, COMP
S=	0	X	X	X	X	LR, COMP
SASAUTOS=	SASAUTOS	X	X	X	X	COMP, LR
SASFRSCR	none					P-222
SASHELP=	SASHELP†	X	X			COMP, LR
SASLIB=	SASLIB	X	X			COMP
SASMSG=	SASMSG†	X	X			COMP, LR
SASMSTORE=	none	X	X	X	X	P-222
SASSCRIPT=	none	X	X	X	X	P-222
SASUSER=	SASUSER†	X	X			COMP, LR
SEQ=	8	X	X	X	X	LR
SEQENGINE=	SASV6SEQ	X	X		X	COMP
SERROR	SERROR	X	X	X	X	LR
SETINIT	NOSETINIT	X	X			LR
SITEINFO=	none	X	X			COMP, LR
SKIP=	0	X	X	X	X	P-222
SMF	NOSMF	X	X			INST
SMFEXIT=	none	X	X			INST
SMFTYPE=	0	X	X			INST
SORT=	0	X	X		X	COMP
SORTANOM=	0	X	X		X	COMP
SORTCUTP=	4M	X	X		X	COMP
SORTDEV=	SYSDA	X	X		X	COMP
SORTEQOP	SORTEQOP	X	X		X	COMP
SORTLIB=	SYS1.SORTLIB	X	X		X	COMP
SORTLIST	NOSORTLIST	X	X		X	COMP
SORTMSG	NOSORTMSG	X	X		X	COMP
SORTMSG=	SYSOUT	X	X		X	COMP
SORTNAME=	SORT	X	X		X	COMP

(*continued*)

† operational value

Table 20.1 *(continued)*

Option name	Default	Specified in				See
		SAS Invocation	**CONFIG file**	**OPTIONS window**	**OPTIONS statement**	
SORTOPTS	SORTOPTS	X	X		X	COMP
SORTPARM=	none	X	X		X	COMP
SORTPGM=	BEST	X	X		X	COMP, LR
SORTSEQ=	none	X	X	X	X	P-222
SORTSHRB	SORTSHRB (interactive), NOSORTSHRB (batch)	X	X		X	COMP
SORTSIZE=	MAX	X	X	X	X	P-222
SORTSUMF	SORTSUMF	X	X		X	COMP
SORTUNIT=	CYLS	X	X		X	COMP
SORTWKDD=	SASS	X	X		X	COMP
SORTWKNO=	3†	X	X		X	COMP
SORT31PL	SORT31PL	X	X		X	COMP
SOURCE	SOURCE (display manager, batch), NOSOURCE (interactive line mode, noninteractive)	X	X	X	X	LR
SOURCE2	NOSOURCE2	X	X	X	X	LR
SPOOL	SPOOL	X	X	X	X	LR
STAE	STAE	X	X		X	COMP
STATS	STATS	X	X		X	COMP
STAX	STAX	X	X			COMP
STIMER	STIMER	X	X			COMP, LR
SUBSYSID=	SAS0	X	X			COMP
SVC0R15=	4	X	X			INST
SVC0SVC=	109	X	X			INST
SYMBOLGEN	NOSYMBOLGEN	X	X	X	X	LR
SYNCHIO	NOSYNCHIO (interactive), SYNCHIO (batch)	X	X			COMP
SYSIN=	none (interactive), SYSIN (batch)	X	X			COMP, P-252
SYSINP=	none	X	X			COMP

(continued)

† operational value

Table 20.1 (*continued*)

Option name	Default	SAS Invocation	CONFIG file	OPTIONS window	OPTIONS statement	See
				Specified in		
SYSLEAVE=	(0,102400)	X	X		X	COMP, LR
SYSPARM=	none	X	X	X	X	LR
SYSPREF=	user profile prefix (TSO), user ID (batch)†	X	X		X	COMP
SYSPRINT=	none	X	X		X	COMP
S2=	0	X	X	X	X	LR
S99NOMIG	NOS99NOMIG	X	X		X	COMP
TAPECLOSE=	REREAD	X	X	X	X	LR, COMP
TCPIPMCH=	none	X	X			COMP
TCPIPPRF=	none	X	X			COMP
TCPSEC=	none	X	X		X	COMP
TERMINAL	TERMINAL (interactive), NOTERMINAL (batch)	X	X			P-252
TRANTAB=	none	X	X	X	X	P-222
USER=	none	X	X	X	X	COMP, LR
VECTOR	VECTOR‡	X	X			COMP
VERBOSE	NOVERBOSE	X	X			COMP, LR
VMCTLISA	160K	X	X		X	INST
VMNSISA	0	X	X			INST
VMNSOSA	0	X	X			INST
VMPAISA=	256K‡	X	X		X	INST
VMPAOSA=	128K‡	X	X		X	INST
VMPBISA=	256K‡	X	X		X	INST
VMPBOSA=	128K‡	X	X		X	INST
VMTAISA=	0	X	X		X	INST
VMTAOSA=	0	X	X		X	INST
VMTBISA=	0	X	X		X	INST
VMTBOSA=	0	X	X		X	INST
VNFERR	VNFERR	X	X	X	X	LR

(*continued*)

† operational value

‡ configuration-file value

Table 20.1 (*continued*)

Option name	Default	SAS Invocation	CONFIG file	OPTIONS window	OPTIONS statement	See
VSAMLOAD	NOVSAMLOAD	X	X		X	COMP
VSAMREAD	VSAMREAD	X	X		X	COMP
VSAMUPDATE	NOVSAMUPDATE	X	X		X	COMP
WORK=	WORK†	X	X			COMP, LR
WORKINIT	WORKINIT	X	X			LR
WORKTERM	WORKTERM	X	X	X	X	LR
YEARCUTOFF=	1900	X	X	X	X	LR

† operational value

Chapter 21 Windows and Window Features

Host-Specific Windows   411

Host-Specific Frames of the FORM Subsystem   416
TSO Print-File Parameter Frame   417
   Field Descriptions   417
IBM 3800 Print-File Parameter Frame   418
   Field Descriptions   418

Command-Line Commands   419

Windowing Options under MVS   423

Display Manager Under MVS – Terminal Support   424
Text Device Drivers   424
Graphics Device Drivers   424
SAS3270 Device Drivers   425
Using a Mouse in the SAS Windowing Environment under MVS   426
   Using a Three-Button Mouse   426
   Using a Two-Button Mouse   426
Appearance of Window Borders, Scroll Bars, and Widgets   426
Improving Screen Resolution on an IBM 3290 Terminal   427

Portable features of the SAS Display Manager windowing environment are documented in *SAS Language: Reference.* Only features that are MVS-specific or that have host-specific aspects are documented in this chapter.

This chapter also includes information about terminals and special devices that you can use with the SAS System under MVS.

Host-Specific Windows

DSINFO

Provides information about a cataloged operating system data set

Syntax

DSINFO *DDname*
DSINFO *'OS-data-set-name'*

DSINFO *continued*

Description

You can invoke the DSINFO window from any display manager window, as well as from other windows in the windowing environment such as SAS/FSP and SAS/AF windows. To invoke the DSINFO window, type DSINFO followed by either a DDname, a fully qualified data set name, or a partially qualified name such as *'.misc.text'*. (See "Specifying Operating System Data Sets" on page 13 for information about using partially qualified data set names.) You can also invoke the DSINFO window by using the X selection-field command in the FNAME window.

If you are referencing a concatenated file, the DSINFO window displays information for the first data set in the concatenation.

Display 21.1
DSINFO Window

```
DSINFO: TSO.VDR.ISPTLIB
 Command ===>

  Volume Serial:        XYZ123      Allocated Cylinders: 6
  Device Type:          3380        Allocated Extents:   1
  Organization:         PO          Used Cylinders:      3
  Record Format:        FB          Used Extents:        1
  Record Length:        80
  Block Size:           6160        Management Class:
  1st Extent Cylinders: 6           Storage Class:
  2nd Extent Cylinders: 0           Data Class:

                    Creation Date:      96/01/23
                    Expiration Date:    **NONE**
```

FILENAME

Displays assigned filerefs and their associated file names

Syntax

FILENAME

MVS Specifics

A DDname that was allocated externally (using the JCL DD statement or the TSO ALLOCATE command) is not listed by the FILENAME window until after you have used it as a fileref in your SAS session.

FNAME

Displays allocated DDnames, their associated data set names, and data set information

Syntax

FNAME *<DDname>*
FNAME *<generic-name*>*

Description

The FNAME window displays allocated DDnames whether they are identified as librefs, filerefs, or other DDnames. You can invoke the FNAME window from any display manager window, as well as from other windows in the windowing environment such as SAS/FSP and SAS/AF windows. To invoke it, type FNAME. If you do not supply the optional DDname, then the FNAME window displays all DDnames that are associated with your session, along with the names of the operating system data sets that are associated with them. If you supply a DDname, it can either be specific or generic. For example, to see only DDnames that begin with S, you would use the following generic specification:

FNAME S*

By entering one of the following selection-field commands, you can perform various functions on the displayed data sets:

B   selects a sequential data set or partitioned data set (PDS) member for browsing.

E   selects a sequential data set or PDS member for editing.

I   includes a sequential data set or PDS member into the PROGRAM EDITOR window.

%   submits a %INCLUDE statement to SAS to include a sequential data set or PDS member.

F   frees (deallocates) an allocated fileref.

M   opens the MEMLIST window, which lists the members in a single PDS.

C   lists the members in a concatenation of PDSs.

X   opens the DSINFO window, which provides data set information.

FNAME   *continued*

Display 21.2
FNAME Window

```
FNAME
 Command ===>

    DDname    Data Set Name                               Org Status  Disp

 _  CONFIG    SAS608.SAS.CONFIG(TSO)                        PO   SHR   KEEP
 _            MVS.SAS608.BNDLCNFG(SASHOST)                  PO   SHR   KEEP
 _  CTRANS    SAS608.SASC.LOAD                              PO   SHR   KEEP
 _  GDEVICE0  SAS608.GDRV.TESTSIO                           PS   SHR   KEEP
 _  ISPCTL0   SYS96071.T084354.RA000.USERID.R0164922       PS   NEW   DELETE
 _  ISPCTL1   SYS96071.T084354.RA000.USERID.R0164923       PS   NEW   DELETE
 _  ISPCTL2   SYS96071.T084354.RA000.USERID.R0164924       PS   NEW   DELETE
 _  ISPLIST   ++ SYSOUT ++                                  PS   MOD   DELETE
 _  ISPLST1   SYS96071.T084354.RA000.USERID.R0164925       PS   NEW   DELETE
 _  ISPLST2   SYS96071.T084354.RA000.USERID.R0164926       PS   NEW   DELETE
 _  ISPMLIB   TSO.VDR.ISPMLIB                               PO   SHR   KEEP
 _            TSO.ISPF.ISPMLIB                              PO   SHR   KEEP
 _  ISPPLIB   DEF.DEPT.ISPPLIB                              PO   SHR   KEEP
 _            TSO.VDR.ISPPLIB                               PO   SHR   KEEP
 _            TSO.ISPF.PREPLIB                              PO   SHR   KEEP
 _  ISPSLIB   TSO.VDR.ISPSLIB                               PO   SHR   KEEP
 _            TSO.ISPF.ISPSLIB                              PO   SHR   KEEP
 _  ISPTLIB   TSO.VDR.ISPTLIB                               PO   SHR   KEEP
 _            TSO.ISPF.ISPTLIB                              PO   SHR   KEEP
```

LIBNAME

Lists all the librefs that are currently assigned in your SAS session

Syntax

LIBNAME

MVS Specifics

A DDname that was allocated externally (using the JCL DD statement or the TSO
ALLOCATE command) is not listed by the LIBNAME window until after you have used it
as a libref in your SAS session.

Display 21.3
LIBNAME Window

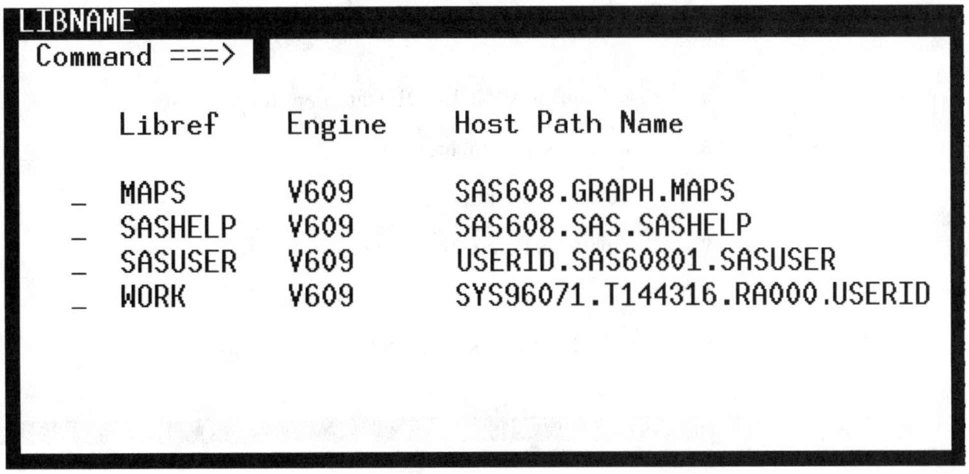

```
LIBNAME
 Command ===>

        Libref     Engine     Host Path Name

     _  MAPS       V609       SAS608.GRAPH.MAPS
     _  SASHELP    V609       SAS608.SAS.SASHELP
     _  SASUSER    V609       USERID.SAS60801.SASUSER
     _  WORK       V609       SYS96071.T144316.RA000.USERID
```

MEMLIST

Displays a member list for a partitioned data set (PDS) or for a series of partitioned data sets in a concatenation

Syntax

MEMLIST *DDname*
MEMLIST *DDname*(*member*)
MEMLIST *DDname*(*generic-name* *)
MEMLIST '*OS-data-set-name*'
MEMLIST '*OS-data-set-name*(*member*)'
MEMLIST '*OS-data-set-name*(*generic-name* *)'

Description

You can invoke the MEMLIST window from any display manager window, as well as from other windows in the windowing environment such as SAS/FSP and SAS/AF windows. You can specify either a generic member name or a specific member name. For example, to list only members whose names begin with TEST, you would use the following generic specification:

    MEMLIST MYPDS(TEST*)

You can also invoke the MEMLIST window by using the M selection-field command in the FNAME window.

By entering one of the following selection-field commands in the MEMLIST window, you can perform various functions on the displayed list of PDS members:

B   selects a member for browsing.

E   selects a member for editing.

I   includes a member into the PROGRAM EDITOR window and makes PROGRAM
        EDITOR the active window.

MEMLIST *continued*

%	submits a %INCLUDE statement for a member.
R	renames a member.
D	deletes a member.
V	verifies a delete or rename command.
C	cancels a rename or delete command.
S	selects a member for browsing (same as B).

Display 21.4
MEMLIST Window

```
MEMLIST: TSO.ISPF.PREPLIB
 Command ===>

   Name       VV.MM  Created   Last Modified  Size   Init   Mod   ID

 _ EDCFP16    01.00  96/02/04  96/02/04 12:18   39     39     0    USERID
 _ EDCJP16    01.00  96/02/05  96/02/05 10:30   37     37     0    USERID
 _ FLMB#P     01.00  96/02/05  96/02/04 12:33   74     74     0    USERID
 _ FLMDDG#P   01.00  96/02/04  96/02/04 11:23   52     52     0    USERID
 _ FLMDEXT    01.00  96/02/04  96/02/04 12:29   18     18     0    USERID
 _ FLMDMN     01.00  96/02/04  96/02/05 10:28   43     43     0    USERID
 _ FLMDSU#P   01.00  96/02/05  96/02/05 10:39   23     23     0    USERID
 _ FLMDXE#P   01.00  96/02/04  96/02/04 12:20   40     40     0    USERID
 _ FLMDXI#P   01.00  96/02/04  96/02/04 12:24   45     45     0    USERID
 _ FLMEB#P    01.00  96/02/04  96/02/06 11:43   33     33     0    USERID
 _ FLMED#P    01.00  96/02/05  96/02/06 11:26   30     30     0    USERID
 _ FLMEDR02   01.00  96/02/05  96/02/05 10:37   28     28     0    USERID
```

Host-Specific Frames of the FORM Subsystem

The FORM subsystem consists of six frames (or windows) that are described in detail in *SAS Language: Reference.* You use these frames to define a form for each printer that is available to you at your site.

Two of the frames in the FORM subsystem contain host-specific information. Both are print-file parameter windows that you use to specify the printer, text format, and destination for your output. Display 21.5 and Display 21.6 show these two frames. Display 21.6 appears only if you select IBM 3800 print-file parameters.

Brief discussions of the fields in these frames follow the displays. For more details, extensive online help is available for the FORM windows. You can access the help facility for general information about the FORM subsystem. You can also request help on specific fields within each frame by moving the cursor to the field and pressing the help function key. Also see "Using the PRINT Command and the FORM Subsystem" on page 99 for more information about using the FORM subsystem.

The TSO print-file parameters in the first frame are the same parameters you would use in a TSO ALLOCATE statement.

TSO Print-File Parameter Frame

```
FORM:  NEW.FORM (E)
 Command ===>

                          TSO Print File Parameters

        Destination: [        ]        Class:  [A]
              Forms: [     ]             UCS:  [     ]
             Copies: [1    ]             FCB:  [     ]
             Writer: [       ]        Outlim:  [        ]


         Parameter options:

           Hold output:   YES  [NO]

                 SELECT IBM 3800 print file parameters


         To select or deselect, place cursor on choice and press ENTER.
```

Field Descriptions

Many of the values that are entered for these parameters are site-specific. The data center personnel at your site can give you information about the Destination, Forms, and Class codes that are used at your site.

Destination	routes the output to a particular device. Destination is a one to eight alphanumeric or national character name that is defined for a device by your site.
Class	refers to the SYSOUT class of the file. The SYSOUT parameter is used to route output to printers and other devices. Class can be any alphanumeric character. Ask your data center personnel which specifications are appropriate for this field.
Forms	are specified by using one to four alphanumeric or national characters. Form numbers are used to request special paper. Ask your data center personnel which values are appropriate for this field.
UCS	requests that a print chain or print train that contains the Universal Character Set be mounted for a device. Ask your data center personnel which values are appropriate for this field.
Copies	specifies how many copies to print. The range is from 1 to 255, with a default value of 1.
FCB	is the forms control-buffer value, which specifies the movement of forms on a device. Ask your data center personnel which values are appropriate for this field.
Writer	specifies the name of a program in the SYS1.LINKLIB library that is to be used to write the output instead of JES2 or JES3. Ask your data center personnel for information about using this parameter.
Outlim	specifies the maximum number of output lines that can be printed. The range is from 1 to 16,777,215. If Outlim is exceeded, the job is automatically terminated.

Hold   requests that output be held in the output queue instead of going directly to
                        the device.

IBM 3800 Print-File Parameter Frame

Display 21.6
IBM 3800 Print-File
Parameter Frame

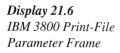

```
FORM:  NEW.FORM (E)
Command ===>


                              IBM 3800 Print File Parameters


          Character tables:  [    ]   [    ]   [    ]   [    ]
               Flash name:   [    ]        Flash count:  [    ]
               Modify name:  [    ]        Modify TRC:   [    ]
                  Formdef:   [       ]        Pagedef:   [       ]

          Options:

               Burst        Optcode=J


          To select or deselect, place cursor on choices and press ENTER.
```

Field Descriptions

This frame requests the following print-file parameters. For more information, consult the
help facility. Also refer to the IBM JCL reference manual for your system for additional
information about these parameters.

Character tables	specifies which character table to use for printing output. Ask your data center personnel which values are appropriate for this field.
Flash name and Flash count	control the use of overlay forms. Ask your data center personnel for details.
Modify name and Modify TRC	control the use of copy modification modules in SYS1.IMAGELIB for printing output. Ask your data center personnel for details.
Burst	requests that your output be torn apart into separate sheets of paper. When Burst is not specified, the default is normal fanfold (continuous) printing.
Optcode	works in conjunction with the character tables option. Ask your data center personnel for details.

Command-Line Commands

Portable command-line commands are documented in *SAS Language: Reference.* This section includes detailed information about only MVS-specific command-line commands.

CLOCK

Displays the current time according to a 24-hour clock

Syntax

CLOCK

Description

The time is shown as *hh.mm* in the lower-right corner of the display. Repeat the command to toggle the clock on and off.

GCURSOR

When applicable, turns the graphics cursor on or off

Syntax

GCURSOR <ON> | <OFF>

Description

This command is used only with 3179G, 3192G, IBM5550, and IBM3472G graphics terminals. When a mouse is attached, the default setting for GCURSOR is ON. Without a mouse, the cursor movement keys are used to position the graphics cursor. The GCURSOR command acts like a toggle switch. Alternatively, you can use the ON and OFF operands.

HOSTEDIT

Temporarily suspends the current SAS session and starts a session of the ISPF editor or browser

HOSTEDIT   *continued*

Syntax

HOSTEDIT | **HED**

MVS Specifics

Under MVS, this command starts a session of the ISPF editor or browser. Under other operating systems, it invokes other host-specific editors.

Note: The HOSTEDIT command works only if you have invoked SAS from the ISPF environment.

You can execute the HOSTEDIT command from the command line of any SAS Display Manager window that involves the SAS Text Editor, such as the PROGRAM EDITOR, LOG, OUTPUT, NOTEBOOK, and BUILD windows, among others.

When the ISPF EDIT session begins, the screen displays the contents of the display manager window from which it was invoked. Depending on how the display manager window was defined when it was created, one of the following actions occurs:

□   If the window can be edited, you are placed in an ISPF EDIT session editing the contents of the display manager window. You can then use the standard ISPF EDIT commands to edit the text or to call up any of the ISPF EDIT models, and you can save changes back to the display manager window from which the HOSTEDIT command was issued.

□   If the window is read-only, you are placed in an ISPF BROWSE session that displays the contents of the display manager window.

□   If the window cannot be edited by the host editor, a message to that effect appears in the display manager window, and no other action occurs.

Special text attributes such as color or highlighting are lost during a host editing session. When the HOSTEDIT command is issued from a display manager window that contains text with these attributes, a requestor window appears. The requestor window gives you the option of either continuing or aborting the HOSTEDIT command.

When you have finished editing in the ISPF EDIT session, do one of the following:

□   To save the contents back to the display manager window, issue the END command.

□   To discard the changes you made, issue the CANCEL command.

□   To save the contents of the window to an external file, use the standard ISPF EDIT commands such as CREATE or REPLACE. Then issue the END or CANCEL command, depending on whether you also want to save the changes back to the display manager window.

In each case you are returned to the display manager window in the SAS session that was suspended.

See Also

□ "Using the ISPF Editor from Your SAS Session" on page 110

INCLUDE

Copies the contents of an external file into the current window

---

Syntax

INCLUDE *fileref*
INCLUDE *fileref(member)*
INCLUDE *'OS-data-set-name'*
INCLUDE *'OS-data-set-name(member)'*

MVS Specifics

This command is available in the PROGRAM EDITOR window as well as in any other window that uses the SAS Text Editor such as the NOTEPAD window. You can also include an external file from the MEMLIST or FNAME windows. You can identify the external file by specifying either a fileref or the operating system data set name. If you specify the operating system data set name, you must enclose it in quotes.

Here are examples of including different forms of filerefs or operating system data set names:

INCLUDE MYPGM
    where MYPGM is a fileref that was previously associated with the external file.

INCLUDE MYPGM(PGM1)
    where PGM1 is a member of the partitioned data set that is associated with the fileref MYPGM.

INCLUDE 'USERID.TEST.PGMS'
    operating system data set name.

INCLUDE 'USERID.TEST.PGMS(AAA)'
    operating system data set name with member specified.

INCLUDE '.TEST.MYPGM'
    where the first level is the value of the SAS system option SYSPREF=, which defaults to the user's system prefix.

See Also

□ "Specifying Operating System Data Sets" on page 13

□ *SAS Language: Reference*

NULLS

Turns NULLS on or off for all input fields of all windows

Syntax

NULLS <ON> | <OFF>

Description

When NULLS is ON, all input fields are padded with null characters instead of blanks. The NULLS command acts like a toggle switch. Alternatively, you can use the ON and OFF operands.

TSO

Issues a TSO command or invokes a CLIST or a REXX exec from the command line

Syntax

TSO *<command>*

Description

The TSO command is similar to the TSO (or X) statement, the TSO (or SYSTEM) CALL routine, the TSO (or SYSTEM) function, and the %TSO (or %SYSEXEC) macro statement. It accepts the following argument:

command
> is a system command. Under MVS, "system command" includes TSO commands, CLISTs, and REXX execs.

To submit a TSO command, or to invoke a CLIST or a REXX exec, use the TSO *command* form of the command. You can use the TSO command from the command line of any display manager window. SAS executes the TSO command immediately.

Under MVS, TSO is an alias for the X command. On other operating systems, the TSO command has no effect, whereas the X command is always processed.

You can use the TSO command to issue most TSO commands or to execute CLISTs or REXX execs. However, you cannot issue the TSO commands LOGON and LOGOFF, and you cannot execute CLISTs that include the TSO ATTN statement.

You can also use the TSO command to go into TSO submode from within a SAS session. To start the submode, enter **TSO** from the command line without specifying a TSO command. When the command is executed, SAS goes into TSO submode and prompts you for TSO commands. Any commands that you enter in TSO submode are processed by TSO; they are not processed by display manager. They can be any length; however, if the command is longer than one line, you must enter a TSO continuation symbol.

To return to the SAS session, enter RETURN, END, or EXIT. Any characters that follow the RETURN, END, or EXIT subcommand are ignored. An END command that occurs within a CLIST terminates the command procedure without ending the TSO submode.

Note: The TSO command processor does not know when or if it is invoking an interactive windowing application. To avoid problems with screen clearing, you may want to invoke ISPF, IOF, or similar facilities directly. For example:

tso ispf

This method works only if you invoked SAS from the TSO READY prompt. It does not work if you were already in ISPF when you invoked your current SAS session.

See Also

□ X command in this chapter

□ TSO statement on page 296 and X statement on page 297

□ TSO CALL routine on page 166 and SYSTEM CALL routine on page 165

□ TSO function on page 172 and SYSTEM function on page 171

□ "Macro Statements" on page 193

X

Enters host-system mode or enables you to submit a host-system command without ending your SAS session

Syntax

X *<command>*

MVS Specifics

The X and TSO commands are identical, with one exception: under an operating system other than MVS, the TSO command has no effect, whereas the X command is always processed. See "TSO" on page 422 for more information.

Windowing Options under MVS

You can use the following SAS system options to customize the windowing environment under MVS:

CHARTYPE=   specifies which character set or screen size to use for a device.

FSBORDER=   specifies what type of symbols to use in window borders and other widgets.

FSDEVICE=   specifies which terminal device driver to use.

FSMODE=   specifies which type of IBM 3270 data stream to use for a terminal.

PFKEY=   specifies which set of function keys to designate as the primary set.

For detailed information about these system options, see Chapter 20, "System Options."

Display Manager Under MVS – Terminal Support

The information in the following sections may be useful to you if you use graphics or special device drivers in the SAS windowing environment.

Text Device Drivers

The SAS System uses two interactive windowing text (nongraphics) device drivers: a non-Extended-Data-Stream (non-EDS) driver and an Extended-Data-Stream (EDS) driver. An EDS device supports IBM 3270 extended attributes such as colors and highlighting, whereas a non-EDS device does not. Note that EDS devices also support the non-EDS data stream. The ability to do graphics on a 3270 terminal implies that it is an EDS device. Examples of EDS and non-EDS IBM terminals are

EDS	Non-EDS
3179, 3290 (LT-1)	3277
3279, 3270-PC	3278 (most)
3278 with graphics RPQ	3290 (LT-2, 3, or 4)

On non-EDS terminals, vertical window borders occupy three display positions on the screen: the first position for the field attribute byte, the next position for the border character itself, and the third position for the attribute byte for the following field. Because a window has both left and right vertical borders, six display positions are used by the vertical borders. Therefore, on an 80-column non-EDS device, the maximum display/editing area in a window is 74 columns.

Vertical window borders on EDS devices occupy two display positions: the border character and the attribute for the next field (left vertical border), or the attribute and the border character (right vertical border). Therefore, on an 80-column EDS device, the maximum display/editing area in a window is 76 columns.

Graphics Device Drivers

There are two 3270 graphics device drivers in the SAS windowing environment: the Programmed Symbol driver and the Vector-to-Raster driver. On terminals that support graphics, these two drivers are used to produce graphics as well as mixed text and graphics. Both graphics drivers communicate with the text driver, which controls the terminal display.

□   The Programmed Symbol graphics driver uses user-definable characters to display graphics. A programmed symbol is a character on the device in which certain pixels are illuminated to produce a desired shape in a position (cell) on the display. A loadable programmed symbol set is a terminal character set that contains these application-defined programmed symbols. (The default symbol set on a device is the standard character set—that is, those symbols that are normally displayed and that can be entered from the keyboard.) Examples of terminals that use programmed symbols to display graphics are the 3279G, 3290, and 3270-PC.

□ The Vector-to-Raster graphics driver is used to produce graphics on terminals that support graphics drawing instructions such as MOVE and DRAW. Examples of these devices are the 3179G/3192G and the IBM5550. The 3179G/3192G terminals also have limited support for programmed symbol graphics.

SAS3270 Device Drivers

When used with Emulus 3270 terminal emulation software on a UNIX workstation, the SAS3270 device drivers provide workstation-like capabilities that can greatly enhance SAS/INSIGHT and SAS/GRAPH software, as well as applications that are developed using SAS/AF software. These capabilities include the following:

use of local workstation memory for graphics
    offers significant performance improvements for SAS/AF applications, because a local copy of graphics is stored in the workstation memory rather than being continually retransmitted from the mainframe.

color loading by RGB value
    enables applications to use more colors than just the standard 8 or 16 graphics colors that they would use on a typical 3270 terminal or terminal emulator.

rubber-banding
    enables you to create, resize, and move objects. For example, you can:

    □ create or size graphics objects by dragging the workstation mouse in the SAS/GRAPH Graphics Editor

    □ easily drag and position objects in the SAS/AF Frame Editor

    □ rotate a plot when using SAS/INSIGHT software

    □ resize or move SAS windows.

dynamic graphics cursor shapes
    enables applications to change the shape of the graphics cursor to indicate the state of the application. For example, the graphics cursor typically changes shape when a user drags an object or rotates a plot.

To use these drivers, specify SAS3270 as the value of the SAS system option FSDEVICE=.

The SAS3270 drivers are compatible with the default 3270 drivers, except that graphics do not work when you use these drivers with the OS/2 Communications Manager 3270 terminal emulator. Therefore, do not specify SAS3270 as the value of FSDEVICE= if users at your site run SAS graphics applications using the 3270 terminal emulator in OS/2 Communications Manager.

Using a Mouse in the SAS Windowing Environment under MVS

The IBM 3179G, 3192G, 3472G, and 5550 terminals are all graphics terminals that support the use of a mouse. The IBM 3179G, 3192G, and 5550 terminals use the three-button IBM 5277 Model 1 optical mouse, whereas the IBM 3472G terminal uses the two-button PS/2® mouse.

SAS recognizes when the mouse is attached and automatically places the graphics cursor under the control of the mouse.

Using a Three-Button Mouse

The IBM 5277 Model 1 optical mouse has three buttons:

leftmost button
> SAS uses the leftmost button as an ENTER key. The keyboard ENTER key is used to select menu items; to grow, shrink, or move windows; to scroll using scroll bars, and so on. Therefore, having the ENTER key on the mouse is useful. The text cursor moves to the location of the mouse cursor whenever you press this mouse button.

center button
> By default, SAS assigns the value of the F15 function key to the center button. You can use the KEYS window or the KEYDEF command to change the definition of this button. The button is designated as MB2. See *SAS Language: Reference* for more information about the KEYS window and the KEYDEF command.

rightmost button
> The rightmost button is a reset button that unlocks the keyboard.

For additional information about using a mouse, refer to the appropriate documentation at your site.

Using a Two-Button Mouse

The 3472G terminal is a multiple-session graphics terminal. This device uses the two-button PS/2 mouse. With the graphics cursor attached, these buttons have the same functions as the leftmost and center buttons on the three-button mouse.

Appearance of Window Borders, Scroll Bars, and Widgets

Depending on the type of terminal, SAS uses either programmed symbols or APL symbols to create window borders, scroll bars, and widgets (radio buttons, push buttons, and check boxes). This can cause SAS display manager windows to look somewhat nicer on some terminals than on others.

□ On devices that support programmed symbols, the SAS windowing environment uses a predefined set of programmed symbols for its window components. Programmed symbols give window components a nicer appearance than APL symbols. These programmed symbols are available for the four most-common character cell sizes: 9 x 12, 9 x 14, 9 x 16, and 6 x 12. Programmed symbols are not used for any device that has a different character cell size (for example, 10 x 14 on a Tektronix® 4205), even though the device supports programmed symbols.

□ On 3270 terminals that do not support programmed symbols, but which support the APL* character set, the SAS windowing environment uses APL symbols. APL is supported only on EDS devices, including all nongraphic 3279 and 3179 terminals, and on many PC 3270 emulators.

Improving Screen Resolution on an IBM 3290 Terminal

The IBM 3290 terminal gives you the ability to change character cell size (and therefore, to change screen resolution). This capability is useful if you are working with graphics, for example.

You use the CHARTYPE= system option to modify the character cell size. For example, on a 3290 terminal that is configured as having 43 rows by 80 columns, CHARTYPE=1 (the default) produces a 62 x 80 display size.

If you specify CHARTYPE=2, the display size will be 46 x 53. Note that if you configure the 3290 as 62 x 160 (the maximum display size available on the 3290), CHARTYPE=2 results in a display size of 46 x 106. This results in a very legible and attractive windowing environment. See "CHARTYPE=" on page 307 for more information about this option.

Note: If you are running in interactive graphics mode under MVS and you receive a message, your display may become corrupted. To correct this and return the screen to its original display, press ENTER in response to the SCREEN ERASURE message. Alternatively, you can configure the 3290 as one logical terminal with a 62 x 160 character cell size.

Tektronix is a registered trademark of Tektronix Inc.

* APL ("a programming language") relies heavily on mathematical-type notation, using single-character operators in a special character set.

429

Part 4
Appendices

Appendix 1   **Accessing V5 and V5SEQ SAS® Data Libraries**

Appendix 2   **Using the INFILE/FILE User Exit Facility**

Appendix 3   **Host-System Subgroup Error Messages**

Appendix 1 Accessing V5 and V5SEQ SAS® Data Libraries

Overview of the V5 and V5SEQ Engines   431

Using the V5 Engine   432
   When to Use This Engine   433
   How to Select the V5 Engine   433
DCB Attributes for the V5 Engine   433
   External Allocation   434
   Internal Allocation   434
Engine/Host Options for the V5 Engine   434
Utilities That You Can Use with V5 SAS Data Libraries   435
CONTENTS Procedure Output   435

Using the V5SEQ Engine   436
When to Use This Engine   436
How to Select the V5SEQ Engine   437
DCB Attributes for the V5SEQ Engine   437
   External Allocation   437
Engine/Host Options for the V5SEQ Engine   438
Utilities That You Can Use with V5SEQ SAS Data Libraries   438
CONTENTS Procedure Output   438

Overview of the V5 and V5SEQ Engines

You use the V5 and V5SEQ engines to access V5 and V5SEQ SAS data libraries, respectively. Table A1.1 summarizes some useful information about these engines.

For information about portable features of the SAS System that are used by these engines, see *SAS Language: Reference*. For information about host-specific features, see the appropriate chapter in this book.

For general information about SAS library engines, see "SAS Library Engines" on page 26 and *SAS Language: Reference*.

Table A1.1
Overview of the V5 and V5SEQ Engines

	V5 Engine	**V5SEQ Engine**

DCB Attributes	DSORG=DA
	RECFM=U
	BLKSIZE=32760
	LRECL=32756
		Tape:
		   DSORG=PS
		   RECFM=U
		   BLKSIZE=32760
		   LRECL=32756
		Disk:
		   DSORG=PS
		   RECFM=U

(continued)

Table A1.1
(continued)

	V5 Engine	**V5SEQ Engine**
Member Types Supported	DATA CAT* GCAT* IMLWK* MODEL*	DATA
Engine/Host Options	BLKSIZE= DISP= SPACE= UNIT= VOLSER=	DISP=
Portable Data Set Options	all	all
MVS-Specific Data Set Options	BLKSIZE=	BLKSIZE= FILECLOSE= FILEDISP=
Portable System Options	n/a	TAPECLOSE=
MVS-Specific System Options	BLKSIZE= DLORGCK= FILEDEV= FILESPPRI= FILESPSEC= FILEUNIT= FILEVOL= NDSVOLS= SYSPREF=	SYSPREF=

* directory-level processing only; that is, RENAME and DELETE functions in PROC DATASETS
and in the DIR window. Read-level access by PROC V5TOV6.

Using the V5 Engine

The V5 engine provides read, write, and update access to Version 5 SAS data sets. This means that you can create new Version 5 data sets in existing Version 5 data libraries, and you can also create new Version 5 SAS data libraries under Version 6.

In contrast to the V6 engine, the V5 engine does not support indexing and compression of observations.

A V5 SAS data library is a direct-access operating system data set (DSORG=DA). A V5 SAS data library can exist only on one volume—that is, on one physical disk pack. If you need a SAS data library on disk to span more than one volume, create a Version 6 SAS data library, a Version 5 sequential SAS data library on disk, or a Version 6 sequential SAS data library on disk.

When to Use This Engine

Use the V5 engine to access SAS data sets that you want to share between Version 5 and Version 6 applications. Additionally, if you rely on the SOURCE records that are maintained with a SAS data set, you must keep your data in a Version 5 SAS data library. Note, however, that any Version 5 data set that you create under Version 6 will not have any SOURCE records associated with it.

How to Select the V5 Engine

There are three ways to select this engine:

□ Specify V5 as the value of the *engine* argument in the LIBNAME statement.

□ For existing Version 5 SAS data libraries, specify no value for *engine* in the LIBNAME statement. SAS then examines the data set attributes and selects this engine automatically. SAS also selects this engine automatically if you omit the LIBNAME statement and use a JCL DD statement or a TSO ALLOCATE command to allocate the library.

□ For a new SAS data library, set the value of the SAS system option ENGINE= to V5. This option tells SAS which engine to use as the default when you allocate a new operating system data set without specifying an engine. Note that you must also specify DISP=NEW.

DCB Attributes for the V5 Engine

The operating system data set label contains DCB information that describes the data set's characteristics. The operating system writes the DCB information when it creates the library, using either values that are supplied by the user, or the values of several SAS system options. Both the SAS System and MVS utility programs use this DCB information during processing.

Whether you allocate a new Version 5 disk-format data library externally (using a JCL DD statement or a TSO ALLOCATE command) or internally (using a SAS LIBNAME statement), you can allow SAS to supply the DCB information for you. If you choose to specify DCB information yourself, then you must specify the following DCB attribute values:

□ DSORG=DA

□ RECFM=U

□ BLKSIZE=32760

□ LRECL=32756

The LRECL= and BLKSIZE= values are the maximum possible values for any operating system data set on the device. The block size and logical record length for individual SAS data sets cannot exceed the BLKSIZE= and LRECL= values for the library as a whole. Therefore, setting the library's value to the maximum possible value for the disk eliminates all library restrictions on the block size and logical record length for the SAS data sets within the library.

The criteria for the maximum allowable logical record length and block size for a SAS data set are as follows:

□ The absolute maximum on the largest possible device is about 32,100 bytes, based on the MVS maximum block size of 32,760 bytes, with additional amounts subtracted for internal SAS System use.

□ On 3375, 3380, and 3390 disks, SAS records the BLKSIZE= value as 32760 and the LRECL= value as 32756; therefore, a SAS data set in the library can have that block size and logical record length if necessary. (Of course, most SAS data sets have a much smaller logical record length, thereby allowing SAS to use a more efficient block size.)

The following sections provide additional information about DCB parameters for the V5 engine. Also see "DCB Attribute Options" on page 275 for more information.

External Allocation

Here is an example of allocating a Version 5 SAS data library externally:

```
alloc fi(sasdata) da(sas.v5data) dsorg(da) recfm(u) lrecl(32756)
      blksize(32760) new
```

Internal Allocation

Here is an example of using the LIBNAME statement to allocate a Version 5 disk-format SAS data library:

```
libname v5data V5 '.v5.sasdata' disp=(new,catlg,delete) space=(cyl,(1,1))
      unit=sysda vol=aca005 blksize=6144;
```

You can override the default value of the BLKSIZE= system option by using the BLKSIZE= option in the LIBNAME statement.

Engine/Host Options for the V5 Engine

The engine/host options that you can supply in the LIBNAME statement correspond to the JCL or TSO parameters that you would specify if you allocated the SAS data library externally. For the V5 engine, you can specify any of the engine/host options shown in Table A1.1 on page 431. (For more information about these options and their values, see the description of *engine/host options* under "LIBNAME" on page 289.) Or you can accept the default values that are specified by the corresponding SAS system options, as follows:

□ If you do not specify a value for DISP=, the default for existing data sets is DISP=(OLD,KEEP,KEEP). For new data sets, the default depends on how you are allocating the library:

　　□ If you are allocating the library with a LIBNAME statement, then you must at least specify DISP=NEW. The default for the complete DISP= specification is DISP=(NEW,CATLG,DELETE).

　　□ Similarly, if you are allocating the library with a TSO command, you must at least specify NEW, and the complete disposition specification defaults to DISP=(NEW,CATLG,DELETE).

    □   If you are allocating the library externally with a JCL statement, disposition defaults to DISP=(NEW,DELETE,DELETE).

□   If you do not specify values for the SPACE= parameters, SAS uses the current values of the SAS system options FILEUNIT=, FILESPPRI=, and FILESPSEC=. The defaults are SPACE=(CYL,(1,1)).

□   If you do not specify a value for VOLSER=, SAS uses the current value of the SAS system option FILEVOL=, if a value for FILEVOL= has been specified at your site.

□   If you do not specify a value for UNIT=, SAS uses the current value of the SAS system option FILEDEV=. The default is SYSDA.

Note: The default values shown are those that are supplied by SAS. Your SAS system administrator may have changed the default values for your site.

For temporary data libraries, you do not need to specify any options, but you can override any of the default values.

Utilities That You Can Use with V5 SAS Data Libraries

You can copy V5 SAS data libraries using the COPY procedure running under Version 5 of the SAS System. If your installation must copy large numbers of V5 SAS data libraries, such as the contents of an entire disk volume, then your SAS Software Representative should contact the Technical Support Division at SAS Institute before attempting to use any utility other than the COPY procedure to copy V5 SAS data libraries.

As long as a SAS data library contains only SAS data sets (members of type DATA), you can also copy it using the COPY procedure running under Version 6 of the SAS System. (See SAS Technical Report P-195 for detailed information about transferring files between host operating systems under Version 5 and Version 6.) If your input library is a Version 6 data library that contains other member types, you will receive warning messages indicating that those files cannot be copied. However, the SAS data sets that you selected will be copied. Similarly, if your input library is a V5 data library that contains members of type CAT, GCAT, MODEL, or IMLWK, you will receive warning messages indicating that those members cannot be copied. However the SAS data sets that you selected will be copied.

Note: There is no room in the Version 5 variable descriptor to save the informat length. If you copy a SAS data set from a Version 6 SAS data library to a Version 5 data library, then copy it back to a Version 6 data library, you lose informat lengths.

You can convert a V5 SAS data library to a Version 6 SAS data library by using the V5TOV6 procedure. See the *SAS Procedures Guide* and "V5TOV6" on page 256 for details.

CONTENTS Procedure Output

The PROC CONTENTS output in Output A1.1 shows information that is generated by the V5SEQ engine.

Output A1.1
PROC CONTENTS
Output Generated
by the V5 Engine

```
                              The SAS System

                           CONTENTS PROCEDURE

Data Set Name: V5DAT.ORANGES              Observations:        4
Member Type:   DATA                       Variables:           5
Engine:        V5                         Indexes:             0
Created:       14:52 Tuesday, March 5, 1996   Observation Length:  44
Last Modified: 14:52 Tuesday, March 5, 1996   Deleted Observations: 0
Protection:                               Compressed:          NO
Data Set Type:                            Sorted:              NO
Label:

                -----Engine/Host Dependent Information-----

          Physical Name:         USERID.V5.DATA
          Release Created:       6.09
          Created by:            USERID
          Last Modified by:      USERID
          Protection:            NONE
          CPU Id:                00-XXXX-XXXXXX
          Blocksize:             23456
          Lrecl:                 44
          Subextents:            1
          Total Tracks Used:     1
          Observations per Track: 1066

                           CONTENTS PROCEDURE

        -----Alphabetic List of Variables and Attributes-----

          #    Variable   Type   Len   Pos
          -----------------------------------
          2    FLAVOR     Num    8     12
          4    LOOKS      Num    8     28
          3    TEXTURE    Num    8     20
          5    TOTAL      Num    8     36
          1    VARIETY    Char   8     4
```

Note: The Last Modified field in Output A1.1 records only the last time the data set was modified under Version 6. If you modify a data set under Version 6, then later modify it under Version 5, the Last Modified date is the Version 6 modification date.

Using the V5SEQ Engine

A Version 5 sequential SAS data library is a physical sequential operating system data set, either on tape or on disk. Because the library does not contain a directory, SAS cannot access an individual data set directly. It must read through all preceding SAS data sets in order to reach a requested data set. In addition, you can use only one SAS data set from a particular sequential SAS data library in a single DATA or PROC step.

When to Use This Engine

Use the V5SEQ engine to read Version 5 SAS data sets in sequential format on tape or disk in Version 6 applications, or to back up Version 6 SAS data sets to tape in the Version 5 sequential format. You may also want to use this engine to write SAS data libraries in the Version 5 sequential format so that they can be read by a Version 5 application either at your site or at another site.

How to Select the V5SEQ Engine

There are two ways to select this engine:

□ Specify V5SEQ as the value of the *engine* argument in the LIBNAME statement.

□ Use a libref of TAPE*xxxx* for sequential format on disk data sets.

DCB Attributes for the V5SEQ Engine

The operating system data set label contains DCB information that describes the data set's characteristics. The operating system writes the DCB information when it creates the library, using either values that are supplied by the user, or the values of several SAS system options. Both the SAS System and MVS utility programs use this DCB information during processing.

The following sections provide additional information about DCB parameters for the V5SEQ engine. Also see "DCB Attribute Options" on page 275 for more information.

External Allocation

If the device specified in a JCL statement is a tape unit, SAS assumes that the library is in sequential format. You can use any DDname for a sequential format SAS data library on tape or disk. Sequential SAS data libraries can occupy up to 255 volumes (physical tapes).

Note: In order to use the TSO ALLOCATE command to allocate a data set on tape, your user ID must have MOUNT authority.

The data set label in a sequential format SAS data library on a standard labeled tape contains this DCB information:

□ DSORG=PS

□ RECFM=U

□ BLKSIZE=32760

□ LRECL=32756

Here is an example of allocating a V5SEQ SAS data library externally:

```
//XYZ DD DSN=MY.TAPE,DISP=(NEW,KEEP),
//        UNIT=TAPE,VOL=SER=XYZ001,LABEL=(1,SL),
//        DCB=(DSORG=PS,RECFM=U,BLKSIZE=32760,LRECL=32756)
```

The BLKSIZE= and LRECL= values are the maximum possible values for any data set on tape. The block size and logical record length for individual SAS data sets cannot exceed the BLKSIZE= and LRECL= values for the library as a whole. Therefore, setting the library's value to the maximum possible value for the disk eliminates all library restrictions on the block size and logical record length for the SAS data sets within the library. You should not override these parameters.

A sequential format SAS data library on disk is a physical sequential operating system data set. The data set label in a sequential format data library on disk contains the following DCB information:

   □ DSORG=PS

   □ RECFM=U

   □ BLKSIZE=*value*, where *value* is the maximum allowable for a SAS data set on the disk device

   □ LRECL=BLKSIZE - 4.

Engine/Host Options for the V5SEQ Engine

The V5SEQ engine supports the following option in the LIBNAME statement:

DISP=OLD | SHR

If you do not specify DISP=, the default value is DISP=(OLD,KEEP,KEEP).

Here is an example of specifying the V5SEQ engine for the existing data library V5.DATA.SEQ:

```
libname V5 v5seq 'v5.data.seq' disp=shr;
```

Utilities That You Can Use with V5SEQ SAS Data Libraries

You can use IEBGENER and ISPF/PDF Screen 3.3 to transfer Version 5 sequential libraries between unlike I/O devices.

You can also copy V5SEQ SAS data libraries using the COPY procedure running under Version 5 of the SAS System. As long as a SAS data library contains only SAS data sets (members of type DATA), you can also copy it using the COPY procedure running under Version 6 of the SAS System. (See SAS Technical Report P-195 for detailed information about transferring files between host operating systems under Version 5 and Version 6.) If your input library is a Version 6 data library that contains other member types, you will receive warning messages indicating that those files cannot be copied. However, the SAS data sets that you selected will be copied. Similarly, if your input library is a V5 data library that contains members of type CAT, GCAT, MODEL, or IMLWK, you will receive warning messages indicating that those members cannot be copied. However the SAS data sets that you selected will be copied.

  Note: There is no room in the Version 5 variable descriptor to save the informat length. If you copy a SAS data set from a Version 6 SAS data library to a Version 5 data library, then copy it back to a Version 6 data library, you lose informat lengths.

CONTENTS Procedure Output

The PROC CONTENTS output in Output A1.2 shows information that is generated by the V5SEQ engine.

```
                              The SAS System

                           CONTENTS PROCEDURE

Data Set Name: X.ORANGES                Observations:          .
Member Type:    DATA                    Variables:             5
Engine:         V5SEQ                   Indexes:               0
Created:        16:00 Tuesday, March 5, 1996    Observation Length:   44
Last Modified:  .                       Deleted Observations:  0
Protection:                             Compressed:            NO
Data Set Type: DATA                     Sorted:                NO
Label:

                -----Engine/Host Dependent Information-----

    Physical Name:    USERID.DATA
    Volume:           XXXXXX
    Created by:       USERID
    Release Created:  6.09
    CPU Id:           00-XXXX-XXXXXX
    Unit:             DISK
    Max blksize:      32760

           -----Alphabetic List of Variables and Attributes-----

              #    Variable   Type   Len   Pos
              -----------------------------------
              2    FLAVOR     Num     8    12
              4    LOOKS      Num     8    28
              3    TEXTURE    Num     8    20
              5    TOTAL      Num     8    36
              1    VARIETY    Char    8     4

                        -----Directory-----

    Libref:        X
    Engine:        V5SEQ
    Physical Name: USERID.DATA

              #  Name     Memtype  Indexes
              ---------------------------
              1  ORANGES   DATA
```

Note: The Last Modified field in Output A1.2 records only the last time the data set was modified under Version 6. If you modify a data set under Version 6, then later modify it under Version 5, the Last Modified date is the Version 6 modification date.

Appendix **2** Using the INFILE/FILE User Exit
Facility

Introduction   *441*

Writing a User Exit Module   *441*
Function Request Control Block   *442*
User Exit BAG Control Block   *443*

Function Descriptions   *445*
Initialization Function   *445*
Parse Options Function   *445*
Open Function   *447*
Read Function   *448*
Concatenation Function   *448*
Write Function   *449*
Close Function   *450*

SAS Service Routines   *451*

Building Your User Exit Module   *453*

Activating an INFILE/FILE User Exit   *453*

Sample Program   *453*

Introduction

The INFILE/FILE User Exit Facility provides an interface for accessing user exit modules during the processing of external files in a SAS DATA step. A user exit module (or user exit) consists of several functions that you write in order to perform special processing on external files. For example, you can write user exits that inspect, modify, delete, or insert records. Here are some more-specific examples of how user exits may be used:

☐   encrypting and decrypting data

☐   compressing and decompressing data

☐   translating data from one character-encoding system to another.

If a user exit is active, SAS invokes it at various points during the processing of an external file.

Writing a User Exit Module

You can write a user exit module in any language that meets the following criteria:

☐   the language runs in 31-bit addressing mode

☐   the language supports standard OS linkage.

Examples of such languages are IBM assembly language and C. See "Sample Program" on page 453 for an example of an exit that is written in assembly language.

Note: In all the figures in this chapter, the field names that are shown in parentheses (for example, EXITIDB in Figure A2.2 on page 443) are those that were used in the Sample Program.

In your user exit module, you should include code for all seven of the functions that are described in "Function Descriptions" on page 445. At the beginning of your user exit module, examine the function code that was passed to you in the Function Request Control Block (described in the next section) and branch to the routine or function that is being requested.

When you write the user exit module, you must follow IBM conventions for assembler linkage, and you must set R15 to a return code value that indicates whether the user exit was successful. Any non-zero return code causes execution to stop. If you want to write an error message to the SAS log, use the SAS LOG service routine. (See "LOG" on page 451.)

If the user exit terminates with a non-zero return code value, you must put the address of a user-defined message string that ends in a null (00x) character in the Pointer to User Error Message (ERRMSG) field of the User Exit BAG Control Block. (See "User Exit BAG Control Block" on page 443.) This message is printed in the SAS log.

Return code values that apply to particular function requests are listed with the descriptions of those functions in later sections of this appendix.

Be sure to take advantage of the SAS service routines when you write your user exit functions. See "SAS Service Routines" on page 451 for details.

Function Request Control Block

The Function Request Control Block (FRCB) provides a means of communication between SAS and your user exit functions. Each time SAS invokes the user exit module, R1 points to a Function Request Control Block (FRCB) that contains, at a minimum, the fields shown in Figure A2.1.

Figure A2.1
Function Request
Control Block Fields

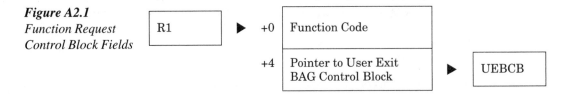

The 4-byte Function Code communicates the current user exit phase to the user exit. It contains one of the following values:

0   indicates the Initialization function.

4   indicates the Parse Options function.

8   indicates the Open function.

12   indicates the Read function.

16   indicates the Concatenation function.

20   indicates the Write function.

24   indicates the Close function.

These functions are described in "Function Descriptions" on page 445. Each time SAS calls the user exit, the user exit should branch to the appropriate exit routine, as determined by the Function code.

User Exit BAG Control Block

In Figure A2.1, the UEBCB (User Exit BAG Control Block) serves as a common anchor point for work areas that SAS has obtained on behalf of the user exit. SAS reserves a user word in the UEBCB for the user exit to use. You can use this word to store a pointer to memory that you allocate for use by all your exit routines. SAS does not modify this word during the lifespan of the user exit. The lifespan is defined as the time period between the Initialization function request and the Close function request.

Figure A2.2 illustrates the structure of the UEBCB and its relationship to other data areas:

Figure A2.2
UEBCB Structure

+0	Exit IDB (EXITIDB)	▶ Used by the SAS System
+4	Exit Entry Point (EXITEP)	▶ Used by the SAS System
+8	Size of the Work Area above the 16M line (MEMALEN)	▶ Size specified by user
+C	Pointer to the Work Area above the 16M line (MEMABV)	▶ Work Area
+10	Size of the Work Area below the 16M line (MEMBLEN)	▶ Size specified by user
+14	Pointer to the Work Area below the 16M line (MEMBEL)	▶ Work Area
* +18	User Word that can be set by the user exit (USERWORD)	▶ Available to user
+1C	Logical Name of the file (DDname) (EDDNAME)	▶ Specified in INFILE or FILE statement
+24	Pointer to routine that creates SAS variables	▶ VARRTN Routine
* +28	Pointer to User Error NULL-terminated string (ERRMSG)	▶ String
* +2C	Flag Byte 1	
+2D	Reserved	

continued next page

* The user exit can update this field.

Figure A2.2
(continued)

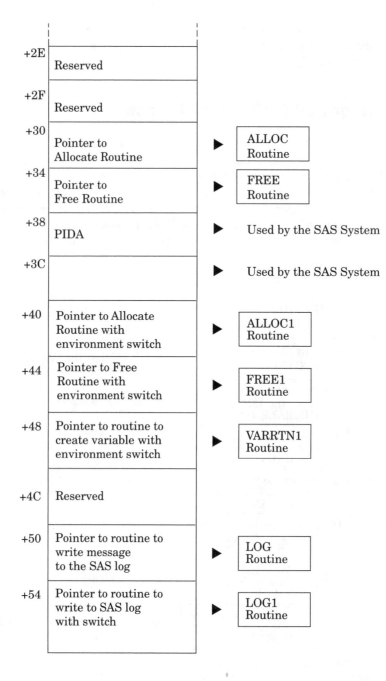

The Flag Byte 1 field can have one of several values. The following list gives the values and their meanings.

'80'x	EX_NEXT	prompt the exit for the next record.
'40'x	EX_DEL	ignore the current record.
'20'x	EX_EOF	end-of-file has been reached.
'10'x	EX_EOFC	this exit supports read/write calls after end-of-file has been reached.
'08'x	EX_ALC	this exit uses the ALLOC/FREE routines.
'04'x	EX_STOR	this exit supports stored programs and views.

Function Descriptions

The following sections provide the information that you need in order to write the functions that are part of the user exit module.

Initialization Function

SAS calls the Initialization function before it calls any of the other functions. In the Initialization function, you specify the amount of virtual memory that your routine will need above and below the 16-megabyte address line. You store the length of the work area that you need *above* the line in the fullword that is pointed to by the INITMALN field of the Initialization FRCB. You store the length of the work area that you need *below* the line in the fullword that is pointed to by the INITMBLN field of the Initialization FRCB. All pointers in the Initialization FRCB point to valid data areas.

In the amount of storage that you request, you should include space for a Local Register Save Area (LRSA) of 72 bytes, plus any other work areas that your Parse Options function and Open function will need.

SAS allocates the memory that you request when it returns from this function, and it stores pointers to the allocated memory in the UEBCB. The pointer to the memory that was allocated *above* the line is stored in the MEMABV field of the UEBCB. The pointer to the memory that was allocated *below* the line is stored in the MEMBEL field.

Figure A2.3 illustrates the Initialization FRCB structure and its relationship with other control blocks:

Figure A2.3
Initialization FRCB

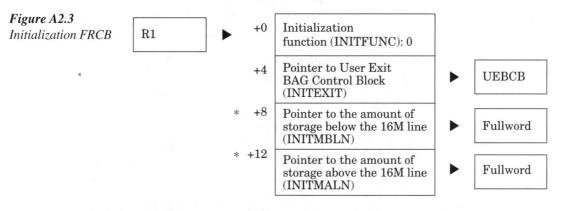

* The user exit can update this field.

Parse Options Function

In the Parse Options function you validate both the name of the user exit and any INFILE or FILE statement options that SAS does not recognize. SAS calls this function once to process the user exit module name. SAS then calls the function for each statement option that it does not recognize so that the function can process each option and value string.

You can use two kinds of statement options in your user exit:

□ options that take a value, such as *name=value*. For example:

```
myopt=ABC
```

Note that quotes are considered part of the value; if you want them to be stripped off, you must provide the code to do so.

□ options that do not take a value.

The first time the Parse Options function is invoked, it should do the following:

□ verify that the virtual storage that was requested during the Initialization function has been allocated

□ initialize both the allocated virtual storage and the two data areas in the UEBCB (User Word and Pointer to User Error Message).

Figure A2.4 illustrates the Parse Options FRCB structure and its relationship to other control blocks:

Figure A2.4
Parse Options
FRCB

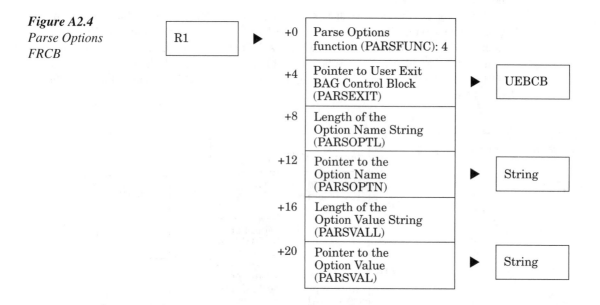

When the Parse Options function receives control, PARSOPTL is set to the length of the option name, and the address of the option name is stored in PARSOPTN. For options that take a value, PARSVALL is set to the length of the value, and the address of the option value is stored in PARSVAL. For options that do not take a value, both PARSVALL and PARSVAL are set to 0.

If an invalid option name or option value is detected, R15 should be set to a return code value of 8.

Open Function

SAS invokes the Open function after INFILE or FILE statement processing opens the associated data set. Figure A2.5 illustrates the Open FRCB and its relationship to other control blocks:

Figure A2.5
Open FRCB

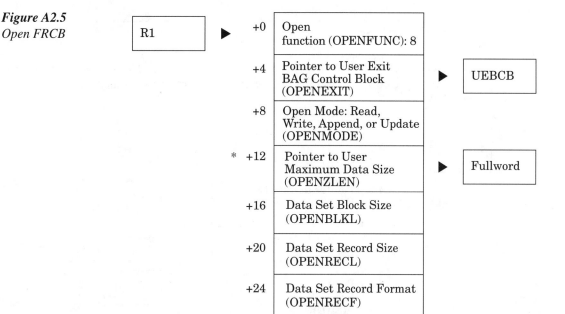

* The user exit can update this field.

The OPENMODE field can be one of the following values:

1	the data set is opened for input mode.
2	the data set is opened for output mode.
4	the data set is opened for append mode.
8	the data set is opened for update mode (read and write).

When this function receives control, the Pointer to User Maximum Data Size field (OPENZLEN) points to a fullword that contains the Data Set Record Size. In this function, set the pointer so that it points to a fullword that you initialize. The fullword should contain the size of the largest record that you expect to process with the Read function. If it contains a lesser value, then truncated records may be passed to the Read function.

The Data Set Record Format field (OPENRECF) can be any combination of the following values:

'C0'x	indicates Undefined format.
'80'x	indicates Fixed format.
'40'x	indicates Variable format.
'10'x	indicates Blocked format.
'08'x	indicates Spanned format.
'04'x	indicates ASA Control Characters format.

The Open function should activate any sub-processes and/or exits and should solicit from them any virtual storage requirements.

In this function, if you turn on the EX_NEXT flag in the UEBCB, SAS calls the Read function for the first record before it reads any records from the file itself.

If you use any SAS service routines (such as the ALLOC and FREE routines) in this function, then you must set the EX_ALC flag in the UEBCB.

Read Function

SAS invokes the Read function during execution of the INPUT statement to obtain the next input record. Figure A2.6 illustrates the Read FRCB structure and its relationship to other control blocks:

Figure A2.6
Read FRCB

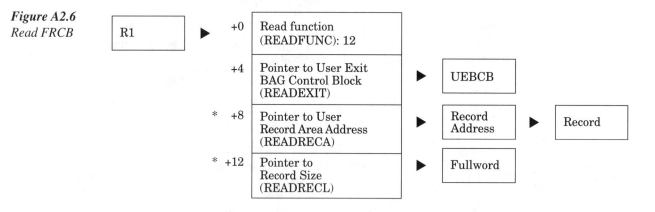

* The user exit can update this field.

When the Read function receives control, the READRECA field (or Pointer to User Record Area Address) points to the address of the current record from the file. The READRECL field points to a fullword that contains the length of the record that is in the Record Area.

In this function you can change the Record Address so that it points to a record that was defined by your user exit. If you do this, then SAS passes your record to the INPUT statement, rather than passing the record that was read from the file. However, in this case you must also update the fullword that the Pointer to Record Size points to: it must equal the actual size of the record that the Record Address points to.

As long as the EX_NEXT flag is on, SAS invokes the Read function to obtain the next record. SAS reads no records from the file itself until you turn off the EX_NEXT flag.

If you set the EX_DEL flag, then SAS ignores the current record, and processing continues to the next record.

Concatenation Function

SAS invokes the Concatenation function whenever a data set in a concatenation of data sets has reached an end-of-file condition and the next data set has been opened. Figure A2.7 illustrates the Concatenation FRCB structure and its relationship to other control blocks:

Figure A2.7
Concatenation
FRCB

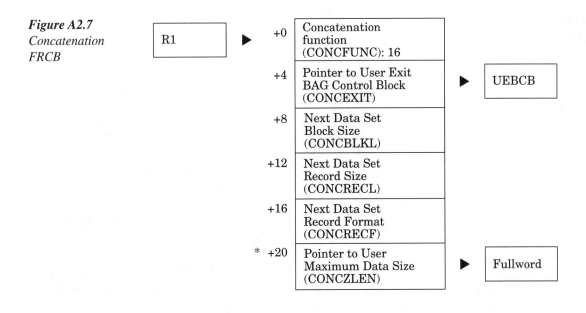

* The user exit can update this field.

In this function you can modify the maximum data size for the next data set by changing the Pointer to User Maximum Data Size so that it points to a fullword that you initialize.

Write Function

SAS invokes the Write function during the execution of the PUT statement whenever a new record must be written to the file. Figure A2.8 illustrates the Write FRCB and its relationship to other control blocks:

Figure A2.8
Write FRCB

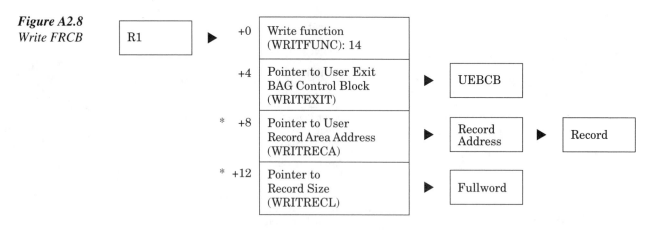

* The user exit can update this field.

When the Write function receives control, the WRITRECA field (or Pointer to User Record Area Address) points to a Record Address. The Record buffer is allocated by SAS and contains the record that was created by the PUT statement.

In this function you can change the Record Address so that it points to a record that is defined by your user exit. If you do this, then SAS writes your record to the file, instead of writing the record that was created by the PUT statement. However, in this case you must also update the fullword that the Pointer to Record Size points to: it must equal the actual size of the record that the Pointer to Record Area points to.

In the Write function, you may also change the setting of flags in the UEBCB. As long as the EX_NEXT bit in the UEBCB is on, SAS calls the Write function to write the next output record. The DATA step is not prompted for any new records to output until the EX_NEXT flag has been set. At any time, if the EX_DEL bit in the UEBCB is on, SAS ignores the current record, and processing continues to the next record.

Close Function

SAS invokes the Close function after it closes the associated data set. In this function, you should close any files that you opened, free any resources that you obtained, and terminate all sub-processes and/or exits that your user exit initiated.

Figure A2.9 illustrates the Close FRCB structure and its relationship to other control blocks:

Figure A2.9
Close FRCB

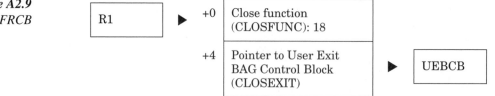

SAS Service Routines

SAS provides four service routines that you can use when writing INFILE/FILE user exits. These service routines allocate memory, free memory, access DATA step variables, or write a message to the SAS log. Whenever possible, use the SAS service routines instead of the routines that are supplied with MVS. For example, use the ALLOC SAS service routine instead of GETMAIN. When you use the ALLOC routine, SAS frees memory when you are finished with it. By contrast, if you use the GETMAIN routine, cleaning up memory is your responsibility, so you also have to use the FREEMAIN routine.

The following list describes the four SAS service routines. You invoke one of these routines by loading its address from the appropriate field in the UEBCB, and then branching to it. All of these routines are used in the "Sample Program" on page 453.

ALLOC routine
  allocates an area of memory from within the SAS memory pool. This memory is automatically freed when the Close function is processed. The ALLOC routine takes the following parameters:

ALCEXIT	a pointer to the UEBCB.
ALCPTR	a pointer to a fullword in which the allocated area address will be stored.
ALCLEN	the amount of memory required.
ALCFLG	a flag byte that controls whether the memory is allocated above or below the 16M line. It has the following values:

  1   allocates the memory below the 16M line.

  0   allocates the memory above the 16M line.

FREE routine
  frees an area of memory that was previously allocated by a call to the ALLOC routine. The FREE routine takes the following parameters:

FREEXIT	a pointer to the UEBCB.
FREPTR	a pointer to the area to be freed.
FREFLG	a flag byte that indicates whether the memory that is to be freed is above or below the 16M line. It has the following values:

  1   the memory is below the 16M line.

  0   the memory is above the 16M line.

LOG routine
  prints a message to the SAS log. The LOG routine takes the following parameter:

LOGSTR	a pointer to a character string that ends with a null.

VARRTN routine

defines or gets access to a SAS DATA step variable. The VARRTN routine takes the following parameters:

VARNAME   a pointer to the name of the variable.

VARNAMEL   the length of the variable name.

VARTYPE   the type of variable that is being defined. It takes the following values:

     1   the variable is numeric (double precision).

     2   the variable is character.

VARSIZE   the size of the variable, if the variable type is character.

VARFLAG   a flag byte that controls whether the variable is considered internal or external. It takes the following values:

     X'01'   the variable is an internal variable; it will not appear in any output data set.

     X'02'   the variable is an external variable; it will appear in the output data set.

VARADDR   a pointer to a fullword into which SAS places the address at which the current value of the variable will be stored. For numeric variables the value is stored as a double precision value. For character variables the stored value consists of three components:

     MAXLEN   is 2 bytes, and represents the maximum length of the character variable.

     CURLEN   is 2 bytes, and represents the current length of the character variable.

     ADDR   is 4 bytes, and is a pointer to the character variable string data.

Here are the return codes for the VARRTN routine:

0   the routine was successful (the variable was created or accessed).

1   the variable already exists as a different type.

2   the variable already exists as a character variable, but with a shorter length.

3   the variable already exists

Building Your User Exit Module

After you have coded your user exit module, you must assemble or compile it and then link it into a load library. The name that you choose for your load module must consist of a four-character prefix, followed by the letters IFUE. Do not use a prefix that is the same as the name of a FILE or INFILE statement option.

After your load module is built, use the LOAD parameter of the SAS CLIST or cataloged procedure when you invoke SAS to tell SAS the name of the load library that contains your user exit module.

Activating an INFILE/FILE User Exit

To activate an INFILE/FILE user exit, you generally specify the first four characters of the name of the user exit module following the DDname or data set name in an INFILE or FILE statement. For example:

```
infile inputdd abcd;
```

Only the first 4 characters of the user exit module name in the INFILE or FILE statement are significant; SAS forms the load module name by adding the constant IFUE to these characters. Therefore, in the previous example, SAS loads a module named ABCDIFUE.

You can also specify the name of the user exit module by using the ENGINE= option in the FILENAME statement.

Note: If you use an INFILE/FILE user exit with a DATA step view, specify the name of the exit in the FILENAME statement that you use to allocate the file, instead of in the INFILE or FILE statement. (If you specify the exit name in an INFILE or FILE statement, the exit is ignored when the view is executed.) For example:

```
filename inputdd 'my.user.exit' abcd;
```

Sample Program

The following sample program illustrates the process of writing an INFILE/FILE user exit. Notice that this is not a trivial program. Writing user exits requires a firm understanding of register manipulation and other fairly advanced programming techniques.

The example uses ESA services to compress data. The data are compressed on output and decompressed on input. *

The example consists of several assembly macros, followed by the assembly language program itself. The macros define how the parameter lists are to be interpreted. Each macro begins with a MACRO statement and ends with a MEND statement. The actual program begins on the shaded line that reads **SASCSRC START** on page 458. Here is the example:

---

* This code is actually implemented in the SAS System, to support the CSRC option on the INFILE and FILE statements. This option is described in "Standard Options for the FILE Statement under MVS" on page 266 and in "Standard Options for the INFILE Statement under MVS" on page 286.

```
          TITLE 'INFILE/FILE USER EXIT TO COMPRESS DATA USING ESA SERVICES'
*----------------------------------------------------------------------
* COPYRIGHT (C) 1991 BY SAS INSTITUTE INC., CARY, NC 27513 USA
*
* NAME:      ==> SASCSRC
* TYPE:      ==> EXTERNAL FILE USER EXIT
* LANGUAGE:  ==> ASM
* PURPOSE:   ==> TO COMPRESS/DECOMPRESS DATA USING CSRCESRV SERVICES
* USAGE:     ==> DATA;INFILE MYFILE CSRC;INPUT;RUN;
*----------------------------------------------------------------------
* - - - - - - - - -
        MACRO
*----------------------------------------------------------------------
* COPYRIGHT (C) 1991 BY SAS INSTITUTE INC., CARY, NC 27513 USA
*
*  NAME     ==> VXEXIT
*  PURPOSE  ==> DSECT MAPPING OF INFILE EXIT TABLE
*----------------------------------------------------------------------
        VXEXIT
*----------------------------------------------------------------------
* MAP OF USER EXIT HOST BAG
*----------------------------------------------------------------------
VXEXIT   DSECT
         SPACE 1
*----------------------------------------------------------------------
* THE FOLLOWING FIELDS MUST NOT BE CHANGED BY THE EXIT ROUTINE
* EXCEPT USERWORD
*----------------------------------------------------------------------
EXITIDB  DS    A
EXITEP   DS    A
MEMALEN  DS    F                 LENGTH OF WORK AREA ABOVE 16M LINE
MEMABV   DS    A                 POINTER TO WORK AREA ABOVE 16M LINE
MEMBLEN  DS    F                 LENGTH OF WORK AREA BELOW 16M LINE
MEMBEL   DS    A                 POINTER TO WORK AREA BELOW 16M LINE
USERWORD DS    A     (USER UPD)  WORD AVAILABLE TO EXIT
EDDNAME  DS    CL8               LOGICAL NAME OF THE FILE
VARRTN   DS    A                 SAS VARIABLE CREATING ROUTINE ADDRESS
ERRMSG   DS    A     (USER UPD)  NULL TERMINATED ERROR MESSAGE POINTER
EFLAG1   DS    XL1   (USER UPD)  FLAG BYTE-1
EX_NEXT  EQU   X'80'             GET NEXT RECORD FROM EXIT
EX_DEL   EQU   X'40'             DELETE THIS RECORD
EX_EOF   EQU   X'20'             EOF OF DATASET REACHED
EX_EOFC  EQU   X'10'             CALL USER EXIT AFTER EOF
EX_ALC   EQU   X'08'             WILL USE ALLOC/FREE ROUTINES
EX_STOR  EQU   X'04'             WILL SUPPORT STORED PROGRAMS
EX_TERM  EQU   X'02'             WILL NEED A TERMINAL CALL
EFLAG2   DS    XL1               FLAG BYTE-2
EFLAG3   DS    XL1               FLAG BYTE-3
EFLAG4   DS    XL1               FLAG BYTE-4
ALLOC    DS    A                 ALLOC ROUTINE
FREE     DS    A                 FREE ROUTINE
PIDA     DS    F                 PID ABOVE
PIDB     DS    F                 PID BELOW
```

```
ALLOC1   DS    A                    ALLOCATE ROUTINE WITH SWITCH
FREE1    DS    A                    FREE ROUTINE WITH SWITCH
VARRTN1  DS    A                    SAS VARIABLE CREATING ROUTINE WITH SWITCH
VXCRAB   DS    A                    CRAB ADDRESS
LOG      DS    A                    LOG ROUTINE WITHOUT SWITCH
LOG1     DS    A                    LOG ROUTINE WITH SWITCH
         SPACE 1
         DS    0D
         SPACE 1
VXEXITL  EQU   *-VXEXIT
*----------------------------------------------------------------
* MAP OF VARRTN FUNCTION CALL
*----------------------------------------------------------------
PARMVAR  DSECT
*
VARNAME  DS    A                    POINTER TO VARIABLE NAME
VARNAMEL DS    F                    VARIABLE NAME LENGTH
VARTYPE  DS    F                    VARIABLE TYPE 1=NUM, 2=CHAR
VARSIZE  DS    F                    SIZE OF VARIABLE IF CHAR
VARFLAG  DS    F                    FLAGS , X'01' - INTERNAL
*                                           X'02' - EXTERNAL
VARADDR  DS    A                    POINTER TO VAR LOC ADDRESS (RETURNED)
*
* FOR CHARACTER VARIABLE IT RETURNS A POINTER TO A STRING STRUCTURE
*
* MAXLEN  DS    H                    MAX LENGTH OF STRING
* CURLEN  DS    H                    CURRENT LENGTH OF STRING
* ADDR    DS    A                    ADDRESS OF STRING DATA
PARMVARL EQU   *-PARMVAR
*----------------------------------------------------------------
* MAP OF ALLOC FUNCTION CALL
*----------------------------------------------------------------
PARMALC  DSECT
*
ALCEXIT  DS    A                    POINTER TO THE EXIT BAG
ALCPTR   DS    A                    PLACE TO RETURN ALLOCATED ADDRESS
ALCLEN   DS    F                    LENGTH OF MEMORY REQUIRED
ALCFLG   DS    F                    FLAG BYTE  1=BELOW 16M, 0=ABOVE 16M
PARMALCL EQU   *-PARMALC
*----------------------------------------------------------------
* MAP OF FREE FUNCTION CALL
*----------------------------------------------------------------
PARMFRE  DSECT
*
FREEXIT  DS    A                    POINTER TO THE EXIT BAG
FREPTR   DS    A                    ADDRESS OF FREEMAIN
FREFLG   DS    F                    FLAG BYTE  1=BELOW 16M, 0=ABOVE 16M
PARMFREL EQU   *-PARMFRE
*----------------------------------------------------------------
* MAP OF INIT EXIT CALL
*----------------------------------------------------------------
PARMINIT DSECT
*
```

```
INITFUNC DS   F                 FUNCTION CODE
INITEXIT DS   A                 USER EXIT BAG ADDRESS
INITMBLN DS   A                 PTR TO AMT OF MEMORY NEEDED BELOW LINE
INITMALN DS   A                 PTR TO AMT OF MEMORY NEEDED ABOVE LINE
PARMINIL EQU  *-PARMINIT
*-----------------------------------------------------------------
* MAP OF PARSE EXIT CALL
*-----------------------------------------------------------------
PARMPARS DSECT
*
PARSFUNC DS   F                 FUNCTION CODE
PARSEXIT DS   A                 USER EXIT BAG ADDRESS
PARSOPTL DS   F                 OPTION NAME LENGTH
PARSOPTN DS   A                 POINTER TO OPTION NAME
PARSVALL DS   F                 OPTION VALUE LENGTH
PARSVAL  DS   A                 OPTION VALUE
PARMPARL EQU  *-PARMPARS
*-----------------------------------------------------------------
* MAP OF OPEN EXIT CALL
*-----------------------------------------------------------------
PARMOPEN DSECT
*
OPENFUNC DS   F                 FUNCTION CODE
OPENEXIT DS   A                 USER EXIT BAG ADDRESS
OPENMODE DS   F                 OPEN MODE
OPENZLEN DS   A                 POINTER TO DATA LENGTH
OPENBLKL DS   F                 DATA SET BLOCK SIZE
OPENRECL DS   F                 DATA SET RECORD LENGTH
OPENRECF DS   F                 DATA SET RECORD FORMAT
PARMOPEL EQU  *-PARMOPEN
*-----------------------------------------------------------------
* MAP OF READ EXIT CALL
*-----------------------------------------------------------------
PARMREAD DSECT
*
READFUNC DS   F                 FUNCTION CODE
READEXIT DS   A                 USER EXIT BAG ADDRESS
READRECA DS   A                 POINTER TO RECORD AREA ADDRESS
READRECL DS   A                 POINTER TO RECORD LENGTH
PARMREAL EQU  *-PARMREAD
*-----------------------------------------------------------------
* MAP OF WRITE EXIT CALL
*-----------------------------------------------------------------
PARMWRIT DSECT
*
WRITFUNC DS   F                 FUNCTION CODE
WRITEXIT DS   A                 USER EXIT BAG ADDRESS
WRITRECA DS   A                 POINTER TO RECORD AREA ADDRESS
WRITRECL DS   F                 RECORD LENGTH
PARMWRIL EQU  *-PARMWRIT
*-----------------------------------------------------------------
* MAP OF CLOSE EXIT CALL
*-----------------------------------------------------------------
```

```
PARMCLOS DSECT
*
CLOSFUNC DS     F                 FUNCTION CODE
CLOSEXIT DS     A                 USER EXIT BAG ADDRESS
PARMCLOL EQU    *-PARMCLOS
*-------------------------------------------------------------------
* MAP OF CONCAT EXIT CALL
*-------------------------------------------------------------------
PARMCONC DSECT
*
CONCFUNC DS     F                 FUNCTION CODE
CONCEXIT DS     A                 USER EXIT BAG ADDRESS
CONCBLKL DS     F                 NEXT DATA SET IN CONCAT BLOCK SIZE
CONCRECL DS     F                 NEXT DATA SET IN CONCAT RECORD LENGTH
CONCRECF DS     F                 NEXT DATA SET IN CONCAT RECORD FORMAT
CONCZLEN DS     A                 POINTER TO DATA LENGTH
PARMCONL EQU    *-PARMCONC
*
*-------------------------------------------------------------------
* MAP OF LOG ROUTINE PARMLIST
*-------------------------------------------------------------------
PARMLOG  DSECT
LOGSTR   DS     A                 ADDRESS OF THE NULL-TERMINATED STRING
PARMLOGL EQU    *-PARMLOG
*
*-------------------------------------------------------------------
* EQUATES AND CONSTANTS
*-------------------------------------------------------------------
EXITPARS EQU    4
EXITOPEN EQU    8
EXITREAD EQU    12
EXITCONC EQU    16
EXITWRIT EQU    20
EXITCLOS EQU    24
EXITP2HB EQU    28   NOT SUPPORTED YET
EXITHB2P EQU    32   NOT SUPPORTED YET
*
*   EXITMODE    VALUES
EXITINP  EQU    1
EXITOUT  EQU    2
EXITAPP  EQU    4
EXITUPD  EQU    8
*   RECFM       VALUES
EXITRECF EQU    X'80'
EXITRECV EQU    X'40'
EXITRECB EQU    X'10'
EXITRECS EQU    X'08'
EXITRECA EQU    X'04'
EXITRECU EQU    X'C0'
&SYSECT  CSECT
         MEND
         DS     0D
VXEXITL  EQU    *-VXEXIT
```

```
            SPACE 1
            MACRO
&LBL        VXENTER &DSA=,&WORKAREA=MEMABV,&VXEXIT=R10
            DROP
&LBL        CSECT
            USING &LBL,R11
            LR    R11,R15              LOAD PROGRAM BASE
            USING VXEXIT,&VXEXIT
            L     &VXEXIT,4(,R1)       LOAD -> VXEXIT STRUCTURE
            AIF   ('&DSA' EQ 'NO').NODSA
            AIF   ('&DSA' EQ '').NODSA
            L     R15,&WORKAREA        LOAD -> DSA FROM VXEXIT
            ST    R15,8(,R13)          SET FORWARD CHAIN
            ST    R13,4(,R15)          SET BACKWARD CHAIN
            LR    R13,R15              SET NEW DSA
            USING &DSA,R13
.NODSA  ANOP
            MEND
*  - - - - - - - - -
            MACRO
&LBL        VXRETURN &DSA=
            AIF   ('&LBL' EQ '').NOLBL
&LBL        DS    0H
.NOLBL  AIF   ('&DSA' EQ 'NO').NODSA
            L     R13,4(,R13)          LOAD PREVIOUS DSA
.NODSA  ANOP
            ST    R15,16(,R13)         SAVE RETURN CODE
            LM    R14,R12,12(R13)      RELOAD REGS
            BR    R14                  RETURN
            LTORG
            MEND
*  - - - - - - - - - - - - - - - - - - - - - - - - - - - - - -
*  - - - - - - - - - - - - - - - - - - - - - - - - - - - - - -
SASCSRC  START
*
* MAIN ENTRY POINT FOR ALL EXITS
*
            USING SASCSRC,R15
            STM   R14,R12,12(R13)
            L     R2,0(,R1)            LOAD FUNCTION CODE
            L     R15,CSRCFUNC(R2)     LOAD FUNCTION ADDRESS
            BR    R15
*
CSRCFUNC DS    0A                      CSRC FUNCTIONS
            DC    A(CSRCINIT)             INITIALIZATION
            DC    A(CSRCPARS)             PARSE CSRC OPTIONS
            DC    A(CSRCOPEN)             OPEN EXIT
            DC    A(CSRCREAD)             READ EXIT
            DC    A(CSRCCNCT)             CONCATENATION BOUNDARY EXIT
            DC    A(CSRCWRIT)             WRITE EXIT
            DC    A(CSRCCLOS)             CLOSE EXIT
*
* INITIALIZATION EXIT
```

```
*
CSRCINIT VXENTER DSA=NO
         SPACE 1
         USING PARMINIT,R1
*
* THIS EXIT RUNS ONLY IN MVS/ESA, WHICH SUPPORTS DECOMPRESSION.
* THE CODE CHECKS FOR IT FIRST. IF NOT ESA, THE INIT FAILS
*
         L     R15,16                 LOAD CVT POINTER
         USING CVT,R15                BASE FOR CVT MAPPING
         TM    CVTDCB,CVTOSEXT        EXTENSION PRESENT
         BNO   NOTESA                 FAIL, NOT ESA
         TM    CVTOSLV0,CVTXAX        SUPPORTS ESA
         BNO   NOTESA                 NOT AN ESA
         DROP  R15
         L     R3,=A(PWALENL)         SET WORK AREA LENGTH...
         L     R2,INITMALN
         ST    R3,0(,R2)              AS ABOVE THE 16M LINE LENGTH
         SLR   R15,R15                GOOD RC
         XC    EFLAG1,EFLAG1          CLEAR
         OI    EFLAG1,EX_ALC          WILL USE ALLOC/FREE ROUTINES
         B     INITX                  RETURN
NOTESA   DS    0H
         LA    R15,BADOS
         ST    R15,ERRMSG             SAVE ERROR MESSAGE
INITX    DS    0H
         SPACE 1
         VXRETURN DSA=NO
BADOS    DC    C'THIS SUPPORT CAN BE USED ONLY IN AN ESA ENVIRONMENT'
         DC    XL1'00'
*
*   PARSE EXIT
*
CSRCPARS VXENTER DSA=PWA
         USING PARMPARS,R4
         LR    R4,R1                  R4 IS PARMLIST BASE
         SPACE 1
         L     R6,PARSOPTL            R6 = OPTION NAME LENGTH
         LTR   R6,R6                  IF 0
         BZ    PARSR                     RETURN OK
         LA    R15,4                  SET BAD OPTION RC
         L     R7,PARSOPTN            R7 -> OPTION NAME
         L     R8,PARSVALL            R8 = OPTION VALUE LENGTH
         L     R9,PARSVAL             R9 -> OPTION VALUE (VAR NAME)
         SPACE 1
*---------------------------------------------*
* OPTION ACCEPTED IS:                         *
*   CSRC   RECL=                              *
*---------------------------------------------*
         C     R6,=F'4'               IF LENGTH NOT 4
*        BNE   PARSX                  RETURN WITH ERROR
         LTR   R8,R8                  IS IT =
         BNZ   PARSRECL               THEN CHECK FOR RECL=
```

```
              CLC   0(4,R7),=CL4'CSRC'        IF NOT 'CSRC'
              BNE   PARSX                     RETURN WITH ERROR
              B     PARSR                     ELSE RETURN OK
        *-------------------------------------------*
        * PARSE RECL=NUM                            *
        *-------------------------------------------*
        PARSRECL DS   0H
              CLC   0(4,R7),=CL4'RECL'        IF NOT 'RECL'
              BNE   PARSX                     RETURN WITH ERROR
              CH    R8,=H'16'                 GREATER THAN 16
              BNL   PARSX                     INVALID VALUE
              BCTR  R8,0                      MINUS 1 FOR EXECUTE
              XC    TEMP,TEMP                 CLEAR
              EX    R8,CONNUM                 CONVERT TO NUMBER
        *CONNUM PACK  TEMP(0),0(R9)
              CVB   R0,TEMP                   CONVERT TO BINARY
              ST    R0,RECL                   SAVE RECL
              SPACE 1
        PARSR  SLR   R15,R15                  RETURN OK
              SPACE 1
        PARSX  VXRETURN DSA=PWA
        CONNUM PACK  TEMP(8),0(0,R9)          *** EXECUTE ****
        *
        * OPEN EXIT
        *
        CSRCOPEN VXENTER DSA=PWA
              USING PARMOPEN,R1
              SPACE 1
              LA    R15,NOINPUT               SET -> NO INPUT ERROR MESSAGE
              L     R4,RECL                   LOAD USER RECLEN
              LTR   R4,R4                     HAS IT BEEN SET?
              BNZ   *+8
              LH    R4,=Y(32676)              SET LRECL=32K BY DEFAULT
              SPACE 1
              LA    R15,DLENBIG               SET -> DATALENGTH TOO BIG MESSAGE
              L     R2,OPENZLEN
              L     R3,0(,R2)                 R3 = DATA LENGTH OF EACH RECORD
              CR    R3,R4                     IF GREATER THAN CSRC MAXIMUM
              BH    OPENX                        RETURN ERROR
              SPACE 1
              ST    R4,0(,R2)                 RETURN LENGTH TO THE SAS SYSTEM
              ST    R4,RECL                   SAVE LENGTH
        *
        * ALLOCATION OF BUFFER FOR INPUT RECORDS
        *
              LA    R1,PARM                   POINT TO PARMAREA
              XC    PARM,PARM                 CLEAR
              USING PARMALC,R1
              ST    R10,ALCEXIT               COPY HOST BAG POINTER
              LA    R15,MEMADDR
              ST    R15,ALCPTR                PLACE TO RETURN MEM ADDRESS
              ST    R4,ALCLEN                 LENGTH OF MEMORY NEEDED
              L     R15,ALLOC                 LOAD MEMORY ALLOCATE ROUTINE
```

```
          BALR  R14,R15              ALLOCATION OF MEMORY
          LTR   R15,R15             WAS MEMORY ALLOCATED?
          BNZ   OPENMEM             IF NOT, OPERATION FAILS
*
* QUERY THE COMPRESS SERVICE
*
          LA    R0,1                USE RUN LENGTH ENCODING
          CSRCESRV SERVICE=QUERY    QUERY IT
          LTR   R15,R15             EVERYTHING OK
          BNZ   OPENERR             IF NOT, FAIL WITH MESSAGE
          LTR   R1,R1               REQUIRE WORK AREA
          BZ    OPENX               IF NOT, END
          LR    R0,R1               SAVE R1
          LA    R1,PARM             POINT TO PARMLIST
          LA    R15,MEMWK           ALLOCATE WORK AREA
          ST    R15,ALCPTR          PLACE TO RETURN MEM ADDRESS
          ST    R0,ALCLEN           LENGTH OF MEMORY NEEDED
          L     R15,ALLOC           LOAD MEMORY ALLOCATE ROUTINE
          BALR  R14,R15             ALLOCATION OF MEMORY
          LTR   R15,R15             WAS MEMORY ALLOCATED?
          BNZ   OPENMEM             IF NOT, OPERATION FAILS
          B     OPENX               RETURN, OPERATION IS DONE
OPENERR   DS    0H
          XC    TEMP,TEMP           CONVERT RC TO DECIMAL
          CVD   R15,TEMP            CONVERT TO DECIMAL
          MVC   MSG(BADESRVL),BADESRV  MOVE IN SKELETON
          UNPK  MSG+BADESRVL-3(2),TEMP  UNPACK
          OI    MSG+BADESRVL-2,X'F0'    MAKE IT PRINTABLE
          LA    R15,MSG             SET MESSAGE
          ST    R15,ERRMSG          SET -> ERROR MESSAGE, IF ANY
          LA    R15,8
          B     OPENX
OPENMEM   DS    0H
          LA    R15,NOMEMORY
          SPACE 1
OPENX     DS    0H
          ST    R15,ERRMSG          SET -> ERROR MESSAGE, IF ANY
*                                   R15 = EITHER 0 OR NONZERO
          VXRETURN DSA=PWA
*
NOINPUT   DC    C'CSRC: DECOMPRESS DOES NOT SUPPORT OUTPUT'
          DC    XL1'00'
NOFIXED   DC    C'CSRC: DECOMPRESS DOES NOT SUPPORT FIXED LENGTH RECORDS'
          DC    XL1'00'
DLENBIG   DC    C'DATASET DATALENGTH > CSRC MAXIMUM'
          DC    XL1'00'
NOMEMORY  DC    C'CSRC: UNABLE TO OBTAIN MEMORY'
          DC    XL1'00'
BADESRV   DC    C'CSRC: NON ZERO RETURN CODE FROM QUERY, RC = '
BADESRVN  DC    H'0'
          DC    XL1'00'
BADESRVL  EQU   *-BADESRV
*----------------------------------------------------------------
```

```
* READ EXIT
*
* THIS EXIT DECOMPRESSES EACH RECORD
*----------------------------------------------------------------
CSRCREAD VXENTER DSA=PWA
         USING PARMREAD,R1
         SPACE 1
         L     R8,READRECL          R8 -> RECORD LENGTH
         L     R9,READRECA          R9 -> RECORD ADDRESS
         L     R3,0(,R8)            R3 = RECORD LENGTH
         L     R2,0(,R9)            R2 = RECORD ADDRESS
         L     R1,MEMWK             LOAD WORK AREA ADDRESS
         L     R4,MEMADDR           R4 = OUTPUT BUFFER
         L     R5,RECL              R5 = OUTPUT BUFFER LENGTH
         CSRCESRV SERVICE=EXPAND
         LTR   R15,R15              EVERYTHING OK
         BNZ   READERR              IF NOT, SET ERROR AND RETURN
         L     R15,MEMADDR          START OF BUFFER
         SR    R4,R15               MINUS LAST BYTE USED
         ST    R4,0(,R8)            LENGTH OF UNCOMPRESSED RECORD
         ST    R15,0(,R9)           SAVE UNCOMPRESSED REC ADDRESS
         SLR   R15,R15              SET GOOD RC
         B     READX                RETURN TO USER
READERR  DS    0H
         XC    TEMP,TEMP            CONVERT RC TO DECIMAL
         CVD   R15,TEMP             CONVERT TO DECIMAL
         MVC   MSG(EXPERRL),EXPERR  MOVE IN SKELETON
         UNPK  MSG+EXPERRL-3(2),TEMP  UNPACK
         OI    MSG+EXPERRL-2,X'F0'  MAKE IT PRINTABLE
         LA    R15,MSG              SET MESSAGE
         ST    R15,ERRMSG           SET -> ERROR MESSAGE, IF ANY
         LA    R15,8
*
         SPACE 1
READX    DS    0H
         VXRETURN DSA=PWA
         SPACE ,
EXPERR   DC    C'CSRC NON ZERO RETURN CODE FROM EXPAND, RC = '
EXPERRN  DC    H'0'
         DC    XL1'00'
EXPERRL  EQU   *-EXPERR
*
*
* CONCATENATION EXIT
*
CSRCCNCT VXENTER DSA=PWA
         SPACE 1
         SLR   R15,R15
         VXRETURN DSA=PWA
*----------------------------------------------------------------
* WRITE EXIT
*
* THIS EXIT COMPRESSES EACH RECORD
```

```
*---------------------------------------------------------------
CSRCWRIT VXENTER DSA=PWA
         USING PARMWRIT,R1
         L     R8,WRITRECL          R8 -> RECORD LENGTH
         L     R9,WRITRECA          R9 -> RECORD ADDRESS
         L     R3,0(,R8)            R3 = RECORD LENGTH
         L     R2,0(,R9)            R2 = RECORD ADDRESS
         L     R1,MEMWK             LOAD WORK AREA ADDRESS
         L     R4,MEMADDR           R4 = OUTPUT BUFFER
         L     R5,RECL              R5 = OUTPUT BUFFER LENGTH
         CSRCESRV SERVICE=COMPRESS
         LTR   R15,R15              EVERYTHING OK
         BNZ   WRITERR              IF NOT, SET ERROR AND RETURN
         L     R15,MEMADDR          START OF BUFFER
         SR    R4,R15               MINUS LAST BYTE USED
         ST    R4,0(,R8)            LENGTH OF RECORD
         ST    R15,0(,R9)           SAVE NEW RECORD ADDRESS
         SLR   R15,R15              SET GOOD RC
         B     WRITEX               RETURN TO USER
WRITERR  DS    0H
         XC    TEMP,TEMP            CONVERT RC TO DECIMAL
         CVD   R15,TEMP             CONVERT TO DECIMAL
         MVC   MSG(WRTERRL),WRTERR  MOVE IN SKELETON
         UNPK  MSG+WRTERRL-3(2),TEMP UNPACK
         OI    MSG+WRTERRL-2,X'F0'  MAKE IT PRINTABLE
         LA    R15,MSG              SET MESSAGE
         ST    R15,ERRMSG           SET -> ERROR MESSAGE, IF ANY
         LA    R15,8
         SPACE 1
         SPACE 1
WRITEX   DS    0H
         VXRETURN DSA=PWA
WRTERR   DC    C'CSRC: NON ZERO RETURN CODE FROM COMPRESS, RC = '
WRTERRN  DC    H'0'
         DC    XL1'00'
WRTERRL  EQU   *-WRTERR
         LTORG
*
* CLOSE EXIT
*
CSRCCLOS VXENTER DSA=PWA
         SLR   R15,R15
         LA    R1,PARM
         XC    PARM,PARM
         USING PARMFRE,R1
         ST    R10,FREEXIT
         L     R15,MEMADDR
         ST    R15,FREPTR
         L     R15,FREE
         BALR  R14,R15
         VXRETURN DSA=PWA
*
R0       EQU   0
```

```
R1        EQU   1
R2        EQU   2
R3        EQU   3
R4        EQU   4
R5        EQU   5
R6        EQU   6
R7        EQU   7
R8        EQU   8
R9        EQU   9
R10       EQU   10
R11       EQU   11
R12       EQU   12
R13       EQU   13
R14       EQU   14
R15       EQU   15
*
          VXEXIT ,
*
PWA       DSECT                      PROGRAM WORK AREA
PWASAVE   DS    32F                  SAVE AREA
TEMP      DS    D
RECL      DS    F
SAVE      DS    32F
PARM      DS    CL(PARMALCL)
MEMADDR   DS    F
MEMWK     DS    F
MSG       DS    CL200
PWALENL   EQU   *-PWA                LENGTH OF CSRC WORK AREA
          CVT DSECT=YES
*
          END
```

Introduction   465

Messages from the SASCP Command Processor   465

Messages from the TSO Command Executor   467

Messages from the Internal CALL Command Processor   469

Appendix **3** Host-System Subgroup Error Messages

Introduction

This appendix provides brief explanations of many of the host-system subgroup error messages that you might encounter during a SAS session. The explanation for each message includes where the message comes from, a short explanation of its meaning, and information about what you can do to correct the possible problem, if anything.

Messages from the SASCP Command Processor

To help you identify and remedy problems when running under TSO, the SAS System provides the following list of messages from the SASCP command processor. SASCP is involved in processing SAS System tasks and is invoked by the terminal monitor program as a standard TSO command processor.

SAST001I COMMAND SYSTEM ERROR +
Entering a question mark in the line following this message produces one of these additional messages:

```
□  NOT ENOUGH MAIN STORAGE TO EXECUTE COMMAND
□  IKJPARS RETURN CODE rc
```

Either the SAS command processor was unable to allocate enough memory to begin execution, or the system failed while it was parsing the command line. This message should not occur under normal conditions; inform your SAS Software Consultant.

SAST002I DATA SET *dsn* NOT IN CATALOG or
SAST002I DYNAMIC ALLOCATION ERROR, IKJDAIR RETURN CODE *rc*
DARC *drc* CTRC *crc*
The SAS command processor was unable to locate a data set that was specified by the TASKLIB operand. This message usually indicates that a data set name was misspelled.

SAST003I MORE THAN 15 TASKLIB DATA SETS SPECIFIED
You have specified more than 15 task-library data sets with the TASKLIB operand. Reduce the number of task-library data sets.

SAST004I *dsn* IS NOT A PARTITIONED DATA SET
For the value of the TASKLIB operand, you have specified a task-library data set that is not a partitioned data set. This message usually indicates a misspelled data set name or a reference to the wrong data set.

SAST005I TASKLIB CANNOT BE OPENED

The SAS command processor was unable to open the task library. You have probably specified an invalid load library as a task-library data set in the TASKLIB operand.

SAST006I SAS ENTRY POINT NAME NOT SPECIFIED

You have not specified a member name for the SAS entry point. Use the ENTRY operand to specify an entry-point name for the SAS System.

SAST007I SAS ENTRY POINT NAME *entry-name* NOT FOUND

The SAS command processor was unable to locate the member name that was specified as the SAS entry point. This message usually indicates that an entry-point name was misspelled. Use the ENTRY operand to specify a valid entry-point name.

SAST007I BLDL I/O ERROR ON TASKLIB

An error occurred during BLDL processing of TASKLIB.

SAST008I OPTIONS FIELD TRUNCATED TO 256 CHARACTERS

The options parameter string that was passed to the SAS System was too long and was truncated to 256 characters. (This string consists of SAS options that you specified as the value of the OPTIONS operand plus any additional SAS options that were supplied automatically within the SAS CLIST.) This message is a warning message.

SAST009I COMMAND SYSTEM ERROR +

Entering a question mark in the line following this message produces one of these additional messages:

```
□   NOT ENOUGH MAIN STORAGE TO INVOKE SAS SUBTASK
□   ATTACH RETURN CODE rc
```

Either the SAS command processor was unable to allocate enough memory to invoke the SAS System, or the system was unable to create the SAS subtask. This message should not normally occur; inform your SAS Software Consultant.

SAST010I *entry-name* ENDED DUE TO ERROR +

This message indicates that the SAS session has terminated abnormally (abended). Entering a question mark in the line following this message produces one of these additional messages:

```
□   USER ABEND CODE uac
□   SYSTEM ABEND CODE sac REASON CODE  rc
```

A user abend code of 999 ('3E7'x) indicates an error condition. You can specify other user abend codes in the SAS ABORT statement. A system abend code should not normally occur; inform your SAS Software Consultant.

SAST011I *entry-name* TERMINATED DUE TO ATTENTION

The SAS session has ended because you pressed the BREAK or ATTN key and then entered the word END in response to the message SAST013D.

SAST012I COMMAND SYSTEM ERROR +

Entering a question mark in the line following this message produces one of these additional messages:

```
□   NOT ENOUGH MAIN STORAGE TO EXECUTE COMMAND
□   STAE RETURN CODE rc
```

Either the SAS command processor was unable to allocate enough memory to invoke the SAS System, or an error occurred during execution of the SASCP command. This message should not normally occur; inform your SAS Software Consultant.

SAST013D ENTER "END" TO TERMINATE SAS, OR A NULL LINE TO CONTINUE

The SAS System displays this prompt when the SAS command processor detects that the BREAK or ATTN key has been pressed. Enter the word END to leave the SAS session, or enter a null line to resume SAS processing.

SAST014I INVALID RESPONSE, MUST BE "END" OR A NULL LINE

You have entered a response other than the word END or a null line after receiving message SAST013D. Enter either the word END or a null line.

SAST015I SASCP INVOKED IN A NON-TSO ENVIRONMENT OR PASSED INVALID PARAMETERS
USE SASCP AS A TSO COMMAND TO INVOKE SAS IN THE FOREGROUND
USE PGM=SAS TO INVOKE SAS IN THE BACKGROUND

SASCP was not invoked as a TSO command, and it could not locate the appropriate TSO control blocks to reconstruct a TSO command environment, either because it was invoked as a background program or because the TSO environment is nonstandard. If you were running under TSO, contact your SAS Software Consultant.

SAST016I PARM FIELD TRUNCATED TO 256 CHARACTERS

The PARM list operand that was passed to the CALL command is too long and was truncated. (The CALL command is used to invoke the SAS System.)

SAST017I INVALID PARAMETER LIST PASSED TO IKJDAIR

An invalid parameter list was passed to the TSO service routine IKJDAIR. This message should not normally occur; inform your SAS Software Consultant.

SAST018I SASCP INVOKED IN A NON-TSO ENVIRONMENT
USE PGM=SAS TO INVOKE SAS IN THE BACKGROUND

SASCP was not invoked under TSO.

Messages from the TSO Command Executor

The TSO command executor is involved with TSO command processors for the X and TSO commands, the X and TSO statements, and the TSO function.

SAST101I ERROR IN PUTGET SERVICE ROUTINE

An error occurred while the TSO command executor was attempting to read a line from the terminal or from the TSO input stack using the TSO service routine IKJPTGT. This message should not normally occur; inform your SAS Software Consultant.

SAST102I INVALID COMMAND NAME SYNTAX

You have specified an invalid command name in one of the following:

□ a TSO or X command

□ a TSO or X statement

□ a TSO or SYSTEM function

□ a TSO or SYSTEM CALL routine.

This message usually indicates that a TSO command name was misspelled.

SAST103I COMMAND *cmd* **NOT SUPPORTED**

You have entered a TSO command that cannot be issued from within a SAS session. To issue the command, end the session, issue the command, and then start a new session.

SAST104I COMMAND *cmd* **NOT FOUND**

The TSO command executor could not locate the TSO command name that was specified. This message usually indicates that a TSO command name was misspelled.

SAST105I *cmd* **ENDED DUE TO ERROR +**

Entering a question mark in the line following this message produces one of these additional messages:

```
□   SYSTEM ABEND CODE sac REASON CODE  rc
□   USER ABEND CODE uac
```

A TSO command that was invoked in one of the following ways ended abnormally with the indicated abend code:

□   a TSO or X command

□   a TSO or X statement

□   a TSO or SYSTEM function

□   a TSO or SYSTEM CALL routine.

SAST106I COMMAND SYSTEM ERROR +

Entering a question mark in the line following this message produces one of these additional messages:

```
□   NOT ENOUGH MAIN STORAGE TO EXECUTE COMMAND
□   ATTACH RETURN CODE rc
```

Either the TSO command executor was unable to allocate enough memory to execute the requested command, or an error occurred during execution of the command executor. This message should not normally occur; inform your SAS Software Consultant.

SAST107I COMMAND SYSTEM ERROR +

Entering a question mark in the line following this message produces one of these additional messages:

```
□   NOT ENOUGH MAIN STORAGE TO EXECUTE COMMAND
□   STAE RETURN CODE rc
```

Either the system was unable to allocate enough memory to execute the requested command, or an abend occurred during execution of the command. This message should not normally occur; inform your SAS Consultant.

SAST108I SEVERE COMMAND SYSTEM ERROR +

Entering a question mark in the line following this message produces one of these additional messages:

```
□   SYSTEM ABEND CODE sac REASON CODE rc
□   USER ABEND CODE uac
```

The TSO command executor encountered severe internal failure. This message should not normally occur; inform your SAS Software Consultant.

SAST109I TSO SUBMODE, ENTER "RETURN" OR "END" TO RETURN TO THE SAS SYSTEM

The SAS System displays this prompt when you enter TSO submode.

SAST110I COMMAND *cmd* TERMINATED DUE TO ATTENTION

You have stopped the execution of the specified TSO command by pressing the BREAK or ATTN key and entering the word END in response to message SAST1112D.

SAST111I SPF COMMAND NOT ALLOWED, SPF ALREADY ACTIVE

You have attempted to issue the TSO ISPF/PDF or SPF command from a SAS session that you invoked under the ISPF/PDF or SPF TSO command processor panel (panel 6). To return to the ISPF/PDF or SPF session, end the SAS session.

SAST112D ENTER "END" TO TERMINATE COMMAND, OR A NULL LINE TO CONTINUE

This prompt is displayed when you press the BREAK or ATTN key during the execution of a TSO command. Enter the word END to terminate the command, or enter a null line to resume the command.

SAST113I INVALID RESPONSE, MUST BE "END" OR A NULL LINE

You have entered a response other than the word END or a null line after receiving message SAST112D. Enter either the word END or a null line.

SAST114I SASTSO NOT SUPPORTED IN NON-TSO ENVIRONMENT

The command that you have entered cannot be executed under the MVS batch TMP. The command can be executed only during an interactive TSO session.

SAST114I COMMAND *cmd* NOT SUPPORTED IN BACKGROUND

You have entered a TSO command that cannot be issued from a background TSO session.

Messages from the Internal CALL Command Processor

The internal CALL command processor implements the TSO CALL command for use by an unauthorized caller outside of the Terminal Monitor Program.

SAST201I COMMAND SYSTEM ERROR +

Entering a question mark in the line following this message produces one of these additional messages:

```
□  NOT ENOUGH MAIN STORAGE TO EXECUTE COMMAND
□  IKJPARS RETURN CODE rc
```

Either the CALL command was unable to allocate enough memory to begin processing, or the system failed while it was parsing the command line. This message should not normally occur; inform your SAS Software Consultant.

SAST202I TEMPNAME ASSUMED AS MEMBER NAME

You have not specified a member name with a CALL command invocation, and the CALL command processor used the member name TEMPNAME.

SAST203I PARM FIELD TRUNCATED TO 100 CHARACTERS

The parameter string that was by CALL to the program was too long and was truncated to 100 characters.

SAST204I DATA SET *dsn* **NOT IN CATALOG**

The CALL command processor was unable to locate the specified program data set. This message usually indicates that a data set name was misspelled. You will be prompted to enter the correct data set name.

SAST204I DATA SET NOT ALLOCATED, IKJDAIR RETURN CODE *rc*
    DARC *drc* **CTRC** *crc*

An error occurred while the data set was being allocated; inform your SAS Software Consultant.

SAST205I MEMBER *mem* **SPECIFIED BUT** *dsn* **NOT A PARTITIONED**
    DATA SET

You have specified a program library in the CALL command that is not a valid load-module library. This message usually indicates that a data set name was misspelled.

SAST206I DATA SET *dsn* **NOT USABLE +**

Entering a question mark in the line following this message produces this additional information:

```
CANNOT OPEN DATA SET
```

The CALL command processor was unable to open the program library. This message usually indicates an invalid load-module library or a misspelled data set name.

SAST207I MEMBER *mem* **NOT IN DATA SET**

The CALL command processor could not locate the member name that you specified in the CALL command. This message usually indicates that a member name was misspelled. You will be prompted to enter the correct member name.

SAST207I BLDL I/O ERROR

An error occurred while searching for the program on the data set; inform your SAS Software Consultant.

SAST208I COMMAND SYSTEM ERROR +

Entering a question mark in the line following this message produces one of these additional messages:

```
□  NOT ENOUGH MAIN STORAGE TO EXECUTE COMMAND
□  ATTACH RETURN CODE rc
```

Either the system was unable to allocate enough memory to invoke the specified program, or an error occurred while it was attaching the program. This message should not normally occur; inform your SAS Software Consultant.

SAST209I INVALID PARAMETER LIST PASSED TO IKJDAIR

The CALL command processor passed an invalid parameter list to the TSO service routine IKJDAIR. This message should not normally occur; inform your SAS Software Consultant.

Glossary

This glossary gives definitions of SAS System and MVS terms that are used in this book. See *SAS Language: Reference, Version 6, First Edition* for SAS System terms that are not listed here. For MVS terms, see the appropriate IBM documentation.

autocall library

a source partitioned data set containing SAS macros.

autoexec file

a file containing SAS statements that are executed automatically when the SAS System is invoked. The autoexec file is usually used to specify SAS system options and to assign librefs and filerefs that are commonly used.

base SAS software

software that includes a programming language that manages your data, procedures for data analysis and reporting, a macro facility, help menus, and a windowing environment for text editing and file management.

batch job

a job submitted to the operating system for batch processing. The job begins with a JCL JOB statement and ends with a JCL null (//) statement.

batch mode

a method of running jobs where jobs are submitted, but not processed immediately. You can use batch mode on mainframes and minicomputers as a method of running SAS programs in which you prepare a file containing SAS statements and any necessary operating system control statements. You then submit the file to the operating system. Unlike interactive mode, batch mode does not require intervention by the user. Execution is completely separate from other operations at your terminal. Batch mode is sometimes referred to as running in the background.

block

a unit of physical storage on DASD or tape that MVS and the SAS System transfer when reading or writing a data set. Blocks are separated from each other by spaces called interblock gaps. The format of the data stored in a block depends on the access method and on the application that created the data.

block size

the number of bytes in a block. See also block.

blocking factor

the number of logical records that fit in one block. See also block.

BMDP

the Version 6 engine for read-only access to BMDP files. An alternate name for this engine is SASBMDPE.

buffer

a temporary storage area reserved for holding data after they are read or before they are written.

carriage-control character

a specific symbol that tells the printer how many lines to advance the paper, when to begin a new page, when to skip a line, and when to hold the current line for overprint.

catalog

See SAS catalog.

catalog entry

See entry type.

cataloged procedure

See SAS cataloged procedure.

CLIST

a command list composed of a planned, executable sequence of TSO commands, subcommands, and command procedure statements that control various system and program operations.

configuration file

an external file containing SAS system options. The options in the file are put into effect when the SAS System is invoked. There may be a user configuration file as well as a system configuration file. Either configuration file can be a sequential data set or a member of a partitioned data set.

data control block (DCB)

the MVS control block that contains information about the physical characteristics of an operating system data set.

data set

under MVS, a collection of information that the operating system can identify and manage as a unit. The term data set under MVS corresponds to files under other systems. In this book, the term operating system data set is used to distinguish an MVS data set from a SAS data set.

A SAS data library is an operating system data set whose internal structure has been specially formatted by the SAS System. See also partitioned data set (PDS), SAS data set, sequential data set, and VSAM data set.

data set label

(1) in a SAS data set, a user-defined field that can consist of up to 40 characters. It can be used for purposes of documenting the SAS data set. (2) under MVS, a format 1 data set control block (DSCB) for a disk data set or an IBM label for a tape data set.

data set option

See SAS data set option.

DATA step

a group of statements in a SAS program that begin with a DATA statement and end with a RUN statement, another DATA statement, a PROC statement, the end of the job, or the line after instream input data that contains one or four semicolon(s). The DATA step enables you to read raw data or other SAS data sets and use programming logic to create a SAS data set, write a report, or write to an external file.

DD statement

a data definition statement that describes an operating system data set to the operating system, including the resources needed for the data set. The way the program can use a data set depends on the parameters in the DD statement.

DDname

a name defined by a JCL DD statement or a TSO ALLOCATE command. DDnames can contain one to eight characters; the first character must be a letter or national character. If you allocate a SAS data library externally using a DD statement, the first time you use the DDname as a libref, the SAS System assigns it to the library. Similarly, if you need to use an external file in a SAS program, you can allocate the file using a DD statement. In this case, the DDname corresponds to the fileref for the external file. See also libref and fileref.

dialog box

a feature of the PMENU facility that appears in response to an action. The purpose of dialog boxes is to obtain information, which you supply by filling in a field or choosing a selection from a group of fields. You can execute the CANCEL command to exit the dialog box.

direct-access storage device (DASD)

a type of I/O device that does not require sequential access. With direct-access (or disk) storage, you can position anywhere in a file and read or write without requiring sequential I/O to locate data.

display manager

See SAS Display Manager System.

display manager mode

an interactive method of running SAS programs in which you edit a group of statements, submit the statements, and then review the results of the statements in various windows.

EBCDIC collating sequence

an ordering of characters in the Extended Binary Coded Decimal Interchange Code (EBCDIC) 8-bit character coding scheme. The following operating systems supported by the SAS System use the EBCDIC collating sequence: CMS, MVS, and VSE.

engine

a part of the SAS System that reads from or writes to a file. Each engine allows the SAS System to access files with a particular format.

There are several types of engines. Library engines control access at the SAS data library level and can be specified on the LIBNAME statement. Native library engines access SAS files created and maintained by SAS Institute Inc., while interface library engines support access to other vendors' files, for example, BMDP files.

View engines enable the SAS System to read SAS data views described by the SQL procedure (native view) or SAS/ACCESS software (interface view). You cannot specify a view engine in a LIBNAME statement. See also native engine.

engine/host option

an option that is specified in a LIBNAME statement. Engine/host options specify attributes that apply to the SAS data library as a whole. See also data set option and SAS system option.

entry

a unit of information stored in a SAS catalog.

entry type

a part of the name for an entry in a SAS catalog that is assigned by the SAS System to identify what type of information is stored in the entry. For example, HELP is the entry type for an entry containing help information for applications developed with the BUILD procedure in SAS/AF software.

external file

an operating system data set created and maintained by MVS from which you can read data or stored SAS programming statements or to which you can write procedure output or output created by PUT statements in a DATA step.

fileref

the name used to identify an external file to the SAS System. You assign a fileref with a FILENAME statement or with operating system control language. For example, under MVS one way to assign a fileref is through a DD statement.

Normally, a DDname and a fileref are the same. The DDname is how the operating system references the file; the fileref is how the SAS System references the file. However, under some circumstances, the DDname used to assign a file is not the same as the name used within the SAS System.

format

the instructions the SAS System uses to write each value of a variable. There are two types of formats: formats supplied by SAS Software and user-written formats created using the FORMAT procedure.

format library

a collection of formats and informats. The format library can be either a FORMATS catalog in a Version 6 SAS data library, or a load library containing SAS formats and informats in load module form. See also load library.

function key

a keyboard key that can be defined to have a specific action in a specific software environment.

gigabyte

2^{30} or 1,073,741,824 (approximately one billion) bytes. The available address space under MVS/XA is 2 gigabytes. See also kilobyte, megabyte, and terabyte.

host

the operating system that provides facilities, computer services, and the environment for software applications.

index

a feature of a Version 6 SAS data set that enables the SAS System to directly and quickly access observations in the SAS data set. The purpose of SAS indexes is to optimize WHERE-clause processing and facilitate BY-group processing, without requiring that the data set first be sorted on the BY variables.

informat

the instructions that specify how the SAS System reads raw data values to create variable values. There are two types of informats: informats supplied by SAS software and user-written informats created using the FORMAT procedure.

instream program

a SAS program submitted in a job stream as part of a batch job.

interactive line mode

a method of running SAS programs without using the SAS Display Manager System. You enter one line of a SAS program at a time. The SAS System processes each line immediately after you enter it.

interface engine

See engine.

ISPF

an interactive dialog that can be used to facilitate many programming tasks. The complete name is the Interactive System Productivity Facility/Program Development Facility.

job

a unit of work performed by the host computer.

job control language (JCL)

statements used to identify your job to the operating system and inform the operating system of the resources such as data sets, time, and memory that your job needs.

job stream

the stream of JCL statements in a batch job. These statements identify operating system data sets, execute programs, and provide data that are processed by the job. See also job control language (JCL).

kilobyte

2^{10} or 1024 bytes. See also gigabyte, megabyte, and terabyte.

library engine

See engine.

libref

the name used to identify a SAS data library to the SAS System. You assign a libref with a LIBNAME statement. Also, you can use a TSO ALLOCATE statement or a JCL DD statement to allocate a data library externally. If you allocate a data library externally, when you reference the data library the SAS System normally assigns a libref that is the same as the DDname. The libref is the first-level name of a two-level name. For example, PERM is the libref in the two-level name PERM.CLASS. The default libref is WORK unless the USER libref is defined. See also DDname and USER library.

line mode

See interactive line mode.

listing file

See SAS procedure output file.

load library

a partitioned data set that contains load modules. These may be modules supplied by SAS Institute or compiled and linked by other sources. See also format library.

load module

a member of a partitioned data set that has been processed by the MVS linkage editor and is in a format that can be loaded by the system loader and then executed.

logical name

a name associated with an operating system data set name. A logical name can be a DDname, fileref, or libref. An example is the logical name SASMSG, which is used in the SAS CLIST and cataloged procedure. See also the entries for DDname, fileref, and libref.

megabyte

2^{20} or 1,048,576 (approximately 1 million) bytes. See also the entries for gigabyte, kilobyte, and terabyte.

member

(1) a SAS file in a SAS data library. (2) a single element of a partitioned data set under the MVS operating system.

member name

(1) the name of a file in a SAS data library. When you reference a file with a two-level name, such as PERM.CLASS, the member name is the second part of the name (the libref is the first part). (2) the name of a single element of a partitioned data set under the MVS operating system.

member type

the classification of a file in a SAS data library that is assigned by the SAS System to identify what type of information is stored in the file. For example, CATALOG is the member type for SAS catalogs in Version 6, and Version 5 catalogs have the member type CAT.

Multiple Engine Architecture (MEA)

a feature of the SAS System that enables it to access a variety of file formats through sets of instructions called engines. See also engine.

multiprogramming system

a system in which many programs can reside in the computer at the same time. Multiprogramming enables the operating system to periodically interrupt an executing program in order for another program to continue.

multitasking

the ability to execute more than one task running inside a single CPU.

native engine

an engine that accesses forms of SAS files created and processed only by the SAS System. See also engine.

nibble

half a byte.

noninteractive mode
a method of running SAS programs in which you prepare a file of SAS statements and submit the program to the computer system. The program runs immediately and occupies your current terminal session.

observation
a row in a SAS data set that contains the specific data values for an individual entity.

operating system data set
See data set.

OSIRIS engine
the Version 6 engine for read-only access to OSIRIS files. An alternate name for this engine is SASOSIRI.

page size
(1) the size of the page of printed output. (2) the number of bytes of data that the SAS System moves between external storage and memory in one logical input/output operation.

partitioned data set (PDS)
a form of data set organization. An MVS partitioned data set consists of one or more separate units of information called members, plus a directory. Each member has a unique name entered in the PDS directory. Partitioned data sets must reside on disk. See also the entries for data set, member, sequential data set, and VSAM data set.

PDS
See partitioned data set (PDS).

permanent SAS data library
a library that is not deleted when the SAS session terminates; it is available for subsequent SAS sessions. Unless the USER libref is defined, you normally use a two-level name to access a file in a permanent library. The first-level name is the libref, and the second-level name is the member name. See also USER library.

permanent SAS file
a SAS file in a SAS data library that is not deleted when the SAS session or job terminates.

PF key
See function key.

physical filename
the name the operating system uses to identify a file. In this book, physical filename is synonymous with operating system data set name.

PMENU facility
a menuing system in the SAS System that is used instead of the command line as a way to execute commands.

portable
describes a computer application that can execute on more than one operating system.

print file
an external file containing carriage-control (printer-control) information. See also carriage-control character.

PROFILE catalog

a SAS catalog in a special SAS data library that contains information used by the SAS System to control various aspects of your SAS display manager session. See also the entry for SASUSER library.

program function key

See function key.

pull-down menu

the list of choices that appears when you choose an item from an action bar or from another pull-down menu in the PMENU facility. The choices in the list are called items.

random access

the ability to retrieve specific records in a file without reading previous records.

raw data

(1) data stored in an external file that have not been read into a SAS data set. (2) in statistical analysis, data (including SAS data sets) that have not had a particular operation, such as standardization, performed on them.

record

under MVS, a logical unit of related data that can be fixed, variable, or undefined in length.

requestor window

(1) a window that the SAS System displays that enables you to confirm, cancel, or modify an action. (2) a window that provides information.

return code

a code passed to the operating system that indicates whether the execution of a command or job step completed successfully.

SAS catalog

a SAS file that stores many different kinds of information in smaller units called entries. Some catalog entries contain system information such as key definitions. Other catalog entries contain application information such as window definitions, help windows, formats, informats, macros, or graphics output.

SAS cataloged procedure

a cataloged procedure supplied with base SAS software. A cataloged procedure is a group of JCL statements used to execute a program. It is packaged so all the JCL statements can be invoked with a single EXEC statement.

SAS command

a command that invokes the SAS System. This command may vary depending on operating system and site.

SAS data file

a SAS data set that stores descriptor information and observations in the same location.

SAS data library

an operating system data set with an internal format defined by the SAS System. The internal format subdivides the DASD space allocated to the operating system data set into space for each SAS file stored in the library. Each file is a member of the library.

SAS data set

descriptor information and its related data values organized as a table of observations and variables that can be processed by the SAS System. A SAS data set can be either a SAS data file or a SAS data view.

SAS data set option

an option that appears in parentheses after a SAS data set name. Data set options specify actions that are applicable only to the processing of that SAS data set. See also SAS system option and engine/host option.

SAS data view

a SAS data set in which the descriptor information and the observations are stored in separate locations. SAS data views store the information required to retrieve data values that are stored in other files.

SAS Display Manager System

a windowing environment in which actions are performed with a series of commands or function keys. It can be used to prepare and submit SAS programs, view and print the results, and debug and resubmit the programs.

SAS file

a specially structured file that is created, organized, and maintained by the SAS System. SAS files reside in SAS data libraries. Examples of SAS files include a SAS data set, a SAS catalog, a stored program, or an access descriptor.

SAS invocation

the process of initializing a SAS session.

SAS log

a file that contains the SAS statements you have submitted and messages about the execution of your program.

SAS procedure output file

a file that contains the result of the analysis or the report produced. Most procedures write output to the procedure output file by default. DATA step reports that contain the FILE statement with the PRINT destination also go to this file.

SAS system option

an option that affects the appearance of SAS output, the handling of some of the files used by the SAS System, the use of system variables, the processing of observations in SAS data sets, the features of SAS System initialization, the SAS System's interface with your computer hardware, and the SAS System's interface with the operating system.

SASHELP library

a SAS data library supplied by SAS software that stores the text for HELP windows, default function key and window definitions, and menus.

SASUSER library

the SAS data library that contains a profile catalog that stores the tailoring features you specify for the SAS System.

sequential access

a method of file access in which the records are read or written one after the other.

sequential data set

a form of data set organization. A sequential data set consists of blocks of data only. The data set does not contain any internal information about how the operating system is to process the data. Sequential data sets can exist on disk or tape. Under MVS, sequential-format SAS data libraries are sequential data sets. See also data set, partitioned data set (PDS), and VSAM data set.

Session Manager

an IBM product that enhances TSO on IBM 3270-series and compatible terminals. Session Manager works by dividing the communication between the terminal and the host computer into streams. All communications of a particular type belong to the same stream. For example, all TSO commands, SAS statements, and so on that you direct toward the computer by pressing ENTER form the TSOIN stream. All communications from the computer to you including TSO messages, the display of TSO commands after you enter them, and so on, form the TSOOUT stream. The division between TSOIN and TSOOUT streams affects the appearance of interactive SAS sessions under Session Manager.

site number

the number used by SAS Institute to identify the site to which the SAS System is licensed. The site number appears near the top of the log in every SAS session.

SPSS

the Version 6 engine for read-only access to SPSS files. Alternate names for the engine are SPSSX and SASSPSS.

statement option

an option specified in a given SAS statement that affects only that statement.

System Management Facility (SMF)

an MVS facility that gives information on the resources the operating system utilizes when it runs a job.

task

a logical process within the SAS System. A task can be a procedure or a DATA step, a window, or a supervisor process.

temporary SAS data library

a library that exists only for the current SAS session or job. The most common temporary library is the WORK library. See also WORK data library.

temporary SAS file

a SAS file in a SAS data library (usually the WORK data library) that is deleted at the end of the SAS session or job.

terabyte

2^{40} or 1,099,511,627,776 (approximately 1.1 trillion) bytes. See also gigabyte, kilobyte, and megabyte.

transport file
a sequential file containing a SAS data library, a SAS catalog, or a SAS data set in transport format as produced by the CPORT procedure or as written by the XPORT engine or the XCOPY procedure. The format of the transport file produced by the CPORT procedure is different from the format of the transport file written by the XPORT engine or the XCOPY procedure. You can use transport files to move SAS data libraries, SAS catalogs, and SAS data sets from one operating system or host to another.

USER data library
a SAS data library associated with the libref USER. When the libref USER is defined, the SAS System uses it as the default libref for one-level names.

view engine
See engine.

VSAM data set
a classification that indicates the way the records in a data set are organized. VSAM stands for Virtual Storage Access Method and is an IBM data access method that provides three ways to organize records in a disk file: Entry-Sequenced Data Set (ESDS), Key-Sequenced Data Set (KSDS), and Relative Record Data Set (RRDS). VSAM allows three types of access to records in VSAM files: sequential, direct, and skip sequential. See also the entries for data set, partitioned data set (PDS), and sequential data set.

VTOC
the volume table of contents for a disk. The VTOC contains the name and location of operating system data sets and, if the VTOC is not indexed, it contains unused space on the disk. The VTOC also contains other information about the data sets, such as date of creation and size.

windowing environment
See SAS Display Manager System.

WORK data library
the temporary SAS data library automatically defined by the SAS System at the beginning of each SAS session or job to store temporary SAS files. When the libref USER is not defined, the SAS System uses WORK as the default library for one-level names.

Index

A

ABEND option, ABORT statement 261
abnormal termination 261–262
ABORT statement 261–262
ACCELERATE= option, ITEM statement 230
ADABAS files, accessing 27
ADB option, OPTIONS procedure 219
ADB SAS view engine 27
AFTER statement 241
ALIAS option, AFTER statement 241
ALIASMATCH= option, PROC PDSCOPY
    statement 224, 225
ALIGN option, FILENAME statement 280
ALLOC SAS service routine 451
allocating external files
    See external files, allocating
allocating SAS data libraries
    See SAS data libraries, allocating
ALTER= data set option 169
alternate load library, DDname 369
ALTLOG= system option 97, 299–300
ALTPRINT= system option 97, 300
ampersand (&), in operating system data set
    names 290
APF option, OPTIONS procedure 219
APPC security 301–302
APPCSEC= system option 301–302
appending to compressed data sets 170
ASA control characters 76
ASCII data, converting to EBCDIC 173
$ASCIIw. format 173
assembler programs, compiling 242–243
asterisk (*)
    in configuration file comments 7
    in ISPF variable names 111
attention handling exit, enabling 385
ATTRIB statement 262–263
AUTHENCR= system option 302–303
autocall libraries
    creating an autocall macro 195–196
    location 367–368
    specifying 198
    specifying in batch mode 194–195
    specifying under TSO 195
AUTOEXEC= system option 303
autoexec.bat, specifying 303
AUTOSCROLL command 160

B

background colors, CIMPORT procedure
    207–208
BACKWARD option, FILE statement 268
BASE engine 26, 45, 290
BEFORE statement 240
BESTw. format 182

binary data
binary data
    converting to EBCDIC 173
    reading and writing 174–175
binary zero, converting to blank 173
$BINARYw. format 173
BKWD option, FILE statement 268
BLKALLOC system option 303–304
BLKSIZE=
    data set option 167, 169
    FILE statement option 266
    FILENAME statement option 275–276
    INFILE statement option 286
    LIBNAME statement option 291
    PROC PDSCOPY statement option 224, 225
    system option 304–306
BMDP control statements 202
BMDP engine 53
BMDP files
    assigning a libref 54
    converting to SAS data sets 213
    example 54–55
    referencing 54
    variable names 213
BMDP= option, PROC CONVERT statement
    212
BMDP procedure
    BMDP control statements 202
    BMDP programs, calling 199–200
    example 203–206
    FORTRAN routines 202
    missing values 202
    PARMCARDS statement 202
    PROC BMDP statement 200–201
    VAR statement 201–202
BMDP programs, calling 199–200
BMDP save file, creating and converting
    203–206
borders, symbols for 329, 423
BOUNDARY= option, PROC RELEASE
    statement 233
BUFND= option, FILE statement 268
BUFNI= option, FILE statement 268
BUFNO= data set option 169
BUFNO= option, FILENAME statement 276
BUFSIZE= data set option 169
BUFSIZE= system option 306
BURST option, FILENAME statement 280

C

CA-DATACOM/DB files, accessing 27
CA-IDMS files, accessing 27
CALL routines
    See also SYSTEM function
    See also TSO commands
    See also TSO function

CALL routines *(continued)*
  See also TSO statement
  See also X statement
  SYSTEM 165–166
  TSO 166
CAPSOUT system option 306–307
carriage control
  ignoring 82, 318
  in print data sets 76
  in transported files 137
  writing to external files 76–77
case sensitivity, OpenEdition MVS commands 89
CATALOG procedure 206–207
CBTCOLOR= option, CIMPORT statement 207–208
CCHHR= option, INFILE statement 286, 288
CENTER system option 19
CHANGE statement 221
character data
  compression table 154
  converting to EBCDIC 173
character variables 115–116
CHARTYPE= system option 307, 423
$CHARZBw. informat 173
CHAR1= option, FILENAME statement 280
CHAR2= option, FILENAME statement 280
CHAR3= option, FILENAME statement 280
CHAR4= option, FILENAME statement 280
CIMPORT procedure
  background colors 207–208
  restoring transport files 207–208
  transporting SAS catalogs 134–135
CLEANUP system option 307–308
CLIST system option 308
CLISTs
  invoking from a SAS session 166, 295–297, 422–423
  SAS input from 308
clock, 24-hour 419
Close FRCB 450
Close function 450
CLOSE= option, FILE statement 266
CLOSE option, FILENAME statement 280
CLOSE= option, INFILE statement 286
CNTLLEV= data set option 169
CNV option, FILE statement 268
code generation
  allocating memory for 309–310
  multiple passes 308–309
CODE= option, BMDP statement 200
CODEPASS= system option 308–309
CODEPCT= system option 309–310
collating sequence
  See also formats
  See also informats
  EBCDIC 144
  stored compiled macro facility 197
colon (:)
  exchanging member names 222
  in EXCLUDE statement 228, 239
  in ISPF variable names 111
  in SELECT statement 239
COMAMID= system option 310–311
COMAUX1= system option 311–312

COMAUX2= system option 312
comma (,), ISPF fixed binary parameters 112
communications access method
  auxiliary 311–312
  specifying 310–311
COMPRESS= data set option 169
compressed data sets 154, 169, 170
Concatenation FRCB 449
Concatenation function 449
CONFIG= system option 7, 312–313
configuration files, filerefs for 312–313
CONTENT= option, BMDP statement 200
CONTENTS procedure
  determining observation length 39–40
  used in debugging 148
  viewing file contents 208–211
CONTENTS statement 206
CONTROLINTERVAL option, FILE statement 268
CONVERT procedure
  BMDP files 213
  missing values 212
  OSIRIS files 213
  SPSS files 215
COPIES= option, FILENAME statement 280
COPYVOLSER option, PROC TAPECOPY statement 247
CPORT procedure
  creating transport files 216
  transporting SAS catalogs 134–135
creating external files
  See external files, allocating
creating SAS data libraries
  See SAS data libraries, allocating
CSRC option
  FILE statement 266
  INFILE statement 286
CSVxxxx messages 147
CTLINTV option, FILE statement 268
CVAF option, INFILE statement 288

D

Data Control Block (DCB) 278
DATA= option, BMDP statement 200
data representation
  characteristics 141
  decimal point 142
  floating-point numbers 141–143
  integers 143
  loss of precision 143
  radix point 142
  SAS variables, maximum integer size 144
  saving space 143
Data Set Control Block (DSCB) 277
data set names
  See also data sets
  fully qualified 13
  nonstandard member names 14
  partially qualified 13
  temporary 14
data set options
  ALTER= 169
  BLKSIZE= 167, 169

BUFNO= 169
BUFSIZE= 169
CNTLLEV= 169
COMPRESS= 169
DROP= 169
FILECLOSE= 169
FILEDISP= 168, 169
FILEFMT= 169
FIRSTOBS= 169
INDEX= 169
KEEP= 169
LABEL= 169
OBS= 169
PW= 169
PWREQ= 170
READ= 170
RENAME= 170
REPLACE= 170
REUSE= 170
SORTEDBY= 170
summary table 169–170
TYPE= 170
WHERE= 170
WRITE= 170
data set type, specifying 170
data sets
  See also data set names
  See also SAS data sets
  allocation error messages 322–323
  allocation unit 326–327
  displaying information about 411–412
  partially-qualified names 388–389
  primary space allocation 325
  redirecting temporary 16–17
  releasing unused space 231–234
  secondary space allocation 325
  sorting 170
  specifying devices for 319
  verifying existence 192, 263–264
  volume serial 327
DATA step debugger 148
DATA system option 19
Data-In-Virtual (DIV) data set 156
DATACLAS= option
  FILENAME statement 279
  LIBNAME statement 291
DATASETS procedure
  See also CONTENTS procedure
  SAS data libraries, managing indexes 216–217
  SAS data sets, appending to SAS data libraries 216–217
  SAS files, copying 216–217
  SAS files, deleting 216–217
  SAS files, listing 216–217
  SAS files, renaming 216–217
date and time
  informat 175
  writing to SAS log 19
DATE system option 18
DBCSTYPE= system option 313
DB2 files, accessing 27
DB2 option, OPTIONS procedure 219
DB2 SAS view engine 27
DC option, PROC PDSCOPY statement 224

DCB (Data Control Block) 278
DCB attribute options 275–277
DCB attributes, allocating 314–315
DCB= option
  FILE statement 266
  INFILE statement 286
DCBDEVT= option, PROC TAPELABEL statement 254
DCBS option, PROC PDSCOPY statement 224, 226
DDB option, OPTIONS procedure 219
DDB SAS view engine 27
DDNAME= option
  PROC RELEASE statement 232
  PROC TAPELABEL statement 254
DDnames
  displaying 413–414
  reserved 23–24
DELETE statement 221
DEN= option, PROC TAPECOPY statement 248
DEST= option, FILENAME statement 280
device character set, specifying 307, 423
device drivers
  EM3179 161
  graphics 424–425
  SAS/GRAPH software 314
  SAS3270 425
  specifying 423
  terminal 330
  text 424
  Vector-to-Raster 424–425
device screen size, specifying 423
device screen type, specifying 307
DEVICE= system option 314
DEVTYPE= option
  FILE statement 267
  INFILE statement 287
DIAG option, SORT statement 235
Dialog Development Models 108
DIALOG statement 230
DICT= option, PROC CONVERT statement 212
DIRDD= option, PROC SOURCE statement 237
directory records, producing 243–244
DISP= option
  FILENAME statement 272–273
  LIBNAME statement 291–292
Display Manager under MVS
  Emulus 3270 terminal emulation 425
  graphics device drivers 424–425
  mouse 426
  Programmed Symbol driver 424–425
  resolution, IBM 3290 terminal 427
  SAS3270 device drivers 425
  scroll bars 426–427
  text device drivers 424
  Vector-to-Raster driver 424–425
  widgets 426–427
  window borders 426–427
DIV (Data-In-Virtual) data set 156
DIV data set pages, update frequency 334–335
DLORGCK system option 314–315

double ampersand (&&), in operating system
data set names 290
double byte character set 313
double quote (""), ISPF fixed binary
parameters 112
DROP= data set option 169
DSCB (Data Set Control Block) 277
DSCB= option
FILE statement 267
INFILE statement 287
DSNAME= option, INVOL statement 249
DSNEXST statement
data sets, verifying existence 263–264
syntax 263
DSNTYPE= option, FILENAME statement
279
DSORG= option, FILENAME statement 276
DSRESV system option 315
DYNALLOC system option 315–316
See also SORT= system option
See also SORTDEV= system option
See also SORTUNIT= system option
See also SORTWKDD= system option
See also SORTWKNO= system option

E

EBCDIC data, converting
formats/informats for 173
to ASCII 173
to binary 173
to character 173
to octal 173
$EBCDICw. format 173
ECHOAUTO system option 18
Emulus 3270 terminal emulation 425
EM3179 device driver 161
encryption 302–303
end-of-file on input 449
ENGINE= system option 316–317
EQUALS option, SORT statement 235
ERASE= option, FILE statement 268
error diagnosis 192
ESTAE exit, enabling 383–384
Ew. format
See also Ew.d informat
scientific notation, writing in 183
Ew.d informat 175–176
See also Ew. format
EX option, PROC RELEASE statement 233
examples
assembler programs, compiling 242–243
BMDP files 54–55
BMDP procedure 203–206
BMDP save file, creating and converting
203–206
control cards for IEBCOPY 244–246
data sets, releasing unused space 234
data sets, verifying existence 263–264
external files, accessing 79
external files, allocating 61–62
external files, writing to 71–72
GETEXEC DATA step function 127–128
INFILE/FILE User Exit Facility 453–464

INFILE statement 79
members, copying 229
members, deleting 222–223
members, renaming 222–223
OSIRIS files 57
printing selected members 242
producing directory records 243–244
PUTEXEC DATA step routine 128–129
redirecting temporary data sets 16–17
REXX exec 127
REXX return codes 129
SAS data libraries, allocating internally 30
SAS system options, redirecting temporary
data sets 16–17
SPSS files 56
tapes, copying multiple files from multiple
tapes 253
tapes, copying multiple files from one tape
253
tapes, copying nonlabeled to nonlabeled 252
tapes, copying standard label to nonlabeled
252
tapes, copying standard label to standard
label 251–252
tapes, listing label information 255–256
EXCHANGE statement 222
EXCLUDE statement
PDSCOPY procedure 227–228
SAS data sets, importing 259–260
SOURCE procedure 239–240
EXPORT option, XCOPY statement 258
EXTENT option, PROC RELEASE statement
233
EXTENTS option, PROC RELEASE statement
233
external files
concatenating 66
copying to a window 421
deallocating 66–67
default maximum block size 317–318
displaying information about 66
FILE user exit facility 91
INFILE user exit facility 91
information about input data sets 82
redirecting SAS input 91
referring to 70
writing your own I/O methods 90
zero-length records 323
external files, accessing
CA-IDMS files 83
concatenated data sets 81
from terminals 80
IMS-DL/I files 83
INFILE statement 78–79
members of a partitioned data set 80
multiple files 81–82
print data sets 82
sequential files 79–80
VSAM files 83–84
VTOC (Volume Table of Contents) 84
external files, allocating
cataloged tape files 63
generation data sets 64–65
HFS files 66
ISAM files 65

on tape 63
SMS PDSE files 66
summary of methods 59–60
uncataloged tape files 63
with FILENAME statement 60, 61
with JCL DD statements 62
with TSO ALLOCATE command 63
external files, writing to
appending to a data set 75, 76
data set attributes 74–75
data set disposition 75–76
FILE statement 71–72
internal reader 74
members of partitioned data sets 73
printers 73
sequential data sets 72–73
temporary data set 74
to print data sets 76–77

F

FCB= option, FILENAME statement 280
FEEDBACK= option, FILE statement 268
FILE= options, CONTENTS statement 206
FILE statement, HFS 270
FILE statement, SAS
BACKWARD option 268
BKWD option 268
BLKSIZE= option 266
BUFND= option 268
BUFNI= option 268
CLOSE= option 266
CNV option 268
CONTROLINTERVAL option 268
CSRC option 266
CTLINTV option 268
data sets, retrieving information about
267–268
DCB= option 266
DEVTYPE= option 267
DSCB= option 267
ERASE= option 268
FEEDBACK= option 268
GENKEY option 268
HFS file options 270
JFCB= option 267
KEY= option 268
KEYGE option 268
KEYLEN= option 269
KEYPOS= option 269
LRECL= option 266
MOD option 266
MVS specifics 264–265
NOPROMPT option 266
OLD option 267
PASSWD= option 269
pipes options 270
RBA= option 269
RC4STOP option 269
RECFM= option 267
RECORDS= option 269
RECORG= option 269
RESET option 269
routing PUT statement output 264–265

RRN= option 269
SEQUENTIAL option 269
SKIP option 269
standard options under MVS 266–267
syntax 264
UCBNAME= option 268
UPDATE option 270
VOLUME= option 268
VSAM options 268–270
FILE statement options, validating 445–446
FILEBLKSIZE(device-type)= system option
317–318
FILECC system option 318
FILECLOSE= data set option 169
FILEDEST= system option 318–319
FILEDEV= system option 319
FILEDIRBLK= system option 319–320
See also FILESPPRI= system option
See also FILEUNIT= system option
FILEDISP= data set option 168, 169
FILEEXT= system option 320–321
FILEFMT= data set option 169
FILEFORMS= system option 321–322
FILEMOUNT system option 322
FILEMSGS system option 322–323
FILENAME statement
ALIGN option 280
BLKSIZE= option 275–276
BUFNO= option 276
BURST option 280
CHAR1= option 280
CHAR2= option 280
CHAR3= option 280
CHAR4= option 280
CLOSE option 280
COPIES= option 280
DATACLAS= option 279
DCB attribute options 275–277
DCB attributes 277–279
DEST= option 280
DISP= option 272–273
DSNTYPE= option 279
DSORG= option 276
FCB= option 280
filerefs, associating with external files
268–270
FLASH= option 280
FLASHC= option 280
FOLD option 281
FORMDEF= option 281
FORMS= option 281
HOLD option 281
ID= option 281
LABEL= option 274
LIKE= option 279
LRECL= option 276
MGMTCLAS= 279
MODIFY= option 281
MVS specifics 270–271
NOMOUNT option 275
NOPROMPT option 275
OPTCD= option 276–277
OUTDES= option 281
OUTLIM= option 281
PAGEDEF= option 281

FILENAME statement *(continued)*
   PARM1= option 281
   PARM2= option 281
   PARM3= option 282
   PARM4= option 282
   PARM5= option 282
   PGM= option 281
   PRMODE= option 281
   RECFM= option 277
   RECORG= option 279
   REUSE option 275
   SMS keyword options 279–280
   SPACE= option 273–274
   standard file options 272–275
   STORCLAS= option 280
   SUBSYS= option 281
   subsystem options 281–282
   syntax 270
   SYSOUT data set options 280–281
   SYSOUT= option 281
   UCS= option 281
   UCSVER option 281
   UNIT= option 274
   VERIFY option 281
   VOLSER= option 274
   WAIT= option 275
FILENULL system option 323
FILEPROMPT system option 323–324
filerefs
   definition 70
   displaying 412
FILEREUSE system option 324
files
   closing 450
   copying 216–217
   deleting 216–217
   listing 216–217
   renaming 216–217
   viewing contents 208–211
FILES statement 251
FILESPPRI= system option 325
FILESPSEC= system option 325
FILESTAT system option 325–326
FILESYSOUT= system option 326
FILEUNIT= system option 326–327
FILEVOL= system option 327
FILSZ system option 327–328
FIRST statement 240
FIRSTOBS= data set option 169
FIRSTOBS= option, PROC CONVERT
   statement 212
fixed-binary parameters, ISPF 111
FLASH= option, FILENAME statement 280
FLASHC= option, FILENAME statement 280
floating point data, reading 179–180
floating-point values, converting to
   hexadecimal 184
FOLD option, FILENAME statement 281
FOOTNOTE statement 282
footnotes in procedure output 282
FORM subsystem
   adding forms 100
   host-specific frames 416–418
   modifying default forms 99–100
   specifying a form 99

FORMAT= option, V5TOV6 statement 256
FORMAT procedure
   formats, user defined 217–218
   informats, user defined 217–218
formats
   See also specific formats
   $ASCIIw. 173
   BESTw. 182
   $BINARYw. 173
   $EBCDICw. 173
   Ew. 183
   HEXw. 184
   $HEXw. 173
   IBM 370 data 174
   IBw.d 174, 185
   $OCTALw. 173
   PDw.d 174, 186
   $PHEXw. 173
   PIBw.d 174
   RBw.d 174, 187
   S370FFw.d 174
   S370FIBUw.d 174
   S370FIBw.d 174
   S370FPDUw.d 174
   S370FPDw.d 174
   S370FPIBw.d 174
   S370FRBw.d 174
   S370FZDLw.d 174
   S370FZDSw.d 174
   S370FZDTw.d 174
   S370FZDUw.d 174
   S370FZDw.d 174
   user defined 217–218
   w.d 188
   ZDw.d 188–189
FORMDEF= option, FILENAME statement
   281
FORMS= option, FILENAME statement 281
FORTRAN routines 202
FRCB (Function Request Control Blocks)
   442–443
FREE, SAS service routine 451
FSBCOLOR system option 328–329
FSBORDER= system option 329, 423
FSDEVICE= system option 330, 423
FSMODE= system option 330–331, 423
FULLSTATS system option 152, 331–332
   See also MEMRPT system option
   See also STATS system option
   See also STIMER system option
function keys
   defining 193
   primary set 360–362, 424
   storing settings 9
Function Request Control Blocks (FRCB)
   442–443
functions, INFILE/FILE User Exit Facility
   Close 450
   Concatenation 449
   Initialization 445
   Open 447–448
   Parse Options 445–446
   Read 448
   Write 449–450

functions, macro
   %SCAN 194
   %SYSGET 194
functions, SAS
   SYSTEM 171–172
   TSO 172

G

generation data sets
   allocating multivolume 37
   definition 33
   external files, allocating 64–65
   SAS data libraries 33
GENKEY option, FILE statement 268
GETEXEC DATA step function 127–128
GHFONT= system option 332
graphic hardware font 332
graphics cursor, turning on/off 419
graphics device drivers 424–425

H

HELP= option, DIALOG statement 230
HELPCOLOR= option, CIMPORT statement
   207–208
hexadecimal binary data, converting 176–177
hexadecimal data, converting to EBCDIC 173
HEXw. format 184
   See also HEXw. informat
$HEXw. format 173
HEXw. informat 176–177
   See also HEXw. format
HFS file options
   FILE statement 270
   INFILE statement 288
hiperspace
   maximum number of pages 333–334
   size 332–333
HIPERSPACE option, LIBNAME statement
   292
HOLD option, FILENAME statement 281
host commands, issuing from SAS session 423
host sort utility
   cutoff for using 373–374
   EQUALS option support 375
   listing control statements 376
   message class 376–377
   message print file 377
   name of 377–378
   OPTIONS statement support 378
   parameter list type 383
   passing parameters to 378–379
   SUM FIELDS=NONE support 380–381
   supporting FILSZ parameter 327–328
host sort-utility anomalies 372–373
host subgroup error messages 149
HSLXTNTS= system option 155, 332–333
HSMAXPGS= system option 155, 333–334
HSMAXSPC= system option 155, 334
HSSAVE system option 334–335
HSWORK system option 335–336

hyphen (-)
   in EXCLUDE statement 239
   in SELECT statement 239

I

IBM packed decimal data
   reading 178–179
   writing 186
IBM 3090 Vector Facility 158
IBM 3290 terminal, resolution 427
IBM 370 data format 174
IBM 370 data informat 174
IBM 3800 Print-File Parameter 416–418
IBw.d format 174, 185
   See also IBw.d informat
IBw.d informat 174, 177–178
   See also IBw.d format
ICExxxxx messages 147
ICHxxxx messages 147
ICS name resolver, enabling 336
ICSRSLV= system option 336
ID= option, FILENAME statement 281
IDCxxxxx messages 147
IDM option, OPTIONS procedure 219
IDMS SAS view engine 27
IEBCOPY control cards 244–246
IECxxxxx messages 147
IKJxxxx messages 147
IMPLMAC system option 157
IMPORT option
   PROC XCOPY statement 258
   XCOPY statement 258
IMS option, OPTIONS procedure 219
IMS SAS view engine 27
IMS-DL/I files, accessing 27
IN= option, XCOPY statement 258
%INCLUDE statement
   including SAS statements 283
   JCLEXCL option 284
   MVS specifics 283
   SOURCE2 option 283
   syntax 283
   S2= option 283–284
INDD= option
   INVOL statement 250
   PROC PDSCOPY statement 224
   PROC SOURCE statement 237–238
   PROC TAPECOPY statement 248
INDEX= data set option 169
INFILE/FILE User Exit Facility
   See also functions, INFILE/FILE User Exit
      Facility
   Close FRCB 450
   closing files 450
   Concatenation FRCB 449
   end-of-file on input 449
   example 453–464
   FILE statement options, validating 445–446
   FRCB (Function Request Control Blocks)
      442–443
   INFILE statement options, validating
      445–446
   Initialization FRCB 445

INFILE/FILE User Exit Facility *(continued)*
  initializing the work area 445
  Open FRCB 447
  opening a data set 447–448
  Parse Options FRCB 446
  Read FRCB 448
  reading input 448
  SAS service routines 451–452
  UEBCB (User Exit BAG Control Block)
    443–444
  user exit modules, activating 453
  user exit modules, building 453
  user exit name, validating 445–446
  Write FRCB 450
  writing output 449–450
  writing user exit modules 441–443
INFILE statement
  BLKSIZE= option 286
  CCHHR= option 286, 288
  CLOSE= option 286
  CSRC option 286
  CVAF option 288
  DCB= option 286
  DEVTYPE= option 287
  DSCB= option 287
  example 79
  external files, reading 284–288
  HFS file options 288
  JFCB= option 287
  LRECL= option 286
  MVS specifics 284–285
  options for data set information 287
  pipe options 288
  RECFM= option 286–287
  standard options under MVS 286–287
  syntax 284
  UCBNAME= option 287
  VOLUME= option 287
  VTOC options 288
INFILE statement, HFS 288
INFILE statement options, validating 445–446
informats
  See also specific informats
  $CHARZBw. 173
  date and time 175
  Ew.d 175–176
  HEXw. 176–177
  IBM 370 data 174
  IBw.d 174, 177–178
  PDTIMEw. 175
  PDw.d 174, 178–179
  PIBw.d 174
  RBw.d 174, 179–180
  RMFDUR. 175
  RMFSTAMPw. 175
  SMFSTAMPw. 175
  S370FFw.d 174
  S370FIBUw.d 174
  S370FIBw.d 174
  S370FPDUw.d 174
  S370FPDw.d 174
  S370FPIBw.d 174
  S370FRBw.d 174
  S370FZDLw.d 174
  S370FZDSw.d 174

  S370FZDTw.d 174
  S370FZDUw.d 174
  S370FZDw.d 174
  TODSTAMP. 175
  TUw. 175
  user defined 217–218
  w.d 173
  ZDBw. 181
  ZDw.d 180–181
Initialization FRCB 445
Initialization function 445
INTAPE option, PROC PDSCOPY statement
  224, 226
integer binary data
  reading 177–178
  writing 185
internal reader, writing to 242–243
INVOL= option
  INVOL statement 250
  PROC TAPECOPY statement 248
INVOL statement
  DSNAME= option 249
  INDD= option 250
  INVOL= option 250
  NL option 250
  NORER option 250
  SL option 250
  tapes, copying 249–250
ISP option, OPTIONS procedure 219
ISPCAPS system option 336–337
ISPCHARF system option 115, 337–338
ISPCSR= system option 338
ISPEXEC CALL routine 107, 108
ISPEXECV= system option 338–339
ISPF
  accessing SAS variables 114–116
  character values passed as numeric 117
  Dialog Development Models 108
  enabling the interface 106
  error messages, writing to SAS log 340
  fixed-binary parameters 111
  invalid SAS variables 116
  invoking ISPF services 106–107
  ISPEXEC CALL routine 107, 108
  message ID 344–345
  null ISPF variables 117
  panel, displaying 346
  parameter lengths, writing to SAS log
    341–342
  parameter lists, writing to SAS log 342
  parameter value pointers, writing to SAS log
    341–342
  parameters longer than 200 bytes 112–113
  parameters, bypassing 113
  parameters, passing to 111–113
  parameters, uppercasing 336–337
  SAS services, SAS/DMI equivalents 109–110
  SAS system options, changing during DATA
    step 109
  SAS system options, list of 109
  software requirements 106
  source code templates 108
  statistics, writing 325–326
  testing applications 117–118
  truncated numeric variables 117

uninitialized variables 117
using SAS formats and informats 337–338
variable-naming conventions 111
variables, passing to ISPF services 338–339
variables, prefix for 347
variables, zero length 339
ISPF editor
copying EDIT models to a SAS session 110
running from a SAS session 110, 419–421
ISPF services, writing non-zero return codes to
SAS log 341
ISPF variable, set by SAS VDEFINE exit 338
ISPLINK CALL routine 107–108
ISPMISS= system option 339
ISPMSG= system option 339–340
ISPNOTES system option 340
ISPNZTRC system option 341
ISPPT system option 341–342
ISPTRACE system option 342
ISPVDEFA system option 342–343
ISPVDLT system option 343
ISPVDTRC system option 343–344
ISPVIMSG= system option 344
ISPVRMSG= system option 344–345
ISPVTMSG= system option 345
ISPVTNAM= system option 345–346
ISPVTPNL= system option 346
ISPVTRAP information, displaying 345
ISPVTRAP system option 346–347
ISPVTVARS= system option 347
ITEM statement
ACCELERATE= option 230
MNEMONIC= option 230

J

JCLEXCL option, %INCLUDE statement 284
JCTUSER field value 192
JFCB (Job File Control Block) 277
JFCB= option
FILE statement 267
INFILE statement 287
JMRUSEID field value 192
Job File Control Block (JFCB) 277
JOBCAT, reserved DDname 23
JOBLIB, reserved DDname 23

K

KEEP= data set option 169
KEY= option, FILE statement 268
%KEYDEF macro statement 193
KEYGE option, FILE statement 268
KEYLEN= option, FILE statement 269
KEYPOS= option, FILE statement 269

L

LABEL= data set option 169
LABEL= option
FILENAME statement 274
LIBNAME statement 292

PROC BMDP statement 200
PROC TAPECOPY statement 248
LABEL2= option, BMDP statement 200
LAST statement 240
LEAVE= option, SORT statement 235
LENGTH= option, ATTRIB statement 263
LENGTH statement
MVS specifics 289
syntax 288
variable length, specifying 288–289
LIBNAME statement
assigning engines to SAS data libraries
289–294
assigning librefs to SAS data libraries
289–294
BLKSIZE= option 291
DATACLAS= option 291
DISP= option 291–292
HIPERSPACE option 292
LABEL= option 292
MGMTCLAS= option 292
MVS specifics 289
SPACE= option 292–293
STORCLAS= option 294
syntax 289
UNIT= option 293
VOLSER= option 294
WAIT= option 294
librefs
DDname as 32
definition 26
listing 414–415
LIKE= option, FILENAME statement 279
LINESIZE= system option 18–19, 348
LIST option, SORT statement 235
loaded data sets 237
LOG, SAS service routine 451
LOG= system option 96, 348–349
LOG window, suppressing automatic scrolling
160
logging
autoexec SAS statements 18
macro reference resolutions 18
macro SAS statements 18
macro trace information 18
NOTES 18
SAS invocation options 18
SAS source statements 18
secondary SAS source statements 18
system news bulletins 18
LRECL= option
FILE statement 266
FILENAME statement 276
INFILE statement 286
LUFIRST= system option 302, 349
LULAST= system option 302, 349–350
LUNAME= system option 302, 350
LUPOOL= system option 302, 350–351
LUPREFIX= system option 302, 351
LUTYPE= system option 302, 352
LU0MODE= system option 302, 352–353
LU0SEC= system option 353
LU62MODE= system option 302, 354

M

macro statements 193
macro variable symbol tables, memory for 357
macro variables
  maximum number of bytes for 198
  maximum size 357
  MVS 192
  portable 191–192
MAPS= system option 354
MAUTOSOURCE system option 157
MAXBLK= option, PROC PDSCOPY statement 226–227
MAXBLOCK= option, PROC PDSCOPY statement 224, 226
MAXIOERROR= option, PROC SOURCE statement 238
member name extensions 320–321
members
  copying 229
  deleting 220–223
  listing 220–223, 415–416
  printing selected 242
  renaming 220–223
  switching names 222
memory
  allocating 451
  freeing 451
  leaving unallocated 388
  limits 355–356
  usage statistics, writing to SAS log 355
MEMRPT system option 152, 355
MEMSIZE= system option 355–356
MENUCOLOR= option, CIMPORT statement 207–208
MESSAGE option, SORT statement 235
messages, host-system subgroup error
  internal CALL command processor 469–470
  SASCP command processor 465–467
  TSO command executor 467–469
messages, partitioned data set containing 369–370
MGMTCLAS= option, LIBNAME statement 292
migrated data sets, recalling 389–390
MINSTG system option 356
missing values
  BMDP procedure 202
  CONVERT procedure 212
MLOGIC system option 18
MNEMONIC= option, ITEM statement 230
MOD option, FILE statement 266
MODIFY= option, FILENAME statement 281
mounting an off-line volume 322
mouse 426
MPRINT system option 18, 117–118
MSYMTABMAX= system option 198, 357
MVARSIZE= system option 198, 357

N

NDSVOLS= system option 358
NE option, PROC PDSCOPY statement 224, 227

NEWMOD option, PROC PDSCOPY statement 224, 227
news bulletins, writing to SAS log 358–359
NEWS= system option 18, 358–359
NEWVOLSER= option, PROC TAPECOPY statement 249
NL option, INVOL statement 250
NOA option, PROC PDSCOPY statement 227
NOALIAS option, PROC PDSCOPY statement 224, 227
NOBLANK option, AFTER statement 241
NOBLKALLOC system option 303–304
NOCAPSOUT system option 306–307
NOCLIST system option 308
NOCLONE system option 154
NODATA option, PROC SOURCE statement 238
NODCBS option, PROC PDSCOPY statement 224, 226
NODLORGCK system option 314–315
NODSRESV system option 315
NODYNALLOC system option 315–316
NOFILECC system option 318
NOFILEMOUNT system option 322
NOFILEMSGS system option 322–323
NOFILENULL system option 323
NOFILEPROMPT system option 323–324
NOFILEREUSE system option 324
NOFILESTAT system option 325–326
NOFILSZ system option 327–328
NOFSBCOLOR system option 328–329
NOFSNRESEQ option, PROC TAPECOPY statement 249
NOFULLSTATS system option 331–332
NOHSSAVE system option 334–335
NOHSWORK system option 335–336
NOISPCHARF system option 115, 337–338
NOISPNOTES system option 340
NOISPNZTRC system option 341
NOISPPT system option 341–342
NOISPTRACE system option 342
NOISPVDEFA system option 342–343
NOISPVDLT system option 343
NOISPVDTRC system option 343–344
NOISPVTRAP system option 346–347
NOLIST option, PROC TAPECOPY statement 249
NOMINSTG system option 356
NOMISS option, BMDP statement 201
NOMOUNT option, FILENAME statement 275
NOOPLIST system option 359–360
NOPRINT option, PROC SOURCE statement 238
NOPROMPT option
  FILE statement 266
  FILENAME statement 275
NOR option, PROC PDSCOPY statement 227
NOREPLACE option, PROC PDSCOPY statement 224, 227
NORER option
  INVOL statement 250
  PROC TAPECOPY statement 249
NOREXXMAC system option 366
NORSASUSER system option 366–367
NOSORTEQOP system option 375

NOSORTLIST system option 376

NOSORTMSG system option 376–377

NOSORTSHRB system option 379–380

NOSORTSUMF system option 380–381

NOSORT31PL system option 383

NOSPOOL system option 158

NOSTAE system option 383–384

NOSTATS system option 384–385

NOSTAX system option 385

NOSTIMER system option 385–386

NOSUMMARY option, PROC SOURCE
statement 238

NOSYNCHIO system option 386

NOS99NOMIG system option 389–390

not sign, bypassing ISPF parameters 113

NOTES system option 18

NOTEST option, PROC PDSCOPY statement
224, 227

NOTRAP813 option, TAPELABEL statement
254

NOTSORTED option, PROC SOURCE
statement 238

NOVECTOR system option 158, 393–394

NOVSAMLOAD system option 394–395

NOVSAMREAD system option 395

NOVSAMUPDATE system option 395–396

null ISPF variables 117

NULL option, PROC SOURCE statement 238

NULLS, turning on/off 422

NUMBER system option 19, 20

numeric data
compression table 154
writing as EBCDIC 188

numeric variables 115
writing as EBCDIC 182

O

OBS= data set option 169

OBS= option, PROC CONVERT statement
212

OBS= system option 359

observations
determining length 39–40
selecting 170
sorting 234–236
specifying a beginning 169
specifying last 169, 359

observations sorting 234–236

octal data, converting to EBCDIC 173

$OCTALw. format 173

OLD option, FILE statement 267

online help 148

Open FRCB 447

Open function 447–448

OpenEdition HFS
access permission 85–86
accessing a particular file 87
concatenating 87
directories, allocating 85
file names in SAS System 86
files, allocating 85
host-specific options 88–89
PATHMODE option 85–86

PATHOPTS option 85–86
piping data to and from SAS System 88

OpenEdition Shell
invoking 89–90
issuing MVS commands 89–90
navigating directories 89–90
X statement 89–90

opening a data set 447–448

operating system abbreviation 192

operating system commands, issuing from SAS
sessions 165–166, 171–172

OPLIST system option 18, 359–360

OPTCD= option, FILENAME statement
276–277

optimizing I/O
buffer number 153
buffer size 153
BUFNO= option 153
BUFSIZE= option 153
catalogs, optimal block size 152–153
data compression, hardware 153–154
data compression, software 154
data sets, optimal block size 152–153
HIPERSPACE engine option 155
hiperspace libraries 155, 156
placing SAS data libraries in hiperspace
155–156
SAS data libraries as virtual I/O data sets
156
separating catalogs and data sets 152–153
SPOOLing 158

optimizing loading of SAS modules
bundled configurations 159–160
working-set size 159–160

optimizing logon procedure 161

optimizing memory
controlling fragmentation 159
limiting virtual memory 158–159
MEMSIZE= option 158–159
out-of-memory conditions 159
PROCLEAVE= option 159
superblocking 159
SYSLEAVE= option 159

optimizing sorting
DFSORT utility 157
SORTCUTP= option 157
SORTPGM= option 157

optimizing window scrolling 160

optimizing 3270 emulators 161

OPTIONS procedure 218–219

OPTIONS statement
MVS specifics 295
SAS system options, changing values
294–295
syntax 295

ORACLE files, accessing 27

ORACLE SAS view engine 27

OSIRIS engine 53

OSIRIS files
assigning a libref 56–57
converting to SAS data sets 214
example 57
referencing 57
variable names 213

OSIRIS= option, PROC CONVERT statement
212
OUT= option
  PROC CONVERT statement 212
  PROC XCOPY statement 258
out-of-memory conditions 363–364
out-of-resource conditions 307–308
OUTDD= option
  PROC PDSCOPY statement 224
  PROC SOURCE statement 238
  PROC TAPECOPY statement 249
OUTDES= option, FILENAME statement 281
OUTLIM= option, FILENAME statement 281
output, controlling destination of 9
OUTPUT window, suppressing automatic
    scrolling 160
OUTTAPE option, PROC PDSCOPY statement
    224, 227
OUTVOL= option, PROC TAPECOPY
    statement 249
OVP system option 19

P

packed hexadecimal data, converting to
    EBCDIC 173
page numbers 20
PAGE option, PROC SOURCE statement 239
PAGEDEF= option, FILENAME statement
    281
PAGENO= system option 20
PAGESIZE= system option 20, 360
PARM= option, BMDP statement 201
PARMCARDS statement 20, 202
PARM1= option, FILENAME statement 281
PARM2= option, FILENAME statement 281
PARM3= option, FILENAME statement 282
PARM4= option, FILENAME statement 282
PARM5= option, FILENAME statement 282
Parse Options FRCB 446
Parse Options function 445–446
partitioned data sets, copying 223–229
  excluding members 227–228
  missing members 228
  selecting members 228
partitioned data sets, default directory block
    allocation 319–320
PASSWD= option, FILE statement 269
passwords
  APPC 301–302
  SAS files 169–170
PATHOPTS option 86
PDS procedure 220–223
PDSCOPY procedure
  partitioned data sets, copying 223–229
  SAS log output 228
PDTIMEw. informat 175
PDw.d format 174, 186
  See also PDw.d informat
PDw.d informat 174, 178–179
  See also PDw.d format
performance statistics
  collecting 152
  writing to SAS log 331–332

period underscore (._), missing values 115
PFKEY= system option 360–362, 424
PGM= option, FILENAME statement 281
PGMPARM= system option 362
$PHEXw. format 173
PIBw.d format 174
PIBw.d informat 174
Pipes options 270
PMENU procedure 230
pound sign (#), in member names 196
precedence of specification 13
print files
  default 389
  default SYSOUT form number 321–322
  initializing 363
PRINT option
  PROC SOURCE statement 239
  SELECT statement 239
PRINT procedure, used in debugging 148
PRINT= system option 96, 362–363
printed output, uppercasing 306–307
printer destination, default 318–319
printer files, SYSOUT CLASS 326
printer line width 19
printer output, controlling 280–281
printers
  IBM 3800 form 416–418
  TSO form 417–418
PRINTINIT system option 363
PRINTTO procedure 230–231
PRMODE= option, FILENAME statement 281
problem solving, MVS environment 147
problem solving, SAS environment
  CONTENTS procedure 148
  DATA step debugger 148
  host subgroup error messages 149
  online help 148
  PRINT procedure 148
  PUT statements 148
  SAS log 147
  SAS software consultant 145
  SAS System documentation 148
  SAS technical support 146
  SITEINFO window 146
PROC BMDP statement 200–201
PROC CIMPORT statement 207–208
PROC CONVERT statement 211–212
PROC COPY statement 154
PROC PDS statement 220–221
PROC PDSCOPY statement 224–227
PROC RELEASE statement 231–234
PROC SORT statement 234–236
PROC SOURCE statement 237–239
PROC TAPECOPY statement 247–249
PROC TAPELABEL statement 254
PROC XCOPY statement 258
procedures
  BMDP 199–206
  CATALOG 206–207
  CIMPORT 134–135, 207–208
  CONTENTS 39–40, 208–211
  CONVERT 212–215
  CPORT 134–135, 216
  DATASETS 216–217
  FORMAT 217–218

OPTIONS 218–219
PDS 220–223
PDSCOPY 223–229
PMENU 230
PRINTTO 230–231
RELEASE 231–234
SORT 234–236
SOURCE 236–246
TAPECOPY 246–253
TAPELABEL 254, 255–256
V5TOV6 256
XCOPY 256–260
PROCLEAVE= system option 363–364
PROCLIB, reserved DDname 23
PROG= option, BMDP statement 201
PROGRAMCOLOR= option, CIMPORT
    statement 207–208
Programmed Symbol driver 424–425
prompting for nonexistent data sets 323–324
PSUP= system option 364
PUT statements, used in debugging 148
PUTEXEC DATA step routine 128–129
PW= data set option 169
PWREQ= data set option 170

R

RBA= option, FILE statement 269
RBw.d format 174, 187
    See also RBw.d informat
RBw.d informat 174, 179–180
    See also RBw.d format
RC4STOP option, FILE statement 269
READ= data set option 170
Read FRCB 448
Read function 448
real binary data, writing 187
RECFM= option
    FILE statement 267
    FILENAME statement 277
    INFILE statement 286–287
RECORDS= option, FILE statement 269
RECORG= option
    FILE statement 269
    FILENAME statement 279
redirecting temporary data sets 16–17
RELEASE= option, PROC RELEASE
    statement 233
RELEASE procedure 231–234
REMOTE= system option 365
RENAME= data set option 170
REPLACE= data set option 170
RESET option, FILE statement 269
resource descriptors, anchor name 386
resource usage statistics, writing to SAS log
    384–385
restricted options tables 12
return codes 108, 192
RETURN option, ABORT statement 261–262
REUSE= data set option 170
REUSE option, FILENAME statement 275
reusing file allocations 324
REXX
    enabling 122, 366

invoking from a SAS session 166, 422–423
    NOREXXMAC option 122
    return codes, example 129
    REXXMAC option 122
    X statement limitations 126
REXX EXEC library, DDname 365
REXX execs
    assigning values to REXX variables 125
    changing host command environment
        125–126
    checking return codes 125
    compared to ISPF edit macros 126
    example 127
    GETEXEC DATA step function 124
    invoking 123
    PUTEXEC DATA step routine 125
    retrieving REXX variables 124
    routing messages to the SAS log 124
REXXLOC= system option 365
REXXMAC system option 158, 366
RIGHT option, AFTER statement 241
RMFDUR. informat 175
RMFSTAMPw. informat 175
routing SAS log output 96
RRN= option, FILE statement 269
RSASUSER system option 366–367

S

S= system option 367
SAS autocall macro facility, performance 157
SAS cataloged procedure 4
SAS catalogs
    converting to transport format 135
    importing in transport format 136
    managing 206–207
    transporting 134–135
SAS clist 4
SAS/CONNECT software, remote session ID
    365
SAS data libraries
    assigning multiple librefs to 38
    block size 303–304
    converting Version 5 to Version 6 256
    copying 44, 236–237
    data sets, estimating size 39–40
    deallocating 38
    default access method 316–317
    default block size 304–306
    disposition 168, 169
    extending to multiple DASD volumes 34–35
    ignoring specified volumes 358
    librefs, definition 26
    listing current librefs 39
    location of default 393
    managing indexes 216–217
    moving 44
    record length 303–304
    SAS index, estimating size 41
    Version 6 utilities 44
    V5, accessing 431–436
    V5SEQ, accessing 436–439
SAS data libraries, allocating
    existing 25

SAS data libraries, allocating *(continued)*
  external 26, 31–32
  generation data sets 33
  internal 26, 28–30
  multivolume 33–36
  multivolume generation data groups 37
  multivolume under SMS environment 36–37
  new 25
SAS data libraries, copying
  excluding members 239–240
  selecting members 239
SAS data sets
  See also data sets
  access level 169
  appending to SAS data libraries 216–217
  block size 167, 169
  buffer number 169
  buffer size 169, 306
  compressing 169
  converting to transport format 132–133
  default block size 304–306
  exporting 256–257
  format of 169
  importing 256–260
  importing in transport format 133
  indexes for 169
  labels 169
SAS DATA step variables, accessing 452
SAS files, transporting
  ASCII data on an EBCDIC host 139
  CIMPORT procedure limitation 138–139
  DCB characteristics 136–137
  via communications software 137
  via tape 138
SAS/GRAPH map data sets 354
SAS input
  from external files 387
  primary 387
SAS library engines
  automatic assignment 32–33
  BASE 26, 45, 290
  BMDP 27, 53
  OSIRIS 27, 53
  REMOTE 27
  SPSS 27, 53
  table of 26–27
  TAPE 26, 49, 290
  V5 27, 431–436
  V5SEQ 27, 431–432, 436–439
  V6 26, 43–48
  V6SEQ 26, 43–44, 49–52
  V606 26, 290
  V607 26, 290
  V608 26, 290
  V609 26, 290
  XPORT 27, 132–134
SAS logs
  changing appearance 18–19
  changing contents 18
  copying 97
  copying to external files 97
  definition 17
  destination for 299–300
  including date and time 18
  listing 218–219

non-display manager mode 348–349
  numbering pages 19
  overprinting 19
  portable system options 18–19
  printer line width 18
  routing output 230–231
  used in debugging 147
  writing to 12, 451
SAS logs, routing
  PRINTTO procedure 230–231
  table of alternate destinations 94
  table of defaults 93
  to default destination 95
  to remote destinations 101
SAS logs, routing to external files
  DD statements 98
  FILE command 97
  PRINTTO procedure 95
  SAS system option 96–97
SAS logs, routing to printers
  PRINT command 100–101
  PRINT command, FORM subsystem 99–100
  PRINTTO procedure 98–99
  PRTFILE command 100–101
SAS output, line size 348
SAS output file in non-display-manager modes 362–363
SAS output page size 360
SAS portable supervisor 364
SAS procedure output, routing
  ALTPRINT= system option 300
  PRINTTO procedure 230–231
  table of alternate destinations 94
  table of defaults 93
  to default destination 95
  to remote destinations 101
SAS procedure output, routing to external files
  DD statements 98
  FILE command 97
  PRINTTO procedure 95
  SAS system options 96–97
SAS procedure output, routing to printers
  PRINT command 100–101
  PRINT command, FORM subsystem 99–100
  PRINTTO procedure 98–99
  PRTFILE command 100–101
SAS procedure output file
  aligning contents 19
  changing appearance 19–20
  definition 19
SAS service routines 451–452
SAS services, SAS/DMI equivalents 109–110
SAS statements, interpreting as REXX statements 158
SAS System
  commands for invoking 4
  invoking in batch mode 4
  invoking under TSO 4
  logging on directly 5
SAS System, customizing
  autoexec files 8
  configuration files 7, 8
  in batch mode 6
  interactively 6

SASUSER library 9, 9–11
  under TSO 6
  with SAS statements 6
  with SAS system options 6
SAS System connection methods
  SAS/CONNECT software 5
  SAS/SESSION 6
  SAS/SHARE software 5
  terminal emulators 5
SAS System documentation, used in
    debugging 148
SAS system files
  parmcards file 20
  summary table 21–23
SAS system options
  ALTLOG= 97, 299–300
  ALTPRINT= 97, 300
  APPCSEC= 301–302
  AUTHENCR= 302–303
  AUTOEXEC= 303
  BLKALLOC 303–304
  BLKSIZE= 304–306
  BUFSIZE= 306
  CAPSOUT 306–307
  changing 11–12
  changing during DATA step 109
  CHARTYPE= 307, 423
  CLEANUP 307–308
  CLIST 308
  CODEPASS= 308–309
  CODEPCT= 309–310
  COMAMID= 310–311
  COMAUX1= 311–312
  COMAUX2= 312
  CONFIG= 7, 312–313
  DBCSTYPE= 313
  default options tables 12
  DEVICE= 314
  displaying settings 12–13
  DLORGCK 314–315
  DSRESV 315
  DYNALLOC 315–316
  ENGINE= 316–317
  FILEBLKSIZE(device-type)= 317–318
  FILECC 318
  FILEDEST= 318–319
  FILEDEV= 319
  FILEDIRBLK= 319–320
  FILEEXT= 320–321
  FILEFORMS= 321–322
  FILEMOUNT 322
  FILEMSGS 322–323
  FILENULL 323
  FILEPROMPT 323–324
  FILEREUSE 324
  FILESPPRI= 325
  FILESPSEC= 325
  FILESTAT 325–326
  FILESYSOUT= 326
  FILEUNIT= 326–327
  FILEVOL= 327
  FILSZ 327–328
  FSBCOLOR 328–329
  FSBORDER= 329, 423
  FSDEVICE= 330, 423

  FSMODE= 330–331, 423
  FULLSTATS 331–332
  FULLSTATS option 152
  GHFONT= 332
  HSLXTNTS= 332–333
  HSMAXPGS= 333–334
  HSMAXSPC= 334
  HSSAVE 334–335
  HSWORK 335–336
  ICSRSLV= 336
  IMPLMAC 157
  in configuration files 7
  ISPCAPS 336–337
  ISPCHARF 337–338
  ISPCSR= 338
  ISPEXECV= 338–339
  ISPMISS= 339
  ISPMSG= 339–340
  ISPNOTES 340
  ISPNZTRC 341
  ISPPT 341–342
  ISPTRACE 342
  ISPVDEFA 342–343
  ISPVDLT 343
  ISPVDTRC 343–344
  ISPVIMSG= 344
  ISPVRMSG= 344–345
  ISPVTMSG= 345
  ISPVTNAM= 345–346
  ISPVTPNL= 346
  ISPVTRAP 346–347
  ISPVTVARS= 347
  LINESIZE= 348
  list of 109
  listing settings 394
  LOG= 96, 348–349
  LUFIRST= 302, 349
  LULAST= 302, 349–350
  LUNAME= 302, 350
  LUPOOL= 302, 350–351
  LUPREFIX= 302, 351
  LUTYPE= 302, 352
  LU0MODE= 302, 352–353
  LU0SEC= 353
  LU62MODE= 302, 354
  MAPS= 354
  MAUTOSOURCE 157
  MEMRPT 355
  MEMRPT option 152
  MEMSIZE= 355–356
  MINSTG 356
  MSYMTABMAX= 357
  MVARSIZE= 357
  NDSVOLS= 358
  NEWS= 358–359
  NOBLKALLOC 303–304
  NOCAPSOUT 306–307
  NOCLIST 308
  NOCLONE option 154
  NODLORGCK 314–315
  NODSRESV 315
  NODYNALLOC 315–316
  NOFILECC 318
  NOFILEMOUNT 322
  NOFILEMSGS 322–323

SAS system options *(continued)*
  NOFILENULL 323
  NOFILEPROMPT 323–324
  NOFILEREUSE 324
  NOFILESTAT 325–326
  NOFILSZ 327–328
  NOFSBCOLOR 328–329
  NOFULLSTATS 331–332
  NOHSSAVE 334–335
  NOHSWORK 335–336
  NOISPCHARF 337–338
  NOISPNOTES 340
  NOISPNZTRC 341
  NOISPPT 341–342
  NOISPTRACE 342
  NOISPVDEFA 342–343
  NOISPVDLT 343
  NOISPVDTRC 343–344
  NOISPVTRAP 346–347
  NOMINSTG 356
  NOOPLIST 359–360
  NOREXXMAC 366
  NORSASUSER 366–367
  NOSORTEQOP 375
  NOSORTLIST 376
  NOSORTMSG 376–377
  NOSORTSHRB 379–380
  NOSORTSUMF 380–381
  NOSORT31PL 383
  NOSPOOL 158
  NOSTAE 383–384
  NOSTATS 384–385
  NOSTAX 385
  NOSTIMER 385–386
  NOSYNCHIO 386
  NOS99NOMIG 389–390
  NOVECTOR 158, 393–394
  NOVSAMLOAD 394–395
  NOVSAMREAD 395
  NOVSAMUPDATE 395–396
  OBS= 359
  OPLIST 359–360
  OPTIONS procedure 12
  OPTIONS window 12–13
  PAGESIZE= 360
  performance-related 157–158
  PFKEY= 360–362, 424
  PGMPARM= 362
  precedence of specification 13
  PRINT= 96, 362–363
  PRINTINIT 363
  PROCLEAVE= 363–364
  PSUP= 364
  redirecting temporary data sets 16–17
  redirecting temporary data sets, example
      16–17
  REMOTE= 365
  restricted options tables 12
  REXXLOC= 365
  REXXMAC 158, 366
  RSASUSER 366–367
  S= 367
  SASAUTOS= 367–368
  SASHELP= 368–369
  SASLIB= 369

  SASMSG= 369–370
  SASUSER= 370
  SEQENGINE= 370–371
  SITEINFO= 371
  SMF option 152
  SORT= 371–372
  sort-related 235
  SORTANOM= 372–373
  SORTCUTP= 373–374
  SORTDEV= 374
  SORTEQOP 375
  SORTLIB= 375–376
  SORTLIST 376
  SORTMSG= 377
  SORTMSG 376–377
  SORTNAME= 377–378
  SORTOPTS 378
  SORTPARM= 378–379
  SORTPGM= 379
  SORTSHRB 379–380
  SORTSUMF 380–381
  SORTUNIT= 381–382
  SORTWKDD= 382
  SORTWKNO= 382–383
  SORT31PL 383
  specifying 11–12
  SPOOL 158
  STAE 383–384
  STATS 384–385
  STATS option 152
  STAX 385
  STIMER 385–386
  STIMER option 152
  SUBSYSID= 386
  summary table 396–410
  SYNCHIO 386
  SYSIN= 387
  SYSINP= 387
  SYSLEAVE= 388
  SYSPREF= 388–389
  SYSPRINT= 389
  S99NOMIG 389–390
  TAPECLOSE= 390
  TCPIPMCH= 390–391
  TCPIPPRF= 391
  TCPSEC= 391–393
  USER= 393
  VECTOR 158, 393–394
  VERBOSE 394
  VSAMLOAD 394–395
  VSAMREAD 395
  VSAMUPDATE 395–396
  WORK= 396
  writing to SAS log 12, 359–360
SAS system options, host-specific 198
SAS system options, portable
  CENTER 19
  DATA 19
  DATE 18
  ECHOAUTO 18
  LINESIZE= 18, 19
  MLOGIC 18
  MPRINT 18
  NEWS= 18
  NOTES 18

NUMBER 19, 20
OPLIST 18
OVP 19
PAGENO= 20
PAGESIZE= 20
SAS procedure output file, aligning
    contents 19
SOURCE 18
SOURCE2 18
SYMBOLGEN 18
SAS variables
    tracing VDEFINEs 343–344
    VDEFINEd 342–343
    VDELETE before VDEFINE 343
SAS variables, accessing with ISPF
    character variables 115–116
    ISPCHARF option 115
    NOISPCHARF option 115
    numeric variables 115
    VDEFINE service 114
    VDELETE service 114
    VRESET service 114
SAS view engines 27
SAS window background colors 328–329
SAS WORK library, libref 396
SASAUTOS= system option 367–368
SASHELP SAS data library, location 368–369
SASHELP= system option 368–369
SASLIB= system option 369
SASMSG= system option 369–370
SASUSER data library, read-only access
    366–367
SASUSER= system option 370
SAS3270 device drivers 425
%SCAN function 194
scientific notation 175–176
    writing in 183
scroll bars 426–427
scrolling, suppressing automatic 160
SELECT statement
    PDSCOPY procedure 228
    SAS data sets, importing 258
    SOURCE procedure 239
SEPARATOR statement 230
SEQENGINE= system option 370–371
sequence numbers, ignoring 367
SEQUENTIAL option, FILE statement 269
sequential SAS data libraries, default engine
    for 370–371
shared disk volumes, exclusive use of 315
SHAREIN option, PROC PDSCOPY statement
    227
SHAREINPUT option, PROC PDSCOPY
    statement 224, 227
sharing data buffers 379–380
single quote ('), ISPF fixed binary parameters
    112
site information file, location 371
SITEINFO= system option 371
SIZE= option, SORT statement 236
SKIP option, FILE statement 269
SL option, INVOL statement 250
slash (/), in HFS file names 86
SMF system option 152
SMFSTAMPw. informat 175

SMS keyword options 279–280
sort library name 375–376
SORT procedure 234–236
SORT= system option 371–372
    See also DYNALLOC system option
    See also SORTUNIT=
sort utility, specifying 379
sort work files
    allocating 315–316
    allocation units 381–382
    device names 374
    minimum size 371–372
    number of 382–383
    prefixes 382
SORTANOM= system option 372–373
SORTCUTP= system option 373–374
SORTDEV= system option 374
SORTEDBY= data set option 170
SORTEQOP system option 375
sorting, host sort-utility anomalies 372–373
SORTLIB, reserved DDname 23
SORTLIB= system option 375–376
SORTLIST system option 376
SORTMSG, reserved DDname 24
SORTMSG= system option 377
SORTMSG system option 376–377
SORTNAME= system option 377–378
SORTOPTS system option 378
SORTPARM= system option 378–379
SORTPGM= system option 379
SORTSHRB system option 379–380
SORTSIZE= option, SORT statement 236
SORTSUMF system option 380–381
SORTUNIT= system option 381–382
SORTWKDD= system option 382
SORTWKnn, reserved DDname 24
SORTWKNO= system option 236, 382–383
SORT31PL system option 383
source code templates, ISPF 108
SOURCE procedure
    AFTER statement 241
    BEFORE statement 240
    EXCLUDE statement 239–240
    FIRST statement 240
    LAST statement 240
    PROC SOURCE statement 237–239
    SAS data libraries, copying 236–237
    SAS log output 241
    SELECT statement 239
SOURCE system option 18
SOURCE2 option, %INCLUDE statement 283
SOURCE2 system option 18
SPACE= option
    FILENAME statement 273–274
    LIBNAME statement 292–293
special characters, as delimiters 194
SPOOL system option 158
SPSS engine 53
SPSS files
    assigning a libref 55
    converting to SAS data sets 215
    example 56
    variable names 215
SPSS= option, PROC CONVERT statement
    212

SQL files, accessing 27
SQL SAS view engine 27
STAE system option 383–384
statements
    ABORT 261–262
    AFTER 241
    ATTRIB 262–263
    BEFORE 240
    CHANGE 221
    CONTENTS 206
    DELETE 221
    DIALOG 230
    DSNEXST 263–264
    EXCHANGE 222
    EXCLUDE 227–228, 239–240, 259–260
    FILE 264–270
    FILENAME 270–282
    FILES 251
    FIRST 240
    FOOTNOTE 282
    %INCLUDE 283–284
    INFILE 79, 284–288
    INVOL 249–250
    ITEM 230
    %KEYDEF 193
    LAST 240
    LENGTH 288–289
    LIBNAME 289–294
    OPTIONS 294–295
    PARMCARDS 20, 202
    PROC BMDP 200–201
    PROC CIMPORT 207–208
    PROC CONVERT 211–212
    PROC COPY 154
    PROC PDS 220–221
    PROC PDSCOPY 224–227
    PROC RELEASE 231–234
    PROC SORT 234–236
    PROC SOURCE 237–239
    PROC TAPECOPY 247–249
    PROC TAPELABEL 254
    PROC XCOPY 258
    SELECT 228, 239, 258
    SEPARATOR 230
    %SYSEXEC 193
    TITLE 295
    TSO 295–297
    %TSO 193
    VAR 201–202
    X 297
STATS system option 152, 384–385
STAX system option 385
STEPCAT, reserved DDname 24
STIMER system option 152, 385–386
storage, minimizing 356
STORCLAS= option
    FILENAME statement 280
    LIBNAME statement 294
stored compiled macro facility
    accessing 197
    collating sequence 197
    definition 196
    host-specific SAS system options 197–198
SUBSYS= option, FILENAME statement 281
SUBSYSID= system option 386

summary table data set option 169–170
symbol tables, maximum memory for 198
SYMBOLGEN system option 18
SYNCHIO system option 386
synchronous I/O, enabling 386
SYSABEND, reserved DDname 24
SYSDEVIC macro variable 191
SYSDEXST macro variable 192
SYSENV macro variable 191
%SYSEXEC macro statement 193
%SYSGET function 194
SYSHELP, reserved DDname 24
SYSIN= system option 387
SYSINP= option, passing to external
    program 362
SYSINP= system option 387
SYSJCTID macro variable 192
SYSJMRID macro variable 192
SYSJOBID macro variable 191–192
SYSLEAVE= system option 388
SYSLIB, reserved DDname 24
SYSMDUMP, reserved DDname 24
SYSnnnnn, reserved DDname 24
SYSOUT, reserved DDname 24
SYSOUT data set options 280–281
SYSOUT= option, FILENAME statement 281
SYSPREF= system option 388–389
SYSPRINT, reserved DDname 24
SYSPRINT= system option 389
SYSRC macro variable 192
SYSSCP macro variable 192
SYSSCPL macro variable 192
SYSTEM function 171–172
    See also TSO commands
    See also TSO statement
    See also X statement
system performance statistics, collecting
    385–386
SYSUADS, reserved DDname 24
SYSUDUMP, reserved DDname 24
SYSUID macro variable 192
SYS99ERR macro variable 192
SYS99INF macro variable 192
SYS99MSG macro variable 192
SYS99R15 macro variable 192
S2= option, %INCLUDE statement 283–284
S370FFw.d format 174
S370FFw.d informat 174
S370FIBUw.d format 174
S370FIBUw.d informat 174
S370FIBw.d format 174
S370FIBw.d informat 174
S370FPDUw.d format 174
S370FPDUw.d informat 174
S370FPDw.d format 174
S370FPDw.d informat 174
S370FPIBw.d format 174
S370FPIBw.d informat 174
S370FRBw.d format 174
S370FRBw.d informat 174
S370FZDLw.d format 174
S370FZDLw.d informat 174
S370FZDSw.d format 174
S370FZDSw.d informat 174
S370FZDTw.d format 174

S370FZDTw.d informat   174
S370FZDUw.d format   174
S370FZDUw.d informat   174
S370FZDw.d format   174
S370FZDw.d informat   174
S99NOMIG system option   389–390

T

TAPE engine   26, 49, 290
TAPECLOSE= system option   390
TAPECOPY procedure
   FILES statement   251
   INVOL statement   249, 250
   PROC TAPECOPY statement   247–249
   tapes, copying   246–247
   tapes, copying multiple files from multiple
      tapes   253
   tapes, copying multiple files from one tape
      253
   tapes, copying nonlabeled to nonlabeled   252
   tapes, copying standard label to nonlabeled
      252
   tapes, copying standard label to standard
      label   251–252
TAPELABEL procedure
   PROC TAPELABEL statement   254
   tapes, listing label information   254
tapes
   close disposition   390
   closing   169
   copying   246–247
   copying multiple files from multiple tapes
      253
   copying multiple files from one tape   253
   copying nonlabeled to nonlabeled   252
   copying standard label to nonlabeled   252
   copying standard label to standard label
      251–252
   listing label information   254, 255–256
TCP/IP
   passwords   391–393
   prefixes   391
   security   391–393
   specifying   390–391
TCPIPMCH= system option   390–391
TCPIPPRF= system option   391
TCPSEC= system option   391–393
TECHNIQUE= option, SORT statement   236
terminal device drivers
   FSDEVICE= system option   330
   SAS/GRAPH software   314
   specifying   423
terminals
   See also Display Manager under MVS
   accessing external files from   80
   device driver, SAS/GRAPH software   314
   device drivers   330
   device drivers, specifying   423
   emulators   5
   Emulus 3270 terminal emulation   425
   full-screen data type   330–331
   IBM 3270   5

IBM 3270, data stream   423
IBM 3290, resolution   427
testing applications with ISPF
   MPRINT system option   117–118
   sample   118–122
TITLE statement   295
TODSTAMP. informat   175
TOTAL= option, PROC RELEASE statement
   232
transport files
   creating   216
   definition   131
   examining in hexadecimal format   140
   restoring   207–208
   XCOPY procedure   257
transport format   131
troubleshooting
   See problem solving, MVS environment
   See problem solving, SAS environment
TSO commands
   issuing from SAS sessions   166, 172, 193,
      422–423
TSO function   172
%TSO macro statement   193
TSO Print-File Parameter   417–418
TSO statement
   CLISTs, invoking from SAS session   295–297
   REXX, invoking from SAS session   295–297
   syntax   296
   TSO commands, issuing from SAS session
      295–297
TSO submode   296
TSO user ID   192
TSOEXEC command   296
TUw. informat   175
TYPE= data set option   170
TYPE= option, PROC RELEASE statement
   233

U

UCBNAME= option
   FILE statement   268
   INFILE statement   287
UCS= option, FILENAME statement   281
UCSVER option, FILENAME statement   281
UEBCB (User Exit BAG Control Block)
   443–444
underscore (_)
   in ISPF variable names   111
   in member names   196
UNIT= option
   FILENAME statement   274
   LIBNAME statement   293
   PROC BMDP statement   201
unloaded data sets   237
UNUSED= option, PROC RELEASE statement
   232–233
UPDATE option, FILE statement   270
User Exit BAG Control Block (UEBCB)
   443–444
user exit modules
   activating   453
   building   453

user exit modules *(continued)*
  FRCB (Function Request Control Blocks)
    442–443
  UEBCB (User Exit BAG Control Block)
    443–444
  writing 441–444
user exit name, validating 445–446
user profile catalog, location 370
USER= system option 393
user-defined windows 230

V

VAR statement 201–202
variables
  excluding 169
  renaming 170
  specifying for processing 169
VARRTN SAS service routines
  SAS DATA step variables, accessing 452
VDEFINE, writing to SAS log 346–347
VDEFINE service 114
VDEFINEd variables, invalid values 339–340
VDELETE service 114
vector facility instructions 393–394
VECTOR system option 158, 393–394
VERBOSE system option 394
VERIFY option, FILENAME statement 281
VOLSER= option
  FILENAME statement 274
  LIBNAME statement 294
VOLUME= option
  FILE statement 268
  INFILE statement 287
VRESET service 114
VSAM data sets 394–396
VSAM options 268–270
VSAMLOAD system option 394–395
VSAMREAD system option 395
VSAMUPDATE system option 395–396
VTAM LU
  acquiring from a pool 350–351
  acquisition, beginning numeric suffix 349
  acquisition, ending numeric suffix 349–350
  name 350
  prefix 351
  protocol 352
VTAM LU 0
  passwords 353
  session mode name 352–353
VTAM LU6.2 session mode name 354
VTOC options 288
V5 engine
  DCB attributes 433–434
  engine/host options 434–435
  external allocation 434
  overview 431–432
  sample output 436
  selecting 433
  using 432–433
  utilities for 435
V5SEQ engine
  DCB attributes 437
  engine/host options 438

  external allocation 437–438
  overview 431–432
  sample output 439
  selecting 437
  using 436
  utilities 438
V5TOV6 procedure
  FORMAT= option 256
  SAS data libraries, converting Version 5 to
    Version 6 256
V6 engine
  DCB attributes 46–47
  engine/host options 47, 48
  overview 43–44
  sample output 48
  selecting 45–46
  when to use 45
V6SEQ engine
  DCB attributes 50
  engine/host options 51
  overview 43–44
  sample output 52
  selecting 49
  when to use 49
V606 engine 26, 290
V607 engine 26, 290
V608 engine 26, 290
V609 engine 26, 290

W

w.d format
  numeric data, writing as EBCDIC 188
w.d informat 173
WAIT= option
  FILENAME statement 275
  LIBNAME statement 294
WERxxxxx messages 147
WHERE= data set option 170
widgets 426–427
window attributes, storing 9
window borders 426–427
windowing options under MVS 423–424
windows
  See also FORM subsystem
  user-defined 230
windows, command-line commands
  CLOCK 419
  GCURSOR 419
  HOSTEDIT 419–421
  INCLUDE 421
  NULLS 422
  TSO 422–423
  X 423
windows, copying contents
  to external files 97, 98
  to printers 98–101
windows, host-specific
  DSINFO 411–412
  FILENAME 412
  FNAME 413–414
  LIBNAME 414–415
  MEMLIST 415–416

WORK data library, placing in hiperspace
335–336
WORK library
compared to USER libraries   16
creating   14–15
deleting temporary data sets   16
redirecting temporary data sets   16–17
sizing   15
WORK= system option   396
WRITE= data set option   170
Write FRCB   450
Write function   449–450
WRKSPCE= option, BMDP statement   201

X

X statement   297
XCOPY procedure
See also CIMPORT procedure
See also CPORT procedure
EXCLUDE statement   259–260
PROC XCOPY statement   258
SAS data sets, exporting   256–257
SAS data sets, importing   256–259
SELECT statement   258
XPORT engine
converting SAS data sets to transport format
132–133
with SAS DATA step   134

Z

ZDBw. informat   181
See also ZDw.d format
See also ZDw.d informat
ZDw.d format
See also ZDBw. informat
See also ZDw.d informat
zoned decimal data, writing   188–189
ZDw.d informat   180–181
See also ZDBw. informat
See also ZDw.d format
zoned decimal data
reading   180–181
with blank zeros   181
writing   188–189

Special Characters

, (comma), ISPF fixed binary parameters   112
/ (slash), in HFS file names   86
._ (period underscore), missing values   115
& (ampersand), in operating system data set
names   290
&& (double ampersand), in operating system
data set names   290
* (asterisk)
See asterisk (*)
- (hyphen)
See hyphen (-)
_(underscore)
See underscore (_)

: (colon)
See colon (:)
(pound sign), in member names   196
' (single quote),
ISPF fixed binary parameters   112

Your Turn

If you have comments or suggestions about *SAS® Companion for the MVS Environment, Version 6, Second Edition*, please send them to us on a photocopy of this page or send us electronic mail.

For comments about this book, please return the photocopy to

SAS Institute Inc.
Publications Division
SAS Campus Drive
Cary, NC 27513
e-mail: yourturn@unx.sas.com

For suggestions about the software, please return the photocopy to

SAS Institute Inc.
Technical Support Division
SAS Campus Drive
Cary, NC 27513
e-mail: suggest@unx.sas.com